encyclopedia
of hair removal

HAIRDRESSING AND BEAUTY INDUSTRY AUTHORITY SERIES

HAIRDRESSING

Mahogany Hairdressing: Steps to Cutting, Colouring and Finishing Hair *Martin Gannon and Richard Thompson*

Mahogany Hairdressing: Advanced Looks *Richard Thompson and Martin Gannon*

Essensuals, Next Generation Toni & Guy: Step by Step

Professional Men's Hairdressing *Guy Kremer and Jacki Wadeson*

The Art of Dressing Long Hair *Guy Kremer and Jacki Wadeson*

Patrick Cameron: Dressing Long Hair *Patrick Cameron and Jacki Wadeson*

Patrick Cameron: Dressing Long Hair Book 2 *Patrick Cameron*

Bridal Hair *Pat Dixon and Jacki Wadeson*

Trevor Sorbie: The Bridal Hair Book *Trevor Sorbie and Jacki Wadeson*

Trevor Sorbie: Visions in Hair *Kris Sorbie and Jacki Wadeson*

The Total Look: The Style Guide for Hair and Make-Up Professionals *Ian Mistlin*

Art of Hair Colouring *David Adams and Jacki Wadeson*

Begin Hairdressing: The Official Guide to Level 1 *Martin Green*

Hairdressing – The Foundations: The official Guide to S/NVQ Level 2 5e *Leo Palladino and Martin Green*

Professional Hairdressing: The Official Guide to Level 3 4e *Martin Green and Leo Palladino*

Men's Hairdressing: Traditional and Modern Barbering 2e *Maurice Lister*

African-Caribbean Hairdressing 2e *Sandra Gittens*

Salon Management *Martin Green*

eXtensions: The Official Guide to Hair Extensions *Theresa Bullock*

The Colour Book: The Official Guide to Colour at NVQ Levels 2 & 3 *Tracey Lloyd with Christine McMillan-Bodell*

BEAUTY THERAPY

Beauty Basics – The Official Guide to Level 1 *Lorraine Nordmann*

Beauty Therapy – The Foundations: The Official Guide to Level 2 *Lorraine Nordmann*

Professional Beauty Therapy: The Official Guide to Level 3 *Lorraine Nordmann, Lorraine Williamson, Pamela Linforth and Jo Crowder*

Aromatherapy for the Beauty Therapist *Valerie Ann Worwood*

Indian Head Massage *Muriel Burnham-Airey and Adele O'Keefe*

The Official Guide to Body Massage *Adele O'Keefe*

An Holistic Guide to Anatomy and Physiology *Tina Parsons*

The Encyclopedia of Nails *Jacqui Jefford and Anne Swain*

Nail Artistry *Jacqui Jefford, Sue Marsh and Anne Swain*

The Complete Nail Technician *Marian Newman*

The World of Skin Care: A Scientific Companion *Dr John Gray*

An Holistic Guide to Reflexology *Tina Parsons*

Nutrition: A Practical Approach *Suzanne Le Quesne*

An Holistic Guide to Massage *Tina Parsons*

The Spa Book: The Official Guide to Spa Therapy *Jane Crebbin-Bailey, Dr John Harcup and John Harrington*

The Complete Guide to Make-up *Suzanne Le Quesne*

The Complete Make-up Artist: Working in Film, Fashion, Television and Theatre *Penny Delamar*

The Essential Guide to Holistic & Complementary Therapy *Helen Beckmann and Suzanne Le Quesne*

encyclopedia of hair removal

A COMPLETE REFERENCE TO METHODS, TECHNIQUES AND CAREER OPPORTUNITIES

GILL MORRIS AND JANICE BROWN

  **THOMSON**

Australia • Canada • Mexico • Singapore • Spain • United Kingdom • United States

THOMSON

Encyclopedia of Hair Removal

Gill Morris and Janice Brown

Publishing Director	**Commissioning Editor**	**Development Editor**
John Yates	Melody Dawes	Tom Rennie
Production Editor	**Manufacturing Manager**	**Marketing Manager**
Fiona Freel	Helen Mason	Natasha Giraudel
Typesetter	**Production Controller**	**Illustrations**
Saxon Graphics Ltd, Derby	Maeve Healy	Oxford Designers & Illustrators
Cover Design	**Text Design**	**Printer**
Harris Cook Turner	Design Deluxe, Bath, UK	Rotolito Lombarda, Italy

Copyright © 2006
Thomson Learning

The Thomson logo is a registered trademark used herein under licence.

For more information, contact
Thomson Learning
High Holborn House
50-51 Bedford Row
London WC1R 4LR

or visit us on the World Wide Web at:
http://www.thomsonlearning.co.uk

ISBN-13: 978-1-84480-266-1
ISBN-10: 1-84480-266-3

This publication has been developed by Thomson Learning. It is intended as a method of studying for the Habia qualifications. Thomson Learning has taken all reasonable care in the preparation of this publication but Thomson Learning and the City & Guilds of London Institute accept no liability howsoever in respect of any breach of the rights of any third party howsoever occasioned or damage caused to any third party as a result of the use of this publication.

While the publisher has taken all reasonable care in the preparation of this book the publisher makes no representation, express or implied, with regard to the accuracy of the information contained in this book and cannot accept any legal responsibility or liability for any errors or omissions from the book or the consequences thereof.

Products and services that are referred to in this book may be either trademarks and/or registered trademarks of their respective owners. The publisher and author/s make no claim to these trademarks.

British Library Cataloguing-in-Publication Data

A catalogue record for this book is available from the British Library

contents

about the authors

Janice Brown and Gill Morris

GILL MORRIS

Background

Electrolysis has been a large part of my professional life and I didn't even like it at college!

Beauty therapy training

North Warwickshire College, Nuneaton, Warwickshire
IHBC International Health & Beauty Therapy Diploma & Electrolysis

Additional training, electrolysis qualifications and memberships

Director and founding director of Habia
Chartered Institute of Marketing: Post Graduate Diploma
Chartered Marketer
City and Guilds 730 Teacher Training Certificate
TDLB D32, D33 Assessors Awards
Diploma in Remedial Electrolysis D.R.E.
Advanced Electrolysis Diploma: Removal of Telangiectasia and Fibrous Blemishes
Member of the previous Institute of Electrolysis
Member of the previous British Association of Electrolysis
Member of the British Institute and Association of Electrolysis
Member of American Electrolysis Association
C.P.E. (America) Certified Practitioner in Electrolysis

Career

For the first 2½ years of my professional career, I worked in a general beauty salon carrying out all treatments. However, my employer was an electrologist specialist and taught me a great deal about the wonders of electrolysis and thereby stimulated my love of the subject. In fact, I loved doing it so much I was known to rub electrolysis appointments out of my colleagues' columns and put them into mine!

After working for other people and having two salons of my own, I left the beauty business for a couple of years but came back with a vengeance when I worked for manufacturer and supplier companies Ellisons and Sterex. During my time with both companies I was heavily involved in research and development and new product development, particularly with the Sterex brand and my work on the development of the Sterex Blend epilator was a career high. I travelled nationally and internationally; lecturing, training, selling and above all learning how others around the world carried out electrolysis. There are too many highlights to mention but the most stimulating or 'nerve racking' was carrying out electrolysis treatment on eyebrows, LIVE on GMTV Breakfast programme and, arguably, the one I look back on with the most pride, apart from my equipment development work, was being invited to present a lecture to American electrologists at the American Electrolysis Association's annual convention and being the first British electrologist to do so.

There are not many electrologists who are Chartered Marketers, but having business training and qualifications gives me the best of both worlds through my company 'The GMT Group', as we can offer both advanced electrolysis training to qualified electrologists and management and marketing training and consultancy across the professional beauty industry.

JANICE BROWN

Background

According to my father, my interest in beauty treatments and hair removal began very early when I plucked all the hairs from my dolls and painted their faces.

Beauty therapy training

1983–1985 Chesterfield College of Arts & Technology Chesterfield, Derbyshire
City & Guilds Beauty Therapy, City & Guilds Electrolysis, National Health & Hygiene Certificate

Additional training, electrolysis qualifications and memberships

City & Guilds 730 Teacher Training
D32 and D33 NVQ Assessor Award D34 NVQ Internal Verifier
Diploma in Remedial Electrolysis D.R.E.
Advanced Electrolysis Diploma: Removal of Telangiectasia and Fibrous Blemishes
Member of the previous Institute of Electrolysis
Member of the British Institute and Association of Electrolysis

Career

My first job was as a beauty therapist with Tao Clinic Ltd. I was employed to increase their beauty work as they were primarily an electrolysis company. However, on my first day, one of the electrologists left and I had to do electrolysis for six straight hours! This amount of electrolysis continued for weeks, which created a very quick learning curve, after which I was sent to London for six weeks, Tao training and suddenly decided I loved it – after hating it at college!

I then worked as salon manager for Tao Sheffield spent a brief time as a sales representative for Babor skin care before being asked back to Tao as an area manager and training manager where I had responsibility for eight branches, plus the training and work standards of the whole group and for all new staff training, including their four-week training programme and regular up-date training.

Following a spell as a lecturer at Doncaster College of Further Education, I returned once more to Tao Clinic Ltd as national manager in charge of 20 branches with a team of area managers. My next move saw me become national training manager for the Fraser Muir Group, under the trading name of 'House of Famuir'. This position involved planning, developing, marketing and delivering of training courses and materials; travelling the world to research new products, including the USA, Canada, the Far East and Europe; testing and advising on potential new products and equipment as well as taking an active role in company public relations, including trade shows, seminars and television appearances. In 2002, with my husband Rob, I took over the House of Famuir from the owner Mr Julian Shuba.

acknowledgements

Janice would like to dedicate this book to her Dad who inspired her always and Gill would like to dedicate this to her Mum who has always been her greatest supporter.

To all hair removal practitioners; those practising now and those who will practise in the future, this book is for you. Never stop learning, always keep your mind open to new ideas but ensure you thoroughly evaluate any new information against a background of sound theory.

We and the publishers also wish to publicly thank the people who helped to make this book possible through either their direct or indirect support:

- first to all our clients, tutors, mentors and students who, over the years, have taught us both invaluable lessons
- ASAH Medico
- Clement Beaumont, Dectro International
- David Smith, Polaris Medical Ltd
- David Wright, human resource consultant and specialist adviser to the health and beauty industry, who wrote Chapter Nine
- Dr James Shuster
- Gemma Morris for logging all images
- Jo Viner Smith, Cancer Research UK
- Nagwa Stanforth, Sukar
- Neenu Batra, KHB Salon
- Samantha Hills, clinical development manager Lynton Lasers, for her invaluable advice
- Wendy O'Hare, Hare & Beauty
- House of Famuir Ltd
- The Carlton Group
- Vitality
- Silhouette International
- Australian Body Care
- Lynton Lasers Limited
- Sterex Electrolysis
- Ellisons
- Sorisa

- Dr Patrick Bowles
- Hair Route Magazine
- Ballet.

Thanks also go to our husbands, Rob and Roy, for their support, help and patience.

Our aim in writing this book is to share our enthusiasm for hair removal and to encourage all readers to take up the training options available, particularly in the field of electrolysis.

We hope that, having read this book, you will appreciate the rewards, both financial and emotional, that can be gained from a career in hair removal and we also hope that any one else reading this book may also be encouraged to consider a career as a hair removal practitioner (HRP).

foreword

Talk about luck! I'm lucky to know both Gill and Janice very well and am delighted to get the two top people in the industry to collaborate on this book.

Gill Morris is one of the founder directors of Habia and her vision has helped structure Habia to its position as the industry authority for hair and beauty. Gill's ever positive approach and can-do attitude simply oozes into her writing style: flowing, challenging and ever so consummate.

Janice Brown is a dedicated professional who always manages to make every thing she does look so easy. When you read this book, you'll soon find Janice's relaxed style permeates her writing.

The *Encyclopedia of Hair Removal* is the first book on the market specifically dedicated to hair removal techniques and its practitioners. This specialism is fast becoming a career route in itself and a book which caters to this area in such a way has been long awaited.

Gill Morris and Janice Brown are well-known and respected within the beauty industry, for their knowledge in hair removal techniques and product knowledge as well as their high standards of training.

Both were also involved in the development of Habia Occupational Standards for hair removal, which includes the epilation, laser, IPL and waxing units. This is testament to their authority on the subject and shows how natural a choice they were to produce this book.

Their extensive teaching and training experience is reflected in the style of writing which is very learner-friendly, easy-to-read and understand. This book is sure to motivate, stimulate and maintain the learner's interest.

Alan Goldsbro, Habia CEO

about the book

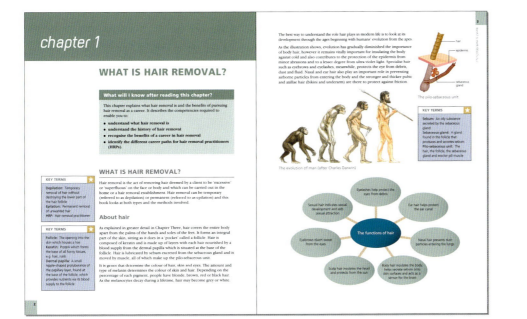

Learning objectives Learning objectives introduce chapters and list those elements that make up the unit and must be achieved in order for you to be accredited with the ~ S/NVQ unit. When you feel confident and competent with the skills/knowledge requirements, you are ready to be assessed. The beauty therapy units relevant to each chapter are identified here.

Spidergrams Spidergram-style diagrams are provided to summarise the skills/knowledge requirement for each element. These provide a useful checklist for you to refer to.

Key terms Definitions of important terms help to improve your understanding of key skills and knowledge requirements.

Tip boxes: Professional and technical The authors' experience is shared through tip boxes which provide positive suggestions to improve your knowledge and skills.

Remember boxes Helpful reminders concerning essential information and practices.

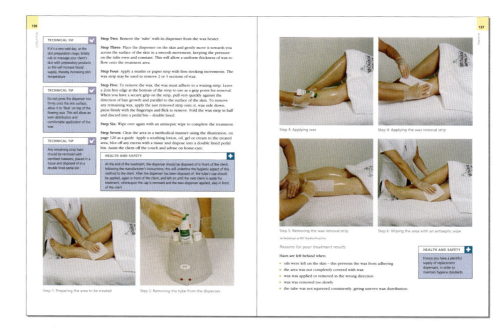

Step-by-step photo sequences Each chapter aims to demonstrate the featured practical skill to enhance your understanding.

Health and safety boxes These boxes draw your attention to related health and safety information for each technical skill.

Record cards A variety of important real-life treatment cards feature throughout the book.

Equipment lists To assist you in preparing for each practical treatment, an essential equipment list is provided.

Practitioner profiles Showcasing career paths of actual hair removal practitioners, they illustrate how they have risen to the top of their field.

Glossary For easy reference, definitions are provided for key words or technical terms.

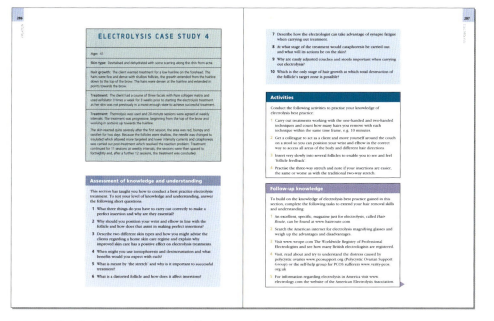

Case studies Describe real-life cases of hair removal treatments and their outcomes.

Activities Suggest interesting activities which will reinforce your learning.

Follow-up knowledge Point you towards useful websites and publications if your want to find out more about topics covered in the chapter.

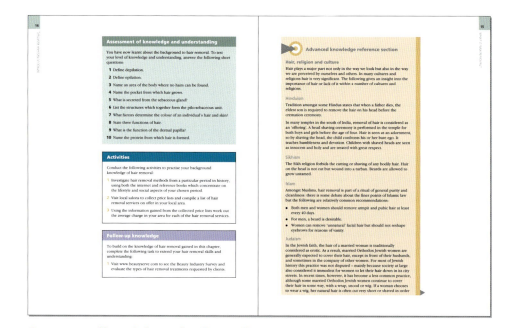

Assessment of knowledge and understanding Review questions are provided at the end of each chapter to assess knowledge and understanding.

Advanced knowledge reference section In-depth articles for the dedicated learner.

part one

introducing hair removal

chapter 1

WHAT IS HAIR REMOVAL?

What will I know after reading this chapter?

This chapter explains what hair removal is and the benefits of pursuing hair removal as a career. It describes the competencies required to enable you to:

- **understand what hair removal is**
- **understand the history of hair removal**
- **recognise the benefits of a career in hair removal**
- **identify the different career paths for hair removal practitioners (HRPs).**

WHAT IS HAIR REMOVAL?

Hair removal is the act of removing hair deemed by a client to be 'excessive' or 'superfluous' on the face or body and which can be carried out in the home or a hair removal establishment. Hair removal can be temporary (referred to as depilation) or permanent (referred to as epilation) and this book looks at both types and the methods involved.

About hair

As explained in greater detail in Chapter Three, hair covers the entire body apart from the palms of the hands and soles of the feet. It forms an integral part of the skin, sitting as it does in a 'pocket' called a follicle. Hair is composed of keratin and is made up of layers with each hair nourished by a blood supply from the dermal papilla which is situated at the base of the follicle. Hair is lubricated by sebum excreted from the sebaceous gland and is moved by muscle, all of which make up the pilo-sebaceous unit.

It is genes that determine the colour of hair, skin and eyes. The amount and type of melanin determines the colour of skin and hair. Depending on the percentage of each pigment, people have blonde, brown, red or black hair. As the melanocytes decay during a lifetime, hair may become grey or white.

KEY TERMS ★

Depilation: Temporary removal of hair without destroying the lower part of the hair follicle
Epilation: Permanent removal of unwanted hair
HRP: Hair removal practitioner

KEY TERMS ★

Follicle: The opening into the skin which houses a hair
Keratin: Protein which forms the base of all horny tissues, e.g. hair, nails
Dermal papilla: A small nipple-shaped protuberance of the papillary layer, found at the base of the follicle, which provides nutrients via its blood supply to the follicle

The best way to understand the role hair plays in modern life is to look at its development through the ages beginning with humans' evolution from the apes.

As the illustration shows, evolution has gradually diminished the importance of body hair, however it remains vitally important for insulating the body against cold and also contributes to the protection of the epidermis from minor abrasions and to a lesser degree from ultra violet light. Specialist hair such as eyebrows and eyelashes, meanwhile, protects the eye from debris, dust and fluid. Nasal and ear hair also play an important role in preventing airborne particles from entering the body and the stronger and thicker pubic and axillae hair (bikini and underarm) are there to protect against friction.

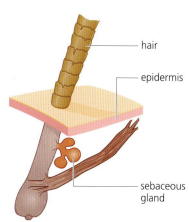

hair

epidermis

sebaceous gland

The pilo-sebaceous unit

The evolution of man (after Charles Darwin)

KEY TERMS ★

Sebum: An oily substance secreted by the sebaceous gland
Sebaceous gland: A gland found in the follicle that produces and secretes sebum
Pilo-sebaceous unit: The hair, the follicle, the sebaceous gland and erector pili muscle

Sexual hair indicates sexual development and aids sexual attraction

Eyelashes help protect the eyes from debris

Ear hair helps protect the ear canal

The functions of hair

Eyebrows divert sweat from the eyes

Nasal hair prevents dust particles entering the lungs

Scalp hair insulates the head and protects from the sun

Body hair insulates the body, helps secrete sebum onto skin surfaces and acts as a sensor for the brain

Sexual hair is the hair that grows in the bikini, underarm and, for males, chest areas. It helps provide indications of sexual development and throughout evolution has played an important part in attracting the opposite sex. There are traditional patterns for both male and female hair growth and any deviation from this can cause immense psychological issues, for example a male beard hair pattern looks great on a man but it is not socially or culturally acceptable on a woman!

In addition to being a key part of our bodies, hair is also an amazing substance:

- Hair is the second fastest-growing tissue in the body (after bone marrow).
- 35 metres of hair fibre is produced every day on the average adult scalp.
- The average scalp has 100,000 hairs. Redheads have the least number of hairs at 80,000; brown- and black-haired people have about 110,000; and blondes have the most hairs at 140,000.
- You have to lose over 50 per cent of your scalp hairs before anyone will notice.
- Over 50 per cent of men, by age 50, have male pattern hair loss, i.e. have gone bald.
- 60 per cent of women by the time they reach menopause (known as the 'change of life' or 'change' between 40 and 55) will have some superfluous facial hair.
- Men and women have the same number of facial hair follicles.
- The diameter of hair is approximately 0.1mm.
- Hair grows faster in warm weather, just like nails.
- Elderly people have slower and thinner hair growth.
- Cutting hair does not influence its growth, whether it is cut with scissors or a razor.

Your hair can reveal a lot about you!

Give a scientist one strand of your hair and they will be able to tell your ethnic origin, what you eat, whether you smoke and details about your diet and lifestyle.

Within its physical and chemical structure, hair holds an accurate record of whatever its owner has eaten or whatever has been applied to it externally – in other words: 'Your hair records what you do'. Since hair only grows 0.3–0.5mm each day, it keeps this life diary for a long time – months or even years. Your hair records whether you smoke, drink or take drugs. It can tell your ethnic origin since different races have different hair structures. The only thing which cannot be seen from a hair is whether you are male or female.

THE HISTORY OF HAIR REMOVAL

Throughout history people have gone to great lengths to remove unwanted hairs.

The earliest references to hair removal come from the ancient civilisations of Mesopotamia (now Iraq), Egypt and Greece. Early writings from Mesopotamia tell of kings asking that maidens 'be brought to me that are clean and smooth', that is hairless. The practice of hair removal, however, may date back as far as the cavemen. Archaeologists have discovered evidence that men shaved their faces as far back as 20,000 years ago, using sharpened rocks and shells to scrape off hair.

During the time of the Turkish (Ottoman) Empire, the harem was an important part of court life. The removal of bodily hair was considered an art, a tradition that has been handed down through the generations. Certain Arabic people still practise total bodily hair removal, especially prior to the wedding night.

Ancient Arabians used string to remove hair, a practice which we now call threading. Egyptians, including Cleopatra, also removed hair: some using bronze razors that have been found in their tombs, but there were other methods, utilising sugar or beeswax.

The Greeks, who equated smooth with civilised, also practised hair removal. Roman men shaved their faces, Julius Caesar is said to have had his facial hairs plucked. Roman ladies plucked their eyebrows with tweezers. A primitive method of hair removal, which actually continues to be used, is rubbing the skin with abrasive mitts or discs to remove the hair.

Early depilatory creams were made from ingredients such as arsenic, quick lime, resin, ivy gum extracts, bat's blood and powdered viper.

WHY REMOVE HAIR?

Through the centuries, hair has been removed by a wide variety of means including dung (a prehistoric version of 'waxing'). Today there are many methods available to remove hair, which we will look at in this book – thankfully dung is no longer one of them!

There are a number of medical reasons why hair needs to be removed, such as in-growing eyelashes, but the main focus of your work as an HRP will be the removal of excess or superfluous hair.

Within different cultures there are many and varied definitions of superfluous hair. Within Buddhism, for example, shaving the head is part of the process of becoming a monk. Across time, how superfluous hair is defined is also changing influenced by styles and trends. During the Elizabethan age, for example, many women removed hair from their hairline as a high forehead was considered extremely fashionable. The amount of facial and body hair which is deemed acceptable or normal can, therefore, significantly differ from one client to another.

It is important for you to understand that your potential clients' attitudes to superfluous hair will be dependent on their social, religious and geographical/

Bust of Cleopatra VII
© Sandro Vannini/CORBIS

Queen Elizabeth I
Fine Art Photographic Library/CORBIS

Buddhist monk

climatic background and their views may vary from your own. It should be noted that you may remove hair from both male and female clients from virtually any part of the body and a crucial aspect of your learning is the study, understanding and acceptance of cultural and social differences.

WHY BECOME A HAIR REMOVAL PRACTITIONER?

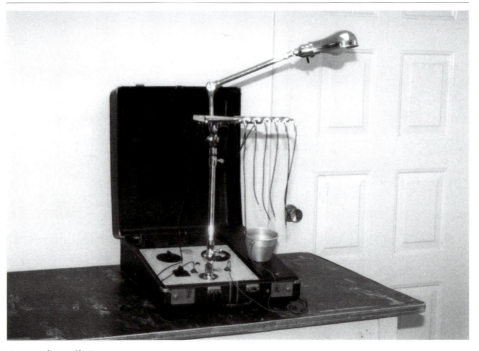

An early epilator Courtesy: International Hair Route Magazine

Hair removal has come a long way

Hair removal, and how to stop hair growing, is a multi-billion pound worldwide industry that is has, over the last ten years, attracted ongoing investment in new technology from major international companies and corporations. This investment in technology and products has meant that more money has also been spent on advertising and promotion, which has provided the consumer with a wider knowledge of hair removal techniques and you, the HRP, with more choice in terms of treatments.

How much money can I earn?

	Electrolysis	'Waxing'/sugaring
Income per hour	£60.00	£60.00
Costs per hour	£2.88	£3.48
Gross profit per hour	£57.12*	£56.52*

*This doesn't include fixed costs, i.e. premises, salaries, etc., and depends on the system used and the number/types of treatments carried out in that hour.

As you can see from the table, with good business management, a career as an HRP, offering a combination of treatments, can earn you a very comfortable living. If you are employed as an HRP, the average annual salary is £18,000–£20,000 which can either be a straight salary or a basic salary plus commission on treatments and/or retail. Further information on how to succeed in the business of hair removal is provided in Part Six.

What career opportunities are available to you as an HRP?

Learning hair removal can be your first step into any number of career paths. As the spidergram illustrates, an HRP can practise in a variety of ways using different combinations of treatment methods:

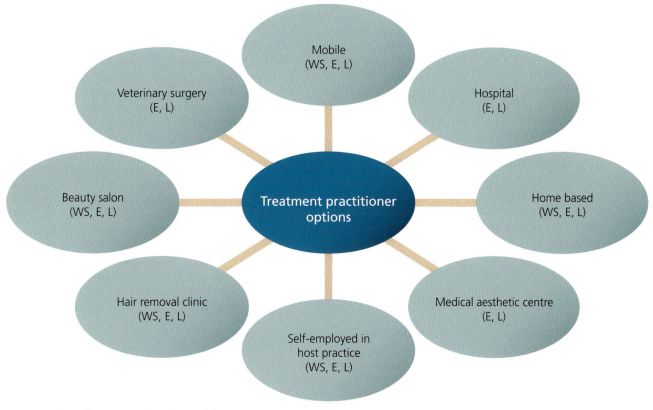

Key: WS = 'waxing' and sugaring, E = electrolysis, L = light

Teaching or assessing is another common career path for HRPs and there are four main educational opportunities:

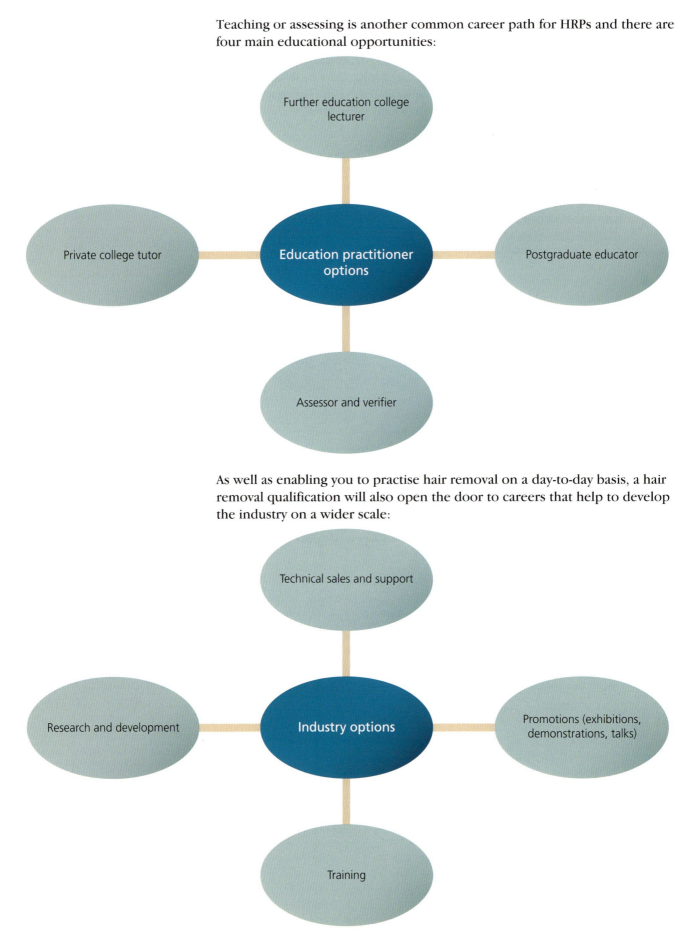

As well as enabling you to practise hair removal on a day-to-day basis, a hair removal qualification will also open the door to careers that help to develop the industry on a wider scale:

Additional training

After you have left college and qualified as an HRP, there are several further qualifications you can pursue to help advance your career:

- Advanced techniques (which are really minor cosmetic surgery procedures)
    - removal of red veins (correct medical term is telangiectasia)
    - removal of skin tags (correct medical term is fibroma)
    - removal of milia (white, pearly nodule trapped under the skin with no pore).
- A teaching qualification, which is a standard prerequisite for becoming a lecturer.
- Business training, to make sure that you have a successful business as well as being one of best HRPs.

How can I achieve job satisfaction?

Hair removal is a 'people business' and, arguably, few jobs offer the rewards that one earns from being a successful HRP. The emotional rewards of being an HRP are rarely matched by any other treatment in the field of salon and clinic treatments. In particular, HRP practitioners have the ability to positively affect clients' self-image and lifestyle, the opportunity to work with people from a wide range of social and cultural backgrounds, for example sports people (male and female), models, grannies, men and women of all ages.

To have this positive effect on clients, you will need all of the following skills; one without the others is not sufficient:

- in-depth anatomy and physiology knowledge
- well-honed interpersonal and communication skills
- technical and practical ability.

Exercising this wide range of skills on a daily basis also ensures that a career in hair removal never becomes dull.

It is unlikely that excess facial and body hair will ever become fashionable and, as human hair continues to grow, a career in hair removal presents a never-ending opportunity, particularly as the industry has progressed towards all-gender hair management. Passing on knowledge and skills to students or colleagues and maintaining lifelong learning as new techniques and equipment become available means an HRP's career is always developing. At the same time, the high earning potential, flexible working hours and unique challenges presented by every client makes hair removal a highly satisfying job.

PRACTITIONER PROFILE

Name Louise Gray

Occupation Hair removal lecturer

Region North west of England

Route to job Higher Diploma in Beauty Therapy at the Abraham Moss College Manchester followed by Certificate in Education at Bolton Institute.

Years in the business After 22 years of dedicated work, I now feel I must have been born with a needle holder in my hand (not a silver spoon)!

Training days It now seems so many moons ago, but my memories of this time are fond and particularly happy. My training was a very rewarding experience: Pam Ledgard gave me the inspiration at the time to specialise as an electrologist. Early in my career I joined the Institute of Electrolysis, Eve Shacklady being my mentor and close friend at this time. I later joined the British Association of Electrolysis (BAE) and became involved for a brief period with the Education Committee of the BAE.

Career path My first experience of working as an electrologist was for the American company Kree International, which I found gave me a great deal of valuable experience working on a wide range of clients. These included transsexuals or – as they are referred to today – gender reassignment clients.

A natural progression into education came in my early twenties, when I was involved as a practical and marking examiner for City and Guilds. I have constantly found teaching electrolysis to be extremely rewarding and have had a number of successes with students; very recently one of my students was the winner of the regional final of the 'Sterex Electrolysis Student of The Year' competition and another of my students was placed second in the national finals of the same competition.

Life as a lecturer Life as a college lecturer involves a fluctuating variety of rewarding, challenging, gratifying, taxing and many other emotions. Ultimately, however, the experience is such a worthwhile one and I wouldn't wish to change this for something else with perhaps more tangible (i.e. monetary!) rewards.

To a prospective lecturer, I would point out the following necessary – some might say obvious – requirements for the job:

- good communications and flexibility
- being well organised and trustworthy
- possessing a particularly thick skin allied with a good sense of humour!
- being unshockable and unshakeable
- appearing to be (if not actually being) confident!
- having the stamina to stand for hours on end!
- (most importantly) having a deep and unwavering love of paperwork!

Someone else's perspective As an ex-student and colleague of Louise's, I felt strongly that I had to add my two-penn'th. Louise has always been a huge inspiration to me, from the day when I first, very shakily, held an epilation probe to the day, very recently, when I needed someone to stand silently behind me. As a tutor she is kind, patient – with a capital P – and very funny, even though she may not always be aware of it! One of the most important qualities that Louise has – for all those who know her – is that she inspires others to give of their best. She inspired me to achieve almost everything that I have achieved in the industry. To sum up: she is an ideal role model, especially for aspiring electrologists.

PRACTITIONER PROFILE

Name Teresa Chilton

Occupation Electrologist

Region Midlands

Route to job I retrained at the age of 39, going to a private college as felt I didn't have 2 or 3 years' time to go to FE.

Years in the business I've been doing electrolysis since 1993.

Training days I did enjoy my training although I found it very nerve racking! But I had a very good teacher! I really enjoyed my training because being a very hairy person myself I appreciated the benefit to others. It is actually a life changing thing as far as I am concerned and have had many clients for whom it has done just that for.

Industry experiences I've not had any bad experiences myself but have seen plenty of bad practice when visiting colleges and also when judging a national electrolysis competition! My first industry experience was working for myself; I had a lady with a very dark moustache. I saw her every week for a long time, but she was happy with the result.

Modality preferred Regarding the method of electrolysis; I use SWD (short wave diathermy) and blend, but mostly SWD.

Fees and clients I charge £9 for 10 min, £12.50 for 15 min and £17 for 30 min. Most of my clients have one of those three. I average about thirty electrolysis clients per week.

Why electrolysis? I feel passionate about electrolysis and it being done correctly, this I know I share with the authors! Again, because I was so hairy and it was such a problem to me, I really appreciate the benefits electrolysis can bring.

Continual professional development I attended the GMT Electrolysis Finishing School and I believe everyone should go on this highly reputable training course or something very like it. Unfortunately there are practitioners who do not carry out electrolysis correctly and, in my opinion, this is because some are not taught correct technique, which makes students hate doing it. If there were more fully competent lecturers, this situation could be avoided.

Advice My advice to students wishing to set up? First and foremost go on the GMT Finishing School course to give them more confidence. After that, I suppose it would very much depend on their age. If they were young, I would say go and work in a salon, one that needs all the skills including electrolysis and not somewhere that doesn't do it!! Get some experience under their belts. However if they were mature, as I was, then I would start in a small way working for myself, making sure I always gave 100 per cent. As the client base grew by word of mouth, I would look to expand, possibly eventually employing someone, or taking an associate, which is what I have done. But I would advise starting small and not shelling out lots of money to open a posh place, only for it to close down. Run before you can walk!!

Client showcase I used to have a client, let's call her Ros. She was of a Mediterranean background and very hairy everywhere. She originally went to her GP with her hirsuitism, only to be told that electrolysis didn't work and caused scarring. A female GP at that!! Ros rang the BAE (British Association of Electrolysis) who gave her my number. She was hairy everywhere, but her main concern was around her nipples. She had so much hair it was like a rug! She was 34 and had never had a relationship because of this problem. We sorted it of course over the course of 2 years. Ros came weekly for all that time and, me being me, I couldn't charge her the full rate every week, so she used to do foreign language lessons for my son as part payment! She had a lot of hairs on her upper lip but she had 4 hairs on the left side of her face which bothered her! I used to epilate those 4 hairs, I could see that she was only concerned about those so didn't mention the upper lip even though I was desperate to treat it. She now has a little boy and is in a happy relationship. So for her electrolysis was life changing.

PRACTITIONER PROFILE

Name Gill Mann

Business Name SkinWise

Region Reading, Berkshire

Route to job I started my career in the beauty industry working for The Sheila Godfrey Clinic where we specialised in electrolysis and then I moved on to offer intense pulsed light (IPL) hair removal treatments using the Epilight system. After moving location for personal reasons, I set up my own aesthetic clinic offering hair removal treatments with the Lumina IPL system and electrolysis. I also offer treatments for thread veins, sun damage, rosacea, acne, fine lines and wrinkles and general skincare advice.

How many years in the business Approximately 10 years.

Did you enjoy your training? I studied at Warwickshire College, Leamington Spa and enjoyed my time training immensely. No bad experiences that I can remember, just many good memories.

First industry experience One of my first IPL clients was someone planning to get married and we were treating her forehead and temples. I covered her eyebrows with microtape, but obviously not enough as I removed hairs from one of her eyebrows. On her wedding day she had to use more eyebrow pencil to cover the gap up. Fortunately, she was amicable about it and the hairs did come back. They say you learn from your mistakes and I certainly did. I tend to put more microtape on now than is needed, but it is better to be safe than sorry.

Types of hair removal equipment used:
1 Electrolysis machines – Apilus, Sterex, Carlton Blend, Rita Roberts
2 Laser/IPL machines – Lumina, Epilight, Aculight, Plasmalite, Lightsheer.

Average charge £15 for 15 mins electrolysis. IPL from £60/£75 per session.

Approximate number of treatments per week Based on a busy four-day week, I have 25 hair removal clients, a mixture of electrolysis and IPL clients.

Why did you choose to focus on hair removal? I went back to college as a mature student and did not feel manicures, pedicures and waxing were for me. I enjoyed electrolysis early on and was thrown in at the deep end working at a specialist clinic. I found specialising in one particular area much more rewarding. At present I also teach electrolysis and the theory of laser and IPL treatments, which gives me the opportunity to pass on my experiences and knowledge to others.

What advice would you give to a student who wants to start a hair removal business? It is important to ensure you research the market for the correct equipment and check out the history of the companies and whether they are likely to stay around. There will be a need for hair removal treatments for many years to come and if a laser company doesn't offer you in-depth training, help with setting up and registering with the Healthcare Commission, I suggest you steer clear of them. Don't be put off by the Healthcare Commission; they are trying to make things easier for Laser/IPL clinics to register. It may be tedious, but clients are more likely to trust clinics who are registered than those who have not bothered to take the time to do so.

Before making any decisions about equipment and opening up your own business, go on some seminars or training courses. Equipment is not cheap, but long term the rewards are well worth the investment.

What postgraduate training have you undertaken?

● BTEC Award in Laser and Intense Pulsed Light Hair Removal. A real insight into how these systems work.
● Laser Safety Effectiveness Course.
● Regular ongoing training with Lynton Lasers, which is imperative. User group meetings twice per year, which enable you to talk to other businesses in the industry and discuss treatments, results, etc.

Assessment of knowledge and understanding

You have now learnt about the background to hair removal. To test your level of knowledge and understanding, answer the following short questions:

1 Define depilation.

2 Define epilation.

3 Name an area of the body where no hairs can be found.

4 Name the pocket from which hair grows.

5 What is secreted from the sebaceous gland?

6 List the structures which together form the pilo-sebaceous unit.

7 What factors determine the colour of an individual's hair and skin?

8 State three functions of hair.

9 What is the function of the dermal papilla?

10 Name the protein from which hair is formed.

Activities

Conduct the following activities to practise your background knowledge of hair removal:

1 Investigate hair removal methods from a particular period in history, using both the internet and reference books which concentrate on the lifestyle and social aspects of your chosen period.

2 Visit local salons to collect price lists and compile a list of hair removal services on offer in your local area.

3 Using the information gained from the collected price lists work out the average charge in your area for each of the hair removal services.

Follow-up knowledge

To build on the knowledge of hair removal gained in this chapter, complete the following task to extend your hair removal skills and understanding:

1 Visit www.beautyserve.com to see the Beauty Industry Survey and evaluate the types of hair removal treatments requested by clients.

Advanced knowledge reference section

Hair, religion and culture

Hair plays a major part not only in the way we look but also in the way we are perceived by ourselves and others. In many cultures and religions hair is very significant. The following gives an insight into the importance of hair or lack of it within a number of cultures and religions.

Hinduism

Tradition amongst some Hindus states that when a father dies, the eldest son is required to remove the hair on his head before the cremation ceremony.

In many temples in the south of India, removal of hair is considered as an 'offering'. A head shaving ceremony is performed in the temple for both boys and girls before the age of four. Hair is seen as an adornment, so by shaving the head, the child confronts his or her bare ego. It teaches humbleness and devotion. Children with shaved heads are seen as innocent and holy and are treated with great respect.

Sikhism

The Sikh religion forbids the cutting or shaving of any bodily hair. Hair on the head is not cut but wound into a turban. Beards are allowed to grow untamed.

Islam

Amongst Muslims, hair removal is part of a ritual of general purity and cleanliness: there is some debate about the finer points of Islamic law but the following are relatively common recommendations:

- Both men and women should remove armpit and pubic hair at least every 40 days.
- For men, a beard is desirable.
- Women can remove 'unnatural' facial hair but should not reshape eyebrows for reasons of vanity.

Judaism

In the Jewish faith, the hair of a married woman is traditionally considered as erotic. As a result, married Orthodox Jewish women are generally expected to cover their hair, except in front of their husbands, and sometimes in the company of other women. For most of Jewish history this practice was not disputed – mainly because society at large also considered it immodest for women to let their hair down in its city streets. In recent times, however, it has become a less common practice, although some married Orthodox Jewish women continue to cover their hair in some way, with a wrap, snood or wig. If a woman chooses to wear a wig, her natural hair is often cut very short or shaved in order to make the wig fit comfortably. For men in some sectors of the Jewish faith it is forbidden to shave the beard or the hair at the sides of the face (sideburns).

Buddhism

Head shaving is part of the process of becoming a Buddhist monk: The Head Shaving Ceremony is about renunciation: from their normal life and self before entering into a monastic lifestyle aimed at the attainment of Buddhahood.

The Far East

In Japan there is a long tradition of great attention to personal hygiene. The main difference between Japanese and Western hair removal practice is that waxing is less commonly used and 'sandpaper' friction strips are particularly popular.

Recently, many of the initial studies into laser hair removal have been carried out in Japan, indicating their interest in this developing method.

It is said that threading originated in China; in fact there are references to 'depilatory string' being used in pre-revolutionary China for people in positions of great power or authority.

The Middle East

Among the ancient Egyptians, a clean-shaven face was a symbol of status. The Egyptians used razors and pumice stones for hair removal. Both men and women shaved themselves bald and then wore very elaborate wigs. Egyptian women used beeswax to remove hair. There is also some evidence that they made a type of depilatory paste using starch, arsenic and quicklime, a very dangerous pastime!

The Egyptians' great interest in hair removal was probably due to their extreme climate, the constant heat encouraged the spread of germs and diseases and the removal of body hair was seen as more hygienic and considered a preventive measure against infection.

The Egyptians' invented sugaring, using a paste that was, and still is, made from sugar and lemon. Sugaring was used as part of a Middle Eastern bridal ritual where, on the eve of the wedding, Lebanese, Palestinian, Turkish and Egyptian brides had all their body hair, except their eyebrows and the hair on their heads, removed by the bridal party. According to lore, the bride maintained her hairless body throughout her marriage as a symbol of cleanliness and respect for her husband.

It is said that tweezers have been found in a tomb dating back to about 3500 BC.

Threading is also said to have its roots in the Far East, where it was used by Arabian women to remove leg hairs.

Europe

Since the times of the ancient Greeks and the Romans, Europeans have had a history of removing hair. The first shave of young Roman men was seen as the arrival of manhood and was used as an offering to the gods. Anglo Saxons used primitive tweezers for plucking hairs from their had bodies. During the Middle Ages, upper class European women wanted to be pale and a thirteenth-century French verse lists some of the requirements of a lady's toilette as supplied by a travelling merchant; among the items included are 'razors and forceps'.

The puritan element in the medieval church prevented most Englishwomen from using cosmetics.

Elizabethan women perceived a high forehead as a sign of great beauty and so many women plucked their hairline in order to achieve the desired effect. It is believed that mothers often used bandages impregnated with vinegar and cat's dung on their daughter's heads as they believed it prevented hair from growing.

It is said that the Duke of Newcastle paid 40 pounds to have his wife's facial hair permanently removed, yet in a letter dated 1755, Horace Walpole refers to the Duke's retirement, saying that he can now 'let his beard grow as long as his Duchess's'.

North America

Native Americans tweezed out their whiskers, hair by hair, between halves of a clam shell. Around 1700, American women applied poultices of caustic lye to burn away hair and no doubt some of the surface of their skin! Around 1800, depilatory creams and powders began to be used.

South America

Brazilian women used the sap from the Coco de Mono tree, a very early type of resin wax to remove hair. Hair removal remains popular, and young girls are often introduced to hair removal by their mothers who regularly visit local waxing salons that use the cold wax method. The women who carry out the waxing treatment are known as 'Depiladoras' (literally, wax women).

part two

the basics

CONSULTATION

This chapter covers the consultation process for hair removal treatments. It describes the competencies required to enable you to:

- **understand each step of the consultation process**
- **conduct a holistic consultation**
- **identify contra-indications for treatments**
- **investigate hair growth.**

When consulting a client it is important to use the skills covered in other chapters:

- **in-depth knowledge of the skin and pilo-sebaceous unit (Chapter Three)**
- **in-depth knowledge of the causes of hair growth (Chapter Three)**
- **in-depth knowledge of temporary hair removal methods and their effects (Chapters Four to Six)**
- **understanding of contra-indications (reasons why treatments cannot take place) (all chapters)**
- **before- and after-treatment procedures (all chapters).**

G15 Provide support to the client

ASSESSING THE CLIENT AND PREPARING TREATMENT PLANS

You may be asking: 'Why do I need to consult with my client?' You may feel you already know what they want and you just want to get them on the couch and get started. This, however, is the wrong approach. You wouldn't expect a doctor to prescribe treatment, for example, without asking you some questions and listening carefully to your answers, would you? There are many reasons why we must consult with our clients before carrying out any treatment:

- to establish a rapport with the client
- to gain the client's trust and confidence
- to identify areas of client concern

- to identify the cause of growth
- to see how previous hair removal methods affect the current growth and treatment plan
- to identify indications and contra-indications
- to promote and sell yourself, your skills, the treatment and associated products.

To put this even more straightforwardly, the consultation is about:

- getting to know each other
- getting to know and understand the client's needs in order to give them the appropriate treatment and products
- gaining relevant information.

The reception area

This is often where first impressions are made and, even if preconceived ideas have been formed by marketing literature, advertising, referrals or other methods of communication, it is in the reception area that a potential client can take one look and decide in a matter of seconds whether they like the look of your establishment or not. If not, they will turn around and walk out.

The first person that your potential client will see will probably be the receptionist, so ensure that this person is skilled in the art of putting people at their ease. The receptionist should be efficient in carrying out their duties, but also effective in their dealings with people.

It may be that in some small businesses there is not a set receptionist, instead two or more members of the team may share the role. This is fine if time is set aside specifically for answering the phone and dealing with customer issues. It is not acceptable, however, for each hair removal practitioner (HRP), in turn with colleagues, to shout 'My turn' and run out of their treatment room, leaving their client, to grab the phone in an out of breath manner. This upsets the client in the salon and makes the potential client on the phone think you are disorganised – making it less likely that they will want to come to you.

The consultation appointment normally lasts for 30 minutes, this should be enough time for you to ask the necessary questions and for the potential client to give you the answers. Therefore, 30 minutes needs to be booked out in the appointment system. Some salons also book out a further 15 minutes at the end of the consultation in case the client wants to start treatment there and then.

Most salons do not charge for a consultation, but for the few that do the fee is normally refunded against the cost of the first treatment. Some business owners believe that by charging a fee it will stop time wasters, however it is generally best to offer the consultation free, as you should endeavour to minimise, wherever possible, the number of reasons for a potential client to go elsewhere.

> **REMEMBER !**
>
> Something as simple as answering the phone in a rush will put potential customers off

> **PROFESSIONAL TIP ✔**
>
> You may consider offering your potential clients a choice or menu of background music

As decoration and music are part of the image of your business, the reception and treatment rooms should be decorated in such a way that it is least offensive for the vast majority of people; the same principle should be applied to background music. Remember it is not your preferences that you should choose but those most likely to appeal to your customers.

Price lists

Ensure price lists are available throughout the reception, not just on the reception desk but on other surfaces around the space and particularly in the toilet – as most clients visit the toilet it can be a useful place to put information. The importance of the toilet must never be underestimated and it must be immaculately clean, with quality fittings, décor and accessories, as clients will often judge the quality of the rest of your business on that small room.

> **REMEMBER** !
>
> Décor colours are subjective: use neutral hues in the reception areas as these are the least offensive to everyone. Accent colours, which can be highlighted using paintings and knick knacks, etc. can be added for a splash of colour

The consultation process

Consultation position

Removing barriers

Make sure you guide potential clients through to the consultation area, remembering they do not know where to go or what to do and may be feeling uncomfortable or even threatened and therefore putting up barriers to free-flow of information.

Seating

'Invisible barriers' can be created by incorrect or unsuitable seating positions, for example, if one person is sitting higher than another, it puts the lower person at a psychological disadvantage. Of course actual 'physical' barriers should also be avoided, for example, tables, couches, etc. between yourself and the potential client.

First impressions count

Be aware the potential client's first impression of you and your business may come from promotional activities, such as leaflets, flyers, advertisements in the newspaper, word of mouth, promotions on a website, e-mail, etc. A client's normal means of communication, from her/his initial interest being stimulated, is the phone, making it a vital business tool. It is essential that the person representing your business on the phone smiles, as smiling positively affects the sound of the voice. The tone of voice should be welcoming and it should demonstrate an interest in what the caller is saying. Alternatively your potential clients may simply just walk into your business.

Personal presentation and image

Remember, whoever greets the potential client, be it yourself or your receptionist, should create the image that you wish to portray for your business. For example, if a clinical image is your choice, then crisp white uniforms may be worn or, if a relaxed environment is preferred, more casual attire may be worn.

Communication

When we communicate with other people, 93 per cent of our message is non-verbal, it is conveyed by what is known as body language. Roughly 40 per cent of this is classed as non-verbal – that is, the

PROFESSIONAL TIP ✔

To empower nervous clients arrange the seating so they sit slightly higher than you

PROFESSIONAL TIP ✔

To salon owners if it is not possible to greet your client personally, leave a clearly visible written or video message

PROFESSIONAL TIP ✔

Image is a means of business communication

KEY TERMS ★

Body language: Any non-verbal communication

position of the body, facial expressions, gestures, etc., just as 50 per cent is classed as body communication and relates to the way we dress, our hair style, make-up, etc. So, please be aware that the following examples are crucial to a successful consultation: open gestures; maintaining eye contact; leaning towards the potential client; nodding; raising eyebrows, etc.

Verbal

The actual words you speak account for only 7 per cent of the received message. You must ensure that the words you use and your body language are saying the same thing, otherwise your client will believe the body language. So if you are tired and sitting in a slumped position, the potential client will believe you are uninterested despite your words to the contrary.

Questioning and listening

You should aim to talk for only 20 per cent of the consultation. Therefore, you will be listening for 80 per cent of the time.

Listening means:

- concentrating on your client's words and body language
- showing interest
- not interrupting
- not saying you 'understand how they feel' or 'don't worry' as this means you are being sympathetic and not empathetic
- not taking the words out of their mouths.

Your questions should be open-ended and positive to illicit as much information as possible. The aim is to guide the client with specific questions.

Gathering information

This is about scene setting – establishing the client's prior knowledge and expectations, describing the treatment from beginning to end, including client responsibilities throughout the course of treatment. Use a consultation sheet/record card as a guide. Remind yourself why you are asking the questions. Your first question should be: Which area do you want treating?

PROFESSIONAL TIP ✔

Remember what it's like not to know – be aware of possible client sensitivities and embarrassment

PROFESSIONAL TIP ✔

Establishing the client's prior knowledge and understanding of the treatment will ensure you do not waste time going through unnecessary explanations

The record card can be completed once all the information has been gathered and you have ascertained that the potential client wants to go ahead with the treatment. Always remember, it is only after the potential client agrees to have treatment that they become 'a client'.

Example of record card systems Sterex Electrolysis

CONDUCTING A HOLISTIC CONSULTATION

A holistic consultation takes into consideration areas of the client's life over and above the specific treatment area, that is to say the whole person and everything that may act upon it. It also involves understanding what type of hair growth the client has and a consideration of what might cause that hair growth.

The following three aspects of a holistic consultation will affect the planning, actual treatment, aftercare procedures and treatment outcomes.

- *Mind* – The potential client's level of concern that their superfluous hair is causing them, in terms, perhaps, of restricting them in social and work activities or negatively affecting their self-image.
- *Body* – The potential client's physical health and mental wellbeing (i.e. food intake, water, caffeine, alcohol, smoking, sleep, stress levels, medication).
- *Lifestyle* – What the potential client's does in and with their life (i.e. exercise, hobby and leisure activities, working environment, holidays, relationships).

Holistic consultation

KEY TERMS ★

Holistic: The whole person, the mind and the environment that the person is in

Treatment appropriate for client's hair growth type?

Client committed to their role in achieving desired treatment outcome?

Treatment appropriate for client's skin type and condition?

Client aware of the equipment to be used in treatment?

Desired outcomes for treatment?

A holistic consultation

Client actively involved in discussion and planning of treatment programme?

Impact of client's health and general fitness on treatment?

Home-care advice?

All possible contra-actions covered?

Client's lifestyle compatible with treatment?

Questioning techniques

Every potential client must answer a number of questions before the correct treatment can be determined. This questioning must be conducted in a private area and all recorded information treated as confidential and securely stored in accordance with the Data Protection Act 1998.

Ask all questions in a sensitive and supportive way and avoid using technical terms or questions which lead to a one word response of 'yes' or 'no'. Aim to make the potential client as comfortable as possible during questioning to ensure an accurate consultation.

Should the consultation reveal that the potential client is unsuitable for treatment, carefully explain this to them and instruct them to seek permission from their GP before commencing treatment.

Standard consultation questions

PROFESSIONAL TIP ✔

Use open-ended questions that begin with who, what, why, when and how

Questions	Information required
What is your desired treatment outcome?	Check this is realistic and match with an appropriate treatment
Which area/s require treatment?	Ensure the potential client highlights every area requiring treatment
When did you first require treatment?	May indicate the cause of hair growth such as puberty, pregnancy or menopause while no obvious cause may reveal an underlying medical issue
What hair removal treatments have you received previously? How satisfactory were the results? If unsatisfactory, why?	Allows you to discuss the benefits your treatment will provide.
What treatments are you currently undergoing for the area (e.g. temporary hair removal methods)?	The treatment area may have deteriorated through neglect or inappropriate treatments – ensure your planned treatment is compatible
Describe your lifestyle	Lifestyle factors directly impact on a client's health
Is your menstrual cycle normal?	A medical problem causing unwanted hair growth may be indicated by an unusual menstrual cycle
Would your commitment to ongoing treatment be hampered by any external issues?	Highlights any impediments which need to be addressed for continuing hair removal treatment
What is your name, address and telephone number?	Necessary if the client needs to be contacted

Types of hair growth

There are three main types of hair growth relevant to hair removal treatments:

1 superfluous or excess hair growth
2 hypertrichosis
3 hirsuitism

Superfluous or excess hair growth

The terms superfluous or excessive refer to hair growth that is normal for any given age, sex or gender but is socially/culturally unacceptable, that is, it is a normal growth pattern for someone of their background but they would prefer not to have it.

Superfluous hair growth can be found on the following areas:

- hairline
- eyebrows
- sides of face
- chest
- axillae (underarm)
- forearm hair
- bikini area
- legs
- toes
- back, ears and buttocks (males).

Hypertrichosis

Hypertrichosis is hormone stimulated growth which is considered abnormal for age, gender and race and is typically seen as:

- strong terminal growth on the chin or face of a female
- strong terminal growth on the back (female)
- strong terminal growth on the breast or chest (female)
- abdomen.

Hirsuitism

Hirsuitism refers to complete male hair growth pattern on females which is hormonally stimulated. Male growth pattern is facial hair, in a beard shape, which is sometimes associated with chest hair and male baldness pattern.

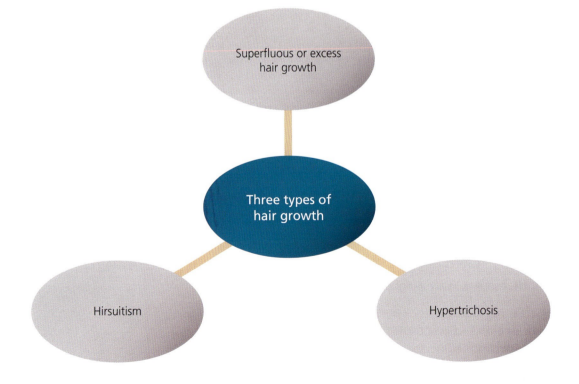

Causes of hair growth

Mechanical stimulation:	Plucking (including 'waxing', threading, sugaring), abrasion.
Normal systemic:	Puberty, pregnancy, menopause, i.e. times of normal hormonal changes in the body.
Abnormal systemic:	Hormone influencing medication: i.e. steroids, contraceptive pill and hormone replacement therapy (HRT) fertility drugs. Disease: e.g. endocrine disorders. Operation: e.g. skin grafts, hysterectomy/oophorectomy. Stress: (may only stimulate hair growth when condition is severe and subsequently triggers a hormonal imbalance, e.g. in anorexia).

TECHNICAL TIP

There is an ongoing debate as to whether topical (externally applied) steroid creams are a cause of hair growth

Clients requiring epilation and light treatments need to provide specific information at the consultation stage and this is explained in the relevant chapters throughout the book.

CONTRA-INDICATIONS AND PRE-TREATMENT PRECAUTIONS

A contra-indication is something which would prevent treatment being carried out. A pre-treatment precaution is something which needs further investigation or medical referral prior to treatment. The same condition can be a contra-indication or a pre-treatment precaution depending on the site of treatment.

This section covers the generic contra-indications and pre-treatment precautions for all hair removal methods. Specific contra-indications and pre-treatment precautions for electrolysis and light treatments are provided in the relevant chapter.

REMEMBER

If in doubt, gain a medical referral

HEALTH AND SAFETY

If a client presents a contra-indication, you must receive a letter of consent from their GP before commencing any treatment. Always practise within the limits of your professional area and do not attempt to diagnose contra-indications when referring a client to their GP

Contra-indications that prevent treatment

- Contagious skin disease, e.g. impetigo.
- Skin cancer (only a contra-indication if on, or close to, the proposed treatment area).
- Allergies (to products used during treatment or if the client has a pre-existing reaction to something else, even if outside of the salon).

Pre-treatment precautions

- Skin disorder, e.g. eczema (would contra-indicate if on the proposed treatment area).
- Allergies (if client has recently experienced an allergic reaction to a substance unrelated to the treatment, their skin may be over-sensitised

and treatment should be delayed until the body has completely recovered).

- Damaged skin, e.g. sunburn and bruising (would contra-indicate if on the proposed treatment area).
- Diabetes, as skin healing may be impaired (for insulin-dependent clients, a doctor's referral is recommended as the symptoms may be more profound than for clients who have diet controlled diabetes).
- Epilepsy (a doctor's referral is required).
- Hyper-sensitive skin.

Be aware that highly strung or very nervous clients can be problematic and may not be suitable for treatment as they can fidget, be over-sensitive to the sensation and make sudden moves. Clients with nervous system dysfunctions may also not be able to detect sensations and this can cause skin areas to be over-treated. Always note the client's body language whilst consulting with them: reassure them if they display discomfort, otherwise they might be deterred from proceeding with a successful treatment.

Investigating the hair growth at the time of the consultation

Once you have established the cause(s) of hair growth and considered any contra-indications and pre-treatment precautions, the next stage is to describe and discuss, with the client, the treatment procedure and plan the client's role and responsibilities within the treatment plan, for example home-care.

Many hair removal methods badly affect hair growth by disrupting the hair growth cycle. In order to plan the treatment and advise the client, it is important to assess the stage of the hair growth as it presents at the time of the consultation and find out whether or not you are seeing the full extent of the hair growth by questioning the client and assessing the area to be treated.

You need to ask a number of basic questions to give you the information you require:

- What hair removal methods have you used previously?
- Over what timescale have previous treatments been used?
- How often were previous treatments used and when was the last time?
- If necessary, are you able to commit to ongoing treatment?
- What is your desired treatment outcome?

DIFFERENT METHODS OF TEMPORARY HAIR REMOVAL AND THEIR EFFECTS

By answering your questions, the client should reveal sufficient information (e.g. desired long-term result of treatment) that will allow you to select an appropriate hair removal method.

Method	Treatment result	Long-term effects
Plucking: tweezing; threading; electronic rotary tweezer	Removes hair from the follicle either individually with tweezers or in groups with an electronic rotary tweezer or by threading. Hairs take from several days up to several weeks to re-grow.	Stimulates blood supply, encourages growth and may distort the follicle.
'Waxing': hot, warm, cool and sugaring	Removes lots of hair from their follicles in one go using products. Hairs take from several days up to several weeks to re-grow.	Stimulates blood supply, encourages growth and may distort the follicle. Cosmetically advantageous as the re-growth is slow compared to cutting and shaving. Quick and easy to achieve results.
Depilatory creams	Chemically dissolves the hair from above the skin surface to fractionally below. Hairs re-grow in 2–4 days.	Can often act as a skin sensitiser; does not stimulate hair growth.
Bleaching	Bleaching is not actually a hair removal method; it is a method of making the hair less noticeable. Bleaching is performed by applying a chemical (bleach) to the area, which removes the pigment from the hair.	Only effective on finer hairs. Often causes skin irritation. Bleaches the skin as well as the hair if great care is not taken. Does not affect the follicle.
Cutting and shaving	Cuts hair off at the skin surface. Hairs re-grow in 1–3 days.	Hair re-grows with a blunt, not tapered end, so cosmetically a disadvantage as hair may appear thicker; does not stimulate growth.
Abrasive methods: discs, pumice stone	Using friction, rubs hair away from above the skin surface often leaving skin very sore and sensitised. Hairs re-grow in 1–3 days.	Only suitable for fine hair and resilient skin; may stimulate blood supply and therefore growth.

Showing the equipment

Depending on their prior knowledge, talk the client through and show them the various pieces of equipment and products that will be used. This puts the client's mind at rest and demonstrates your knowledge and professionalism.

Talking through the treatment procedure

Explain in detail what will be done and why, the sensation the client will feel and the benefits and after-effects; use visual aids where necessary to reinforce your explanations. A reference book can be created in the salon with photographs of treatments in progress and before and after shots (keeping client's anonymity at all times by covering the eyes during photography). In particular, the use of skin and hair diagrams and commercially available posters are invaluable to aid client understanding.

Discussing the client's role in the treatment

It should be emphasised to your client that they have a part to play in this treatment, for example they must follow the instructions given by the HRP with regard to home-care procedures and hair management. The importance of the client attending regularly for appointments must be stressed at this stage.

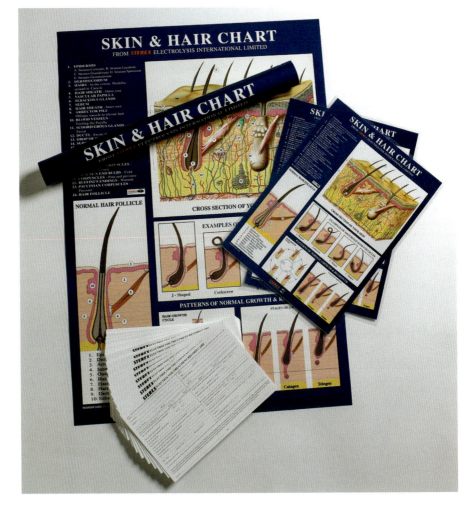

Skin and hair charts   Sterex Electrolysis

Selling

Throughout the process of the consultation you will be selling yourself, the treatment and the home-care products.

The aim of the consultation is to have happy, informed and confident clients who are aware of the treatment plan, their role within it and the outcome they can expect.

Assessment of knowledge and understanding

You have now learnt how to conduct a hair removal consultation. To test your level of knowledge and understanding, answer the following short questions:

1 Who needs to have the most information about the other, the potential client or the therapist?

2 What is the aim of the consultation and why is it important?

3 List the three aspects you must ascertain during a 'holistic' consultation.

4 List the three types of hair growth.

5 List two causes of hair growth.

6 What is the difference between a contra-indication and a pre-treatment precaution?

7 What do you believe are the differences between 'effective' and 'efficient' behaviour?

8 List two general contra-indications to hair removal treatments.

9 Define depilation.

10 List two effects of tweezing.

Activities

Conduct the following activities to practise your knowledge of hair removal consultations:

1 Carry out a 'mock' consultation with a member of your family or a friend, having previously given them a list of hair growth causes to choose from. Tell them NOT to tell you the cause of hair growth they have chosen until you ask the appropriate question(s).

2 When next out in a social situation note the body language of a couple near to you and try and evaluate their relationship and mood.

3 Research into a contra-indication of your choice to explain further the reasons why the condition prevents treatment in the proposed treatment area.

4 Contact salons in your area to ask which methods of hair removal they offer, then create a chart detailing the popularity of the various methods.

5 Create your own visual aid to explain hair growth to potential clients.

Follow-up knowledge

To build on the knowledge of consultations gained in this chapter, complete the following tasks to extend your hair removal skills and understanding:

1 On the internet, using search engines, find and research websites relating to conditions which a potential client may present with, which may prevent or restrict treatment, for example diabetes.

2 Using search engines, find out additional information on body language.

3 Using the internet, find out which are the most accepted and recognised 'calming' colours.

Advanced knowledge reference section

Polycystic ovaries, other conditions and special circumstances which affect hair growth

In this section, there are detailed descriptions of five conditions which adversely affect hair growth and skin condition. It is important that HRPs are aware of these conditions and how they will impact on treatment in order to give accurate advice and treatment plans.

1 Polycystic ovaries and polycystic ovarian syndrome.

2 Menopause.

3 HRT (hormone replacement therapy).

4 Endometriosis.

5 Infertility and in-vitro fertilisation (IVF).

Polycystic ovaries and polycystic ovarian syndrome

As an HRP you will relatively frequently come into contact with sufferers of these conditions, so it is important that you understand their condition in order to give a professional and appropriate service. The disorder was first discovered in 1935 by Drs Stein and Leventhal and, consequently, polycystic ovarian syndrome or PCOS is also known as Stein-Leventhal syndrome.

Polycystic ovaries are ovaries which have many cysts just below their surface. The ovary thickens and cysts are formed because the graafian follicles fail to produce mature ova; the immature ova become trapped below the surface because of hormonal imbalances and ovulation consequently cannot occur from these follicles. The result is a build-up of small cysts and eventually the ovaries become enlarged.

Roughly 25 per cent of British women, examined by ultrasound, are found to have polycystic ovaries. Fortunately, only a small proportion of these women develop the syndrome.

The condition is known as a syndrome – a term that denotes a collection of symptoms of the same disorder.

PCOS affects millions of women of all ages. Although it usually starts in the teenage years, it is often only discovered around 30–40 years of age, when infertility issues bring it to light. As is common with many disorders, women may be unaware that they have polycystic ovaries, while others will have a long list of symptoms. The cause of the syndrome is not yet established, although there is some evidence of a hereditary link.

Symptoms include:

- irregular or absent ovulation
- irregular or absent menstruation
- reduced fertility or frequent miscarriages
- weight gain particularly around the abdomen, upper arms and neck; the increase in weight can be quite rapid and it is invariably difficult to lose weight
- acne or excessively oily skin, particularly prone to hard cysts on the chin
- excess hair growth on the face and body, commonly found on the chin, breasts, middle of the chest and abdomen
- thinning scalp hair
- emotional problems and depression
- insulin resistance.

The excess hair growth associated with PCOS occurs as a result of the hormonal imbalances; there are three hormones produced by the ovaries; oestrogen, progesterone and androgens, one of the androgens is testosterone. Testosterone is thought to be a male-only hormone but, in fact, both men and women produce it; the only difference is that men produce far more. These hormones produced by the ovaries are controlled by follicle stimulating hormone (FSH) and luteinising hormone (LH), which are produced in the pituitary gland in the brain. In a balanced state, the oestrogen and progesterone suppress the androgens, so any fluctuation or imbalance of oestrogen, progesterone, FSH or LH will allow the androgens to stimulate hair growth.

The emotional problems experienced by a PCOS sufferer can be profound. Taken individually any one of these symptoms would be difficult to deal with emotionally. Fluctuating hormones alone can cause mood swings; when they are experienced along with a collection of symptoms, sufferers frequently struggle with depression and heightened emotional issues and a feeling of being out of control of their bodies. Providing a professional hair and skin care management treatment schedule can go a long way towards increasing the client's feeling of wellbeing and hopefully help them to feel more in control and positive.

As if the problems already described weren't enough, people with PCOS also suffer insulin resistance. Their body tissue resists the effects of insulin which causes the pancreas to produce more insulin in compensation. As a consequence, in a high number of sufferers diabetes is a factor, contributing to the hormonal imbalance and the weight gain because the excess insulin produced turns to sugar and is stored as fat. Managing weight has a very positive effect on these symptoms and recent research has shown that a diabetic-style low GI (glycaemic index) is effective, however each person is individual and should take advice from a nutrition expert.

Treatment and relevance to hair removal treatment

Clients with the condition or symptoms of PCOS should always seek medical advice. There is no specific cure but management of the symptoms can have very positive results. It is common for doctors to prescribe the contraceptive pill to regulate menstruation. Research into this subject is ongoing.

Successful treatment of this excess hair growth is very much dependent upon the hormonal balance of each client. If the PCOS client has quite severe symptoms, the best result that can be achieved will generally only be hair management, regardless of the method used. This is because the androgens will keep stimulating new growth. Consequently, even with electrolysis, you will never achieve permanent hair removal in some cases. None the less, good results can be achieved in managing the hair growth with both laser/light treatments and electrolysis. Costs are clearly going to be an issue for a client who will require long-term treatment, it is worth considering giving significant discounts to these clients. Providing you treat them professionally and explain fully the expected outcomes, you will have a long-term and loyal client.

Therefore, clients wishing to have laser/light or electrolysis treatment should be advised that the hormonal changes due to the PCOS may delay or reduce the effectiveness of treatment. Remember to check regularly that your client has not changed their medication.

Treatment notes

It is important to help PCOS clients to feel more in control and better about themselves. Skin treatments, skin care advice and relaxation treatments in addition to the hair removal will help the overall successful outcome of treatment. Although each client will have an individual response to the condition, in general, clearing hairs quickly and allowing the client some time free from any hair growth works well and helps with the psychological effects of the syndrome. This can be achieved by laser or light treatment followed by electrolysis to permanently remove any remaining hairs. When treating with electrolysis only it is best to clear the whole area, leave for 10 to 14 days and then re-treat. This method allows the client a period of time when they are totally free from hair growth and ensures you are always treating the follicle in the anagen stage of growth. Re-growth can be managed by shaving.

More information can be found at www.pcos-support.org and www. verity-pcos.org.uk. Verity is the self-help organisation for women whose lives are affected by PCOS.

Menopause

The menopause is one of the most dramatic changes in hormonal balance during the course of a woman's life. A hormonal imbalance at this time is one of the major causes of excess facial hair growth in women. It is therefore important for HRPs to understand the changes which are occurring in their clients and the effects of those changes on the skin and hair growth.

The average age of the natural menopause is 51 years, but it can occur much earlier or later. Menopause begins because the ovaries contain only a few remaining egg cells, they cannot then respond to the pituitary hormones: FSH and LH and so less oestrogen and progesterone are produced. The resulting low or fluctuating levels of ovarian hormones, particularly oestrogen, are thought to be the cause of many of the symptoms experienced by women during the menopause.

The fluctuation of the ovarian hormones allows the androgens to take prevalence and, as a consequence, facial hair growth is stimulated. This facial hair growth is very common in women experiencing the menopause.

Menopause means the last menstrual period. Periods stop because the low levels of oestrogen and progesterone do not stimulate the endometrium in the normal cycle. Hormone levels can fluctuate for several years before eventually becoming so low that the endometrium stays thin and does not bleed.

Physical symptoms include:

- hot flushes
- night sweats
- palpitations
- insomnia
- joint aches
- headaches
- increase in facial hair growth
- decrease in body hair growth
- skin changes.

The hormonal changes involved bring about changes in the skin and in hair growth. The production of collagen (a protein found in skin, hair, nails and tendons) is affected by falling oestrogen levels, and so the skin may become dryer, thinner, less elastic, more prone to bruising and skin itching may occur. Occasionally, a 'crawling' sensation may be experienced, but it is unclear whether this is due to skin changes or changes in the peripheral nerves.

Hair thinning, dryness and the growth of unwanted hair can be explained by the lack of oestrogen and the relative excess of androgens during the menopause (the adrenal glands continue to produce some androgens including testosterone, the effect of which is no longer suppressed by oestrogen). Hair loss may be dependent on age rather than hormone related.

Psychological symptoms include:

- mood swings
- irritability
- anxiety
- difficulty concentrating,
- forgetfulness.

These psychological symptoms may be related to hormonal changes, either directly or indirectly. Other factors such as sleep disturbance from night sweats, etc. may contribute.

Treatment and relevance to hair removal treatment

Hormone replacement therapy (HRT) is a relatively common hormone medication prescribed to relieve some of the symptoms of the menopause. It is generally administered in either slow release patches or tablets. Since many problems associated with the menopause are believed to be due to reduced oestrogen levels, the main component of HRT is oestrogen. One of the other components may be progesterone.

HRT has also been shown to be beneficial for the treatment and prevention of osteoporosis for women who have, or are thought to be at risk of osteoporosis.

It can take some time for the balance of hormones to be stabilised after a woman begins taking HRT to relieve the symptoms of the menopause. Women are advised to allow 3–6 months on HRT to ensure adequate effect, after which time they may find that the drugs need to be adjusted and a further 3–6 months will have to be allowed to fully assess the effects. During this second 3–6 month period, the body will still be undergoing hormonal changes and, as a consequence, there may be changes in hair growth. Therefore, clients wishing to have laser/light or electrolysis treatment should be advised that the hormonal changes due to HRT may delay or reduce the effectiveness of treatment. If, however, the client has been receiving HRT therapy for longer than 6 months, the hormones should have been stabilised and treatment outcomes should be better. Remember to check regularly that your client has not changed their medication.

Treatment notes

Not all women take HRT, but it is likely that all women will experience some hormone disturbance during their menopause and so they should be advised that the outcomes of laser/light or electrolysis treatment may not be ideal until their hormones regain balance.

We should always take great care of any client's skin during all hair removal treatments, however, with menopausal clients we should be aware that the skin can be very dry, sensitive and bruise easily. Hydrating and moisturising treatments should be recommended.

Endometriosis

The endometrium is the tissue that lines the uterus (the womb). During the menstrual cycle, the endometrium thickens in readiness for the fertilised egg to be implanted. If pregnancy does not occur, the lining is shed during menstruation or a 'period'. Endometriosis is a condition where the cells that are normally found lining the uterus are also found in other areas of the body, usually within the pelvis. Each month this tissue outside of the uterus, under normal hormonal control, is built up and then breaks down and bleeds in the same way as the lining of the uterus. This internal bleeding into the pelvis, unlike a period, has no way of leaving the body. This leads to inflammation, pain and the formation of scar tissue. Endometrial tissue can also be found in the ovary where it may form cysts, called 'chocolate' cysts.

Endometriosis is a very common condition affecting some 2 million girls and women in the UK. endometriosis often goes undiagnosed for years and is most frequently only diagnosed during investigations for infertility, which could be the reason why it is often thought to be a disease of career women, in their thirties, who have delayed childbearing. However the facts are that endometriosis can occur at any time from the onset of menstrual periods until the menopause. It is extremely rare for it to be first diagnosed after the menopause, but not unknown. For the majority of women, the condition ceases at the menopause.

Endometriosis can only be diagnosed by a laparoscopy. This is an operation in which a telescope (a laparascope) is inserted into the pelvis via a small cut near the navel. This allows the surgeon to see the pelvic organs and any endometrial implants and cysts.

Symptoms of endometriosis include:

- painful and/or heavy and prolonged periods, often with clotting
- infertility
- irregular periods
- pain, before periods, during or after sexual intercourse, ovulation pain and during internal examination
- fatigue
- problems when opening bowels.

The majority of women with the condition will experience some of these symptoms. Some women with endometriosis will have no symptoms at all.

The amount of endometriosis does not always correspond to the amount of pain experienced. Chocolate cysts on the ovary can be pain free and only discovered as part of fertility investigations. A small amount of endometriosis can be more painful than a severe level of disease. It depends, largely, on the site of the endometrial deposits.

Treatment and relevance to hair removal treatment

Treatment is generally by hormonal medication. The medication prescribed aims to stop ovulation and allow the endometrial deposits to regress and die. The medication used stimulates either pseudo-pregnancy or pseudo-menopause.

One of the possible side effects of the drugs prescribed for endometriosis is hormonal imbalance and consequently an increase in hair growth on the body and/or face, particularly with prolonged or repeated treatment. Therefore, clients wishing to have laser/light or electrolysis treatment should be advised that the hormonal changes due to their medication may delay or reduce the effectiveness of hair removal treatment. The endometriosis treatment is not generally long term and, as a result, the hormone balance may be restored approximately 3 months after stopping treatment. Remember to check regularly that your client has not changed their medication.

Infertility treatment and in-vitro fertilisation (IVF)

Infertility treatment invariably involves hormonal medication; it is possible that this medication may, as a side effect, disrupt the normal hormone balance and therefore it has the potential to be a cause of unwanted hair growth. It is, however, not a common cause. It is beneficial to have some knowledge of the medical treatments, should you have a client undergoing these procedures.

Fertility drugs are often the first step in the treatment of infertility. The drugs are used to promote ovulation by stimulating the pituitary gland to produce more FSH, which triggers ovulation.

IVF involves eggs being gathered from the woman's ovaries and mixed with the man's sperm in a dish in the laboratory. 'In vitro' is a Latin term literally meaning 'in glass'. It refers to the glass container in the laboratory where fertilisation takes place. Although this is usually a dish, in the popular mind it was thought to be a test tube – hence the term 'test-tube baby'. Thousands of IVF babies have been born worldwide since the technique was first used successfully in 1978.

Treatment and relevance to hair removal treatment

Treatment involves the use of drugs to 'down-regulate' (switch off) the pituitary gland for about two to three weeks, then drugs are injected which stimulate the ovaries to produce multiple eggs. Once the stimulated follicles are ready, a further drug is injected to bring about the final maturation of eggs in the follicles. The eggs are then collected and put together with the sperm. Some of the fertilised eggs are then put back into the uterus.

Given the amount of hormonal medication used, fertility treatment is a potential cause of hair growth. It is not advisable to begin laser/light or electrolysis treatment during any form of fertility treatment. Laser/light or electrolysis treatment should be deferred until the fertility treatment is concluded.

Treatment notes

If the client has already started laser/light hair removal prior to the fertility treatment, medical advice should be sought to establish whether or not the drugs are photo-sensitive. If the drugs are photo-sensitive then laser/light treatment should be stopped.

If electrolysis has started prior to the fertility treatment, there is no reason why treatment should not continue, however the client should be advised that the hormonal changes due to the medication prescribed for fertility treatment may delay or reduce the effectiveness of the electrolysis. It is also advisable to ask the client to confirm with their consultant that electrolysis may continue.

KEY TERMS ★

Androgens are the only hormones which can stimulate hair growth

part three

anatomy and physiology

chapter 3

ANATOMY AND PHYSIOLOGY

What will I know after reading this chapter?

This chapter covers the knowledge of anatomy and physiology needed for hair removal. After studying this chapter you should be able to:

- **understand the basics of the major physiological systems of the human body**
- **recognise the links between the hair and the rest of the body**
- **identify the hair as part of the integumentary system**
- **understand the principles of the hair growth cycle**
- **be aware of the factors affecting hair growth and development**
- **appreciate how the circulatory systems contribute to the health of hair**
- **comprehend the effects of hormone secretion on hair growth**
- **realise the importance of a holistic approach to treatment of the hair.**

BT16 Epilate the hair follicle using diathermy, galvanic and blend techniques

INTRODUCTION

Anatomy refers to the science of the structure of living organisms and physiology refers to the science associated with their functions.

Hair neither grows nor works on its own. Like all other parts of the human body, hair needs the rest of the body for its continued survival and the production and maintenance of hair relies totally on its links with the body as a whole.

Therefore, it is necessary to study anatomy and physiology before the treatment of any form of hair removal, in order to gain an understanding of the various body systems that make up a human organism and the ways in which they contribute to the development and wellbeing of the hair.

THE HUMAN ORGANISM

Each human organism starts life as a single cell or zygote formed by an ovum (egg cell) and sperm cell during fertilisation. The ovum and sperm cells each contain 23 chromosomes which form the basis for the development of the zygote into an embryo, then a foetus and eventually a fully formed person.

Chromosomes consist of genes which in turn contain a coding, in the form of DNA (deoxyribonucleic acid), for particular human characteristics for example hair colour and its thickness.

Although every cell in the body has a nucleus containing all 46 chromosomes and with them all the coding for the development of a complete person, individual cells are able to switch on the particular characteristic they need and switch off those that are not needed, for example genes for hair colour will only be active in cells of the hair whilst genes for eye colour are only active in the cells of the iris, etc. This process is known as differentiation.

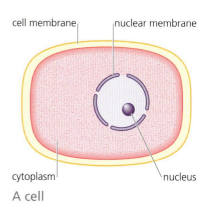

A cell

The four types of human tissue

Cells are like building blocks. Each individual cell is able to subdivide – by a process of simple cell division known as mitosis – allowing for growth and repair. As cells develop, they begin to group together and specialise (differentiate) to form tissue. There are four different types of tissue: epithelial, connective, muscular and nervous tissue. Each tissue type contains groups of cells that have gone through a process of differentiation and specialise in a basic function of the body associated with protection, connection, movement and sensitivity respectively.

Individual cells begin to specialise (differentiate) and form into groups. Groups of specialist cells form tissue. There are four different types of tissue:

1 epithlieal – for protection
2 connective – connecting other tissues and parts of the body's systems
3 muscular – for movement
4 nervous – for sensation.

Epithelial tissue

Simple epithelial tissue – flat scale-like cells arranged in a single row:

- some cells secrete a fluid, e.g. sebum (skin's natural oil)
- some cells secrete a watery substance known as mucus
- some cells contain hair-like structures called cilia.

Compound – comprised of multiple layers of cells:

- stratified – many layers of cells that are either dry and hardened, e.g. the top layers of skin, or wet and soft, e.g. lining of the tongue
- transitional – expandable layers of cells e.g. lining of bladder.

KEY TERMS ★

Cell: Microscopic part of an organism
Chromosome: Part of a cell containing genes
Differentiation: A process whereby cells specialise
Zygote: a fertilised ovum

TECHNICAL TIP ✔

All human cells contain 46 chromosomes, 23 from each parent. Chromosomes consist of genes that contain the mix of inherited characteristics that make each of us unique individuals

KEY TERMS ★

Mitosis: Simple cell division
Tissue: Groups of specialist cells
Epithelial tissue: Groups of cells providing a protective function

Connective tissue

- Areolar – semi-solid layers of cells which connect and protect.
- Adipose – insulating layer of fat cells.
- Lymphoid – semi-solid layers of cells that are able to engulf bacteria.
- Elastic – semi-solid cells which form stretchable fibres.
- Fibrous – cells that form strong fibres, e.g. tendons and ligaments.
- Cartilage – solid cells forming protective coverings and discs.
- Bone – solid formation of cells as part of the skeletal system.
- Blood – fluid in structure and contains water and cells.

Muscular tissue

Skeletal muscular tissue:

- striated in appearance and attached to the bones of the skeleton
- responsible for voluntary movement, e.g. walking.

Visceral muscular tissue:

- smooth in appearance and associated with internal organs
- responsible for involuntary movement, e.g. digestion.

Cardiac muscular tissue:

- tissue exclusive to the heart and responsible for the heartbeat.

Nervous tissue

Neurons – long, delicate cells that form into bundles of nerves and make up the:

- sensory organs, e.g. eyes, ears, skin, nose, tongue, that pick up a stimulus
- sensory nerves that send a message to the brain
- neurons in the brain that interpret the message, e.g. sight, sound, touch, etc.
- motor nerves that send messages to the body to respond to the original stimulus.

Neuroglia – supportive cells which fill the spaces between neurons:

- cells which provide a structural framework
- cells which 'mop up' damaged neurons and eliminate foreign particles.

Glands are formed from epithelial tissue:

- exocrine glands – secrete a substance into a duct, e.g. a sweat gland
- endocrine glands – secrete a substance into the blood, e.g. hormones.

Organs are formed from two or more tissue types, e.g. heart, skin, lungs, etc.

Glands and organs

As groups of tissue develop, they join to form glands and organs.

- Glands are made up of epithelial tissue and produce substances that assist the body in a specific way, for example they produce mucus, sweat, sebum (the skin's natural oil), cerumen (ear wax), tears, digestive juices, bile (aids the absorption of fats in the digestive system) and hormones (chemical messengers).

- Organs are made up of two or more types of tissue and are therefore multi-functional, for example the heart and lungs, brain, skin, liver, stomach, kidneys and bladder.

Glands and organs group together to form the body's systems:

- *Integumentary system* consisting of the skin, hair and nails; offering a protective covering to the human body helping to keep the vital organs in and harmful invaders out.

- *Skeletal and muscular systems* consisting of bones and muscles; providing the human form and the functions of voluntary and involuntary movement.

- *Circulatory and respiratory systems* consisting of the heart and lungs together with veins and arteries; enabling every cell of the body to take in and use oxygen and nutrients and produce and expel carbon dioxide and waste.

- *Digestive system* consisting of the stomach, intestines and the accessory organs including the liver, gall bladder and pancreas; performing the vital functions associated with the ingestion, digestion and absorption of nutrients and the elimination of the associated waste.

- *Genito-urinary system* consisting of the male and female genitalia, kidneys and bladder; ensuring the survival of the species through reproduction and the survival of each individual human being through the maintenance of the body's fluid balance by controlling the production of urine.

- *Nervous system* consisting of the brain, spinal cord and nerves; offering a means to control the body and its functions through electrical messages.

- *Endocrine system* consisting of glands which produce chemical messengers in the form of hormones; informing the body of the changes that need to take place as a human develops throughout life.

It is important to have a basic understanding of the way in which the body develops and functions in order to appreciate that the body works as a whole and, therefore, any part can only be well if the whole is well. The next few paragraphs will provide a brief summary of the roles played by the specialised cells described above. The subsequent sections look in greater detail at how these cells, as glands and organs, work together in the major systems of the body.

KEY TERMS ⭐

Genitalia: the reproductive organs

THE ORGANS OF THE HUMAN BODY

Skin hair and nails

The cells of the surface of the skin, hair and nails are formed from stratified keratinised epithelial tissue. This means that they are hard, dry and formed from the protein keratin, offering a protective covering that helps keep harmful invaders out and necessary organs in.

Bones and muscles

Specialised cells form a dense solid connective tissue that develops into bones whilst other cells specialise to form various types of muscles responsible for voluntary and involuntary movement. Together the cells that produce the bones and muscles provide the body with form and function.

Heart and lungs

Specialist cells forming the four different types of tissue make up the heart and lungs. Epithelial tissue forms the protective linings, connective tissue forms blood, cardiac muscular tissue allows the heart to pump and nervous tissue ensures messages are sent to and from the brain to coordinate activity.

Stomach and intestines

Peristaltic action is produced by involuntary muscular tissue (visceral) found along the digestive tract. This contributes to the churning action of the stomach and the movement of nutrients and waste through the intestines. Mucus secreted from the epithelial linings assists this process.

Liver, gall bladder and pancreas

These are multi-functional organs and glands formed from specialist cells and tissue, which act as vital support systems for the rest of the body. The liver helps to detoxify the blood. The gall bladder and pancreas produce substances that aid the absorption of nutrients from the digestive organs to the blood.

Kidneys and bladder

The kidneys are formed from groups of connective and epithelial tissue that specialise in the filtration of waste from the blood and the subsequent formation of urine. Urine is passed to the bladder for storage by involuntary muscular action where nervous tissue detects the amount stored.

Sexual organs

The ovaries in a female contain the ova (eggs) and the testes in a male contain the sperm. Ova and sperm are cells that contain 23 chromosomes each which, if fertilisation takes place, form one cell containing all the 46 chromosomes needed to initiate the formation of a new human being.

Endocrine glands

Formed from epithelial tissue, endocrine glands produce chemical messengers in the form of hormones. The endocrine glands include, pituitary, pineal, thyroid, parathyroid, thymus, adrenal, islets of Langerhans in the pancreas, and the ovaries and testes. Hormones are able to initiate changes in the body.

KEY TERM ★

Peristalsis: Involuntary movements (constriction and relaxation) of intestinal muscles which propel nutrients and waste through the intestine

Brain and spinal cord

Bundles of nerve cells form the nervous tissue responsible for the brain and spinal cord. Sensory nerves link the eyes, ears, skin, tongue and nose to the brain for recognition of the senses associated with sight, sound, touch, taste and smell. Motor nerves then send messages from the brain to the body.

THE MAJOR SYSTEMS OF THE HUMAN BODY

In order to learn about the structure and function of hair, it is also necessary to have an understanding of the structure and function of the skin and the other systems that have a direct effect on its wellbeing – the respiratory, and circulatory nervous and endocrine systems – and those that have an indirect effect – the skeletal and muscular, digestive and genito-urinary systems. Once we have this understanding, we can begin to appreciate the links between the systems and the vital contribution they all make to the body as a whole. If you think back to the section on a holistic consultation in Chapter Two, you will realise why this understanding is important to work as an HRP.

As part of the integumentary system, hair plays an important role in helping to maintain its functions, which in turn contribute to the health and wellbeing of the body as a whole. No system, organ, gland, tissue or indeed cell operates in isolation; they are all inter-dependent and rely heavily on one another for support. In order to gain a greater perspective of this, it is useful to have an awareness of how the systems of the body interact and what affects such interactions have on the development of the hair. We will now consider the integumentary, skeletal/muscular, respiratory, circulatory, digestive, genito-urinary, nervous and endocrine systems in turn in order to see how they impact on the hair. Later in the chapter, we will take an in-depth look at the integumentary system, as this is the system containing the skin and the hair. We will also consider in more detail the circulatory, nervous and endocrine systems, as these are the systems that have the greatest influence on the hair.

Integumentary system

What is the integumentary system?

The integumentary system consists of the skin, hair and nails, which together form the largest organ of the body. The skin is in a constant state of renewal, shedding old skin, hair and nails as new skin, hair and nails grow.

PROFESSIONAL TIP ✔

When removing hair using any type of treatment, attention must be paid to the surrounding skin. Any resulting trauma to the skin as a result of the hair treatment will require additional aftercare

What does the integumentary system do?

As a whole, the integumentary system provides the entire body with a waterproof outer covering that is resilient and flexible, and contributes to the unique appearance of each person.

How does the integumentary system affect hair?

Hair forms an integral part of the integumentary system and as such contributes to its functions. In turn the hair relies on the skin's structure for its development. If the skin is functioning well, the hair will develop well.

Skeletal and muscular systems

origin of gastrocnemius on femur

Achilles' tendon

insertion of muscle is through the Achilles' tendon on the calcaneum

Skeletal muscle

cranium
facial bones } skull
clavicle
sternum
acromion process
ribs
scapula
trunk
humerus
radius
ulna
ilium
sacrum
coccyx
eater trochanter
pubis
carpals
phalanges
metacarpa
ischium
lower appendage
femur
patella
tibia
fibula
metatarsals
tarsals
phalanges
anterior

head of humerus
vertebral column

posterior

The major bones of the human skeleton

What are the skeletal and muscular systems?

Bones and muscles are active living tissue, which are capable of both growth and repair. They experience periods of rapid growth prior to adulthood, when growth eventually ceases. However, development of bone and muscle continues throughout life.

What do the skeletal and muscular systems do?

The bones provide the body with a structural framework to which the muscles are attached by tendons. Muscles provide the body with support by maintaining posture. Together, the bones and muscles are responsible for movement.

How do the skeletal and muscular systems affect hair?

Bones contain bone marrow which is responsible for the production of new red blood cells. These blood cells are responsible for carrying nutrients within the blood which are transported to all the cells of the body including the hair. Without the nutrients, the hair would be unable to develop.

A tiny muscle known as the arrector pili muscle is attached to the hair root. They control the position of the tiny hairs on the body, allowing them to lie flat against the skin, or stand upright. This movement is responsible for creating 'goose bumps' when it contracts. This muscle and the hair assist in maintaining correct body temperature.

KEY TERMS ★

Arrector pili muscle: Small involuntary muscle in the skin responsible for goose bumps

---

REMEMBER !

There are three types of muscular tissue: *skeletal* which is responsible for voluntary movement e.g. walking, *visceral* which is responsible for involuntary movement e.g. swallowing and *cardiac* which is responsible for the movement of the heart when it beats

---

Respiratory system

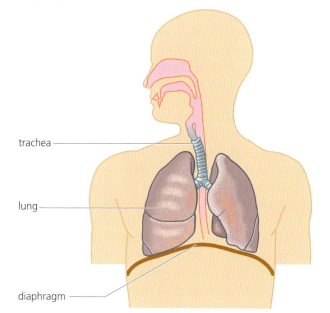

trachea

lung

diaphragm

The respiratory system

What is the respiratory system?

The respiratory system is responsible for breathing. It coordinates the flow of oxygen and carbon dioxide in and out of the body, in order to maintain the life of each cell, tissue type, gland and organ.

What does the respiratory system do?

The respiratory system processes the body's life force. It facilitates the intake of oxygen from the air with the inward breath and the output of carbon dioxide with the outward breath. This process is repeated many thousands of times throughout the course of the day and night and is vital to life.

How does the respiratory system affect hair?

Oxygen breathed into the body via the respiratory system is processed and taken to the cells of the hair and surrounding tissue. In order to replicate – through mitosis – cells need to produce the energy to sustain such action. Oxygen is the main ingredient needed. Without adequate oxygen, the cells that form the hair will die.

Circulatory systems

What are the circulatory systems?

The body's circulation consists of two complementary systems – the blood circulation and the lymphatic circulation – which work together to provide the body with a transportation system.

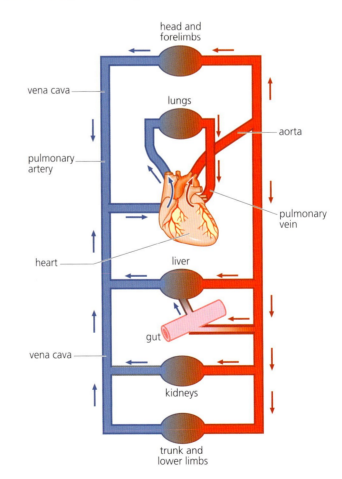

Blood circulation

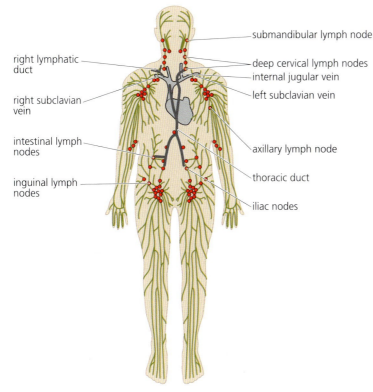

Lymphatic circulation

What do the circulatory systems do?

The blood circulation is a two-way system transporting vital substances *to* the cells and carrying unwanted substances *away* from the cells. The lymphatic circulation is a one-way system supporting the blood circulation by transporting substances *away* from the cells that the blood is unable to take. Together, the circulatory systems contribute to the immune functions of the body as they contain cells that are able to fight harmful invaders such as bacteria and viruses, whether these are breathed in, swallowed or enter the body through the skin due to cuts, etc.

How do the circulatory systems affect hair?

Blood circulation is responsible for transporting oxygen, water and nutrients to the cells of the hair for growth and development. Blood also transports chemical messengers in the form of hormones that inform the hair cells about when and how to grow. Lymphatic circulation supports the blood circulation by transporting the waste products associated with cellular function away from the hair cells.

TECHNICAL TIP ✔

If the hair root which lies within the skin is traumatised in any way, blood rushes to the site and a reddening of the skin appears – known as an erythema. If further trauma occurs then blood spotting may be a contra-action. Bleeding takes place when damage has been caused; the blood cells then act to stem the flow of blood by creating a clot to defend the area until new cells are developed

Digestive system

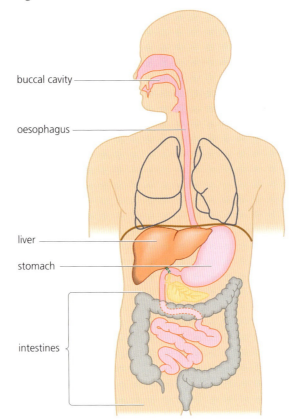

buccal cavity

oesophagus

liver

stomach

intestines

The digestive system

What is the digestive system?

The digestive system is a continuous tube which starts as the alimentary canal at the mouth and ends as the anus at the bottom of the torso, changing in its composition slightly and its shape vastly as it winds its way through the body. Accessory organs in the form of the liver, pancreas and gall bladder all connect with the alimentary canal to offer support in the processes involved with the ingestion of food and elimination of subsequent waste.

What does the digestive system do?

The digestive system as a whole is responsible for the ingestion (eating and drinking) and digestion (breaking down) of food, the absorption of digested nutrients into the blood and the production and elimination of waste (faeces).

How does the digestive system affect hair?

In order for the cells of the body including those of the hair to develop, they need nutrients to fuel the energy needed to perform their functions. In other words, hair simply cannot grow without these nutrients. Blood transports the nutrients to the cells which then combine with oxygen in a process known as oxidation to produce the necessary energy. Cellular reproduction takes place allowing for growth and development.

TECHNICAL TIP ✔

A large percentage of each hair is formed from the protein we take into the body through the digestive system from the foods we eat. Protein is found in eggs, cheese, meat, fish, soya, lentils, peas, beans, etc. and is broken down into different types of amino acids. In the structure of the hair, the amino acids form chains

Genito-urinary system

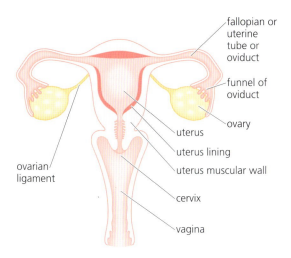

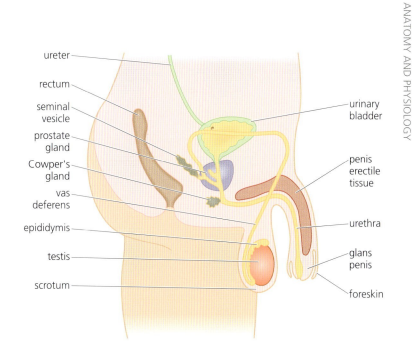

Female and male reproductive organs

What is the genito-urinary system?

This is a combined system that includes the male and female genitalia and the closely linked urinary organs, comprising the kidneys and bladder and connecting tubes.

What does the genito-urinary system do?

The male and female genitalia perform the vital functions associated with reproduction by developing ova in females and sperm in males. The kidneys collect the body's cellular waste and produce urine which is transported via the ureter tubes and stored in the bladder before being excreted out of the body via the urethra tube situated in the male penis and close to the female vagina.

How does the genito-urinary system affect hair?

The male testes and female ovaries not only produce sperm and ova, they also produce male and female hormones. Each person, regardless of their sex, produces both male and female hormones but in differing quantities. Male hormones have the effect of stimulating the growth of hair whilst female hormones do the opposite.

The urinary organs process the waste products associated with cellular activity in the hair cells, which have been transported to the kidneys from the cells via the blood.

TECHNICAL TIP ✔

Coarse hair grows on and around the genitals to protect these vital organs. Removal of such hair requires great care and attention: (i) to prevent undue damage and pain to the area, (ii) to stop possible cross-infection occurring from bacteria associated with urine and faeces that may be in the area and (iii) to avoid any possible misinterpretation of actions

Nervous system

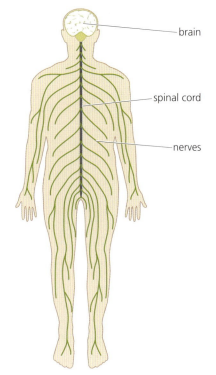

brain

spinal cord

nerves

The nervous system

What is the nervous system?

The nervous system is the main system controlling the body. It consists of the central nervous system (brain and spinal cord), the peripheral nervous system (cranial and spinal nerves) and the autonomic nervous system, which together coordinate activity within all of the body systems by creating electrical impulses.

What does the nervous system do?

The nervous system allows the body to detect external and internal changes through the sensory organs – the eyes, nose, ears, tongue and skin – and to make use of the information received to form a response by stimulating the muscles and organs into action.

How does the nervous system affect hair?

The central nervous system controls the growth cycle of hair through the DNA of each cell. The peripheral nervous system supplies the hair on the skin with pain detectors in the form of sensory nerves that alert the brain to potential harm. The autonomic nervous system picks up on changes, such as fall in body temperature, and alerts the tiny muscles that are attached to the hair to contract, thus forming goose bumps. This action lifts the hair slightly trapping a layer of warm air close to the skin.

TECHNICAL TIP ✔

The tiny involuntary arrector pili muscles attached to the hair are also activated by emotions such as fear. A client may experience goose bumps just prior to having their underarms waxed!

Endocrine system

Gland	Position	Hormones	Functions
Pituitary anterior	Brain – front region	Adrenocorticotrophic hormone (ACTH) Thyroid stimulating hormone (TSH) Gonadotrophins Follicle stimulating (FSH) Luteinising (LH) Growth (GH) Prolactin Melanin stimulating (MSH)	Controls the outer cortex of the adrenal gland Controls the thyroid gland Control the ovaries in females and testes in males Stimulates secretion of oestrogen and spermatozoa Stimulates secretion of progesterone and testosterone Promotes growth of the skeletal/muscular systems Promotes growth of reproductive organs and stimulates milk production Promotes production of melanin in the skin/hair
Pituitary posterior	Brain – back region	Antidiuretic hormone (ADH) Oxitocin	Regulates fluid balance by decreasing urine production Stimulates contraction of uterus and mammary glands during child birth
Pineal	Brain	Melatonin	Associated with the circadian rhythms e.g. wake and sleep
Thyroid	Neck	Thyroxine (T4) and Triiodothyronine (T3) Calcitonin	Regulate metabolism, growth and differentiation of cells Stimulates storage of calcium and phosphorus in the bones and release of excess in urine when levels are high
Parathyroid	Neck	Parathormone	Stimulates reabsorption of calcium and phosphorus from the bones and decreases amount lost in urine when levels are low
Thymus	Behind sternum	Thymosins	Stimulate the production of T-lymphocytes to help protect the body against antigens (harmful substances)
Adrenal cortex	Top of kidneys – outer section	Glucocorticoids Mineralocorticoids Sex corticoids	Stimulate metabolism, development and inflammation Regulate mineral concentration in the body Stimulate sexual development
Adrenal medulla	Top of kidneys – inner section	Adrenalin	Prepares body for 'fight or flight'
Islets of Langerhans	Pancreas	Insulin Glucagon	Reduces blood sugar levels by promoting storage of excess sugar (glycogen) in the liver and muscles Increases blood sugar levels by promoting the release of sugar (glycogen) from the liver and muscles
Ovaries	Female	Oestrogen Progesterone	Responsible for secondary sexual characteristics in females
Testes	Male	Testosterone	Responsible for secondary sexual characteristics in males

Note It is necessary to be aware that both males and females produce both male and female hormones in varying quantities. A dominance in male hormones results in the development of male characteristics in females and a dominance of female hormones in men results in the development of female characteristics in males.

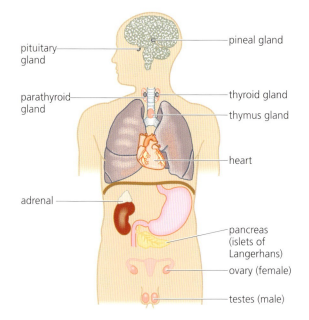

Glands of endocrine system

What is the endocrine system?

The endocrine system is closely linked to the nervous system and consists of a set of ductless glands responsible for producing hormones. Hormones are chemical messengers that are able to inform cells to perform specific functions within the body.

What does the endocrine system do?

The release of hormones has a controlling effect on the whole body, initiating processes associated with homeostasis, growth and sexual development. The endocrine system has a slower controlling action on the body than the nervous system which is designed for quicker responses.

How does the endocrine system affect hair?

The release of hormones has a controlling action on the growth and development of hair and the changes that occur in hair growth patterns associated with sexual development, that is puberty, pregnancy and menopause. Relevant hormones are transported to the hair cells by the blood; they are picked up by target cells that are capable of reading their specific message. The cell is thus instructed to develop in a certain way.

TECHNICAL TIP ✔

An imbalance in hormone release in the body can lead to an imbalance in hair growth and development, resulting in unexpected and unwanted changes in hair growth, including excess or superfluous hair or partial or total hair loss

A CLOSER LOOK AT THE INTEGUMENTARY SYSTEM

The hair forms part of the integumentary system together with the skin and nails.

The skin

A human being consists of organs and glands, and bones and muscles, all of which are covered and held in place by the skin.

Lying directly above the muscles and under the skin is a layer of fatty tissue known as the hypodermis or subcutaneous layer. The skin itself consists of two main sections known as the dermis and epidermis.

- The dermis is the main body of skin. It is made of connective tissue which, in turn, is connected by a basement membrane to the epidermis.
- The epidermis forms five distinct layers of epithelial tissue that make up the surface of the skin.

Hypodermis

The hypodermis is formed from two types of connective tissue, areolar and adipose. Areolar tissue forms a loose network of cells providing strength to protect underlying structures, elasticity to cope with an increase or decrease in body size and support for the blood vessels and nerve endings which service it. Adipose tissue contains fat cells that provide the body with a source of insulation, protection and energy.

- Fat is a poor conductor of heat, so fat cells retain body heat helping to maintain the correct body temperature of 36.8 degrees centigrade.
- Excess fat from our diet is stored within the hypodermis and is genetically programmed to accumulate in specific areas after puberty, for example the abdomen in males and the hips and thighs in women, providing a protective cushioning for these areas.
- Stored fat can be reabsorbed by the blood and used as a source of energy when there is a lack of food for example when dieting.

Dermis

As the main body of the skin, the dermis is often known as the true skin. It is formed from areolar connective tissue and contains many vital structures including circulatory vessels, nerves, two types of glands – sebaceous and sweat glands – and tiny involuntary muscles (arrector pili muscles) together with the hair and hair follicle.

The bulk of the dermis is known as the reticular layer. It contains protein fibres – collagen – elastin and reticulin which contribute to the skin's resilience, elasticity and strength.

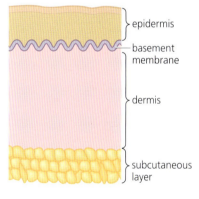

> epidermis
— basement membrane
> dermis
> subcutaneous layer

Skin

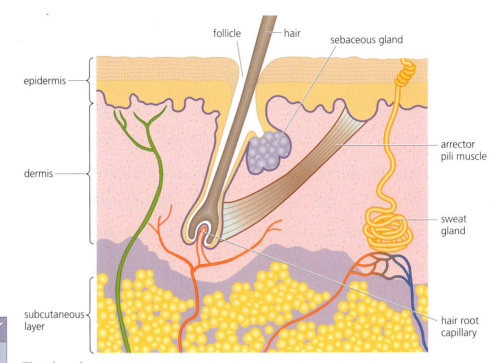

The diagram is labelled: follicle, hair, sebaceous gland, epidermis, dermis, arrector pili muscle, sweat gland, subcutaneous layer, hair root capillary

The dermis

The reticular section of the dermis also contains a host of specialised cells including:

- fibroblasts – responsible for the production of areolar tissue, collagen, elastin and reticulin fibres
- phagocytic cells – which help to defend the body by destroying bacterial invaders
- mast cells – which produce histamine when the skin is damaged or irritated, allowing more blood to flow to the area for assistance.

Circulatory vessels

A blood supply is vital to maintain the structure and function of the cells of the integumentary system as a whole and circulatory vessels link the dermis with the blood and lymph supply of the body. Blood vessels supply the skin cells with oxygen and nutrients and remove carbon dioxide, whilst lymphatic vessels remove cellular waste that the blood is unable to deal with. This process is known as cellular respiration and metabolism and it ensures the survival of the cells of the integumentary system.

Nerves

The integumentary system contains a complex network of nerves linking the skin, hair and nails with the central nervous system (the spinal cord and brain). Sensory nerves in the skin are able to detect various sensations associated with touch and pain and identify changes in pressure and temperature.

The tissues of the skin are bathed in a fluid known as tissue or interstitial fluid. This fluid provides a vital link between the individual cells and the circulatory systems for blood and lymph, allowing substances to pass back and forth. As such, tissue fluid contains mineral salts and this means it is an electrolyte. Electrolytes are substances that are capable of conducting electrical impulses. This assists with the flow of electrical impulses created by the body to and from the nervous system as well as those created, for example, by the electrical machine used for the removal of hair. The drier and more dehydrated the skin is, the less of a conductor it becomes.

Glands

Sebaceous glands

Sebaceous glands produce an oily substance called sebum. They are formed from epithelial tissue and are generally attached to a pocket within which hairs grow, called a hair follicle. Sebum produced in the gland is secreted up through the dermis and epidermis via the hair follicles, exiting onto the surface of the skin through a pore. Sebum provides a natural lubricant for the skin and hair maintaining the skin's suppleness and the hair's lustre. Sebum is also slightly antiseptic and helps to create a barrier on the skin's surface known as the acid mantle. Sebaceous glands are found all over the body except for the soles of the feet and palms of the hands. They are subject to hormonal changes which means they can become over-active during puberty resulting in oily skin and hair.

Sweat glands

Sweat glands are collectively known as sudoriferous glands. There are two types, eccrine and apocrine.

- Eccrine sweat glands are found all over the body but are more numerous on the palms of the hands and soles of the feet. Their function is to produce the liquid we call sweat or perspiration in response to a rise in body temperature. The sweat passes up through the dermis and epidermis via a sweat duct and exits the skin through a sweat pore. As the sweat evaporates it has a cooling effect.
- Apocrine sweat glands are found mainly in the underarm, nipple and genital areas of the body. They are inactive in children and develop in puberty. These glands open onto hair follicles and, as the sweat is broken down by bacteria present on the surface of the skin, the characteristic smell associated with body odour results.

Arrector pili muscles

There are tiny muscles attached to the hair follicles and the base of the epidermis. They are comprised of smooth visceral muscular tissue and are under involuntary control. They therefore respond automatically to changes in temperature. As core body temperature drops below 36.8°C, the muscles contract, pulling the skin into 'goose bumps' while lifting the corresponding hairs. This has the effect of trapping a layer of warm air, helping to increase body temperature.

KEY TERMS ★

Acid mantle: Protective covering to the skin formed from sweat, sebum and cells of the stratum corneum
Sudoriferous glands: Sweat glands
Eccrine glands: Sweat glands found on most parts of the body
Apocrine glands: Sweat glands that open onto a hair follicle and are activated at puberty

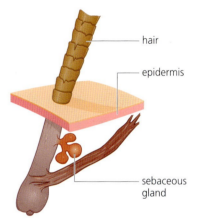

hair
epidermis
sebaceous gland

A sebaceous gland

PROFESSIONAL TIP ✔

Sweat production is also stimulated by emotional factors. The glands may be activated into producing an increased amount of sweat when we experience emotions such as fear and nervousness resulting in the characteristic 'sweaty palms'

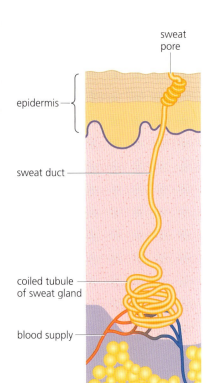

An eccrine sweat gland

KEY TERMS ★

Epidermis: Uppermost section of skin formed from five distinct layers
Keratinocytes: Cells that produce keratin
Germinal matrix: Living, reproducing part of the hair

The papillary layer

Above the reticular section of the dermis lies the thinner papillary section. Comprising areolar connective tissue, the papillary layer contains tiny conical projections called papillae that surround the hair follicle and line the base of the epidermis. The papillae contain blood vessels and nerves which provide the hair follicle and the epidermis with a vital blood supply for cellular respiration and metabolism and a nerve supply for sensation.

Epidermis

The uppermost section of the skin, the epidermis, is made up of five distinct layers or strata of cells which collectively form stratified epithelial tissue.

A basement membrane forms the connection between the dermis and the epidermis, through which the tiny papillae penetrate.

The epidermis provides the outermost section of the skin, from which individual hairs protrude and onto which sebum and sweat are released. The surface skin cells, hairs, sweat and sebum serve to form a protective barrier that is both resilient and strong enough to withstand superficial attack.

Over a period of approximately one month, the cells of the epidermis travel up from the basement membrane to the surface changing as they enter each distinct layer. Most skin cells are known as keratinocytes. Keratinocytes are cells capable of producing the protein keratin which is responsible for forming the surface of the skin, hair and nails.

The layers of the epidermis can be divided into sections or zones including a germinating (growing) and a keratinisation (hardening) zone. The

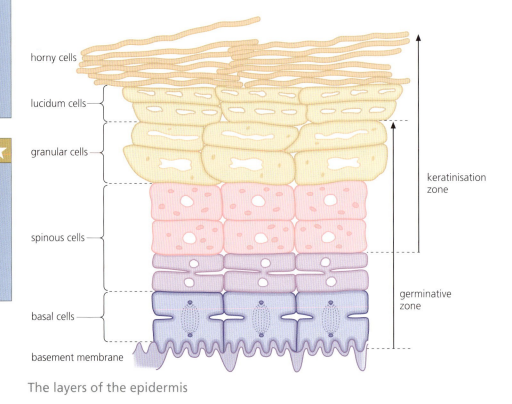

The layers of the epidermis

keratinocytes in the germinating zone are healthy, living, reproducing cells. However, when they reach the keratinisation zone, they begin to undergo a series of changes. These changes result in the hardened and dead cells that are continuously being shed from the skin's surface in a process known as desquamation.

The germinating zone consists of:

- The stratum germinativum which forms a basal (base) layer of cells from which the hair and nails develop. The cells receive a rich blood supply from the underlying papillary layer of the dermis, allowing simple cell division to take place (mitosis). As a result of new cells being produced, old cells are gradually pushed up to form the next layer.

- The stratum spinosum or prickle cell layer is formed by the old cells from the basal layer that have been pushed up and are beginning to mature. As the cells develop through this layer, the production of keratin starts to change the shape of the cells, which become spiky in formation hence the name prickle cell.

The keratinisation zone consists of:

- The stratum granulosum or granular layer of cells is formed as more keratin is produced in the cells, turning the cells from spiky to granular in formation as they continue their progress upwards.

- The stratum lucidum or clear layer of cells is formed as the granular cells harden further, start to flatten and, as a result of enzyme action, lose their colour. The stratum lucidum tends to be thicker on the palms of the hands and soles of the feet as these cells contribute to the waterproofing function of the skin.

- The stratum corneum or horny layer of cells is formed as the clear cells push upwards producing a covering of completely hardened cells. Because of the perpetual renewal of cells at the deeper levels of the epidermis, these surface cells are constantly being shed. If this process is hindered, the hardened cells will remain on the surface forming an uneven surface, for example when the skin is oily. Likewise, if the surface cells come under pressure they will develop into a thick, hard layer offering the body additional protection, for example the hard skin on the soles of the feet.

Like the dermis, the epidermis also contains some specialised cells including:

- Melanocytes are star shaped cells found in the stratum germinativum which produce the colour pigment melanin. Melanin is produced in abundance in dark skins, providing added protection, while it is totally lacking in albino skins, which are pale and vulnerable as a result. The ultra violet rays of the sun activate increased production within the melanocytes causing the additional melanin to rise, darkening the skin and producing a suntan. Melanocytes, however, cannot cope with excessive exposure to the sun's rays, which will cause the skin to burn. The skin's links with the nervous system alert the body to this situation, providing a sensation of pain. Mast cells in the dermis will produce histamine in response to this skin irritation; the skin will turn pink as more blood is sent to the area to soothe and restore it.

TECHNICAL TIP ✔

Much of the integumentary system is made from protein. A diet that has a balanced protein intake will help to ensure the health and well-being of the skin, hair and nails

TECHNICAL TIP ✔

We shed in the region of 4% of our total skin cells every day, which is approximately 18kg of skin in an average lifetime! These hardened dead skin cells form a large percentage of household dust

TECHNICAL TIP ✔

Nails develop from the stratum germinativum as hard clear layers of keratinised cells, providing additional protection to the extremities of the body

TECHNICAL TIP ✔

The palms of the hands and soles of the feet are void of sebaceous glands and hair and as a result absorb more water than other areas of the skin. When the hands or feet are immersed in water for any length of time, the skin appears to wrinkle up

KEY TERMS ★

Melanin: Colour pigment found in the skin and hair
Melanocyte: Cells responsible for producing melanin
Melanocyte stimulating hormone (MSH): Hormone produced in the anterior lobe of the pituitary gland

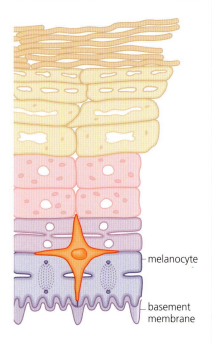

A melanocyte

● Langerhan cells are specialised cells whose function is to absorb potentially harmful foreign bodies from the surface of the skin, passing them through the various layers to be picked up by the circulatory systems (blood and lymph) for safe removal from the body.

SKIN FACTS

The skin is the largest organ of the body and together with the hair and nails performs many vital functions including protection, temperature regulation, absorption, secretion, excretion, sensation and the production of vitamin D to help maintain homeostasis.

FACT: Acid mantle creates a protective barrier formed from a combination of surface dead skin cells (stratum corneum), sweat and sebum, which collectively have an antiseptic, bactericidal effect on the skin.

FACT: Melanin produced in the stratum germinativum as a direct result of exposure to the sun's rays protects underlying structures. Melanin moves up the layers and has the effect of darkening the skin.

FACT: Hair and nails form hardened protrusions that create protective coverings. Both hair and nails originate from the stratum germinativum where cells differentiate to form the specific protective structures.

FACT: Fat cells in the hypodermis provide a protective layer that cushions the body against damage and insulates the body by retaining heat. Fat cells also provide a vital energy reserve when required by the body.

FACT: Sweat is produced in the skin when core body temperature rises. The heat of the skin evaporates the sweat producing a cooling effect on the body. Small amounts of waste products are also excreted with sweat.

FACT: Goose bumps are produced by the arrector pili muscle in response to a drop in core body temperature. This has the effect of trapping warm air beneath the slightly lifted hairs.

FACT: Absorption of moisture takes place on the surface of the skin and is controlled by the acid mantle and the cells of the stratum lucidum. The skin is able to absorb substances like essential oils into the dermis.

FACT: Secretion of the skin's natural oil sebum from the sebaceous glands contributes to the suppleness of the skin and the lustre of the hair. Sebaceous glands respond to hormonal changes becoming over- or under-active.

FACT: Sensations associated with touch, i.e. changes in pressure, pain and temperature are picked up by sensory nerve endings in the skin, relayed to the central nervous system and interpreted by the brain.

FACT: Vitamin D is produced in the skin by a chemical reaction when the skin is exposed to the sun. Vitamin D helps the body store calcium which is vital for the maintenance of the bones.

The thickness of the layers that form the skin varies across the body. Skin is thickest on the soles of the feet and thinnest over the eyelids.

As a result of the structure of the skin, individuals experience a number of differences in its development and function. For example, variations may be:

● inherited, i.e. related to genetic factors such as race, etc.

● hormone related, i.e. imbalances during puberty, pregnancy, menopause, etc.

- stress related, i.e. due to lack of sleep, excess worry, etc.
- diet related, i.e. a result of a lack of protein, lack of water, etc.
- degenerative, i.e. ageing
- illness related, i.e. a side effect of medication, due to pain, etc.
- environment related, i.e. exposure to harsh weather, air conditioning, etc.
- chemical related, i.e. exposure to pollutants, etc.
- care related, i.e. the result of the use of skin care products, etc.
- disease and disorder related or caused by microbes, i.e. viruses, bacteria and fungi or parasites such as worms, insects and mites.

Microbes are infectious and may be spread from person to person in a process known as cross-infection. Cross-infection may occur as a result of personal contact, for example touch, coughs and sneezes, or through contact with an infected instrument, for example tweezers. Diseases and disorders may be classified as being:

- local or topical – affecting one part or a limited area of the body
- systemic – affecting the whole of the body or several of its parts
- congenital – present in the body from the time of birth
- acquired – developed since birth
- acute – sudden but short in duration
- chronic – long in duration.

SKIN SAMPLER A–Z OF SKIN DISEASES AND DISORDERS

Acne – common inflammatory disorder of the sebaceous glands.

Acne rosacea – redness of the nose and cheeks characterised by the shape of a butterfly. Caused by the dilation of minute capillaries in the skin. Papules and pustules accompany this disorder.

Acne vulgaris – chronic acne, usually occurring in adolescence, with the formation of comedones, papules and pustules on the face, neck and upper parts of the trunk.

Albinism – the inherent absence of melanin in the skin, hair and eyes.

Allergy – a disorder in which the body becomes hypersensitive to particular antigens evoking an allergic reaction which may be local or general.

Asteatosis – under-activity of sebaceous glands causing excessively dry, scaly and often itchy skin.

Blister – a separating of the epidermis and dermis caused by friction resulting in a painful swelling containing fluid.

Boil technically known as a furuncle – bacterial inflammation of the hair follicle and surrounding skin. A pus formation develops, which comes to a head in the case of a boil or increases and so becomes an abscess.

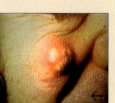
A boil

Bulla – a large blister.

Carbuncles – a collection of boils.

Chloasma – small patches of dark skin colouration which appear as a result of melanocyte action being stimulated. Caused by hormone imbalance and commonly associated with the contraceptive pill.

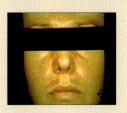
Chloasma

Combination skin – so called because different areas experience differing conditions, e.g. dry forehead and oily skin over the central panel of the face.

Comedones commonly referred to as blackheads – the opening of a pore becomes blocked with excess dried sebum, dead skin cells, sweat and dirt oxidising to form a blackened plug. More common in areas with more sebaceous glands such as the centre panel of the face.

Cysts – found in the sebaceous glands as a small painless lump. Epidermal cysts appear anywhere on the body and are easily infected; pilar cysts appear on the scalp.

Dehydrated skin – skin lacking in moisture as a result of poor body fluid balance.

Dermatitis – inflammatory condition resulting in red, itchy and swollen skin resembling eczema. Usually activated by an allergic reaction to a substance on the skin.

Dermatosis – refers to any skin disease, especially one not characterised by inflammation.

Dermatosis papulosa nigra – a skin disease seen chiefly in black skin with multiple papules occurring over the cheek bones and sometimes progressing more widely over the face.

Dry skin skin lacking in moisture due to under-active sebaceous glands and/or the use of harsh products or exposure to extreme temperatures resulting in a breakdown of the acid mantle leaving the skin vulnerable and tight.

Eczema – there are five variations of eczema and all are forms of inflammation resulting in reddening of the skin due to dilation of capillaries. Fluid accumulates in the skin causing swelling, itching and small blisters (vesicles). Weeping skin develops that dries with scabs and crusts.

Ephelides – commonly referred to as freckles – small flat irregular patches of melanin found on the face and the body. The melanin accumulates in small isolated areas instead of being evenly distributed.

Erythema – reddening of the skin due to dilation of the blood capillaries in the dermis.

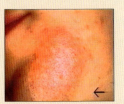

Excoriation – destruction and removal of the surface of the skin by scratching.

Fissures – cracks in the epidermis which exposes the dermis.

Erythema

Herpes simplex – a recurring viral infection commonly known as a cold sore. Characterised by inflammation and vesicles that are itchy, painful and may weep tissue fluid.

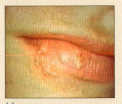

Hyperpigmentation – increase in skin pigmentation.

Hyperidrosis – excessive perspiration.

Hypopigmentation – decrease in skin pigmentation.

Herpes

Impetigo – highly contagious skin infection starting with a red spot which becomes a blister, quickly breaking down and discharging, with a yellow crust developing. The crust spreads. Commonly affected areas include the face, hands and knees.

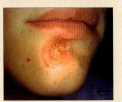

Inflammation – redness, heat, swelling pain and loss of function of the affected area.

Lentigines – flat, brown spots on the skin caused by increased melanin production.

Impetigo

Lesion – an area of tissue with impaired function as a result of damage and/or disease.

Leucoderma – loss of melanin resulting in white patches of skin.

Macule – flat, coloured area of skin.

Mature skin – skin that is ageing either prematurely because of harsh products or exposure to extreme temperatures, or naturally due to the passing of time and gradual decline of the skin's functions, resulting in crêpey skin, lines and wrinkles, dropped contours and changes in hair growth and skin and hair colour.

Melanoma – tumour of melanocytes in the skin.

Milia – small, harmless pinhead cysts.

Miliaria rubra – heat rash also known as prickly heat due to obstruction of the sweat ducts.

Moles – darkened, raised area of skin varying in size, shape and colour.

Naevus – clearly defined malformation of the skin either present at birth or as a result of injury to the skin. Examples of naevi present at birth include capillary naevus/port wine stain, a permanent purplish discolouration of the skin; strawberry naevus, a raised red lump composed of small blood vessels. An example of a naevus occurring as a result of injury is spider naevus, a central dilated blood vessel with smaller capillaries radiating from it.

Normal skin – well-balanced skin with all of its functions working in harmony.

Oedema – swelling as a result of an excessive amount of fluid in the tissues.

Oily skin – an over-secretion of the sebaceous glands causes an excess of sebum present on the surface of the skin resulting in blockages including open, blocked and enlarged pores, comedones, papules and pustules.

Papilloma – a benign growth on the surface of the skin.

Papule – a small raised area of unbroken skin. Solid and painful to touch, often developing into a pustule.

Pediculosis – infestation of lice.

Pediculosis corporis – infestation of the skin of the body by lice.

Psoriasis – a recurring scaly eruption of the skin. Red patches develop covered by a scale which can be itchy.

Pustule – often referred to as a whitehead, spot or pimple. Raised pus filled area of skin often developing from a papule.

Scab – a hard crust of dried blood, tissue fluid or pus that develops over a sore, cut or scratch.

Scabies – highly contagious disease caused by an infestation of a mite which burrows into the skin. Characterised by itchy spots.

Scale – flakes of dead epidermal cells shed from the skin.

Scars – replacement tissue formed over the site of an injury. Keloid scar – harmless mass of excess tissue forming in the scar of an injury. More common in black skins.

Seborrhea – over-active sebaceous glands causing oily skin with enlarged, blocked pores, comedones and pustules.

Sore – a term commonly used to describe any form of ulcer or open wound of the skin.

Spider naevi – stellate haemangiomas. See *naevus*, above.

Skin tag – tiny, loose growths of skin. Colourless and painless, they develop on the neck, groin, armpits and trunk at any age but most commonly in ageing women.

Steatomas or wens – cysts or tumours of the sebaceous glands.

Telangiectasia – dilated/broken capillaries appearing as red spots that may become spidery in appearance, known as telangiectasia angioma.

Tinea – ringworm fungal infection of the skin characterised by lesions of partial or complete rings and may cause intense itching.

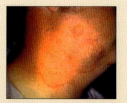

Ringworm

Tinea barbae – ringworm fungal infection of the skin under the bearded area and neck.

Tinea capitis – ringworm fungal infection of the scalp.

Tinea corporis – ringworm fungal infection of the body.

Tinea pedis – ringworm fungal infection of the feet commonly referred to as athlete's foot.

Tumor – swelling associated with inflammation.

Tumour – any abnormal swelling and/or growth of tissue which may be benign (harmless) or malignant (harmful).

Ulcer – a break in the skin that fails to heal and is often accompanied by inflammation.

Urticaria – technical term for hives, which are also referred to as nettle rash – characterised by an itchy rash from the release of histamine from mast cells. Individual swellings (wheals) appear as a common and immediate response to allergens.

Vesicle – a small blister. Vesicles are present in many disorders including eczema and herpes.

Vitiligo – white patches of skin caused by the destruction of melanocytes.

Warts – a benign growth on the skin caused by a viral infection. Common warts occur mainly on the hands and face and plantar warts or verrucas occur on the soles of the feet.

Wheal – a localised area of swelling.

Xanthoma – a yellowish skin legion. Crops of small yellow papules that occur anywhere on the body are known as eruptive xanthomata and larger flat lesions are known as plane xanthomata. **Telangiectasia** commonly referred to as dilated/broken capillaries appearing as red spots that may become spidery in appearance known as telangiectasia angioma.

Having a basic knowledge of the skin and the part it plays as a major organ of the body helps in the understanding of the important contributory role played by the hair.

Hair

Hair grows from the largest organ of the body – the skin. Each hair develops from the hair follicle as part of the stratum germinativum layer of the epidermis and forms three distinct types of hair depending on: (i) the needs of the body; (ii) the health and wellbeing of the body; and (iii) the time of life. The hair provides a protective covering for the whole body, except for the lips, soles of the feet, palms of the hands and parts of the sexual organs. Hair follicles are formed in the body at approximately eight weeks of gestation and develop to produce lanugo hair which, in turn, forms into vellus and terminal hairs.

From early development, hair plays an important role in the protective functions of the body, offering the first line of defence through insulation, camouflage, entrapment and cushioning.

- Scalp and body hair help to keep the body warm as well as form a protective covering helping to guard against the sun's harmful rays.
- Eyebrows and eyelashes help to prevent sweat and dust from entering the eyes, whilst tiny hairs in the nose and ears are able to entrap harmful particles preventing them from entering further into the body.
- Areas of coarse hair help to cushion the body against superficial knocks and blows.
- Pubic hair protects the delicate underlying organs whilst underarm hair provides protection for underlying glands.

Lanugo hair

Lanugo hairs are fine and soft and present all over the body of a foetus from the third to fifth month of gestation. They are lacking in pigment and act as a temporary protective covering. Lanugo hairs are shed from the body during the final trimester and replaced with a second generation of lanugo hair followed by vellus and terminal hairs which offer greater levels of protection for specific areas of the body.

Vellus hair

Vellus hairs are thin (approximately 0.1mm) and short (less than 2cm). They form a downy covering of a large majority of the body. Vellus hairs have shallow roots and are generally lacking in pigment. If stimulated, vellus hairs in certain regions of the body may be transformed into terminal hairs.

Terminal hair

Terminal hairs are thicker (up to 0.6mm) and longer (more than 2cm). They develop from deep seated roots and are found protecting more vulnerable areas of the body. Terminal hairs are pigmented and form the coarse covering of vulnerable areas associated with:

- the scalp, eyelashes and eyebrows in children; present at birth and known as asexual hair
- the axilla (underarms) and pubic hairs which develop at puberty together with the hair of the lower legs and forearms in males and females and classified as ambisexual hair
- the coarse facial and body hair in males post puberty and the coarse male pattern hair growth that may be present in females as a result of hormone imbalance, e.g. menopause, known as sexual hair.

As part of the integumentary system, each hair type grows out of a hair follicle, the walls of which are a continuation of the epidermal stratum germinativum. As the hairs exit the skin via a follicular pore, they are hardened structures made up of two or three layers of keratinised cells collectively known as the hair shaft.

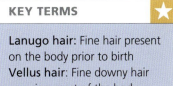

TECHNICAL TIP

The tiny hairs in the nose are known as cilia. As these hairs trap foreign particles, irritation is caused within the nose. The brain is alerted to the irritation through nerve cells and in turn initiates a sneeze reflex, forcibly expelling the unwanted particles

KEY TERMS

Lanugo hair: Fine hair present on the body prior to birth
Vellus hair: Fine downy hair covering most of the body
Terminal hair: Thick, coarse hair protecting underlying structures

TECHNICAL TIP

The presence of primary lanugo hairs at birth is a sign of prematurity

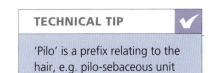

TECHNICAL TIP

'Pilo' is a prefix relating to the hair, e.g. pilo-sebaceous unit

TECHNICAL TIP

Under-active sebaceous glands result in dry skin and hair; a factor largely associated with the ageing process. Skin moisturisers and hair conditioners help to mimic sebum, restoring lost moisture

KEY TERMS ★

Follicle (hair): Tubular pocket in which a hair grows
Hair bulb: Base of the follicle

Depending on the type of hair, the follicle creates a shallow or deep indentation within the dermis where it is affected by the associated structures including:

- *Sebaceous glands* – the hair follicle in combination with a sebaceous gland forms a pilosebaceous unit. Sebum produced in the gland makes its way up the hair follicle and exits the skin via a follicular pore. Sebum acts as a natural lubricant for the skin and hair and contributes to the lustre associated with healthy hair.

- *Sweat glands* – apocrine sweat glands open onto hair follicles in the axilla (underarm) and groin and are activated during puberty. The production of sweat in these glands is thicker than sweat produced in the eccrine glands. It contains waste products of cellular metabolism together with pheromones, which are aromatic molecules associated with sexual attraction. Pheromones are produced at puberty to mark the start of the reproductive years when the attraction between males and females is vital in ensuring the survival of the species.

- *Arrector pili muscles* – attached to both the hair follicle and the base of the epidermis, these tiny muscles are formed from visceral muscular tissue and are responsible for the involuntary action associated with 'goose pimples' in response to changes in body temperature.

- *Circulatory vessels* – a rich blood and lymphatic supply is available to the hair follicle through the papillae in the papillary layer of the dermis. These tiny projections ensure that vital nutrients are transported to the hair and waste products are effectively eliminated as part of the processes associated with cellular respiration and metabolism. When hairs are forcibly tugged out of the skin, blood spotting may result. Blood has been forced to the surface by the aggressive action.

- *Nerve supply* – nerve endings pick up sensations pertaining to the hair such as the removal techniques associated with waxing. Sensory nerves detect the 'pulling' action in the form of electrical impulses which are then relayed to the brain. The nervous tissue in the brain interprets the sensation as pain.

Structure of the hair

Each hair follicle is made up of a permanent upper follicle and an impermanent lower follicle which together contribute to the formation of the different types of hairs and are directly associated with their health and welfare. The structures associated with the upper and lower hair follicles include:

- the outer root sheath, forming the descending projection of the hair follicle

- the vitreous membrane which forms a connection between the hair follicle and the cells of the dermis

- the dermal papilla and cord which connect the whole unit with the underlying blood supply

- the hair bulb which contains the germinating matrix from which the hair develops

- the inner root sheath which forms the impermanent length of the hair follicle.

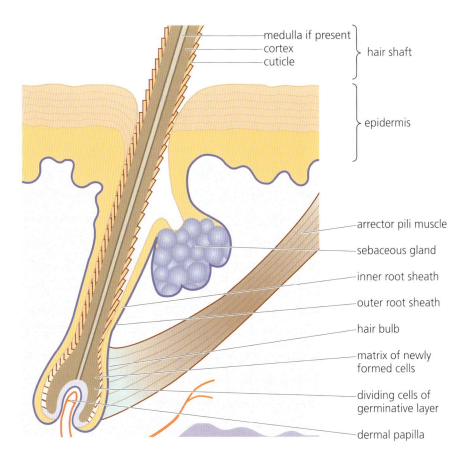

medulla if present
cortex } hair shaft
cuticle

epidermis

arrector pili muscle

sebaceous gland

inner root sheath

outer root sheath

hair bulb

matrix of newly formed cells

dividing cells of germinative layer

dermal papilla

Cross-section of the hair follicle and hair

Outer root sheath

The outer root sheath, or external follicle wall, is the permanent upper section of the hair follicle, forming a descending wall from the epidermal cells. It consists of cells from the stratum spinosum on the inside and cells of the stratum germinativum which together provide a continuous bond with the epidermis, encasing the hair throughout its development within the skin. The outer root sheath extends to contain the 'bulge' region in which stem cells help to activate the cycles of hair growth.

Vitreous membrane

This is a transparent jelly-like substance that forms the basement membrane between the epidermal and dermal layers. This membrane surrounds the whole of the pilosebaceous unit, providing a connection between the epidermal and the papillary and reticular layers of the dermis.

Dermal papillae, cord and hair bulb

Tiny projections known as dermal papillae associated with the papillary layer of the dermis provide rich blood and lymphatic supplies that are necessary for growth and the development of the hair and follicle via the dermal cord.

TECHNICAL TIP ✔

Stem cells are cells that have not undergone the process of differentiation and have therefore not yet become specialised cells with specific functions

Hair bulb and germinating matrix

The hair bulb forms the developing base of the hair follicle to which blood transports nutrients, for example food, water and oxygen, and lymph transports waste products away for efficient cellular respiration and metabolism. In addition, the blood supply transports chemical messengers in the form of hormones which instruct the hair bulb on hair growth and development.

The hair bulb forms a bulbous end to the hair follicle, the lower portion of which contains the germinating matrix or 'growing root'. The cells within the germinating matrix are capable of replicating themselves through a process of simple cell division (mitosis). Hormones command these cells to reproduce new cells by mitosis, pushing the old cells upwards as they begin to differentiate to develop the hair follicle and inner root sheath in much the same way as the cells in the skin form the layers of the epidermis. Melanocytes are also present in the hair bulb, producing the colour pigment melanin which the matrix cells ingest thus determining the natural colour of hair as it grows.

Inner root sheath

The inner root sheath, or internal follicle wall, is the impermanent lower section of the hair follicle forming the ascending wall from the cells within the hair bulb as a hair follicle and the hair grow together. It is made up of three layers:

- an outer layer of flattened cells, known as Henle's layer, which is continuous with the outer root sheath
- a middle layer of square cells, several cells deep, known as Huxley's layer
- an inner layer, known as the cuticle, continuous with the outer layers of hair cells and serving to secure it within the follicle.

The hair itself then forms three layers:

- Cuticle – outer layer of overlapping flat keratinised cells which interlinks with the cuticle of the inner root sheath.
- Cortex – middle layer comprised of several rows of completely keratinised spindle-shaped cells providing the hair with strength.
- Medulla – inner layer of incompletely keratinised cells which is only present in thick terminal hair.

The link between the inner root sheath and the hair itself is discontinued when the hair reaches the sebaceous gland. Here the sheath disintegrates to allow the hair to eventually exit the skin freely as the shaft.

TECHNICAL TIP

The thicker, coarser terminal hairs are composed of a medulla, cortex and cuticle, whilst downy vellus hairs lack a medulla

TECHNICAL TIP

Hair chemistry – hair is made up of the protein keratin which contains molecules made up of smaller units called amino acids joined together in chains. Also present are water, fats, pigments, vitamins and minerals including zinc

PRINCIPLES OF HAIR GROWTH

Hair growth is cyclical, which means that it undergoes a number of changes throughout its development. The hair growth cycle is not synchronised, each hair will enter a phase of the cycle at a different time. There are three main stages involved with the hair growth cycle including:

- Anagen – active, growing phase. This phase lasts from 2 to 8 years depending on the region of the body; 90 per cent of all hairs are in the anagen phase.
- Catagen – changing, regression phase. This is a short phase lasting 2–3 weeks when the matrix cells stop reproducing.
- Telogen – resting, quiescent phase. This lasts for approximately 3–4 months, allowing the hair to become completely detached and eventually fall out.

Stage one – anagen

The whole process of hair growth commences with the anagen stage when the hair cells present within the germinating matrix section of the hair bulb are activated into reproducing replicas of themselves. This is initiated through activity within the dermal papilla and cord. Hormones present in the blood supply associated with the dermal papilla are picked up by target cells within the hair bulb via the dermal cord. These target cells are able to interpret the hormonal message and activate the cells to replicate themselves through the simple cell division associated with mitosis. As the cells reproduce further, they build to form the ascending inner root sheath which in turn forms a continuous external bond with the descending outer root

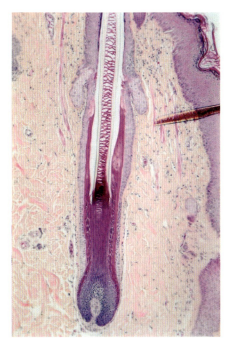 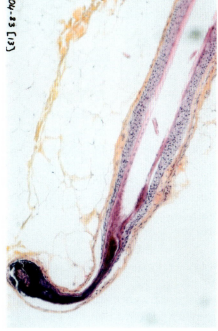 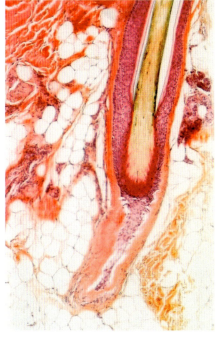

anagen catogen telogen

Histological sections of the hair follicle at different phases

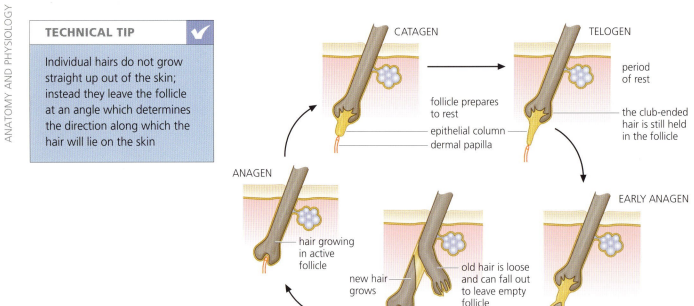

The hair growth cycle

TECHNICAL TIP ✔

Individual hairs do not grow straight up out of the skin; instead they leave the follicle at an angle which determines the direction along which the hair will lie on the skin

PROFESSIONAL TIP ✔

Hair is one of the fastest growing tissues in the body

TECHNICAL TIP ✔

Sometimes the anagen phase of hair growth commences before a hair in the telogen phase has been shed

TECHNICAL TIP ✔

It is normal for an adult to shed in the region of 50–100 hairs from their scalps each day

KEY TERMS ★

Congenital: A condition present at birth
Menopause: The cessation of the menstrual cycle

sheath. The inner root sheath moulds the developing hair shaft and holds it firmly in place. The inner root sheath cuticle contains downward facing cells which interlock with upward facing cells of the hair cuticle. This forms a continuous bond until the permanent section of the hair follicle is reached. During this development process, keratinisation takes place in the Henle layer, followed by the cuticle and finally the Huxley layer of the inner root sheath. This results in a hardening process which forms the layers of the hair shaft that protrude out onto the surface of the skin. As the hair shaft passes the sebaceous gland, sebum is secreted providing an oily covering to the extending hair shaft.

Stage two – catagen

As the hair shaft exits the skin forming a fully formed hair, the cells of the matrix gradually stop reproducing and the hair bulb begins to ascend the hair follicle whilst the dermal papilla is dragged upwards. The outer root sheath shrinks as a result of a process of programmed cell death known as apoptosis that occurs naturally as part of the normal development associated with the catagen stage. The cells undergo a process of regression whereby changes take place that gradually revert the follicle back to an immature level of functioning.

Stage three – telogen

The outer root sheath shrinks back to its permanent level forming a clubbed hair root. This means that the hair shaft is free of all connections with the hair follicle and is able to be shed from the skin. The whole cycle of hair growth is able to commence afresh.

When the hairs are actively growing during the anagen phase of hair growth, stem cells from the bulge region of the follicle migrate along the outer root sheath and take up position on the outside of the hair bulb. During the catagen stage, the stem cells come into contact with the papilla and begin to mature and differentiate forming into specialised cells. As a result, the cells acquire the ability to reproduce a new hair follicle. These cells produce the ascending part of the hair follicle including the inner root sheath and the new hair. The start of the anagen phase is initiated towards the end of the telogen phase.

Factors affecting hair growth

Everything has the potential to affect hair growth from the genetic make-up of our cells to the way in which we take care of our bodies and the type of environment we are exposed to. However, it is the links with the rest of the body that initiate the various levels of changes in hair growth including the following influences from the body's main systems.

- The central nervous system, responsible for coordinating genetic programming and activating the body systems through the formation of electrical impulses.
- The respiratory system, responsible for processing the oxygen vital for cellular survival from the air breathed into the body and ensuring the release of cellular waste in the form of carbon dioxide with the outward breath.
- The digestive system, responsible for processing the nutrients necessary for efficient and effective cellular function.
- The endocrine system, responsible for the release of hormones as chemical messengers informing parts of the body to effect changes as a process of human survival and development.
- The circulatory systems, responsible for transporting oxygen, nutrients and hormones to the cells and waste products away from the cells.
- The urinary system, responsible for the elimination of cellular waste from the body in the form of urine.

As a result of this whole body activity, the causes of hair growth fall into three distinct categories: congenital, topical and systemic.

Congenital

The term congenital refers to a condition that is present from birth, that is, it is genetically programmed to be present. Inherited hair growth patterns fall into the category of normal congenital hair growth. However, there are certain abnormal congenital conditions which present abnormal patterns of hair growth as a symptom. Such conditions are rare and require medical treatment.

Topical

Topical hair growth is local to particular areas of the body. Continuous stimulation of an area of the skin can, in some circumstances, be the cause of changes in both skin and hair and lead to topical hair growth. For example, if blood circulation is stimulated it may increase cellular activity in the stratum germinativum, causing the skin to thicken and the hair to grow coarser and deeper as a result. In these situations, the body is attempting to protect the area under attack more effectively.

Systemic

The term systemic refers to the body as a whole. Systemic hair growth can be classified as both normal and abnormal. Changes in hair growth associated with puberty, pregnancy and menopause are classified as being normal systemic changes.

- During puberty, the brain alerts the endocrine glands to produce sex hormones which are secreted into the blood supply, picked up by target cells and have the effect of stimulating changes in the growth pattern of hair follicles of both sexes in certain areas of the body associated with ambisexual hair, such as terminal hair growth in the pubis and axilla.

- During pregnancy, changes in the secretion of hormones associated with the development of the foetus sometimes create an imbalance which may result in a thickening of vellus hair growth. This hair growth reverts back to normal as hormone secretions normalise after pregnancy.

- During menopause the brain calls for a decrease in the levels of female hormones being produced in the body which in turn initiates the cessation of the female menstrual cycle and fertility. An imbalance in hormone levels occurs as androgens (male hormones) become more dominant, resulting in male characteristics such as male pattern hair growth.

These changes are activated by the secretion of hormones in line with the natural life cycles of human development. However, abnormal secretions of hormones from either over- or under-active endocrine glands can lead to abnormal systemic hair growth, including excessive hair growth and partial/total hair loss that is neither expected nor desired. This type of hair growth is a distressing symptom of a medical condition that requires clinical diagnosis and specialist advice in its treatment.

The distribution, colour, texture and shape of hair are associated with genetic factors and differ among the various races around the world, for example:

- People of Caucasian and northern European descent generally have straight or loosely waved scalp hair with light to medium amounts of facial/body hair distribution.

- People of Latin descent have scalp hair that is coarser, straighter and darker than that of Caucasians, with a heavier distribution of facial and body hair growth.

- People of eastern descent have scalp hair that is very coarse and straight and there tends to be only a light distribution of facial/body hair present.

- People of Afro-Caribbean descent have scalp hair that is tightly curled with a light distribution of facial/body hair growth.

KEY TERMS

Andropause: The male equivalent of the female menopause

REMEMBER

Always think about the judgements that may be made when a woman develops male pattern hair growth. Think about the effect those judgements have on her levels of self-esteem and confidence. Think about the very real benefits that can be gained from a sympathetic HRP offering a realistic and successful method of hair removal and corresponding after care advice

Hair also contributes to the unique appearance associated with each individual person and as such contributes greatly to the way we feel about ourselves, affecting how attractive we and other people view us to be. In particular, hair plays an important role in the recognition of a person and to a lesser extent in identifying which part of the world they may be from. Hair also features highly in a person's non-verbal communication and harsh judgements are often made based on excessive hair growth or extremes of hair loss as well as hair style and colour.

Differing views on the attractiveness of body hair vary within the different cultures of the world as well as with the changing fashions of the time. This is one reason why the need for hair removal techniques forms a large part of an HRP's working life. Determining the correct choice of hair removal technique will depend largely on the underpinning knowledge associated with anatomy and physiology as well as the information gained from a client consultation. Therefore, a combination of theoretical knowledge and practical skill is a basic requirement of all HRPs.

A–Z OF HAIR FACTS

Alopecia – loss of hair caused by hair follicles being unable to produce new hairs.

Anagen – growing stage of hair development.

Canities – white hair, which is due to a lack of melanin forming in new hairs. Associated with ageing and/or hormone imbalance.

Catagen – changing stage of hair development.

Club hairs – hairs have a club end due to the disintegration of the hair bulb during the telogen stage of hair growth.

Corkscrew hairs – distortion of the hair follicle resulting in tightly curled hair shaft.

Curly hair – emerges from flattened follicles.

Embedded hairs – hairs that do not emerge from the skin. The skin grows over the follicle trapping the hair below resulting in a small lump on the surface of the skin.

Folliculitis – Barber's rash – affects areas of facial hair growth and is characterised by redness and swelling in the hair follicles.

Hairy naevus – malformation of the skin containing a hair.

Hirsutism – abnormal androgen-dependent hair growth characterised by male pattern coarse pigmented hair growth in females.

Hypertrichosis – increase of vellus hair growth.

Idiopathic hirsutism – excess hair growth with cause unknown.

In-growing hairs – hairs that grow just beneath the surface of the skin. Prone to becoming infected.

Involuted hair – hair follicle infolds upon itself during catagen.

Lanugo hair – fine foetal hair.

Pediculosis capitis – infestation of the scalp by head lice.

Pili multigemini – two or more hairs growing from the same follicle each having a separate papilla and root sheaths.

Re-growth hairs – hairs that re-grow after treatment.

Straight hair – emerges from round follicles.

Sycosis – inflammation of the hair follicles commonly affecting the beard area of men in their thirties or forties.

Superfluous hair – unwanted hair growth as a result of heredity, hormonal changes and/or stimulation to the area.

Telogen – terminating stage of hair development.

Terminal hair – coarse, pigmented hair.

Tinea barbae – ringworm fungal infection affecting the face and neck.

Tombstone hair – when a new anagen hair in the same follicle as an old telogen hair has been treated with epilation, the telogen hair is removed and the anagen hair as it progresses to the surface becomes thicker and darker than normal. Resulting tombstone hairs naturally fall out as a result of the prior treatment.

Vellus hair – soft downy hair.

Virgin hairs – hairs that have not been treated.

Wavy hair – emerges from oval hair follicles.

In addition, healthy hair growth is dependent on a healthy lifestyle, which should include a balance between rest and activity as well as food and fluid:

- Rest allows the regeneration of cells to occur more effectively.
- Activity stimulates the circulation necessary for cellular respiration and metabolism.
- A diet that is well balanced and varied helps to restock cellular reserves for energy production and cellular renewal.
- Fluid intake prevents dehydration and ensures effective cellular activity.

General care of the whole body adds to this with good posture ensuring better breathing and consequently a greater cellular uptake of oxygen. Observing the body's need to release faeces and urine ensures waste is effectively eliminated from the body as part of excretion, preventing a build-up of harmful toxins in the body.

To understand this more effectively, it is useful to look at certain body systems in more detail including the circulatory systems and the controlling systems.

A CLOSER LOOK AT CIRCULATORY SYSTEMS OF THE BODY

The body's circulation is made up of two complementary systems: the blood and lymphatic systems. These two circulations work together to provide the whole body with a transportation system.

Blood circulation is a two-way system that:

1 transports vital resources such as oxygen, water, nutrients and hormones *to* every cell of the body for cellular respiration and metabolism via arteries

2 transports waste products associated with cellular metabolism and respiration such as carbon dioxide and broken down cells and hormones *away* from every cell of the body via veins.

The lymphatic circulation is a one-way system which supports the blood circulation by:

1 transporting unwanted substances away from the cells that the blood is unable to deal with.

The circulatory systems comprise of:

- the heart, which is the centre of the circulatory systems
- the fluids, blood and lymph, forming the transportation media
- vessels forming a complex network of tubes for transportation.

Heart

The heart is located in the thorax between the lungs and slightly towards the left side of the body. It is a hollow, muscular organ that acts like a pump. The heart is divided into four sections or chambers separated by a muscular wall known as the septum. Valves form connections between the chambers.

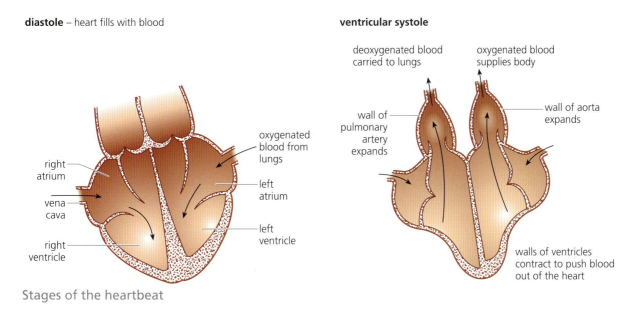

diastole – heart fills with blood

right atrium

vena cava

right ventricle

oxygenated blood from lungs

left atrium

left ventricle

ventricular systole

deoxygenated blood carried to lungs

oxygenated blood supplies body

wall of pulmonary artery expands

wall of aorta expands

walls of ventricles contract to push blood out of the heart

Stages of the heartbeat

Blood

Blood is a fluid connective tissue containing cells that are suspended in a fluid called plasma. There are three main types of blood cells.

- Erythrocytes – red blood cells. These blood cells contain haemoglobin which is responsible for carrying oxygen and carbon dioxide.
- Leucocytes – white blood cells. These blood cells form part of the body's defence mechanism helping to engulf and destroy cellular waste and harmful invaders.

● Thrombocytes – platelets. These blood cells assist with the healing and protective functions of the blood as they are responsible for forming blood clots at the site of an injury.

Plasma is made up of approximately 90 per cent water in which chemical substances are dissolved or suspended allowing the transportation of water, nutrients and hormones to take place.

When the skin is damaged in any way it loses its protective function and blood rushes to the area to assist.

● Thrombocytes coagulate to control the loss of blood by forming a protective covering known as a scab

● Leucocytes deal with any harmful substances that may accompany injury, for example dirt, bacteria, etc.

Subsequently, the blood flow to the area continues to be stimulated to assist in the healing process.

● Erythrocytes bring fresh nutrients to the site so that the edges of the wound can rejoin. Epidermal cells reproduce through mitosis and fibroblasts in the dermis produce protein fibres to replace those lost and damaged.

As new dermal tissue is formed, it domes up into the newly formed epidermal layer. This has the effect of dislodging the protective scab which eventually drops off. The resulting skin may exhibit scarring as the replacement skin tends to be denser. This scar tissue is present for varying lengths of time post injury. Wound repair is normally more efficient when a person is young and/or fit and healthy.

Lymph

The cells of the body are bathed in a fluid known as tissue or interstitial fluid. This fluid is derived from blood plasma and acts as a link between the blood and the cells, allowing substances to pass back and forth. However, some substances that cannot be picked up by the blood form liquid lymph.

Blood vessels

Blood is circulated around the body by a network of vessels known as arteries and veins.

● Arteries always carry blood *away* from the heart. They are thick walled, hollow tubes that subdivide to form smaller vessels known as arterioles.

● Veins always carry blood *towards* the heart. They are thin walled, hollow tubes that subdivide to form smaller vessels known as venules.

Tiny vessels known as capillaries form at the end of arterioles and venules and provide the link between the blood circulation system and the cells.

Lymphatic vessels

Lymph is circulated around the body by a network of lymphatic vessels that start as small tubes called lymphatic capillaries (similar to blood capillaries) and provide the link between the lymphatic circulation system and the cells. These capillaries develop into larger tubes that follow the course of veins through the body. These tubes pass through nodes, tissue and ducts before connecting with the veins.

- Nodes consist of lymphatic connective tissue which acts as a filtering system for lymph. They are found in strategic areas of the body and contain cells responsible for defending the body against antigens by producing antibodies.

- Tissue consists of lymphatic connective tissue and forms the spleen, tonsils and adenoids, thymus gland, lacteals and appendix. These structures support the defensive actions of the nodes.

- Ducts – two ducts collect filtered lymph before draining it into the veins. The thoracic duct collects lymph from the left side of the head, neck and thorax, the left arm, both legs and the abdominal and pelvic areas of the body, draining it into the left subclavian vein. The right lymphatic duct collects lymph from the right side of the head, neck and thorax, as well as the right arm, draining it into the right subclavian vein.

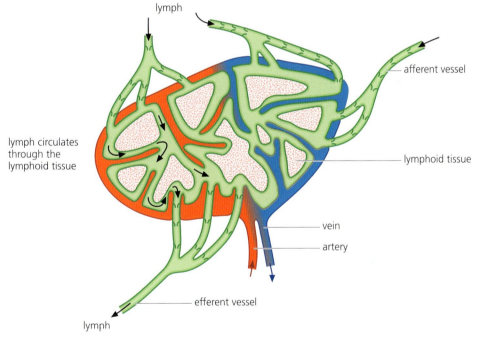

Lymphatic nodes, tissue and ducts

Circulation and hair growth

The body's circulatory systems create a transport network that is vital to the growth and development of the hair. This is because the blood delivers important nutrients and hormones – and at times medication in the form of prescribed drugs – to the skin and hair follicles, and the blood and lymph transport waste products away.

- Nutrients – oxygen, water and nutrients in the form of glucose, amino acids, fats, minerals and vitamins are transported to the cells of the integumentary system for growth and development. Efficient breathing, balanced water intake and diet are needed to ensure the hair growth cycle is maintained efficiently throughout life.

- Hormones – chemical messengers that are vital components in the efficient renewal of the hair growth cycle. Target cells in the integumentary system receive the relevant hormones and respond to their message, initiating the different stages of hair growth development throughout life. Hormones are produced in the endocrine glands, secreted into the blood and transported to the relevant cells for action.

- Drugs – prescribed drugs taken orally, will be processed by the digestive system, absorbed into the blood and transported to the relevant cells for action. Topical drugs in the form of creams will penetrate the skin and be picked up by the circulating blood. Injected drugs enter the blood circulation directly.

- Waste – associated with cellular respiration (carbon dioxide) and cellular metabolism (general waste products, e.g. urea and uric acid) together with used hormones, used drugs and old broken down cells are transported away from the cells by the circulatory systems. Waste products may be taken to the lungs, so that waste can leave the body through the outward breath (carbon dioxide), to the liver to be broken down further or to the kidneys to be excreted out of the body in urine.

The controlling systems of the body: The nervous and endocrine systems

The nervous and endocrine systems have a controlling function over the body through the production of electrical impulses (nervous system) and the secretion of hormones (endocrine system). Together, they act as the communication centres of the body.

- The nervous system communicates using electrical messages in the form of impulses which are fast acting.
- The endocrine system communicates using chemical messengers in the form of hormones which are slower to act.

The fast-acting nervous system stimulates immediate responses, such as reflex actions, whilst the slower-acting endocrine system is responsible for gradual changes within the body, such as growth.

A CLOSER LOOK AT THE NERVOUS SYSTEM

The nervous system controls the body using electrical impulses, allowing it to detect external and internal changes and to make use of the information received to form a response. It forms vital links with all of the systems of the body, providing them with the ability to feel and respond. Nerve cells called neurons facilitate this action:

- sensory neurons carry impulses to the brain
- motor neurons carry impulses away from the brain.

The central nervous system, which consists of the brain and spinal cord, coordinate these impulses through the peripheral nervous system, which includes:

- 12 pairs of cranial nerves servicing the face and neck and responsible for the senses associated with smell, sight, taste, balance and hearing as well as such functions as breathing, eating, speaking and feeling
- 31 pairs of spinal nerves servicing the rest of the body with functions associated with feeling and movement of the corresponding areas of the body.

The autonomic nervous system controls the body further by responding to the effects of stress:

- the sympathetic nervous system prepares the body for activity
- the parasympathetic system prepares the body for rest.

A CLOSER LOOK AT THE ENDOCRINE SYSTEM

The endocrine system consists of a set of ductless glands which are widely spaced around the body. Each one is responsible for the production of hormones.

Hormone production

The hormones secreted by the endocrine glands are chemical substances formed from components of the food we eat. They are either protein based or fat based. Hormones have the ability to affect changes in other cells and are secreted directly into the bloodstream and transported to the various systems of the body. Target cells receive the hormones and allow the body to respond to the message and initiate the appropriate changes.

Hormone secretion

The secretion of hormones is controlled in three ways.

1 A structure in the brain called the hypothalamus produces releasing hormones which regulate the hormone secretion of the pituitary gland. As a result the pituitary gland produces hormones which control some of the other endocrine glands and body systems direct.

2 The nervous system controls some endocrine glands directly when a quick response is required, for example the sympathetic nervous system stimulates the production of adrenalin in the adrenal gland in response to a stressful situation.

KEY TERMS

Hormones: Chemical messengers
Endocrine gland: Ductless glands secreting hormones directly into the blood
Homeostasis: Physiological stability

3 The internal environment of the body controls the action of some endocrine glands, for example the brain is alerted through the nervous system when blood sugar levels rise or fall. This initiates the production of hormones in the islets of Langerhans in the pancreas which are able to restore the blood sugar levels back to normal.

Hormones are circulated around the body in the blood stream before reaching the target cells of the appropriate organs. Once hormones have completed their task the resulting waste product is passed back into the circulatory systems and taken to the liver to be broken down further before being transported to the kidneys to be excreted from the body in urine.

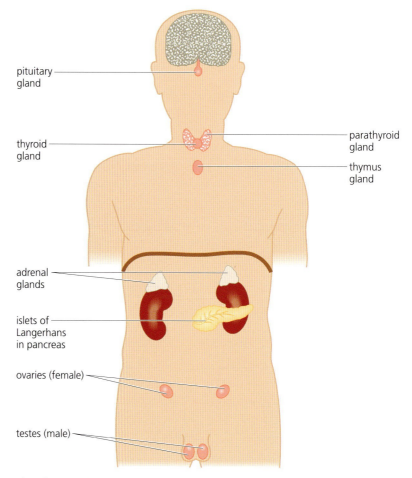

pituitary gland

thyroid gland

parathyroid gland

thymus gland

adrenal glands

islets of Langerhans in pancreas

ovaries (female)

testes (male)

The endocrine system

Hormone balance

The functions of the endocrine glands are controlled, communicated and maintained by links between the nervous and endocrine systems. The three main functions are homeostasis, growth and development, and sexual development.

Homeostasis

The maintenance of a constant state of equilibrium. Communication between the nervous and endocrine systems will pick up on changes within the body

Table of hormones

Gland	Hormone	Underactive	Overactive
Pituitary anterior	ACTH	Adrenal cortex irregularities	
	TSH	Thyroid gland irregularities	
	FSH and LH	Failure to start puberty	Infertility
	GH	Lack of growth	Excessive growth including hair
	PRL	Failure of breast milk production	Infertility, hirsutism
	MSH	Loss of pigmentation	Increased pigmentation
Pituitary posterior	ADH	Fluid loss	Fluid retention
	OT	Loss of maternal behaviour	Increased maternal behaviour
Pineal	Melatonin	Loss of body rhythms – disturbed cycles	
		Inability to sleep	Tiredness
Thyroid	T3	Increased metabolism and weight loss	Decreased metabolism and weight gain
	T4	Possible hair loss	Possible hair growth
	Calcitonin	Raising of calcium levels	Lowering of calcium levels
Parathyroid	Parathormone	Lowering of calcium levels	Raising of calcium levels
Thymus	Thymosins	Lowered immunity	Raised immunity
Adrenal cortex	Glucocorticoids	Weak and wasted muscles	Obesity, hirsutism, osteoposrosis
	Mineralocorticoids	Low blood pressure, weakening and wasting	High blood pressure
	Sex corticoids	Weakening and wasting of muscles	Male characteristic in females & vice versa
Adrenal medulla	Adrenalin	No ill effect due to sympatheric nervous system intervention	Adverse effects of stress i.e. Headaches, sweating, nausea etc.
Islets of langerhans	Insulin	Raised blood sugar levels	Low blood sugar levels
	Glucagon	No ill effects due to compensation by other hormones e.g. GH	Raised blood sugar levels
Ovaries in females	Oestrogen Progesterone	Underactivity of male hormones and/or over-activity of female hormones in males will result in the development of secondary sexual female characteristics.	
Testes in males	Testosterone	Underactivity of female hormones and/or over-activity of male hormones in females will result in the development of secondary sexual male characteristics	

and initiate suitable responses to ensure the correct levels of the following are maintained:

- body temperature
- blood pressure
- fluid balance
- blood sugar levels
- mineral balance.

Growth and development

The correct hormone balance is important for:

- rapid growth and development in the first year of life
- slow, steady growth and development during childhood
- rapid growth and development during puberty
- cessation of growth and the maintenance of development in adulthood.

Sexual development

Hormone balance is also vital at the following times:

- puberty and the onset of fertility in males and females
- pregnancy and the development of a new organism in females
- menopause and the cessation of the menstrual cycle and female fertility.

Endocrine conditions affecting hair growth

Acromegaly

Excessive growth hormone (somatrophin) is produced in the pituitary gland after normal growth has been completed and causes enlargement of the hands and feet and facial features. This condition may increase male hormone androgen secretion, which in turn has an effect on hair growth potentially resulting in hirsutism.

Anorexia nervosa

An eating disorder whereby failure to eat results in a person becoming undernourished and severely underweight. Severe loss of weight causes hypertrichosis with increased vellus hair growth attempting to offer the body additional protection. In addition, the ovaries fail to function properly which has the effect of reducing the oestrogen levels. This has a knock-on effect of stimulating the male hormone androgens in the body which can in turn stimulate excessive hair growth in the form of hirsutism.

Congenital adrenal hyperplasia

This is a group of inherited disorders that relate to the adrenal glands. It is characterised by a deficiency in cortisol and aldosterone production and an over-production of androgens. This has the effect of causing early or inappropriate male characteristics including hair growth.

Cushings syndrome

Hypersecretion of the glococorticoid hormones – cortisol – and sex corticoid hormones – androgens – from the cortex of the adrenal glands is responsible for a series of symptoms including hirsutism, obesity, high blood pressure, diabetes and osteoporosis.

Drugs

The side effects of some drugs often include excessive hair growth. These drugs include:

- *Oral contraceptive pill* – contain androgen progestins and may cause hirsutism.
- *Anabolic steroids* – synthetic forms of androgen hormones that have the effect of enhancing masculine traits in men and stimulating male characteristics in females including hirsutism.

- *Danazol* – synthetic progesterone that inhibits the secretion in the pituitary gland of the gonadotrophins. May be prescribed for heavy menstrual periods and endometriosis. May contribute to hirsutism.
- *Cortisone* – a naturally occurring corticosteroid that may be used to treat disorders of the adrenal glands such as Addisons disease and removal of adrenal glands. May contribute to hirsutism.
- *Cyclosporin* – immunosuppressant drug that may be used to prevent and treat rejection of a transplanted organ or bone marrow. May contribute to hypertrichosis.
- *Minoxidil* – may be used in the treatment of high blood pressure. May contribute to hypertrichosis.
- *Diazoxide* – may be used to treat high blood pressure and conditions in which blood sugar levels are low. May contribute to hypertrichosis.
- *Tamoxifen* – may be used in the treatment of breast cancer to inhibit the effect of oestrogen. May contribute to hirsutism.
- *Phenytoin* – may be used in the treatment of epilepsy. May contribute to hirsutism.

TECHNICAL TIP

Minoxidil may be used topically in the form of a lotion in an attempt to restore hair growth

Excessive exercise

Excessive amounts of physical exercise can result in low levels of body fat in women and may also have an effect on the ovaries, limiting their function and reducing oestrogen levels. This in turn can stimulate the circulating androgen hormones with the development of male characteristics including hirsutism.

Hyperprolactinemia

Increased levels of prolactin PRL in the blood from the pituitary gland may stimulate the ovaries to produce more androgens, resulting in male characteristics including the male pattern hair growth associated with hirsutism. May be caused by disease of the hypothalamus and/or pituitary gland.

Insulin resistance also known as Syndrome X

This is the inability of the hormone insulin to control blood sugar levels effectively. High blood sugar levels produce excessive levels of androgens by stimulating ovarian androgen production and can prove to be a contributory factor in hirsutism. This condition results in Type 2 diabetes mellitus.

TECHNICAL TIP

Research has shown that at least 30 per cent of women with polycystic ovarian syndrome (PCOS) have insulin resistance

Menopause

The phase which marks the end of childbearing years in a woman, usually between the ages of 45 and 55. The breasts and ovaries decrease in size and become less responsive to follicle stimulating hormone (FSH) and luteinising hormone (LH) from the pituitary gland. As a result, the ovaries produce less oestrogen, progesterone and androgens. However, the adrenal gland still produces androgens and this can have the effect of stimulating male pattern hair growth associated with hirsutism.

Ovarian hyperthecosis

Abnormal cellular activity in the ovaries that elevates production levels of androgens resulting in the onset of male characteristics, including male pattern hair growth associated with hirsutism.

Polycystic ovarian syndrome (PCOS)

A collection of symptoms that affects up to 20 per cent of women. A build-up of cysts develop on the ovaries (polycystic ovaries) as a result of undeveloped follicles, which can prevent ovulation from taking place. The cysts gradually enlarge the ovaries and have an effect on their production of hormones having a knock on effect on the rest of the body and resulting in a set of symptoms that contribute to the syndrome. The cause is uncertain; however, PCOS may be associated with any of the following:

- genetic predisposition to the syndrome
- abnormality of the hypothalamus and pituitary link
- hyperandrogenism – over-production of male hormones
- obesity
- environmental chemical pollution – hormone disruptors
- highly processed foods
- insulin resistance
- chronic inflammation.

Symptoms include irregular periods, infertility, acne, obesity, hirsutism (including excess hair growth on the chin, breasts, chest and abdomen), high blood pressure, fluctuating emotions and multiple hormone imbalances. PCOS is discussed in greater detail in the Advanced Knowledge section of Chapter Two.

Pregnancy

Changes in hormone levels during pregnancy may result in changes in hair growth, and hypertrichosis can occur with a thickening of vellus hair on the abdomen, chest and face as well as changes in hair growth on the arms and legs. Scalp hair may also thicken. These changes may continue for up to six months post pregnancy, returning to normal as hormone secretions become more balanced.

Premature menopause

May accompany auto-immune disorders such as thyroid disease and diabetes. These conditions may interfere with the normal functioning of the body's organs, including the ovaries, resulting in a reduction of female hormones and a stimulation of male hormone androgens.

Puberty

In both males and females, this phase is associated with a major release of male and female sex hormones. These are secreted in response to the nervous and endocrine systems' interaction.

TECHNICAL TIP ✔

The term syndrome simply refers to a set of symptoms that occur together. PCOS is one of the most common causes of excessive and unwanted hair growth in women. Each of the associated symptoms in isolation is very distressing but when they occur together they have the potential to create extreme distress

TECHNICAL TIP ✔

If the ovaries are removed during a hysterectomy then menopause will occur within days regardless of age

- The hypothalamus is stimulated to produce corticotrophin releasing hormones (CRH) and gonadotrophin releasing hormones (GnRH) stimulating the pituitary gland.
- The pituitary gland releases adrenocorticotrophic hormones (ACTH) to stimulate the adrenal glands and the gonadotrophins LH and FSH as well as prolactin (PRL) to stimulate the ovaries in females or testes in males.
- The adrenal glands, ovaries and testes are subsequently stimulated to produce male hormones (androgens) and female hormones (oestrogen and progesterone).

The differences in males and females are dependent on the balance between the male and female sex hormones. Males have a predominance of male hormones and females have a predominance of female hormones. Androgens have the effect of stimulating the growing phase of hair development whilst oestrogen and progesterone control the resting phase of hair growth.

Puberty marks the onset of sexual development and with it the body changes synonymous with adulthood including the growth of ambisexual hair in both males and females and sexual hair in males. An imbalance in male and female hormones may result in sexual hair growth in females, known as hirsutism.

Obesity

Fat cells can be insulin resistant. In an obese female there may be an increase in insulin production and as a direct result the pituitary gland, ovaries and adrenal glands may be stimulated causing an increase in LH (stimulating the ovaries) from the pituitary gland and androgens from the ovaries and adrenal glands. Hirsutism may result.

Stress

Stressful situations alert the brain to activate the hypothalamus that links the nervous and endocrine systems of the body.

- The hypothalamus releases corticotrophin releasing hormone (CRH). This stimulates the pituitary gland.
- The pituitary gland then releases adrenocorticotrophic hormone (ACTH) which in turn stimulates the adrenal cortex.
- The adrenal cortex releases the hormone cortisol which helps the body maintain resistance to stress by helping to control blood sugar levels and increase the burning of protein and fat for energy.

However, long-term stimulation of the adrenal cortex can also stimulate increased androgen release causing possible hair growth disturbances.

Thyroid and parathyroid disorders

Hormones produced in the thyroid gland are stimulated by the production of thyroid stimulating hormone (TSH) in the pituitary gland and include thyroxine (T4) and triiodothyronine (T3). These hormones are responsible for metabolism and the development and the differentiation of cells. This hyposecretion and hypersecretion of T3 and T4 hormones may contribute to changes in hair growth. In addition, the hormones calcitonin and

TECHNICAL TIP

Tumours on the ovaries, adrenal or pituitary glands will result in varying degrees of malfunction. Hirsutism may be a resultant symptom

REMEMBER

Excessive hair growth is in itself a stressor. Think about the amount of stress that may be caused by worrying about hair growth and the knock-on physiological effects this may have on the body as a whole

parathormone, which together help to regulate the balance of calcium and phosphorous, are also thought to be involved in the control of hair growth.

Virilisation

Hypersecretion of androgens in the adrenal cortex can result in females developing male characteristics, including temporal balding, muscle bulk, deepening of the voice and hirsutism.

> **KEY TERMS** ★
>
> **Hypothalamus:** The part of the brain that links the nervous and endocrine systems

---

HORMONE PRODUCERS

Hypothalamus – the hypothalamus provides the link between the nervous and endocrine systems. It produces hormones that start and stop the release of pituitary hormones.

Pituitary gland – master gland of the endocrine system which produces hormones that have an effect on some of the other glands, including ACTH for the adrenal glands, TSH for the thyroid gland, FH and LH and PRL for the testes and ovaries. The pituitary gland also produces hormones that have an effect on the whole body systems, including MSH for the integumentary system, GH for the skeletal and muscular systems and oxytocin and ADH for the genito-urinary systems. Any imbalance can seriously affect hair growth.

Pineal gland – known as the third eye gland, this gland produces the hormone melatonin which is believed to have an influence on the 'cycles of life'. Melatonin helps to control sleep patterns, as it is secreted when the sun goes down, making the body feel sleepy. Secretion stops in sunlight. It is also believed to have an effect on the onset of puberty and menopause which subsequently may affect changes in hair growth.

Thyroid gland – produces the hormones T3 and T4 in response to the pituitary gland which have an effect on the metabolism and the body's ability to break down food and store it as energy. Too little secretion of these hormones results in decreased energy levels and weight gain – known as hypothyroidism. Too much secretion results in lots of energy and weight loss – known as hyperthyroidism. Both situations may affect hair growth. Hirsutism may accompany weight gain and weight loss and hypertrichosis may accompany weight loss.

Parathyroid glands – together with the thyroid gland, these glands produce hormones to regulate the levels of calcium and phosphorous levels in the body. This is thought to have an effect on the development of hair growth and may offer an underlying contributory cause.

Thymus gland – the thymus gland produces hormones known as thymosins which are needed to stimulate the production of T-lymphocytes which help fight infection. This gland is larger in children than in adults. It is believed to have an inhibiting effect on the development of the secondary sexual characteristics and as such may contribute to the changes in hair growth during puberty.

Adrenal gland – the outer portion or cortex produces steroid hormones in response to the pituitary gland. Glococorticoids (cortisol) help regulate blood sugar levels, mineralocorticoids (aldosterone) control fluid balance and sex corticoids (androgens) control sexual development. These hormones contribute greatly to hair growth and development and are responsible, or contributory in some circumstances, for hirsutism. The inner portion, or medulla, produces adrenalin which together with cortisol assists the body when under stress.

Islets of Langerhans – responsible for producing insulin and glucagon which together help to control the body's blood sugar levels. Insulin encourages excess sugar to be stored in the liver and muscles and glucagon informs the liver to release its store when blood sugar levels are low. Type 1 diabetes occurs when the pancreas does not produce enough insulin and Type 2 diabetes occurs when the body is resistant to insulin. Diabetes contributes to hirsutism.

Testes – responsible for producing sperm and hormones. Testes produce a dominance of male hormones, especially testosterone, which is responsible for secondary sexual characteristics in males, including male pattern hair growth.

Ovaries – responsible for producing ova and hormones. Ovaries produce a dominance of female hormones, oestrogen and progesterone, which are responsible for secondary sexual characteristics in females including initiating the onset of the menstrual cycle at puberty and the cessation of the menstrual cycle at menopause. Any imbalance in female hormones may result in a dominance of male hormones, which can lead to the male pattern hair growth associated with androgen induced hirsutism.

A holistic approach

Many factors affect the growth and development of hair and these need to be taken into consideration when determining the choice and suitability of hair removal treatment. Considering the body as a whole will help to determine the needs of one small part, and medical guidance is often required in order to give clients the best possible treatment advice.

Assessment of knowledge and understanding

You have now learnt about anatomy and physiology and its relevance to hair removal. To test your level of knowledge and understanding, answer the following questions:

Cells and tissue

1 What do groups of cells form?

2 Name the four different types of tissue.

3 Which does differentiation mean?

4 What types of tissue are bones and blood?

5 Name the two types of movement offered by muscular tissue.

6 Which type of tissue forms glands?

7 Which tissue type is responsible for sensation?

8 What are organs made from?

9 Name five substances formed from glands.

10 Name five organs.

Body systems

1 What is the name given to the system that contains the hair, skin and nails?

2 Which body systems contribute to the shape of the body?

3 Which body system processes oxygen and carbon dioxide?

4 Name the two circulatory systems.

5 Which circulatory system is two-way?

6 Which body system is concerned with ingestion, digestion, absorption and elimination?

7 Which system deals with cellular waste?

8 Which two systems are closely linked and exhibit differences in a male and female?

9 What does the nervous system use to control the body?

10 What are hormones?

Skin

1 Name the top section of skin. How many layers does it consist of?

2 Which section of the skin do papillary and reticular layers form?

3 What does the hypodermis contain?

4 What is sebum and where is it produced?

5 Name the two types of sweat glands. Which are activated at puberty?

6 What is the acid mantle and what is it formed from?

7 How do the arrector pili muscles contribute to controlling the temperature of the body?

8 What is melanin and where is it found?

9 What is keratin?

10 What are mast cells in the skin responsible for?

Hair

1 What is the pilo-sebaceous unit?

2 What are lanugo hairs?

3 Where are terminal hairs found on the body?

4 Name the layers of the hair and root sheath.

5 How do the sebaceous glands contribute to the hair?

6 What does the 'bulge' region contain?

7 Describe vellus hair.

8 Name the three stages of the hair growth cycle.

9 What are the definitions of superfluous hair, hypertrichosis and hirsutism?

10 What are the differences between congenital, topical and systemic hair growth?

Circulatory systems

1 Name the two components that form blood.

2 What is lymph derived from?

3 Name three nutrients carried in blood.

4 What does lymph transport?

5 What are erythrocytes commonly known as and what is their function?

6 What is the function of lymph nodes?

7 What is the name given to white blood cells?

8 Name the two lymphatic ducts.

9 What is the difference between arteries and veins?

10 Describe the process of wound healing.

Controlling systems

1 What is the difference between the nervous and endocrine systems?

2 Which structures make up the central nervous system?

3 Which parts of the nervous system do the cranial and spinal nerves form?

4 What are hormones?

5 Which structure links the nervous and endocrine systems in the brain?

6 What is the sympathetic nervous system responsible for?

7 What are hormones formed from?

8 Name the five sensory organs.

9 What is the difference between sensory and motor neurons?

10 Which part of the autonomic nervous system prepares the body for rest?

Hormones

1 Why is the pituitary gland also known as the master gland?

2 What does the hypothalamus produce to activate the endocrine system?

3 Which glands do the hormones ACTH and TSH have an effect on?

4 Which glands produce corticoid hormones?

5 Name the three types of corticoid hormones.

6 Name the male and female hormones produced in the testes and ovaries.

7 The hormones T3 and T4 are produced in the thyroid gland; what do they have an effect on within the body?

8 Which endocrine glands produce hormones that help to maintain calcium and phosphorous levels in the body?

9 What are androgens?

10 Where are the glands situated that produce hormones that have a regulatory effect on blood sugar levels?

Activities

1 Make stick-on labels for each of the organs of the body. Draw an outline of the human body. Stick on the labels.

2 Make a chart to include the following headings:

- body system

- associated organs

- functions

- effects on the hair.

Use this for revision.

3 Research the skin disorders in more detail and make a chart for reference detailing the following:

- disorder

- symptoms

- cause

- whether or not it is a contra-indication to treatment.

4 Make a chart to include examples of the following:

- different types of hair

- different colours of hair

- different stages of hair growth.

5 Check the beating of your heart by trying the following activities.

- Find the pulse in your neck by pressing the fingers of your right hand against the left side of you neck. What you are feeling is the force of the heart pumping blood into an artery during each beat of the heart.

- Count the number of beats in the space of one minute.

- Jog on the spot for at least one minute, then check your pulse again by counting the number of beats per minute.

- Notice how your pulse rate has risen in response to the need for more oxygen as you jogged.

- Check your pulse again after a further ten minutes. Notice how it has returned to normal, as your body's need for oxygen has decreased.

6 Make a note of how your body responds in stressful situations and compare this with the response your body has to more peaceful situations.

7 Make a chart using the following headings:

- puberty

- menstruation

- pregnancy

- menopause.

Under each heading list the changes that take place in the body during these cycles of life and link the corresponding endocrine activity.

8 Make yourself a chart with the following headings:

- endocrine gland

- hormones

- effects on the body

- effects on hair growth.

Use this for revision.

Advanced knowledge reference section

Hirsutism: Causes and treatment

H. Christina Hanley, M.D.

Hirsutism can be defined as excess facial and body hair. To the woman who has it, the hair may be a devastating condition or she may nonchalantly accept it as the norm for her ethnic or family group. Today, however, women are increasingly self-conscious about unwanted hair, especially as the media tend to promote smooth-skinned, hairless movie stars and models as the standard.

Attempts have been made to quantify hair growth, such as the chart produced by Farriman and Gallwey. A woman, herself, is able to make a much better subjective assessment as to her degree of hirsutism in her family/cultural setting than we are able to do with objective criteria.

The body is completely covered with hair, except the lips, the palms of the hands and the soles of the feet. The number of hair follicles is fixed before birth, and is dependent on genetic factors. These hairs are vellus hairs – they are fine and light – as opposed to the terminal hairs of eyebrows and on the head. Vellus hairs are transformed into terminal hairs when subjected to androgens. A low level of androgen (male-type hormones) produces pubic and axillary hairs and the few strands around the brown circles of the nipple. When there is a higher circulating level of androgen, terminal hair appears over the shoulders, over the sacral area and the upper abdomen (a diamond-shaped extension of the normal pubic triangle). Terminal hairs on the arms and legs vary in their response to androgens so are not a reliable indicator of hirsutism. The amount of terminal hair increases with age. Usually, for women, androgen production does not increase as the years go by, so increased hirsutism must be attributed to the duration of exposure to androgens.

A woman may have hirsutism as the only manifestation of disease, or it may be one sign of virilism; others include acne, obesity, irregular periods or no periods, deepening of the voice, masculinisation including an increase in muscle mass, and temporal balding.

Causes of hirsutism

Androgens are produced in the adrenal gland, the ovaries and, by conversion of precursors, in the periphery (mainly fat and muscle) tissues. If one or more sites increase their production, or if the hair follicles are more sensitive to a normal amount of circulating androgen, hirsutism results. The causes of hirsutism are listed below.

1 Excess production of male-type hormones:

- ovaries – polycystic ovarian disease; Stein-Leventhal
- adrenals – congenital adrenal hyperplasia; adrenal tumour
- peripheral sites (muscle and fat) convert precursors to active androgen
- combination of the above
- pituitary disease: Cushing's disease; high prolactin levels.

2 Increased sensitivity of the hair follicles to androgen stimulation.

3 Medication:

- dilantin – seizures
- minoxidil – hypertension, baldness
- diazoxide – hypoglycemia, hypertension
- cyclosporine – immunosuppression, e.g. organ transplant

- steroids – multiple uses
- androgens – body building
- birth control pills.

4 Other hormone imbalances – hypothyroidism HAIR-AN Syndrome (hirsutism, androgenisation, insulin resistance, and acanthosis nigricans).

5 Racial/familial predisposition.

6 Idiopathic – polycystic ovarian syndrome (POCS) is a very common cause of hirsutism, and some researchers feel its prevalence is as high as 5 per cent of the younger female population. It is not one entity, but a heterogeneous disorders that has one of three features:

- increased LH to FSH ratio
- higher concentration of androgen than oestrogen within the ovary, reflecting a block in the conversion of androgen to oestrogen
- failure of the follicles to mature and dry up so that they continue to produce hormones, become cystic and hence give the disease its name.

Clinically, these patients present with anovulation (sparse periods or infertility) and hyperandrogenism (hirsutism and acne). Obesity occurs in only 40 per cent of sufferers. If an ultrasound of the pelvis is performed, the ovaries may be of normal size or anything up to five times larger than normal. Laboratory tests show an elevated free testosterone and a high LH/FSH ratio. Polycystic ovarian disease is usually diagnosed in adulthood, but the symptoms date back to the teenage years.

7 A small number of hirsute women have an enzyme defect in the pathway leading to the manufacture of cortisol, the major product of the adrenals. The pituitary, in an attempt to make more cortisol, secretes more ACTH, forcing the adrenals to increase all the hormones before the block, so the androgens DHEA and androstenedione rise to high levels. This picture is seen in congenital adrenal hyperplasia, a recessive hereditary disorder, which if the block is only partial, does not manifest symptoms until the teenage years or later.

Steps in the pathway leading to hirsutism – from the hair follicle to the hypothalamus

Hair follicle

Several stimuli convert vellus hair into terminal hair: androgens, local factors, and insulin-like growth factors. Obesity causes insulin-resistance in the peripheral tissues; the body, in an effort to prevent diabetes mellitus, produces more insulin and these high circulating levels of insulin work on the hair follicle and increase hirsutism.

Androgens

The body synthesises several androgens. Androstenedione and dehydroepiandrosterone are weak androgens, but are readily converted into the more potent testosterone. Despite the low potency of the weak androgen, when it is present in large amounts, it can be very effective. Testosterone, in turn, enters cells where it is changed into a very potent hormone, dihydrostestosterone. The enzyme necessary is 5 a-reductase, found only within cells. Radionuclide studies have shown this reaction is highly concentrated in the pilo-sebaceous unit of the skin. The enzyme is also found, of course, in the organs which require masculinisation: the prostate, testes, penis and scrotum. A hirsute woman may convert testosterone to dihypotestosterone at the same rate as a man does, that is four times faster than a normal woman.

Sex Hormone Binding Globulin (SHBG)

Testosterone circulates in the blood stream in a free state (1–2 per cent) or bound to the carrier proteins albumin and sex hormone building globulin (SHBG). Since bound hormone is not active, any increase or decrease is SHBG will cause the androgens to be less or more active. SHBG is increased by oestrogens and excessive thyroid hormone, and decreased by androgen, glucocorticords, growth hormone excess and obesity. Thus a vicious cycle is set up: androgen lowers the total SHBG, allowing more to be free and therefore active. Previously total testosterone was measured in the blood. Now, the emphasis is placed on *free* testosterone. In hyperandrogenic states, the total testerose could be normal or low (secondary to androgen-induced lowering of the SHBG) while the free testosterone is markedly elevated.

Adrenal glands and ovaries

The principal adrenal androgens are the testers dehydroepiandrost-erone (DHEA) and dehydroepiandrosterone sulfate (DHEA-S), accounting for 70 per cent and 95 per cent respectively of the level of these hormones circulating in the bloodstream. Of this, 30 per cent of the DHEA and 5 per cent of the DHEA-S is produced by the ovaries. Consequently, DHEA-S has become a convenient marker of adrenal androgen production. The ovary secretes testosterone itself, and also androstenedione (its marker) and estradiol. The latter two are converted in peripheral tissues by an aromatase enzyme to testosterone. Thus, the ovary contributes 25 per cent of total testosterone production, the adrenal another 25 per cent and the remaining 50 per cent comes from the conversion of precursors. Traditionally, stimulation tests and suppression tests have been done on hirsute patients to identify the organ responsible for the excess androgen. The pituitary hormone, ACTH, which stimulates the adrenal gland, was given, and when a hyperresponse occurred – a rise in the androgen level over three times normal – the adrenal was the putative source. Similarly, dexamethane was given to suppress the adrenals so that they were not required to produce androgen. If the androgen level fell to low or undetectable, the adrenals were again felt to be the overproducer. Parallel tests done for the ovary were a stimulation test with human chorionic gonadotropin (HCG), a more readily accessible hormone than the pituitary luteinising hormone (LH) which is the body's ovarian stimulator. Suppression was accomplished with oestrogen or oral contraceptives. The situation today is not so clear-cut. Dexamethasone administration can decrease *ovarian* androgen secretion in hirsute women. Conversely, the oestrogen-progesterone combination of birth control pills can alter adrenal androgen secretion. The ovaries also appear to increase androgen production in response to a primary adrenal problem, and indeed lead to polycystic ovarian syndrome. Despite the fact that this overlap makes diagnosis more difficult, it makes treatment more flexible.

Pituitary

ACTH (adrenocorticotropic hormone) is the pituitary hormone which regulates adrenal function. There is a negative feedback – when sufficient cortisol is released into the bloodstream, the pituitary damps down the secretion of ACTH. The adrenal androgens, although stimulated by ACTH, do not have a role in shutting off ACTH release. LH or luteinizing hormone, does have a negative feedback control with progesterone and androgen secreted from the ovary. FSH (follicle stimulating hormone) of the pituitary and ovarian oestrogen, have the same push–pull mechanism.

Hypothalamus

The pituitary, in the old days, was thought to be the master gland of the body, controlling all the others. Today we know that it, in turn, is regulated by the hypothalamus which secretes hormones to release the pituitary hormones. FSH and LH appear to share a releasing hormone, termed gonadotropin releasing hormone (GnRH, so called to distinguish it from GRH – growth hormone releasing hormone).

Sites of intervention

Rationally, attempts have been made to block steps in the cascade of events from androgen production to the effect on the hair follicle. Analogues of GnRH have been investigated and used in prostate cancer as it is hormone dependent. Since an analogue has the same action as the original hormone, these compounds cause an initial surge (e.g. of androgen when used for ovarian suppression) as they attach to the pituitary cells for LH and FSH, but they do not come off the cells again so the correct stimulatory message cannot get through. The result is a fall in circulating FSH and LH, and the consequent failure to manufacture hormones in the ovary, both oestrogen and androgen. Glucocorticoids and oestrogen–progesterone agents (birth control pills) have long been prescribed to suppress adrenal or ovarian function and by signalling the pituitary, stopping the secretion of the appropriate tropic hormone (ACTH and FSH-LH). Because of the crossover in the source of androgen production and in the action of oestrogen–progesterone compounds and corticosteroids, either group of medicines or both can be used. Glucocorticoids, however, are the treatment for congenital adrenal hyperplasia substituting for the cortisol that cannot be made and thereby suppressing ACTH secretion. Alteration of the binding of androgens to SHBG is a theoretical intervention practically; oestrogen increases the level of SHBG, thereby binding more androgen and leaving less in the free state. Antiandrogen agents are the more current therapies on the scene and act by binding to the androgen receptor, thereby preventing the true androgen from attaching and activating its message. Another antiandrogen effect is to prevent the enzymatic action of 5 a-reductase in converting testosterone to its potent end-product dihydrotestosterone. Antiandrogens act locally or at specific end-organ sites, such as the skin, and thereby do not have systemic actions and side effects.

Drug treatment

GnRH agonists (also known as LHRH analogues):

- Leuprolide (Lupron) – *1mg daily subcutaneously*
- Zoladex – *3.6mg subcutaneouly every month as a depot preparation*
- Buserelin – *1.2mg nasal spray*

The GnRH analogues or agonists are potent inhibitors of FSH and LH, decreasing ovarian production to castration levels. Initially, there may be a flare of target hormones, which would not be realistically reflected in an increase in hirsutism. Total suppression is achieved in 1–3 weeks. Its effects are completely reversible whenever the drug is discontinued. The side effects are the same as those of oestrogen withdrawal or deficiency: hot flushes, disturbed sleep, tiredness, dry vagina and urethra causing painful intercourse and urination, loss of head hair, depression and a very important side effect: osteoporosis. These can all be prevented by adding oestrogen to the regime, but in such cases there appears to little advantage in using a injectable substance (GnRH agonist) plus an oestrogen instead of an oestrogen–progesterone combination which can be taken orally.

Combination of oestrogen–progesterone pills or birth control pills decrease free testosterone by suppressing FSH and LH, by increasing SHBG and by modestly lowering DHEA-S. Since progestins vary in their androgenicity, ethynodiol diacetate, which has the least androgenic activity, is chosen in preference to norethindrone acetate and norgestrel, which have the highest. These combination pills are most useful in treating polycystic ovarian disease. Since suppression of the LH/FSH axis is needed, the higher oestrogen dose is used rather than the lower dose found to be effective in contraception. Charts are available of oral contraceptive combinations showing the dosages in different trade-name preparations. For therapy in polycystic ovarian disease, Demulen 1/50 is an excellent choice. It is used in cyclic treatment for one year, causing continuous anovulation and suppression of ovarian functions so that the enlarged ovaries shrink to normal size. Upon withdrawal of the medication at the end of one year, 70 per cent of women are fully treated; of the remaining 30 per cent, 70 per cent will respond to a second year of treatment. However, in all those treated, whether the disease eventually responds to treatment or not, up to 90 per cent experience an improvement in their hirsutism. Improvement signifies a slowing in the rate of growth of the abnormal hair – hair that is already present will have to be removed by electrology. Because of the lag time in hair growth, any improvement will not be evident before three months of treatment and it may require six to nine months before effectiveness can be fully assessed. The side effects of oestrogen (although low in incidence) are legion – some minor, some lethal: thrombophlebitis, heart attacks, strokes, hypertension, gall bladder disease, nausea, vomiting, abdominal bloating, breakthrough bleeding, no periods after treatment, chloasma, cholestatic jauntice, migrane headaches, glucose intolerance up to diabetes mellitis, vaginal yeast infections, intolerance to contact lenses. Progestins produce discomfort rather than serious complications: nausea, vomiting, oedema and weight gain, change in menstrual flow, breast engorgement, mood swings.

Glucocorticoids are used to treat congenital adrenal hyperplasia or functional adrenal hyperplasis. For the former, treatment is required for life; for the latter, since it may be a cyclic disease like polycystic ovarian disease, treatment is prescribed for one year. The drug of choice is prednisone. The dosage for desamethasone is so variable that cortisone excess, Cushing's syndrome, frequently occurs. Prednisone 5mg is prescribed at bedtime, taking advantage of the knowledge that ACTH secretion starts at 2 a.m., resulting in an early morning (7 a.m.) rise in cortisol. Bedtime prednisone blocks the secretion of ACTH and its sequelae, and a total lower dosage can be used. As stated before, corticosteroids can also be used to suppress ovarian androgen secretion. The response rate in controlling hirsutism is also very high with this modality. Again, the side effects are numerous, some of great significance and at a higher rate of incidence than with oral contraceptives. Luckily, they occur infrequently with the low dose used for this purpose. Potential side effects are: disfigurement (moon-face, buffalo hump, central obesity, broken veins, bruises, acne, even hirsutism), fluid retention, low potassium, diabetes mellitus, susceptibility to infection, peptic ulcer, osteoporosis, myopathy or muscle weakness, cataracts. When corticosteriods are abruptly stopped, severe adrenal insufficiency can result, but, usually, a higher maintenance dose is given.

Antiandrogens inhibit the binding of androgens to the receptor.

1 *Cimetidine* (Tagamet®) is a weak antiandrogen, not really useful in the treatment of hirsutism, and its action is more noticeable as a side effect of ulcer therapy, especially in men (i.e. impotence).

2 *Cyproterone acetate* (not available in the United States, but used in the treatment of hirsutism in Europe for over 25 years) blocks androgen synthesis, and peripheral androgen receptors. It possesses progestational activity so it suppresses LH secretion from the pituitary.

The dosage is usually 10mg orally per day (the range is 2–200mg per day). Hair growth is diminished in 70–100 per cent of women, higher doses being more effective. It has also had success with acne and baldness. Side effects include nausea, weight gain, breast tenderness, breakthrough bleeding, headache, decreased libido and depression. Pregnant rats given cyproterone produced male foetuses with maldeveloped genitalia causing fears about its use in women who may become pregnant.

3 *Spironolactone* (Aldactone®) was originally marketed as a diuretic, but has limited uses in that field. Its efficacy as an antiandrogen was noticed through its ability to decrease testosterone production, increase the rate of testosterone metabolism, inhibit dihydrotestosterone binding to the androgen receptor and retard the conversion of testosterone to dihydrotestosterone by its effect on 5 a-reductase. Spironolactone is a stronger antiandrogen than cyproterone, but also has progestational effects. The dosage is 50–100mg by mouth twice a day. Cyproterone acetate is taken up in adipose tissue and then slowly released, thus rendering the patient susceptible to menstrual irregularity. A reversed sequential regimen was developed to avoid this side effect. This consists of giving cyproterone acetate on days 5–15 of the cycle in doses initially of 50–100mg per day. Ethynyl estradiol is given in a dose of 50μg daily for days 5–26 of the cycle. Dose reduction is possible once effective remission of hirsutism occurs. A combination oral contraceptive (Diane) containing cyproterone acetate (2mg) and oestrogen ethinyuloestradiol (50μg) is sometimes used for maintenance. Side effects include nausea, fatigue, irregular menses and headache. Because of its previous use as a diuretic, high serum potassium and low blood pressure have been postulated, but do not occur in practice. Spironolactone like cyproterone interrupts the masculinisation of a male foetus so contraception should be practised by a woman previously infertile with polycystic ovarian disease as ovulation is induced with spironolactone.

4 *Flutamide* (Eulexin®) was made available in the United States for the treatment of prostate cancer and has been used under investigation for that purpose since 1972. It differs from the previous agents in that it is nonsteroidal so possesses no progestational oestrogenic, corticosteroid or antigonadotropin activity. It is a potent, selective antiandrogen. The dosage is 250mg three times a day, after meals, taken orally. Side effects include nausea, diarrhoea, dizziness, breast tenderness.

Elevated liver enzymes occurred in 5 per cent of patients taking excessive doses of the drug (1500mg per day) but reversed within six weeks of stopping the medication. Impotence does not occur with this drug as it might with a steroid antiandrogen. Flutamide is also very effective in the treatment of acne and seborrhoea. Nilutaminde is a compound similar to Flutamide but has much higher toxicity. Antiandrogens, by their nature, cause menstrual irregularities, so are used in combination with oestrogen alone (ethinyl estradiol) or with oestrogen–progesterone agents. A phenomenon caused by the *nonsteroidal* androgens is an elevation of the serum testosterone. The antiandrogen interrupts the androgen's negative feedback on the pituitary, leading to a rise in LH and consequently testosterone. However, the effects of the testosterone are blocked at the receptor level. A newer agent, Casodex, is being reviewed as it does not cross the blood/brain barrier so does not affect the hypothalamus–pituitary causing the rise in LH and testosterone.

Topical application of antiandrogens

Creams or lotions would be the ideal route for administering antiandrogens. Their effect would be solely at the end-organ, and indeed, only the areas of skin where unwanted hair was growing. Systemic side effects could be avoided, and the only conceivable problem would be contact dermatitis. Trials have been done with progesterone and spironolactone. Numerous drug treatments are now available for the treatment of hirsutism as the search continues, based on physiological principles, for the optimal agent with the greatest efficacy and the lowest side level of effects. Even should that agent be found, the basic treatment for hirsutism is electrological removal – this is the only method that can get rid of the terminal hairs already present.

H. Christina Hanley, M.D., reproduced from *Hair Route Magazine*, www.hairroute.com

part four

depilation

chapter 4

WAXING

What will I know after reading this chapter?

This chapter covers waxing treatments. It describes the competencies required to enable you to:

- **understand what waxing is**
- **identify the different types of waxing treatments**
- **recognise the specific requirements of a waxing consultation**
- **prepare clients for treatment**
- **perform waxing treatments**
- **complete waxing treatments.**

BT6 Remove hair using waxing techniques

The next three chapters will look at three methods of 'mass plucking': waxing, sugaring and threading. This chapter will concentrate on waxing. As the issues that arise with waxing are, generally speaking, the same as sugaring and threading, this chapter is somewhat longer and covers these common issues in depth.

KEY TERMS ★

Waxing: Temporary removal of hair by mass plucking using product

In recent years waxing has become one of the most popular methods of temporary hair removal and it is consistently rated by beauty industry surveys as one of the most common treatments. The name 'wax' comes from the fact that the first commercially made product used beeswax. 'Waxing' is now used as a general term and it covers products made from other ingredients including honey and glucose syrup. This form of treatment involves the application of hot, warm or cool wax to the skin. The hairs become stuck or embedded into the wax and are removed (depilated) when the waxing product is pulled from the skin.

Wax treatments can be divided into three general types:

- hot wax
- warm wax
- sugaring.

Each type has a different method of treatment application and they will be discussed individually throughout Part Four. Threading is not a wax treatment but it is included in Part Four because it is a method of temporary hair removal and follows the same consultation, pre- and post-treatment procedures.

CONSULTATION

As with all hair removal treatments, when providing waxing treatments you must follow the general consultation advice and procedures discussed in Chapter Two. There are also a number of additional consultation processes specific to waxing which must be followed and are discussed here.

Example of waxing record card

JAYGEE'S

Family name:	Date of birth:
First name:	Address:
Home tel:	Doctor's name:
Mobile:	Address:
E-mail:	Tel:

Have you had previous waxing treatment?: Yes ☐ No ☐

If yes, how many treatments did you have? _____ Over what period? _____

Any skin reactions? _____

When was your last treatment? _____

On what area do you require treatment? _____

Tick area(s) that require treatment

☐ Eyebrows

☐ Face

☐ Underarm

☐ Forearm

☐ Bikini line

☐ Legs

☐ Back

☐ Chest

What other temporary measures have you used? _____ Over what period of time?_____

How often? Have you/do you use a hair growth inhibitor?: _____

Present condition of skin in area to be treated, to include blemishes etc: _____

Related medical information (conditions which restrict or contra-indicate treatment):

Are you taking medication: Yes ☐ No ☐ If Yes, please specify

Patch test carried out Date: _____ Result: _____

I declare that I have answered all the above questions truthfully

Client signature………………………………… Date…………………………

Important considerations when carrying out a consultation for waxing treatment are the clients social, work and holiday commitments, which will indicate to you the best time to carry out waxing treatment in order to get the best result at the right time for the client. The client's record card plays a key role in waxing consultations and you must ensure each stage is completed and entered onto the card. Permanent information is recorded on the front while all current and changeable information (such as treatment progress) should be recorded on the rear of the record card on an ongoing basis.

When conducting your consultation, ask the following questions and enter the responses onto the record card.

What are your name, address and contact details?
It is important that the client is identified with both their first and family names for insurance purposes. It is also important that you can contact a client should you need to change an appointment. For marketing purposes, the client's details are also useful.

What is your date of birth?
This information allows you to establish your client's stage of life and its hormonal influences; it also further identifies the client, should you have another client of the same name. Knowing your client's birthday will also allow you to send special birthday greetings and/or special offers.

What is your doctor's name and address?
This is important information should you wish to discuss any issues regarding the treatment. (The doctor will not discuss any confidential client information with you unless the client has authorised them to do so.)

Have you had previous waxing treatment?
This will indicate to you the client's prior knowledge, which will enable you to give the appropriate information. You will also need to be aware of any contra-actions (reactions to treatment which may prevent you continuing treatment) from previous treatments, why the client did not continue and the results of the previous treatment.

On what area/s was your previous treatment?
This question provides a prompt to ensure that you do not make any assumptions about the area the client is concerned about but that you find out, direct from them, the area to be treated.

Are you using any other temporary methods?
This will help to indicate the current stage of hair growth and establish whether you are seeing the full extent of it. The client's answers will also indicate how the other temporary removal methods have stimulated the growth and allow you to describe fully to the client the probable outcome of waxing treatment.

Pre-treatment precautions

Before commencing a waxing treatment, examine the condition of the skin in the area to be treated. Take note of the general skin condition, paying particular attention to the following as they will restrict or require adaptation of the treatment:

PROFESSIONAL TIP ✓

Never be in a rush to ask and record a potential client's address, etc. Remember this is a consultation and the individual may not decide to have the treatment until you have explained more about it. Our advice is to leave personal information until the end

---

REMEMBER !

It is important to inform the client that, if there are hairs just under the skin at the time of treatment, they will quickly appear; this is not re-growth but the growth of hairs not long enough for removal at that time

- allergic reactions
- bruising
- cuts and abrasions
- eczema and psoriasis
- heat rash
- skin disorders
- sunburn
- warts and moles.

Waxing removes dead skin cells from the surface of the skin and as a consequence will lighten natural tans and may completely remove some self-tan treatments. You must advise your clients of this effect as they may then choose to delay treatment.

Blemishes

Make a particular note on the record card of any blemishes and their position. You should also point out to your client any blemishes, for example scars, pigmentation marks and any other imperfections which are currently present on the proposed treatment area. This will prevent any future misunderstanding should your client only notice the blemish at a later date and blame you and your waxing treatment.

Contra-indications

While completing the record card, ensure you check the client for all of the contra-indications discussed in Chapter Two. There are also a number of contra-indications specific to waxing which must be checked:

- *Diabetes*: In some texts it is suggested that a diabetic client is contra-indicated to waxing due to reduced skin healing and even loss of sensation. Whilst there are undoubtedly more considerations when treating a diabetic client, the symptoms are generally controlled by diet and or medication. Every one of your clients should be treated with the same care and precautions, that is: keep the heat levels as low as possible to effectively remove the hairs, use a wax suitable for sensitive skin and take great care of the skin prior to, during and after waxing treatment.
- *Medication*: In particular you need to know about any medication which has an affect on the skin, for example steroid creams, which may have caused skin thinning. If the client is unsure of any skin side effects, ask them to check with their GP.
- *Hepatitis* (inflammation of the liver): Hepatitis has many causes, two of which are infection by amoeba (bacteria) and viruses. You should be concerned about hepatitis as it is highly infectious. Hepatitis B is of particular risk to hair removal practitioners (HRPs) as it is extremely easy to contract.
- *Heart conditions*: It is important that you are aware of any heart condition as the client may be on blood thinning medication, which could have an impact upon treatment. If bleeding occurs, the blood flow will take longer

HEALTH AND SAFETY

If a potential waxing client reports an allergy to sticking plasters, a waxing treatment should not be carried out on them as it is highly probable they will also be allergic to or at least react to the wax. This is because the substance used to make the plasters stick is colophony, which is a resin from spruce trees, and the same ingredient is used in wax. Alternative methods of hair removal should be advised

TECHNICAL TIP

Recording existing blemishes, scars and pigmentation disorders prior to commencing treatment; this will prevent your client, at a later date, wrongly accusing you of causing them

TECHNICAL TIP

Many medications affect hormonal balance and are often listed as precautions to waxing, e.g. contraceptive pill, HRT. Whilst this is important when you are permanently removing hair, hormonal medication has no bearing on temporary methods

HEALTH AND SAFETY

It is recommended that all hair removal practitioners be inoculated against hepatitis B

than normal to stop. As circulation is affected with heart conditions, the client's healing capacity may be impaired.

- *Epilepsy*: Epilepsy does not necessarily contra-indicate treatment. It is important to find out if a client is epileptic for two reasons:

  1 It may contra-indicate treatment if their epilepsy stimulus is stress or if you think there is a possibility that you could stimulate a seizure (fit) with treatment.

  2 It is important that you discuss with your client the frequency and stimulus of attacks as well as the form the attacks take, as you need to be able to recognise that the client has had a seizure, should it occur in the salon. Not all attacks produce violent seizures. Clients are often disorientated following an attack and it may be that the disorientation is the first thing that you notice.

Patch test

If your client has known sensitivities (things she/he is sensitive to) and reactions or has never had a waxing treatment before, it is advisable to carry out a test patch. To do this, you will need to prepare the area to be tested in the same way as for treatment. All the products that will be used during the treatment – skin sanitiser, wax and after wax solution – should be applied to an area of approximately 2cm², as a control area, and the after-effects noted for a minimum of 24 hours.

Apply a small amount of wax and all other pre- and post-treatment products to be used to an area of the skin approximately the size of a 2p piece which can be covered up in the event of an allergic reaction, for example the inside of the forearm. Remove the wax and apply post-treatment products in the normal way. Ask the client to leave the test patch area alone and return to the salon the next day for you to evaluate the reaction. Should no adverse reaction be seen, a full treatment can take place. The area where the patch test was carried out, the date and any effects of the patch test must be recorded on the record card and signed by the client and HRP.

Client's signature

Ensure that the client signs and dates the record card to confirm that they have answered all the questions truthfully. In the case of minors, this card must be signed by a parent or guardian.

Monitoring ongoing treatment

The rear of the card is where details of individual treatments should be recorded.

The following information is recorded in these columns:

- *Date*: To track treatments and ensure the client is receiving regular treatment.

REMEMBER

If in any doubt always seek medical approval before undertaking treatment

---

KEY TERMS

Patch test: A small trial area which will help you to assess the reaction to treatment

---

HEALTH AND SAFETY

Even though a patch test is small, the usual pre- and post-treatment procedures required by health and safety regulations must be carried out: the wearing of PPE (personal protective equipment) which includes disposable gloves

Reverse of record card

Date	Area	Wax method & type	Treatment reactions	Therapist comment & signature	Client signature

- *Area*: Should another HRP treat your client, they can see what has been treated and how. The card also records any new areas treated.
- *Wax method and type*: For reference purposes and in case of subsequent treatment adjustments, record which method of waxing was used, i.e. hot, warm, roller, etc. Also record the type of wax, i.e. azulene, honey, etc.
- *Treatment reactions*: This section of the card allows you to record any treatment reactions, good or bad, which will influence your choice of wax method and type for subsequent treatments.
- *Therapist comment and treatment reactions*: Allows you to record any additional comments on the treatment and the HRP's signature makes it clear exactly who has carried out which treatments.
- *Client signature*: Confirms that the recorded details are correct.

> **REMEMBER**
>
> Client information is confidential; therefore record cards should not be left where other people can gain access to them and must be stored in accordance with the Data Protection Act 1998

HOT WAX TREATMENT

Composition

Wax ingredients may include beeswax, pine resin, palm wax, plant extracts. It is available in the following product forms:

- pellets
- bricks
- broken chunks
- diskettes
- pure beeswax or with additives, i.e. azulene.

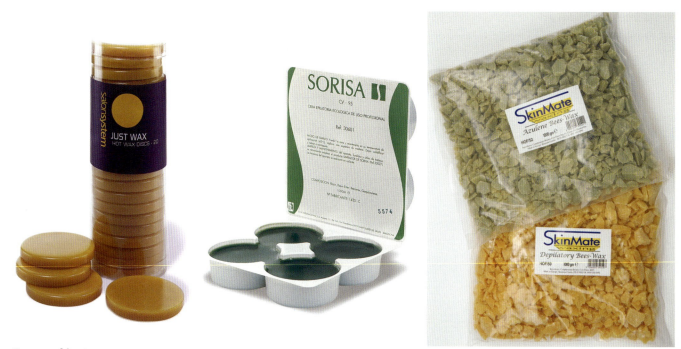

Types of hot wax
House of Famuir Ltd www.hofbeauty.co.uk

The advantages and disadvantages of hot wax treatment compared to other waxing methods

Advantages	Disadvantages
✓ More efficient and effective than other wax methods, particularly on short and strong hairs i.e. bikini, underarm.	✗ More skill required to apply.
✓ Recent resurgence in popularity due to various bikini applications, i.e. Brazilian.	✗ Equipment more expensive.
	✗ Not suitable for heat sensitive skin.
✓ Less breakage of hairs, therefore, longer lasting results.	✗ Takes some time to become proficient at the technique.
✓ Results in smoother skin, due to the exfoliating effect, as hot 'wax' adheres to skin surface more effectively than other methods.	✗ Creates more erythema (redness) than other 'waxing' methods.
	✗ Heat treatments must be avoided for longer, post-treatment, than other 'waxing' methods.
✓ The re-growth is slower.	

Consultation

When administering a hot wax treatment, you must first follow the general consultation guidelines discussed earlier in this chapter and in Chapter Two and make sure you include the specific hot waxing issues discussed in the following subsections.

Test patch

If your client has known sensitivities (things she/he is sensitive to) and reactions or has never had a waxing treatment before, it is advisable to carry out a test patch. To do this, you will need to prepare the area to be tested in the same way as for treatment. All the products that will be used during the treatment – skin sanitiser, wax and after wax solution should – be applied to an area of approximately 2cm², as a control area, and the after-effects noted for a minimum of 24 hours.

Apply a small amount of wax and all other pre- and post-treatment products to be used during treatment (size of a 2cm² piece) to an area of the skin which can be covered in the case of an allergic reaction e.g. inside forearm. Remove wax and apply post treatment products in the normal way. Ask the client to leave the test patch area alone and return to the salon the next day for you to evaluate the reaction. Should no adverse reaction be seen, a full treatment can take place.

Contra-indications and pre-treatment precautions

The conditions listed here are typical precautions and would only become contra-indications and prevent treatment if they were severe or extensively covered the area to be treated. They are discussed in more detail earlier in this chapter and in Chapter Two:

- cuts
- abrasions/open skin
- recent scar tissue (less than 6 months old)
- bruising
- moles or warts
- erythema and oedema
- pre- or post-ultra violet exposure.

In addition to the standard list of hair removal contra-indications, the following are specific contra-indications for hot waxing:

- fragile or thin skin
- hyper-sensitive skin.

Area specific contra-indications

- *Eyebrow treatments*: communicable eye infections such as styes and conjunctivitis.
- *Facial treatments*: herpes simplex (also known as cold sores) which are extremely infectious. Also clients who are using strong acid products such as Retin-A, Renova or Accutane as these medications tend to weaken the skin and tearing of the skin may occur when the wax is removed. This also applies for 2–4 weeks after a course of micro dermabrasion treatments.
- *Underarm/bikini area*: lymphatic swelling in the area to be treated.
- *Legs*: varicose veins.
- *Bikini area*: urinary and genital infections.

> **REMEMBER**
>
> Ensure you understand the difference between contra-indications and pre-treatment precautions when consulting with a potential client

HEALTH AND SAFETY ✚

Dirty laundry should be stored in a covered container whilst awaiting laundering

Equipment and materials

Couch

As the client's size, agility and areas of the body to be treated differ, a fully adjustable couch is advisable. They are also more comfortable for the HRP when carrying out treatment.

- Adjustable couches can be electric, hydraulic or manual.
- Couches should be covered with a protective covering from which wax can be easily removed, i.e. plastic.
- Clean towels or gowns should be available to cover the client if necessary.
- In order to maintain hygiene, a layer of couch roll should be placed the full length of the couch on top of the plastic covering.

Trolley

Some brands of waxing products have their own specifically designed trolleys. These are by no means essential but do look good. However, trolleys:

- should be secure, stable and have castors (preferably lockable)
- have enough shelving for all the equipment and products
- are more useful when they come with an integral power pack which includes plug sockets and an optional magnifier lamp holder
- ideally, should have shelves with an edging rail or safety lip to prevent the wax heater accidentally slipping off.

The shelves of the trolley should be wiped over between clients with disinfectant, or covered with a new piece of disposable couch roll for each client.

Wax heater

There are a variety of wax heaters available in different colours, shapes and sizes. Which type of heater is best is often a matter of personal choice, however they should all:

- be thermostatically controlled
- meet all health and safety requirements and be in good working order
- be wipeable with disinfectant between treatments
- have a lid to keep out airborne particles.

Positioning of equipment

Ensure that your wax heater and trolley are close enough to the area to be treated, are positioned so as to prevent spillage and drips, and will not restrict your movements or cause a hazard in the treatment room or separate storage area, as applicable.

Items required

You can buy waxing products individually or in the starter kits which most suppliers offer, and which can often be cheaper. However you buy, you must

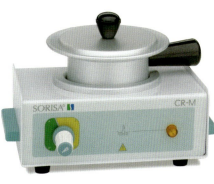

Types of wax heater

make sure you have the following items as well as the actual waxing products:

- skin sanitiser
- powder
- cotton wool/tissues, in a container with lid
- application tool of choice, i.e. spatula
- sterilised tweezers
- after-wax soothing lotion, oil, gel or cream
- pedal bin with lid – double lined (i.e. with two bin liners)
- equipment cleaner
- clean towels
- disinfected scissors.

Treatment planning

Once you have uncovered your client's hair removal history, you can plan and discuss the treatment appointments and likely outcomes. Key considerations when planning the treatment are the client's:

- social commitments
- work commitments
- holiday commitments.

Treatment planning will ensure the client has the best results at the time they are needed and is discussed further in Chapter Two.

Preparation of the treatment area

In order to ensure a safe, hygienic and efficient environment, the treatment room and equipment should meet the following criteria.

PROFESSIONAL TIP ✔

Always have more than one pair of sterilised tweezers available in case one pair is accidentally dropped or contaminated

REMEMBER !

Waxing is one of the most popular treatments on offer in most salons. Clients therefore have a vast choice of salons: by creating the right atmosphere, giving excellent service and paying attention to detail, you will encourage the client to return to your salon

- Lighting should be adequate to carry out treatment.
- The treatment room should be at a comfortable temperature, taking into account that the client will be in various stages of undress.
- There should be good ventilation.
- The ambience, or feeling of the treatment room should be suitable for both a professional environment and relaxation.
- The floor covering should be easy to clean.
- The room should be set up to ensure client privacy is maintained at all times.
- All tools and equipment must be clean and have been sterilised before use.
- Work surfaces should be disinfected regularly.
- Disposable items are preferable wherever possible.
- High standards of personal hygiene should be maintained.

Preparation of the therapist

How you look, how you act and the impression you give must be of the highest standard, you are your own best advert – remember someone is seeing you for the first time and will judge you and your business on how you look and how you present yourself. The following are some 'must do' presentation and hygiene rules.

- Always wear clean and pressed clothing or a uniform.
- Always wear a disposable plastic apron.
- Always wear disposable gloves (single use).
- Have disposable surgical masks available, if required.
- Wear comfortable supportive shoes with a low heel.
- Always present a hygienic and professional appearance, i.e. hair tied back, minimal jewellery – watch and wedding ring only.

Hand exercises should also be conducted on regular basis. Examples of some useful exercises the therapist can practise are illustrated.

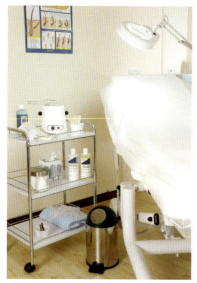

The wax treatment area

HEALTH AND SAFETY ✚

Disposable surgical masks help prevent cross-infection from airborne spores and should be worn when you or your client has a cold

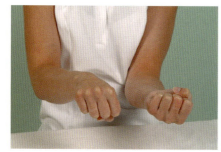

Rotate wrists clockwise then anti-clockwise to loosen the wrists

With backs of hands facing, clench the fingers together. Pull fingers apart, nut maintain contact

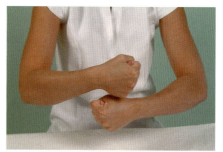

Rotate fists in a circular motion

Finger-pad resistance – press against each other one by one

Place palm together and apply slight pressure, maintaining contact

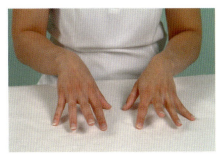

Place alternate fingers down on a hard surface, as if playing the piano

Treatment preparation

Before preparing the client for treatment you must complete each of these steps:

1 Switch on the wax heater so that the wax is at the correct temperature (approx. 60°C) and consistency for your client's appointment time.

2 If the client has had a previous treatment with you, before preparing the client and commencing treatment, the client's record card must be retrieved from its confidential and secure storage facility and be on hand in the treatment room.

3 Accompany the client into the treatment room and assist and/or direct the client with the removal of any necessary garments and, if required, help him or her on to the couch.

4 Ascertain from the client any changes which may affect the treatment and its outcomes, using your record card as a point of reference. This should include any reactions or feedback from the last treatment, any changes in medication and health, stress related issues (i.e. work or personal).

5 Once you and your client are happy to continue, prepare the client for treatment.

Treatment preparation is an important part of the treatment as a whole and should be carried out thoroughly. The following steps will guide you through a typical preparation procedure of yourself and the client for a hot wax treatment:

1 Sanitise your hands by washing with anti-bacterial soap or water-free hand cleanser.

2 Put on single use disposable gloves.

3 Apply skin sanitising product to clean cotton wool and wipe over the area to be treated, in order to sanitise the area and remove any oils or cosmetic products on the skin.

4 Blot treatment area dry with clean tissue.

5 Dispose of cotton wool and tissue in pedal bin (double lined).

6 A light dusting of powder should be applied to the treatment area against the hair growth with a clean cotton wool pad.

> **REMEMBER**
>
> Switch on the heater in good time for the wax to reach working temperature and to coincide with your client's appointment time. In the case of early morning clients, the use of plug socket timers that will turn on your heater at a pre-determined time before you arrive, will be extremely useful

> **PROFESSIONAL TIP**
>
> Never try and remember the client's details, always check the record card before you commence treatment

Hand cleanser

Sterex Electrolysis

Disposable gloves

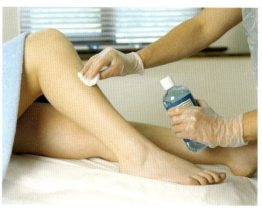

Preparing the area to be treated

Testing the wax on the wrist

TECHNICAL TIP ✔

Visual removal indicator (VRI): the surface of the wax becomes dull when the wax is ready for removal

Temperature test

Test the wax on the inside of your wrist to ensure that it is at a comfortable temperature. If the temperature is comfortable for you, apply a 2cm² area of wax on the area to be treated to ensure that it is comfortable for your client.

TECHNICAL TIP ✔

If your wax heater has not been switched on for a sufficient length of time, you may find the wax is too cool and therefore too thick. You can quickly increase the thermostat control to a higher level for a short period of time and this will more rapidly get the wax to the correct working temperature. Remember the thermostat must be reduced once the temperature has been achieved, in accordance with manufacturer's instructions

Treatment application

Step One: Wax is heated to working temperature and applied onto the skin, against the direction of hair growth, in strips. A variety of wax application tools may be used: wooden spoon, wooden spatula, metal spatula, etc.

Step Two: One end of the strip should be made slightly thicker to provide a grip point for removal. The treatment area is divided into sections and the wax is applied to alternate sections to allow for skin cooling. When the wax has cooled to the correct removal temperature – it is still pliable, but not tacky and dull after approximately 30 seconds to 1 minute (always follow the manufacturer's instructions) it can be removed.

Step Three: Flick up the thicker edge of the wax strip first, then, when you have a secure grip, remove the rest of the strip quickly by holding it firmly between the thumb and forefinger, pulling very quickly, in a 'flicking action', against the direction of hair growth and parallel to the surface of the skin, whilst supporting the skin with the other hand.

Step Four: Immediately after the strip has been removed, firmly place your free hand on the area. This pressure detracts from any sensation the client may be feeling and acts to soothes the area. To remove any remaining wax, apply the just removed strip onto it by applying firm pressure with a finger and flick the strip to remove. Fold the wax strip in half and discard into the double lined pedal bin.

Step Five: Clear the area in a methodical manner using the illustrations as a guide. Any remaining stray hairs should be removed with your sterilised tweezers. The hairs should be placed in a tissue and disposed of in a double lined pedal bin.

Step Six: Apply a soothing lotion, oil, gel or cream to the treated area; blot off any excess with a tissue and dispose of in a double lined pedal bin. Assist the client off the couch and remind them of their home-care responsibilities, giving a home-care leaflet to reinforce your advice.

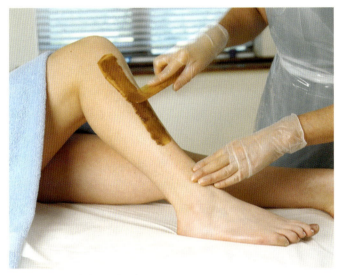

Step 1: Applying the hot wax

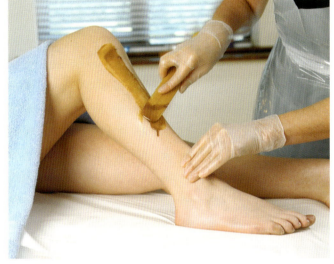

Step 2: The 'grip' area

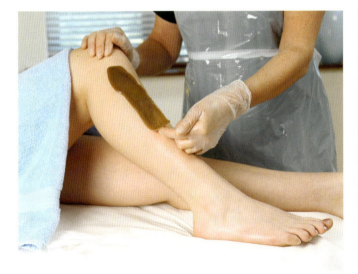

Step3 : Flicking

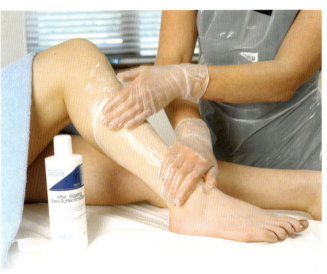

Step 5: Applying aftercare product

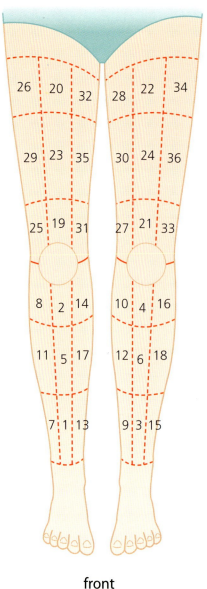

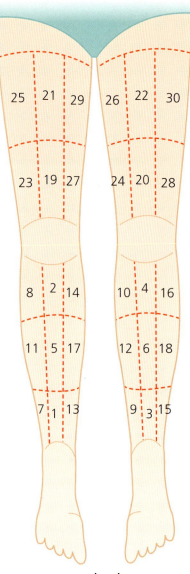

front   back

The sections of the leg

Reasons for poor treatment results

Hairs are left behind after treatment when:

- oils or other products were left on the skin as this prevents the wax from adhering to the hairs
- the area was not completely covered by wax
- wax was applied or removed in the wrong direction
- wax was removed too slowly
- wax was applied too thinly.

Waxing treatment session timings: Industry standards

Area	Time
Half leg wax	30
Bikini line wax	15
Arm wax	30
Full leg wax	50
Half leg, bikini, underarm	60
Full leg, bikini, underarm	75
Underarm wax	15

Home-care advice

Home-care advice leaflet

JAYGEE'S

Waxing home-care

Please read these home-care notes carefully and follow our recommendations. We have taken great care to protect you from infection and, in addition to our normal salon routine, we have applied a soothing antiseptic lotion after your treatment. It is important for you to take extra care of the waxed area, especially within the first 24–48 hours. When a large number of hairs have been removed the area could be prone to infection if not cared for.

PLEASE NOTE: If you experience persistent redness or discomfort, or have any questions, do not hesitate to contact your hair removal practitioner.

The following should be avoided for the first 48 hours following treatment:

- sunbathing
- sunbed treatments
- very hot baths
- friction from tight clothing
- perfumed body lotion or creams.

For underarm waxing
- deodorants and anti-perspirants.

For facial waxing:
- application of make-up (first 4–8 hours only).

We recommend that you use soothing antiseptic after-wax lotion daily for 3–4 days after treatment, which should be purchased from your hair removal practitioner.

WARM WAX

Warm wax treatments are very popular and can be applied using a variety of methods:

- spatula wax method
- roller wax method
- tube wax method.

A range of areas can be treated using warm wax methods:

- eyebrows
- upper lip
- underarm (axillae)
- forearms
- bikini lines
- legs
- male areas.

The advantages and disadvantages of warm wax treatment compared to hot wax

Advantages	Disadvantages
✓ Easy technique to master	✗ Not as effective as hot wax on short hairs
✓ Can be used on any part of the body	
✓ Can be used on any hair type	✗ More risk of hair snapping off due to less heat involved
✓ Most widely used method of hair removal, therefore pricing is cost effective	
✓ More suitable for clients with heat sensitive skin	

Composition of warm wax

As a depilatory wax, most warm waxes are a blend of types of beeswax and resins. Ingredients are selected according to their adhesion (ability to stick), melting point, flexibility, odour and skin reaction potential. The most commonly found ingredients are:

- Rosin – this is the chief ingredient of warm wax and is the residue left after distilling off the volatile oil from extracts of various species of pine.
- White and yellow beeswax – purified wax from the honeycomb of the bee. Commonly called white wax when bleached and yellow when unbleached.
- Microcrystalline wax – a wax derived from petroleum which has very fine crystals.
- Glyceryl rosinate – Glycerine derived from resin for softening purposes.

Waxes are often blended with some of the following:

- fatty acids

- candelilla wax – hydrocarbons of *Euphorbia Cerifera*
- ceresine – wax
- plasticides – these increase flexibility.

The molecules of wax are held together in a disorganised manner. The material is non-crystalline, in other words not solid. As a result, wax has a range of melting point temperatures, so it is important to follow the manufacturer's instructions.

Additions

There are a variety of additional products available which, when added to the base product, gives the wax different properties. These different properties, some of which are listed below, make the end product suitable for a variety of different skin types and hair types:

- honey
- white (titanium dioxide)
- green (chlorophyll)
- aromatherapy, e.g. tea tree
- azulene
- fragrances may also be added to wax, e.g. fruit fragrances.

The working temperature of warm wax is usually 40–45°C, but it is important to always follow the manufacturers instructions.

Consultation

When administering a warm wax treatment, you must first follow the general consultation guidelines discussed earlier in this chapter and in Chapter Two, and make sure you include the following specific warm waxing issues.

- During the consultation, it is important to establish the client's needs and expectations in order that you can effectively schedule treatments to meet those needs and ensure the client has a realistic view of the treatment outcomes.
- It is particularly important that the treatment outcomes are realistic, especially when some hairs are not quite long enough, for example if they are only just emerging from the skin or are just under the skin. This indicates that the cycle of growth has been disturbed by previous treatments, and that hairs from more than one growth are present on the area.
- Whilst longer hairs will be removed effectively and not re-grow for 2–4 weeks, the ones which are just emerging from the skin will be left behind and will grow quite quickly, which will give the client the impression that the waxing treatment was ineffective unless this was fully explained.

Contra-indications and pre-treatment precautions

The conditions listed here are typical precautions and would only become contra-indications and prevent treatment if they were severe or extensively covered the area to be treated. They are discussed in more detail earlier in this chapter and in Chapter Two:

couch
trolley
wax heater
wax
skin sanitiser
powder
cotton wool
tissues
sterilised tweezers
after-wax soothing lotion
pedal bin with lid
equipment cleaner
clean towels
couch roll
disinfected scissors
wax removal strips
roller heads (required for roller cassette method only)
disposable spatula (required for spatula method only)
variety of applicator sizes (required for tube method only)

- cuts
- abrasions/open skin
- recent scar tissue (less than 6 months old)
- bruising
- moles or warts
- erythema and oedema
- immediately before or after ultra violet exposure.

The following would also contra-indicate treatment:

- fragile or thin skin
- hyper-sensitive skin.

Area specific contra-indications

- *Eyebrow treatments*: communicable eye infections such as styes and conjunctivitis.
- *Facial treatments*: herpes simplex (also known as cold sores) which are extremely infectious. Also clients who are using strong acid products such as Retin-A, Renova or Accutane as these medications tend to weaken the skin and tearing of the skin may occur when the wax is removed. This also applies for 2–4 weeks after a course of micro dermabrasion treatments.
- *Underarm/bikini area*: lymphatic swelling in the area to be treated.
- *Legs*: varicose veins.
- *Bikini area*: urinary and genital infections.

Equipment and materials

Couch

- As the client's size, agility and areas of the body to be treated differ, a fully adjustable couch is advisable; this can be electric, hydraulic or manual.
- The couch needs to be covered with a protective covering from which 'wax' can be easily removed, i.e. plastic.
- In order to maintain hygiene, a layer of couch roll should be placed the full length of the couch on top of the plastic covering.
- Any towels which are to be used to cover the client must be freshly laundered.

Trolley

- The trolley should be secure, stable and have castors (preferably lockable).
- It should have enough shelving for all the equipment and products.
- The shelves of the trolley should be wiped over between clients with disinfectant, or covered with a new piece of disposable couch roll for each client.
- Ideally the shelves should have an edging rail or safety lip to prevent the wax heater accidentally slipping off.

Wax heater

Warm wax heaters
Clean and Easy

There are many wax heaters on the market; whichever one you choose, it should:

- be thermostatically controlled, meet all health and safety requirements and be in good working order
- be wiped with disinfectant between treatments
- have a lid to keep out airborne particles.

Positioning of equipment

Ensure that your wax pot and trolley are close enough to the area to be treated, positioned to prevent spillage and drips, and that it will not restrict your movement or cause a hazard.

The three methods of warm wax – spatula, roller and tube waxing – all require different heaters and different techniques. Consider carefully which method or methods you will offer before making a purchase.

> **REMEMBER** !
>
> Heaters are generally designed to heat the wax within their own container, with its lid resting on the wax container itself as opposed to the heater. Check with the manufacturer before pouring wax directly into the heater, as this is generally not considered to be good practice because thorough cleaning of the heater is not possible with this method

Warm wax products

Items required

All warm wax methods require the following equipment in addition to the major items listed above:

- skin sanitiser
- powder
- cotton wool (in a container with lid)
- tissues
- sterilised tweezers
- after wax soothing lotion, oil, gel or cream
- pedal bin with lid (double-lined)
- equipment cleaner
- clean towels
- couch roll
- disinfected scissors
- wax removal strips.

Additional equipment

The three methods of warm waxing require the following additional items:

- for the roller cassette method, a variety of roller head sizes
- for the pot wax method, a disposable spatula
- for the tube method, a variety of applicator sizes.

Treatment planning

Once you have uncovered your client's hair removal history, you can plan and discuss the treatment appointments and likely outcomes. Key considerations when planning the treatment are the client's:

- social commitments
- work commitments
- holiday commitments.

Treatment planning will ensure the client has the best results at the time they are needed.

Preparation of the treatment area

Preparation will ensure that you can provide safe, hygienic and efficient treatments.

The treatment room should

- be adequately lit to carry out treatment
- be at a comfortable temperature, taking into account that the client will be in various stages of undress
- be well ventilated

- have an ambience that is conducive to both a professional and a relaxing environment, e.g. with relaxing music perhaps
- have a floor covering that is easy to wipe and is level
- be set up to ensure that client privacy is maintained at all times.

Preparation of the therapist

It is important to present a professional image. It is particularly important to maintain a high standard of personal hygiene.

- Always wear clean and pressed clothing or a uniform.
- Put on a single-use disposable plastic apron for each client.
- Use a new pair of disposable gloves (latex or vinyl) for each client.
- Have disposable surgical masks available, in case they are required.
- Wear comfortable supportive shoes with a low heel to protect your posture and avoid accidents.
- Always present a professional, hygienic and practical appearance, i.e. hair tied back, minimal jewellery (watch and wedding ring only).

> **PROFESSIONAL TIP** ✔
>
> The client must feel confident about the therapist and this can be achieved by:
> - a professional appearance
> - good organisational skills
> - a reassuring and positive approach to consultation and treatment

> **PROFESSIONAL TIP** ✔
>
> Never try and remember the client's details, always check the record card before you commence treatment

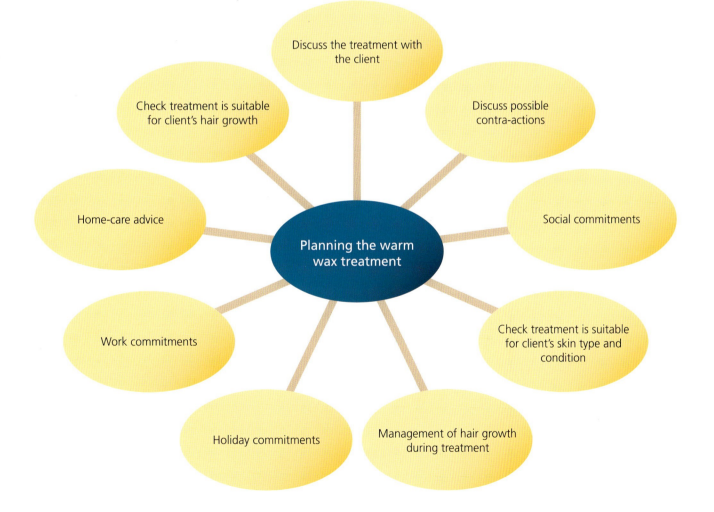

REMEMBER !

Switch on the heater in good time for the wax to reach working temperature and to coincide with your client's appointment time. In the case of early morning clients, the use of plug socket timers that will turn on your heater at a pre-determined time before you arrive, will be extremely useful

REMEMBER !

It is an insurance for you and a good practice requirement that you complete the record card after each treatment and ensure the client signs it each time

PROFESSIONAL TIP ✔

A light dusting of powder prevents the wax from sticking to the skin and lifts the hairs to assist with wax coverage

PROFESSIONAL TIP ✔

With warm wax, apply with the direction of growth

HEALTH AND SAFETY ✚

Wax is warm and sticky – remember to keep your wax pot or heater covered to prevent contamination by airborne particles and bacteria

Treatment preparation

Before preparing the client for treatment you must complete each of these steps:

1 Switch on the wax heater so that the wax is at the correct temperature (approx 40–45°C) and consistency for your client's appointment time.

2 If the client has had a previous treatment with you, before preparing the client and commencing treatment, the client's record card must be retrieved from its confidential and secure storage facility and be on hand in the treatment room.

3 Accompany the client into the treatment room and assist and/or direct the client with the removal of any necessary garments and, if required, help him or her on to the couch.

4 Ascertain from the client any changes which may affect the treatment and its outcomes, using your record card as a point of reference, e.g. any reactions and feedback from the last treatment, change in medication and health, stress (job or personal issues).

5 Once you and your client are happy to continue, prepare the client for treatment.

Treatment preparation is an important part of the treatment as a whole and should be carried out thoroughly. The following steps will guide you through a typical preparation procedure of yourself and the client for a warm wax treatment:

1 Sanitise your hands.

2 Put on single use disposable gloves.

3 Apply skin sanitising product to clean cotton wool and wipe over the area to be treated, in order to sanitise the area and remove any oils or cosmetic products on the skin.

4 Blot treatment area dry with clean tissue.

5 Dispose of cotton wool and tissue in pedal bin (double lined with 2 bin liners).

6 A light dusting of powder should be applied to the treatment area against the hair growth with a clean cotton wool pad. Test the wax on the inside of your wrist to ensure it is at a comfortable temperature. If the temperature is comfortable for you, apply a 2cm^2 area of wax on the area to be treated to ensure it is comfortable for the client.

TECHNICAL TIP ✔

If your wax heater has not been switched on for a sufficient length of time, you may find the wax is too cool and therefore too thick. You can quickly increase the thermostat control to a higher level for a short period of time and this will more rapidly get the wax to the correct working temperature. Remember the thermostat must be reduced once the temperature has been achieved, in accordance with manufacturer's instructions

Treatment application

Warm wax treatments can be applied using a variety of methods:

- spatula wax method
- roller wax method
- tube wax method.

SPATULA WAX METHOD

Treatment application

The following steps lead you through the step-by-step process of removing hair with warm wax, applied by the spatula method.

Step One: Prepare yourself and the client by putting on the appropriate PPE and cleansing the client's skin.

Step Two: Dip a new spatula into the wax, remove excess and apply to the area to be treated holding the spatula at a 45° angle.

Step Three: Place your spatula on the skin and gently move it towards you across the surface of the skin in a smooth movement, this will allow a uniform thickness of wax to flow on to the treatment area.

Step Four: To remove the wax, the wax must adhere to a waxing strip. Select a wax removal strip (fabric or paper); place it onto the wax in a firm, downward stroking movement in the sequence that you applied the wax and in the direction of hair growth. Leave a 2cm free edge at the bottom of the strip to use as a grip point for removal.

Step Five: When you have a secure grip on the strip, pull very quickly in a 'flicking movement' against the direction of hair growth and parallel to the surface of the skin.

Step Six: To remove any remaining wax, apply the just removed strip on to it, wax side down, press firmly with the finger tips and remove quickly, parallel to the skin's surface. Fold the wax strip in half and discard into a pedal bin – double lined.

Clear the area in a methodical manner using the illustration on page 120 as a guide.

Step Seven: Any remaining stray hairs should be removed with sterilised tweezers, then placed in a tissue and disposed of in a double lined pedal bin.

Step Eight: Apply a soothing lotion – oil, gel or cream – to the treated area, blot off any excess with a tissue and dispose into a double lined pedal bin.

REMEMBER

Wax is heat sensitive; once it has been spread it can lose heat very quickly, particularly if the client and/or room are cold, therefore it is important to ensure that both are warm prior to waxing

PROFESSIONAL TIP

If it's a very cold day, at the skin preparation stage, briskly rub or massage your client's skin with the preparatory products as this will increase blood supply, thereby increasing skin temperature.

HEALTH AND SAFETY

When using the spatula method, the spatula must be replaced:
- for each client
- when it comes into contact with any blood spotting
- when changing treatment area on the same client

HEALTH AND SAFETY

A spatula must never be placed back into the wax container if it has been in contact with blood spotting

TECHNICAL TIP

Ensure you do not apply too much pressure with the spatula, as this will scrape the skin, nor too little pressure, which will result in too thick a layer

Step 1: Preparing the area to be treated

Step 2: Getting the right amount of wax onto the spatula

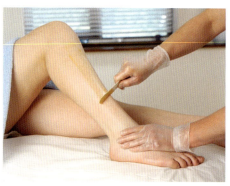

Step 3: Applying wax with the spatula

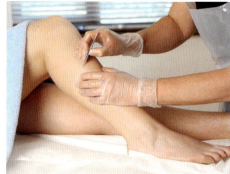

Step 4: Applying the wax removal strip

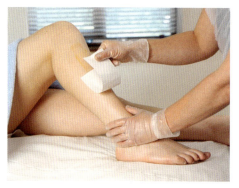

Step 5: Removing the wax removal strip

Step 7: Removing stray hairs with tweezers

Step 8: Applying of aftercare product

Reasons for poor treatment results

Clients consider they have had a poor treatment if there are any hairs left behind: after all that is what they have paid to have removed. Hairs are normally left behind when:

- oils were left on the skin, preventing the wax from adhering
- the area was not completely covered with wax
- wax was applied or removed in the wrong direction
- wax was removed too slowly
- the waxing strip did not adhere to the wax sufficiently.

> **HEALTH AND SAFETY** ✚
>
> Great care should be taken when moving the waxing pot or trolley around the treatment area once it has heated; the wax is fluid and, if spilt, could easily cause damage to floor, furniture, furnishings and practitioner

> **HEALTH AND SAFETY** ✚
>
> If using surgical spirit to clean your wax heater, ensure that the heater has cooled down: surgical spirit is an alcohol and therefore highly flammable

Home-care advice

Home care advice leaflet

JAYGEE'S

Waxing home-care

Please read these home-care notes carefully and follow our recommendations. We have taken great care to protect you from infection and, in addition to our normal salon routine, we have applied a soothing antiseptic lotion after your treatment. It is important for you to take extra care of the waxed area, especially within the first 24–48 hours. When a large number of hairs have been removed the area could be prone to infection if not cared for.

PLEASE NOTE: If you experience persistent redness or discomfort, or have any questions, do not hesitate to contact your hair removal practitioner.

The following should be avoided for the first 48 hours following treatment:

- sunbathing
- sunbed treatments
- very hot baths
- friction from tight clothing
- perfumed body lotion or creams.

For underarm waxing

- deodorants and anti-perspirants.

For facial waxing:

- application of make-up (first 4–8 hours only).

We recommend that you use soothing antiseptic after-wax lotion daily for 3–4 days after treatment, which should be purchased from your hair removal practitioner.

ROLLER WAX

Before commencing a roller wax treatment, ensure you have completed all of the consultation, preparation and planning steps for warm wax methods outlined earlier in the chapter.

Roller wax cartridges are available in 80 or 100ml sizes. The 80ml size are generally supplied separately from the roller heads, whereas the 100ml size usually have a fixed roller head attached. This is then disposed of with the empty cartridge.

The advantages and disadvantages of a roller application of warm wax compared to hot wax

Advantages	Disadvantages
✓ Cross-infection risk is reduced	✗ Hygiene procedures are time consuming
✓ Range of roller head and cartridge sizes – reduces wastage	✗ Not as effective as hot wax on short hairs
✓ Roller system ensures a consistently thin flow of wax, making it an economical option	✗ More risk of hair snapping off due to less heat being involved
✓ Risk of dripping and spilling of wax is absolutely minimal	
✓ Easy technique to master	
✓ Can be used on any part of the body	
✓ Can be used on any hair type	
✓ More suitable for clients with heat sensitive skin	

Treatment application

The following steps lead you through the step-by-step process of removing hair with warm wax, applied using a roller.

Step One: Prepare the equipment.

Step Two: Put on the appropriate PPE.

Step Three: After checking the client's details on the record card, sanitise the area to be treated.

Step Four: Remove the wax cartridge from the heater using the roller head. Wait 10 seconds for two air bubbles to rise before applying wax, this will indicate that the wax is ready to use and will flow freely into the roller. Place the roller head on the skin, hold it at a 45° angle and gently move it towards you across the surface of the skin in a smooth movement. This will allow a uniform thickness of wax to flow on to the treatment area.

Step Five: To remove the wax, the wax must adhere to a waxing strip. Select a wax removal strip (fabric or paper), place it onto the wax in a firm, downward stroking movement, following the sequence of wax application

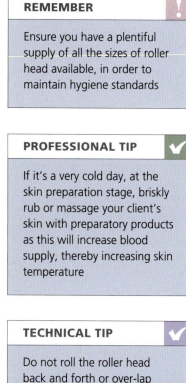

REMEMBER !

Ensure you have a plentiful supply of all the sizes of roller head available, in order to maintain hygiene standards

PROFESSIONAL TIP ✔

If it's a very cold day, at the skin preparation stage, briskly rub or massage your client's skin with preparatory products as this will increase blood supply, thereby increasing skin temperature

TECHNICAL TIP ✔

Do not roll the roller head back and forth or over-lap wax; one thin coat of wax is all that is necessary

PROFESSIONAL TIP ✔

The wax strip may be used to remove 2 or 3 sections of wax

TECHNICAL TIP ✔

The quicker your roller head passes over the skin, the less wax is applied. Your aim is to apply the thinnest layer possible

and direction of growth. Leave a 2cm free edge at the bottom of the strip to use as a grip point for removal. When you have a secure grip on the strip, pull very quickly against the direction of hair growth and parallel to the surface of the skin. To remove any remaining wax, apply the just removed strip on to it, wax side down, press firmly and remove. Fold the wax strip in half and discard into a pedal bin – double lined. Clear the area in a methodical manner.

Step Six: Any remaining stray hairs should be removed with sterilised tweezers, placed in a tissue and disposed of in a double lined pedal bin.

Step Seven: Apply a soothing lotion, oil, gel or cream to the treated area, blot off any excess with a tissue and dispose into a double lined pedal bin. Assist the client off the couch and advise on home-care.

> ### HEALTH AND SAFETY ✚
>
> At the end of the treatment, the roller head should be taken off the cartridge and any remaining wax cleaned away using wax removing solution, washed in hot soapy water and placed in disinfectant solution, following the manufacturer's instructions. A disinfected roller head should be placed on the wax cartridge ready for the next client

Step 1: Roller wax equipment

Step 2: Putting on PPE – gloves

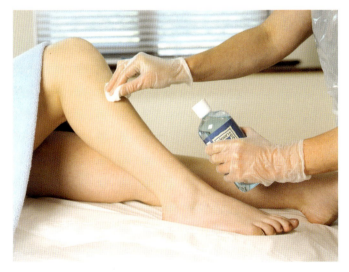

Step 3: Preparing the area to be treated

Step 4: Applying the wax with the roller

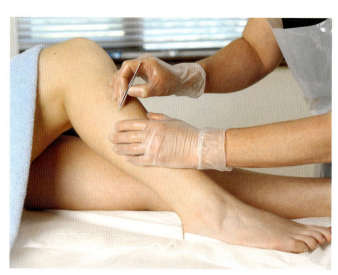

Step 6: Removing stray hairs with tweezers

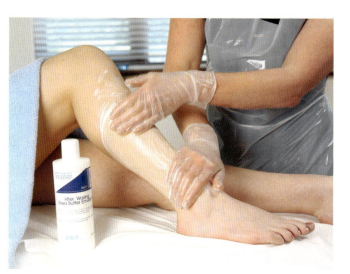

Step 7: Applying aftercare product

TECHNICAL TIP ✔

Do not press the roller head too firmly onto the skin surface; allow it to 'float' on top of the flowing wax. This will allow an even distribution and comfortable application of the wax

Roller heads are available in a range of sizes

House of Famuir Ltd www.hofbeauty.co.uk

Good practice for effective roller wax treatment

- The amount of skin covered with wax will depend on the temperature and your experience. For example, an experienced practitioner, when treating a half leg, will apply wax to the entire front and side areas of both legs and then remove. Alternatively, a less experienced practitioner will simply apply 2 or 3 applications of wax and remove them before applying additional wax.

- Once the heated cartridge is removed from the heater it will begin to cool quite quickly, particularly if you are not using a thermal sleeve and the wax will not flow as easily. If you have more than one of the large-size cartridges heated, you can alternate them during treatment to maintain the wax flow.

- Some manufacturers supply a thermal sleeve in which to place the wax cartridge. In addition, to retaining heat, they offer some protection to the practitioner's hands – useful if they are overly heat sensitive.

- Place the cartridges into the heater with the roller heads facing the back when not in use, this prevents any wax on the actual roller from cooling which could prevent the roller from flowing freely.

- Replace the cartridge if the wax level gets too low (see manufacturer's instructions). As if there is only a small amount of wax in the cartridge, the wax can overheat.

- Avoid squeezing the cartridge when applying the wax; this will cause too much wax to be distributed on to the skin.

- Avoid over-lapping the applied wax. Apply one thin layer of wax, and then remove the roller immediately.

HEALTH AND SAFETY ✚

Wax cartridges are purchased with wax inside and you should not refill them as this will invalidate the manufacturer's guarantee. Refilling could also invalidate your insurance as the wax may not be compatible with your heater, causing the wax to overheat and potentially resulting in burns on the client's skin.

Reasons for poor treatment results

Hairs are left behind when:

- oils were left on the skin – this prevents the wax from adhering
- the treatment area was not completely covered with wax
- wax was applied or removed in the wrong direction
- wax was removed too slowly
- too much wax was applied
- the skin was too cold during treatment.

Home-care advice

The aftercare procedure for roller waxing is identical to spatula waxing, both in terms of salon procedures and home-care advice.

A thermal sleeve for a roller wax cartridge

House of Famuir Ltd www.hotbeauty.co.uk

TUBE WAX

The advantages and disadvantages of tube wax application compared to hot wax

Advantages	Disadvantages
✓ Risk of cross-infection is minimal and hygiene procedures straightforward	✗ Not as effective as hot wax on short hairs
✓ Risk of dripping and spilling wax is absolutely minimal	✗ Greater risk of hair snapping off due to less heat being involved
✓ Can be used on any part of the body	✗ If the correct and consistent pressure is not applied to the tube, the application of wax will be erratic
✓ Can be used on any hair type	
✓ More suitable for clients with heat sensitive skin	

Before commencing a tube wax treatment, ensure you have completed all of the consultation, preparation and planning steps for warm wax methods outlined earlier in the chapter.

Treatment application

Tube wax is applied in a consistently thin layer and therefore is prone to cooling more quickly. All wax is heat sensitive – once it has been spread, it can lose heat very quickly, particularly if the client and/or the room is cold. Therefore, it is important to ensure that both are warm prior to waxing, and consequently the amount of skin covered with wax will depend upon the temperature and your experience. For example, an experienced practitioner, when treating a half leg, will apply wax to the entire front and side areas of both legs and then remove. Alternatively, a less experienced practitioner will simply apply two or three strips of wax and remove before applying additional wax.

Step One: Prepare the area to be treated by wiping over with an antiseptic wipe.

TECHNICAL TIP ✔

If it's a very cold day, at the skin preparation stage, briskly rub or massage your client's skin with preparatory products as this will increase blood supply, thereby increasing skin temperature

TECHNICAL TIP ✔

Do not press the dispenser too firmly onto the skin surface; allow it to 'float' on top of the flowing wax. This will allow an even distribution and comfortable application of the wax

TECHNICAL TIP ✔

Any remaining stray hairs should be removed with sterilised tweezers, placed in a tissue and disposed of in a double lined pedal bin

Step Two: Remove the 'tube' with its dispenser from the wax heater.

Step Three: Place the dispenser on the skin and gently move it towards you across the surface of the skin in a smooth movement, keeping the pressure on the tube even and constant. This will allow a uniform thickness of wax to flow onto the treatment area.

Step Four: Apply a muslin or paper strip with firm stroking movements. The wax strip may be used to remove 2 or 3 sections of wax.

Step Five: To remove the wax, the wax must adhere to a waxing strip. Leave a 2cm free edge at the bottom of the strip to use as a grip point for removal. When you have a secure grip on the strip, pull very quickly against the direction of hair growth and parallel to the surface of the skin. To remove any remaining wax, apply the just removed strip onto it, wax side down, press firmly with the fingertips and flick to remove. Fold the wax strip in half and discard into a pedal bin – double lined.

Step Six: Wipe over again with an antiseptic wipe to complete the treatment.

Step Seven: Clear the area in a methodical manner using the illustration, on page 120 as a guide. Apply a soothing lotion, oil, gel or cream to the treated area, blot off any excess with a tissue and dispose into a double lined pedal bin. Assist the client off the couch and advise on home-care.

HEALTH AND SAFETY ✚

At the end of the treatment, the dispenser should be disposed of in front of the client, following the manufacturer's instructions; this will underline the hygienic aspect of this method to the client. After the dispenser has been disposed of, the tube's cap should be applied, again in front of the client, and left on until the next client is ready for treatment, whereupon the cap is removed and the new dispenser applied, also in front of the client

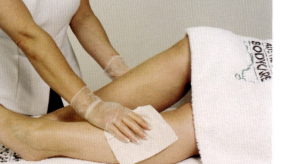

Step 1: Preparing the area to be treated

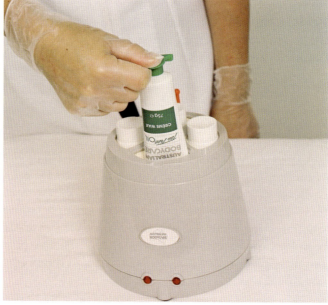

Step 2: Removing the tube from the dispenser

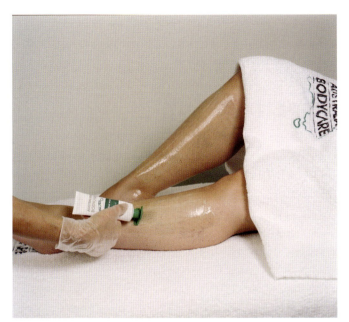

Step 3: Applying wax

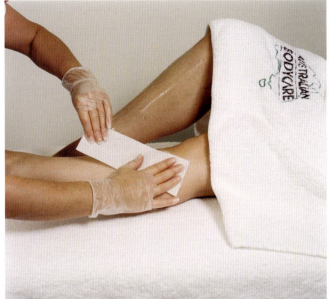

Step 4: Applying the wax removal strip

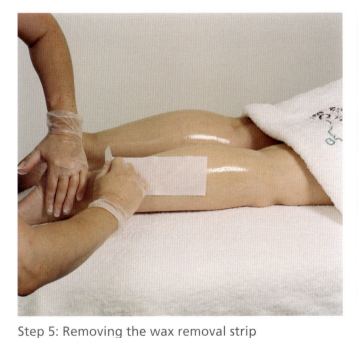

Step 5: Removing the wax removal strip

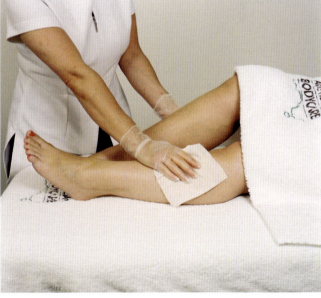

Step 6: Wiping the area with an antiseptic wipe

'As Simplsimple as ABC' Astralian Body Care

Reasons for poor treatment results

Hairs are left behind when:

- oils were left on the skin – this prevents the wax from adhering
- the area was not completely covered with wax
- wax was applied or removed in the wrong direction
- wax was removed too slowly
- the tube was not squeezed consistently, giving uneven wax distribution.

HEALTH AND SAFETY ✚

Ensure you have a plentiful supply of replacement dispensers, in order to maintain hygiene standards

TECHNICAL TIP ✔

Use a mirror and eyebrow brush as aids to discuss the desired eyebrow shape with your client. The client should be in an upright position during the discussion; when lying down, the skin can settle in a different way to when upright, and therefore it is possible to create the wrong shape

Home-care advice

The aftercare procedure for tube waxing is identical to spatula waxing, both in terms of salon procedures and home-care advice.

WAXING TREATMENT AREAS

Before treating any of these areas, ensure you have followed all the necessary consultation, preparation and treatment planning steps outlined earlier in this chapter and in Chapter Two.

Each area to be treated requires specific knowledge regarding application. Before applying any wax you should first examine the direction of hair growth on the area to be treated. This will affect where you position yourself and your client.

Eyebrow waxing

Waxing provides a good alternative to tweezing for the eyebrow area because it removes all the hairs, including the fine vellus ones, which gives a smooth area for make-up. Waxes for sensitive skin such as white wax or azulene are more suitable for eyebrows.

Consultation

Prior to waxing treatment, consult with the client to ascertain how they would like their eyebrows shaped in accordance with the general consultation steps discussed earlier and in Chapter Two. In addition, there are some standard consultation guidelines for eyebrow waxing that can be followed.

● In order to assess the standard shape and demonstrate the natural line of the eyebrow to the client, an imaginary line is drawn up from the side of the nose, through the tear duct and up to the eyebrow. This is the standard starting point of the eyebrow.

● A second imaginary line is drawn from the side of the nose, through the outer corner of the eye and beyond until it intersects with the existing

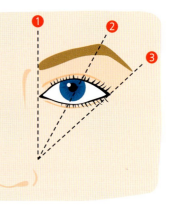

Use these guidelines when defining the eyebrow shape:
1. Start;
2. Point of arch;
3. End point of eyebrow

Guidelines for defining the eyebrow shape:
(1) start, (2) point of arch, (3) end

eyebrow; that is where the eyebrow should end. The internal shape and thickness of the eyebrow is dependent on client choice.

- Hair should not be removed from above the eyebrow, as it adversely affects the natural shaping as indicated by the orbital ridge.

- Once the desired eyebrow shape has been agreed with your client, prepare the area for treatment.

TECHNICAL TIP ✔

When waxing eyebrows and upper lips, strips should be cut down to an appropriate smaller size or they can be purchased from specialist suppliers

---

Treatment application

1 Prior to normal sanitising procedures, thoroughly remove all make-up from the area.

2 For less experienced practitioners petroleum jelly may be applied carefully to the hairs you wish to leave behind; this will prevent the wax sticking to those hairs and so prevent them being accidentally removed.

3 Position the client comfortably on the couch, bearing in mind that you need easy access to the area to be treated: the head should be tilted back as far as is comfortable, this can be assisted by either a rolled towel under the neck or the client may put their head slightly over the edge of the couch or chair.

4 Turning the client's head slightly away from you and using an appropriate size applicator (small or fine), apply and remove wax in small sections and check constantly to ensure the desired shape is being achieved. As the skin tissue around the eye is fine and thin, particularly on more mature clients, the skin must be well supported when removing the strip.

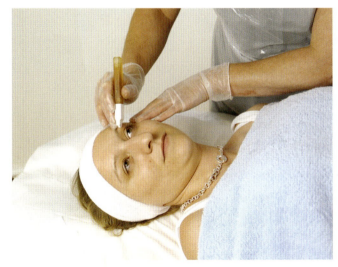

Applying roller wax to the eyebrow   Removing wax removal strip from the eyebrow

Upper lip waxing

Treatment preparation

1 Prior to normal sanitising procedures, thoroughly remove all make-up from the area.

2 Waxes for sensitive skin are more suitable for this area, for example white wax or azulene.

3 Using an appropriately sized applicator, apply the wax to one of three sections: one section is the centre of the upper lip and there is one either side.

4 Remove the wax and repeat application and removal for the remaining two sections.

> **TECHNICAL TIP** ✔
>
> Over a period of time, the treatment area may enlarge as waxing can stimulate the surrounding finer growth

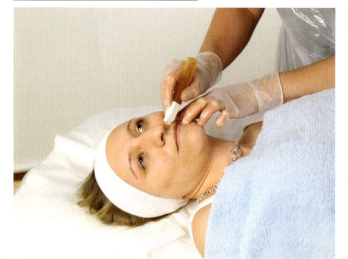
Applying roller wax to upper lip – side

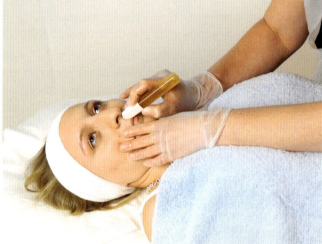
Application of roller wax to upper lip – middle

Underarm (axillae) waxing
Treatment preparation

1 Ensure client's underwear is protected with disposable paper or a towel.

2 Position the client by putting their arm above or behind their head, supporting the elbow with a pillow or rolled up towel, if necessary.

3 Waxes for stronger hairs are more suitable for this area, for example chlorophyll.

4 When removing the wax, you may need to ask a female client to hold her breast away from the underarm. Always support the skin carefully, but do not press too hard on the skin as there are numerous glands in this area.

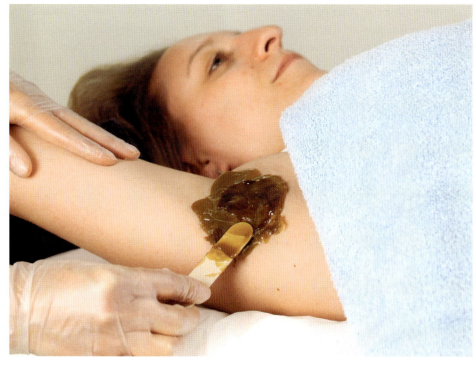

Applying hot wax to the underarm

EQUIPMENT LIST
couch
trolley
wax heater
strong wax (e.g. chlorophyll)
skin sanitiser
powder
cotton wool
tissues
sterilised tweezers
after-wax soothing lotion
pedal bin with lid
equipment cleaner
clean towels
couch roll
disinfected scissors
wax removal strips
disposable paper

TECHNICAL TIP ✔

Assess the direction of growth thoroughly as it is common on underarms for the hair to be multi-directional. Ensure that your wax application is applied in small sections, paying particular attention to the direction of growth. Numerous strips of wax will have to be applied, if the hair grows in many directions

TECHNICAL TIP ✔

Underarm and bikini line hair is very strong terminal hair, the root of which has a very rich blood supply, which may travel up the follicle as the hair is removed, showing as tiny blood spots. This is normal and in no way indicates a poor treatment

EQUIPMENT LIST
couch
trolley
wax heater
wax
skin sanitiser
powder
cotton wool
tissues
sterilised tweezers
after-wax soothing lotion
pedal bin with lid
equipment cleaner
clean towels
couch roll
disinfected scissors
wax removal strips
disposable paper

Forearm waxing

Treatment preparation

1 Discuss with the client the exact area to be treated.

2 The client may be positioned sitting upright on the treatment couch or sitting on the opposite side of the treatment couch to the practitioner, either is suitable.

3 In both cases, rest the client's arm on a firm cushion or pillow, which is covered in a wipeable material with a sheet of couch roll on top. This will ensure comfort for the client and helps to position the client correctly for treatment.

4 Assess the direction of growth and ensure that your wax application is applied in sections, paying particular attention to the directions of growth.

5 As with other areas, the wax must be removed parallel to the treatment area. In the case of the forearm remember the surface area is curved. When removing the wax, also ensure that you are holding the skin taut.

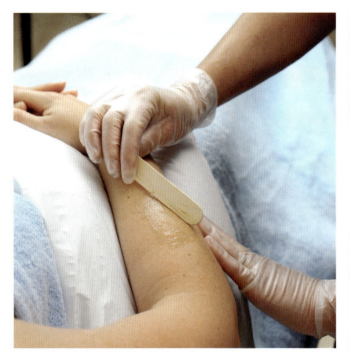

Applying the spatula wax to the forearm

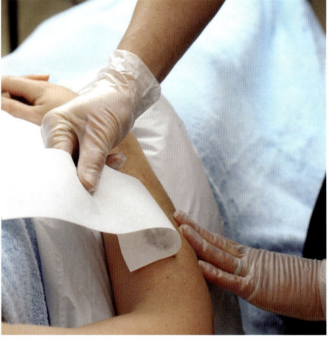

Removing wax removal strip from the forearm

EQUIPMENT LIST
couch
trolley
wax heater
strong wax (e.g. chlorophyll)
skin sanitiser
powder
cotton wool
tissues
sterilised tweezers
after-wax soothing lotion
pedal bin with lid
equipment cleaner
clean towels
couch roll
disinfected scissors
wax removal strips
disposable paper

Abdomen waxing

Treatment preparation

1 Ensure underwear is protected with disposable paper and position the client so that you can comfortably reach the area to be treated.

2 If the abdominal skin is not firm, that is flabby, you may need to ask the client to support the skin on either side of the treatment area when the wax is applied and removed.

3 Waxes for stronger hairs are more suitable for this area, for example chlorophyll.

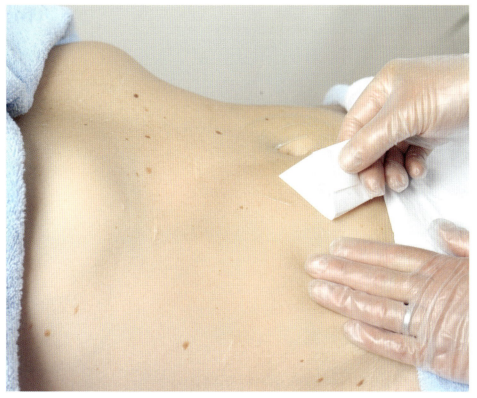

Removing wax from the abdomen using small strips

Bikini waxing

Consultation

In addition to your standard consultation procedures, you must discuss with the client the 'bikini' area that she would like treated: how high or low should the bikini line be – just below the line of underwear, higher or from the whole area?

Treatment preparation

1 Ensure the client is wearing disposable pants, or if they wear their own underwear protect it with tissues or disposable paper.

2 Position the client and yourself so that you can comfortably reach the area to be treated. The hairs to be removed and their direction will dictate how the client and her legs are positioned on the couch, for example the client may kneel on the couch to afford the practitioner access to the hairs, particularly in cases where the client wants all pubic hair removed.

3 You may need to ask the client to assist you by stretching and supporting the skin when the wax is applied and removed.

4 To reduce discomfort and excess pulling, trim hair to approx 1–2cm in length using disinfected scissors.

5 The normal rules of application of wax apply, that is, if hair grows in many directions a greater number of smaller strips will need to be applied.

EQUIPMENT LIST
couch
trolley
wax heater
strong wax (e.g. chlorophyll)
skin sanitiser
powder
cotton wool
tissues
sterilised tweezers
after-wax soothing lotion
pedal bin with lid
equipment cleaner
clean towels
couch roll
disinfected scissors
wax removal strips
disposable paper

Application of hot wax to bikini area

PROFESSIONAL TIP ✔

Maintain extreme professionalism and distance during this treatment and never be too chatty or friendly, as this may be misinterpreted and make the client feel uncomfortable

Brazilian or Hollywood waxing

Brazilian waxing is the most common term used to describe a technique where the majority of hair is removed from the bikini area, leaving only a very small downward strip from the pubis bone. Hollywood waxing is the most common term used for a technique where all of the hair is removed from the bikini line area.

Both techniques have become extremely popular. Some clients report that these waxing techniques make them feel more feminine and sexually attractive while others feel they are more hygienic. They are, without question, the most efficient way to achieve a totally smooth bikini line and are especially popular with models and beach fans, as even the skimpiest bikinis can be worn. However, a home skin care regime that helps prevent in-growing hairs must be advocated to these clients.

Consultation

Carefully consult the client in accordance with the procedures discussed earlier in the chapter and in Chapter Two, with a particular emphasis on questioning regarding urinary infections, past or present. As with all waxing, the skin is temporarily left in a vulnerable state with the follicles open. If the client has a urine infection or similar, the infection could easily be spread to the treated area, particularly when going to the toilet.

During consultation there are additional issues specific to Brazilian and Hollywood waxing which must be considered.

- There are potential legal implications regarding touching in sexual areas.
- There are health and safety issues related to working in the genital area.

- Be sensitive over staff feelings towards carrying out this treatment. Ensure that staff are not forced into carrying out these treatments, directly or indirectly.
- Be aware of a client's wrongful interpretation of your actions during the treatment procedure, i.e. any actions which could be perceived as sexual assault.
- Be scrupulous about contaminated waste disposal (double lined pedal bin for feminine wipes, hair removal practitioner's disposable apron and gloves, etc.).

It is also extremely important to remember that minors (people under the age of 16 years) should not receive any treatment without parental consent.

Treatment preparation

It is advisable to ask the client to shower or bathe prior to arriving for treatment. If this is not possible, feminine hygiene wipes should be available for the client to use and then disposed of in a pedal bin (double lined).

Ask the client to put on disposable thong panties. These can be adjusted, as necessary, to access all areas and in particular, can be moved inside the 'lips' of the vagina.

Decide on the most appropriate type of wax for the client. There is an ongoing debate over which is the best wax to use: hot wax or warm wax with soothing ingredients such as titanium dioxide. There are advantages and disadvantages to each.

Hot wax:

- Grips strong hairs more efficiently, and, of course, bikini line hairs are strong.
- It also, however, heats the area more; clearly this area is very sensitive and, as a consequence, more reactive.
- Hot wax also requires more skill to achieve effective procedure.

Warm wax:

- With titanium dioxide, there is a relatively low temperature on application which can avoid over heating and excess reaction.
- Warm wax may not grip the shorter hairs as effectively.

Treatment application

Step One: Prepare the area for treatment.

Step Two: Apply the hot wax.

Step Three: Use a soothing hand, after strip has been removed.

Step Four: Carefully position the client to access the underneath area.

Step Five: Partial removal – Brazilian.

Step Six: Complete removal – Hollywood.

EQUIPMENT LIST
couch
trolley
wax heater
wax
skin sanitiser
powder
cotton wool
tissues
sterilised tweezers
after-wax soothing lotion
pedal bin with lid
equipment cleaner
clean towels
couch roll
disinfected scissors
wax removal strips
disposable paper

HEALTH AND SAFETY

Gloves should always be worn when administering Brazilian and Hollywood treatments

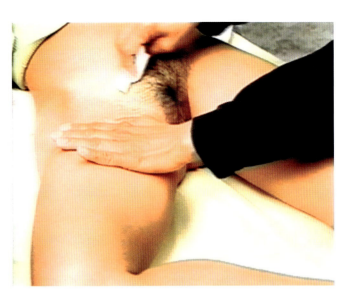

Step 1: Preparing the area to be treated

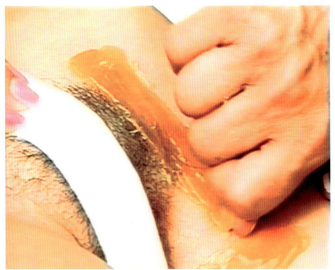

Step 2: Applying the hot wax

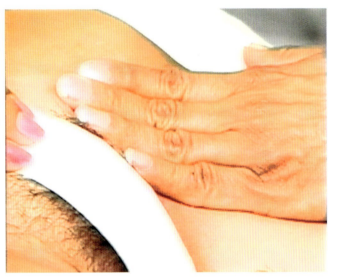

Step 3: Using a soothing hand after the strip has been removed

Step 4: Accessing the underneath area

Step 5: Partial removal – Brazilian

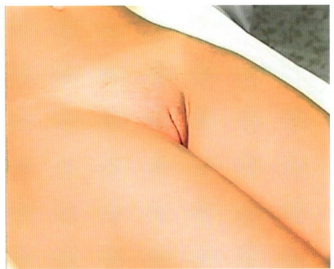

Step 6: Complete removal – Hollywood

Note: Gloves should always be worn when administrating Brazilian and Hollywood treatments

Home-care advice

Cross contamination is more likely to occur with bikini waxing. The client's after-care procedures should be even more stringent with an emphasis on cleanliness, particularly after using the toilet. In addition, clients should avoid friction, for example from tight clothes, bodily contact and heat.

A careful and thorough consultation may help the HRP to be aware whether there are likely to be any potential problems with cross contamination, for example urinary tract diseases, STIs (sexually transmitted infections) etc. However, not all clients will be aware if they have these.

Discuss with the client the implications of aftercare:

- keeping the area meticulously clean, particularly after visiting the toilet
- wearing loose undergarments for 24–48 hours post treatment
- avoiding heat or friction, i.e. tight clothes and bodily contact, for 24–48 hours post treatment
- applying aftercare, as instructed by the HRP.

Leg waxing

Leg waxing can be a half leg wax – most commonly from the ankle to the knee, but can also be from the knee to the bikini line. A lower leg wax would normally include the top of the foot and toes. A full leg wax is from the toes up to the bikini line. A three-quarter leg wax may also be requested, this would include the area from ankle to the mid-thigh – it would not include the bikini area.

Treatment preparation

1 Ensure the client is comfortably positioned on the treatment couch and clothing is protected; the skin has been sanitised and prepared for treatment and the direction of hair growth has been investigated.
2 When removing hair from the knee, the client should bend their knee, placing the foot flat on the treatment couch and wax should be applied in small sections and removed immediately.
3 When treating the lower leg, from ankle to knee, discuss with the client how far above the knee they would like the hair removal to finish.
4 If the client requires the removal of hair from the feet and toes, this should be done whilst the leg is in the position shown in the illustration, that is with the ankle extended and the foot flat on the couch. Support and angle the toe, which will stretch the skin, ensuring complete coverage by the wax.

TECHNICAL TIP

If the client does not agree to the aftercare regime, treatment should not be carried out

PROFESSIONAL TIP

If you feel that your client is just saying she will carry out the aftercare procedures you demand but has no intention of actually doing so, then don't treat. Your business will be the better for it

TECHNICAL TIP

The normal rules for the application of wax apply, i.e. if the hair grows in many directions a greater number of smaller strips will need to be applied

TECHNICAL TIP

There is an ongoing debate as to whether topical (externally applied) steroid creams are a cause of hair growth

PROFESSIONAL TIP

Removal of hairs from above the knee may be charged as a three-quarter leg wax depending on how far the removal goes. Hairs removed up to mid-thigh would certainly be classed as a three-quarter leg wax and charged accordingly

EQUIPMENT LIST

couch

trolley

wax heater

strong wax (e.g. chlorophyll)

skin sanitiser

powder

cotton wool

tissues

sterilised tweezers

after-'wax' soothing lotion

pedal bin with lid

equipment cleaner

clean towels

couch roll

disinfected scissors

wax removal strips

disposable paper

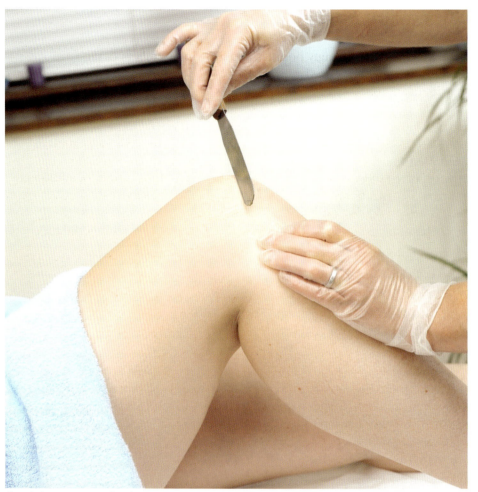

Applying wax to the knee

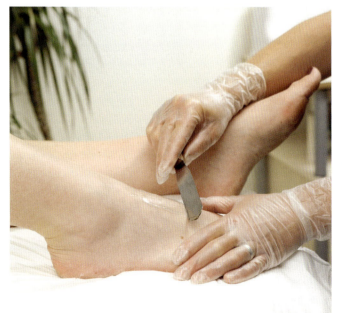

Applying wax to the feet

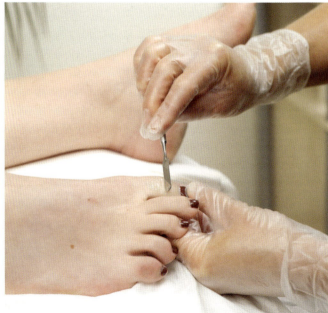

Applying wax to the toes

MALE WAXING

Male waxing is increasingly popular and growing numbers of men are requesting, in addition to the areas already discussed, having their chest, shoulders and back waxed.

Consultation

In addition to the usual consultation steps, there are a number of additional issues to be considered when providing male waxing services. As is the case with Brazilian waxing on females, the following should be considered prior to treatment:

● There are potential legal implications regarding touching in sexual areas, particularly when practitioner and client are of the opposite sex.

● There are health and safety issues relating to working in the genital area.

● Consider staff feelings towards carrying out this treatment. Ensure that staff are not forced into carrying out these treatments, directly or indirectly.

● Be aware of a client's wrongful interpretation of your actions during the treatment procedure, i.e. the risk of a sexual assault charge, or of the HRP being sexually assaulted by the client.

● Be scrupulous about contaminated waste disposal (double lined pedal bin for feminine wipes, hair removal practitioner's disposable apron and gloves, etc.).

People under the age of 16 years (minors) should not receive any treatment without parental consent. The repercussions of treating – and therefore touching – this area without consent cannot be underestimated.

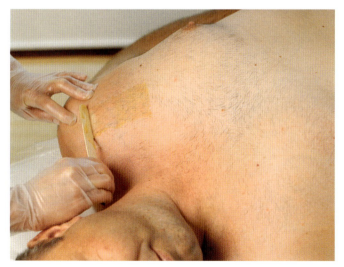

Applying warm wax to a male chest with a spatula

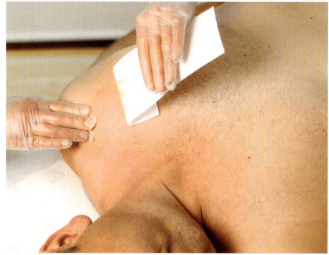

Removing wax removal strip from male chest

Treatment application

The general rules are still relevant and wax should be applied:

- following the direction of the hair growth, depending on the wax method used
- against the direction of hair growth for hot wax and with the direction of hair growth for all other methods
- with the client lying on his stomach for a back and shoulder wax and on his back for a chest wax.

The male 'buttock' area is often referred to as back, sack and crack (BSC) which crudely defines the treatment areas of the buttocks, the scrotum and between the buttocks. This is becoming a popular treatment with clients reporting that they feel 'freer', more hygienic and more sexually attractive. It is particularly popular with male models and dancers, who are required to wear skimpy underwear, and body builders, who like to remove hair from the buttocks – being hair free shows muscle definition better, particularly when competing and wearing a G-string.

Some HRPs feel uncomfortable about offering this service; it is not a requirement within the standards, but it is becoming more requested in the industry. Generally speaking, salon owners allow HRPs to decide themselves whether or not they wish to carry out this treatment.

Positioning of client for BSC

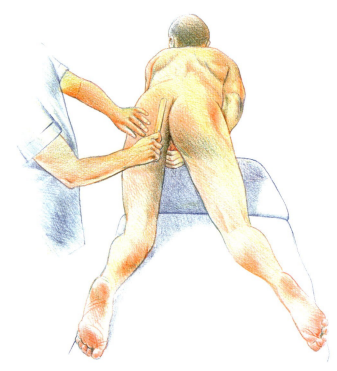

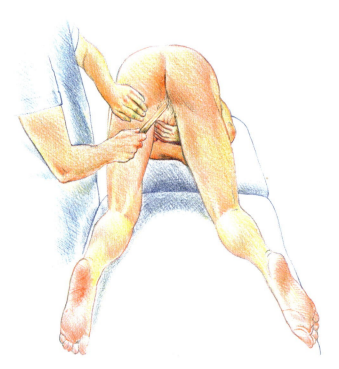

Position for buttocks (back) and between the buttocks ('crack'), application and removal, client to support genitals and hold slightly forward

Position for back of scrotum ('sack'), application and removal, client to support genitals and hold forward which helps to make the skin taut and smooth, making the application and removal of wax easier

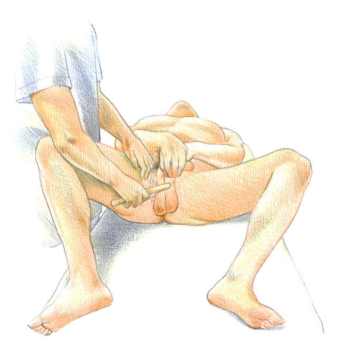

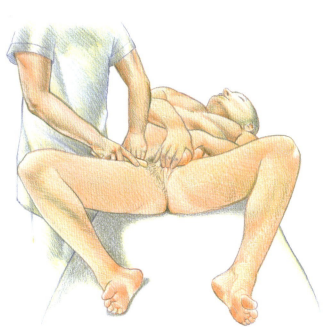

Position for front of scrotum, application and removal, client to hold genitals away from the treated area

Position for front side, application and removal, client to hold and support genitals away from side being treated

WAXING – CASE STUDY 1

Age: 26	
Gender: Female	
Treatment area: Bikini and half leg wax	
Skin sensitivity: Medium	
Type of hair growth: Coarse, dark and dense	
Type of wax and why: Azulene wax due to its soothing qualities	
Method of wax: Warm wax	
Frequency of treatment: First treatment at this salon, usual salon fully booked and client going on holiday tomorrow	
Hair management: Waxing every three to four weeks. Occasionally uses home wax kit	

Re-growth issues: Growing faster over the years and hairs have distorted. Hair present after one week. Many different growths present on the area, some hairs too short for treatment

Comments: Prior to commencing treatment it was fully explained to the client that some hairs were too short to be effectively removed and consequently some hairs would be apparent quite soon after treatment. She stated that she didn't mind, she just needed them doing for her holiday. The treatment was completed with good results. The HRP pointed out that as she expected some of the hairs which were just emerging from the skin, could be felt but not seen and would grow back fairly quickly.

Four weeks later: The salon received a letter from the customer's solicitor. Stating that the client was seeking compensation as her holiday had been spoiled because she had so many hairs left, she could not wear swim wear. Unfortunately, although the HRP had explained this in detail, she did not write the information on a record card.

The client was awarded compensation.

WAXING – CASE STUDY 2

Age: 28

Gender: Female

Treatment area: Half leg

Skin sensitivity: Good

Type of hair growth: Fine, dark and sparse

Type of wax and why: Natural organic. No skin problems

Method of wax: Warm roller wax. Client saw article in magazine about roller wax and requested it

Frequency of treatment: 3 times per year

Hair management: Shaving occasionally when going out and/or wearing a skirt or dress

Re-growth issues: None, lasts ages

Comments: Client very happy, pleased with results. Has other treatments

WAXING – CASE STUDY 3

Age: 35

Gender: Female

Treatment area: Bikini

Skin sensitivity: Heat sensitive over time

Type of hair growth: Coarse

Type of wax and why: Standard beeswax/warm wax with titanium dioxide. Lower heating temperature therefore goes on cooler and quicker and reduces heat reaction

Method of wax: Hot to warm wax. Changed due to sensitivity to heat

Frequency of treatment: Every 6 weeks – 119 treatments to date

Hair management: Shaving occasionally if cannot get to salon.

Re-growth issues: Terrible ingrowing hairs

Comments: Discussing electrolysis as alternative to waxing due to ingrowing hairs. Meanwhile continuing with AHA skin products on bikini area

PRACTITIONER PROFILE

Name: Wendy O'Hare

Occupation: Beauty therapist and owner of Wendy O'Hare Skin Care

Business name: Director, Hare & Beauty Ltd

Region: Stratford Upon Avon

Wendy came into the beauty industry later than most. Twelve years ago, and at the age of 33, Wendy trained as a beauty therapist in New Zealand, while her husband worked for a local university. Beauty therapy had always been of great interest to Wendy, but circumstances had led her down a different route. So when the opportunity arose to follow her dream, Wendy embraced it.

Wendy undertook intensive beauty therapy training, and even in the early days had a keen interest in waxing. Wendy was not only involved with waxing as part of the curriculum, but was also heavily involved with the development of the disposable dispenser and tube waxing method. The synergy between working as a professional beauty therapist and the development of a unique and revolutionary waxing system highlighted to Wendy the importance of cleanliness, speed, skill and hygiene with this treatment.

On returning to the UK after three years in New Zealand, Wendy was asked to work for a well-known beauty company as a representative, to educate and sell the disposable applicator (tube) waxing system which was then being introduced to the UK. However, after three years, Wendy decided to set up her own exclusive beauty salon in Stratford upon Avon. After five years of successful trading, Wendy has developed a reputation for absolute professionalism.

'… providing a complete beauty clinic service is so important in our industry, no one part can make a successful clinic on its own, however if you get a fundamental treatment such as waxing wrong, then you're in big trouble.'

As part of Wendy's commitment to providing a quality service, she has always been pro-actively involved with the development of new products.

'… new technology and the re-invention of existing treatments are the way forward, without new products and commitment to improving treatments, the beauty industry will always be viewed as a cottage industry.'

Wendy was also instrumental in setting up Hare & Beauty Ltd, a company dedicated to developing new products to improve working practices and products within the salon environment. Two such products are TT-Hy waxing for Australian Body Care and 'eggpot' spatula waxing.

Wendy's philosophy is speed, hygiene and professional practice.

'… waxing as a treatment needs to start from first impressions, and that starts from the moment your client walks into the room. A dirty wax pot, trolley, couch, floor and even wall say something about the therapist and the salon. Yes, waxing is very messy, but it's only as messy as the user.'

Wendy goes on to say that the wax should be on the client's skin, in the correct amount and at the right temperature. Wax application, if done professionally, illustrates both skill and experience, giving confidence to your client and gaining respect for the therapist. Likewise, the professional removal of wax also highlights skill and wins respect. If wax is applied so thickly that removal sprays the client's clothes, the HRP should pursue a further training course. Bad technique reflects bad practice and will eventually lose clients.

'Waxing is all about confidence without being over-confident. Confidence shows control and skill while over-confidence can result in bruising and complaints.

'With so much choice available in wax and method of application, it's personal choice what you use; however, all the points above are relevant to any system and hygiene is becoming paramount.

'Waxing should be treated with respect and care as it involves the removal of skin tissue, hair follicle, sebum and blood, all of which could harbour infection or could act as a conduit for infection. Think about issues like these. Would you like to be waxed with the same spatula or dispenser that has just been used on the previous client? Thinking about your own safety will make you a better HRP on all levels. If you don't think your methods are as safe as they can be then don't carry out the treatment.

'Do not get blasé about waxing. Even if it's your most regular client always check for contra-indications. Do not be afraid to refuse to wax a client if you feel that they will react badly. Your client may not understand at first, but if you clearly explain that it could result in skin damage, she/he will respect your decision. This type of attitude only increases your reputation, even if your client doesn't understand at first. Remember you are the HRP, you've been trained and you know best.

'Just because a waxing treatment is not a relaxing treatment there is no need to ignore the following: always ensure that the treatment room is immaculate and inspires a calm feeling when your client enters. The couch should be clean and professionally laid out. Hygiene, as mentioned many times, should be your primary concern whatever method you use. Obviously, you also need to perform a treatment which is perfect. Gloves should always be worn, and any disposable components of the treatment should be disposed of in front of your client and at the end of the treatment.

'Removal techniques vary greatly from therapist to therapist, but remember your objective is to remove the hair from the follicle leaving the skin smooth, wax free and with minimal trauma.

'Always cleanse and soothe the skin with a good quality product. Offer aftercare advice every time. The time you forget this will be the one time your client goes out and has a sunbed session, causing potential burning and skin pigmentation problems.

'Advise your clients to use specific products at home, which help repair and condition the skin, which of course you will retail to them.'

Wendy's advice is that, whatever you do, give a 110 per cent as this will reward you in the end. Clients will share an excellent waxing treatment with their friends and family; likewise a bad one is shared too! Consider which testimonial you would rather have.

Assessment of knowledge and understanding

You have now learnt how to conduct hot wax and warm wax treatments. To test your level of knowledge and understanding, answer the following short questions:

Hot wax

1 State the procedure for a test patch and say why it is necessary.

2 Why must the client follow the aftercare procedures?

3 What is the purpose of placing a hand on the treated area immediately after removing a hot wax strip?

4 Why is it important to use skin sanitising products prior to waxing treatments?

5 List three reasons why poor results may occur after waxing treatments.

6 List two advantages of hot wax.

7 List two disadvantages of hot wax.

8 List one specific contra-indication for the following areas:

   a Bikini line;

   b Face.

9 State how the temperature of the wax should be tested prior to application on the client.

10 What can cause the wax to become brittle?

Warm wax

1 Compare and contrast the different applications of warm wax and evaluate their advantages and disadvantages.

2 List the extra precautions to be taken when carrying out Brazilian waxing and state why they are necessary.

3 List four reasons for poor treatment results and say how they can be avoided.

4 List four things a client should avoid following a waxing treatment.

5 Under what circumstances would it be necessary to carry out a patch test?

6 What are the key considerations when planning the timing of a wax treatment?

7 Why is it important to wear disposable gloves for waxing treatment?

8 How often should a roller head be changed?

9 What is the special requirement for treating people under 16 years of age?

10 List two contra-indications and two precautions to waxing on the underarms.

Activities

Conduct the following activities to practise your knowledge of hot wax treatments:

1 Plan a waxing treatment for Mrs Smith who is going on holiday in 6 weeks' time and has never waxed before and has been shaving for the last 10 years.

2 Using diagrams to illustrate, design a waxing treatment area to include the required equipment.

3 Research supply companies and discover the costs of equipment for your hot waxing treatment area.

4 Discover how many of your friends, relatives, neighbours, have had a hot wax hair removal treatment? (Ask only those *not* involved with your course or who have modelled for you or your colleagues.)

5 Draw the body and per area:

a list the contra-indications to hot wax

b in another colour, list the pre-treatment precautions for hot wax.

Conduct the following activities to practise your knowledge of warm wax treatments:

6   Research and visit a trade exhibition to gather information on as many brands of warm wax as possible. Make a list of questions before you go and ask everyone the same set of questions in order to evaluate the market.

7   Suggest ways in which you would improve the ambience of a treatment room.

8   Describe ways of increasing client comfort during treatment.

9   Carry out a risk assessment on a wax treatment area within a local salon or college.

Follow-up knowledge

To build on the knowledge of hot waxing gained in this chapter, complete the following tasks to extend your hair removal skills and understanding:

1   Using a range of trade sources, i.e. beauty therapy suppliers gather information about wax additives and evaluate their treatment benefits.

2   Using search engines on the internet, try and discover if 'home use' hot wax kits are available in shops or via mail order.

To build on the knowledge of warm waxing gained in this chapter, complete the following tasks to extend your hair removal skills and understanding:

1   Investigate the UK home strip waxing market through the internet and consumer press.

2   Investigate postgraduate waxing courses in areas not covered by the National Occupational Standards for Beauty Therapy.

Advanced knowledge reference section

Shaving and its effect on hair growth

We have previously been led to believe that shaving causes hair to grow faster and thicker. Young men are encouraged to start shaving as early as possible because it is believed that it will increase their beard growth. Many beauty therapists and hair removal practitioners are told that shaving will stimulate hair growth and so dissuade their clients from shaving in-between waxing and electrolysis treatments.

The fact is that shaving does not stimulate hair growth. Shaving is merely a form of cutting and we are always advising our clients to cut the hairs with scissors in between treatments. The only difference between cutting with scissors and a razor is that the razor will cut off the hair closer to the skin: neither will stimulate hair growth.

After shaving there is an illusion of an increased speed of growth, because once the hair has been cut off at the level of the skin it only needs to grow 1–2mm before the hair is apparent to the close observer. If the hair is already 2cm long and grows an extra 2mm in the same period of time as the shaved hair, the extra growth would go un-noticed. If we observe a man has a beard it would be difficult, even from day to day, to notice any growth in the beard hair. If, however, a man is clean shaven in the morning, it will be easy to detect even the slightest growth by the end of the day.

Hairs which have been shaved give the appearance of being thicker because the razor leaves a long angled cut at the end of the hair which gives a blunt and thick appearance to the hair shaft, particularly because it is being compared directly against the colour of the skin.

Shaving and cutting affect only the dead hair shaft above the surface of the skin. In order to stimulate hair growth, the follicle itself must be stimulated. Even very vigorous shaving on a daily basis has no effect on the follicle.

In 1928 Dr Mildred Trotter of Washington University School of Medicine carried out a study, by observing three girls who shaved their legs from ankle to knee twice weekly for eight months. A microscopic examination of the shaved hairs revealed that there was no increase in the diameter or colour of the hair after the shaving, providing evidence that shaving does not affect hair growth.

M. Trotter, *Anatomical Record*, December 1928, 37: 373–9

chapter 5

SUGARING

What will I know after reading this chapter?

This chapter covers sugaring treatments. It describes the competencies required to enable you to:

- **consult with the client**
- **plan the treatment**
- **prepare clients for sugaring treatments**
- **treat the client using sugaring techniques**
- **understand the different types of sugar**

INTRODUCTION

Sugaring is one of the oldest methods of removing body and facial hair. It has been practised for thousands of years by generation upon generation of Middle Eastern women.

What is sugaring?

Sugaring is a form of mass plucking. It is a pliable paste made from pure natural ingredients, and can be removed using strips or by hand.

CONSULTATION

As with all hair removal treatments, when providing sugaring treatments you must follow the general consultation advice and processes discussed in Chapter Two. There are also a number of additional consultation processes specific to sugaring which must be followed and they are discussed here.

The client's record card plays a key role in sugaring consultations and you must ensure each stage is completed and entered onto the card. Permanent information is recorded on the front while all current and changeable information (such as treatment progress) should be recorded on the rear of the record card on an ongoing basis.

> **TECHNICAL TIP** ✔
>
> As sugar paste is water-soluble, spillages can easily be removed using warm water. It is also easily wiped from couches, floors and clothing

Sugaring products

JAYGEE'S

Family name:	Date of birth:
First name:	Address:
Home tel:	Doctor's name:
Mobile:	Address:
E-mail:	Tel:

Have you had previous sugaring treatment?: Yes ☐ No ☐

If yes, how many treatments did you have? _____ Over what period? _____

Any skin reactions/allergies? _____

When was your last treatment? _____

On what area do you require treatment?

☐ Eyebrows

☐ Face

☐ Underarm

☐ Forearm

☐ Bikini Line

☐ Legs

☐ Back

☐ Chest

What other temporary measures have you used? _____ Over what period?_____

How often? _____ Have you/Do you use a hair growth inhibitor?: _____

Present condition of skin in area to be treated, to include blemishes etc: _____

Related medical information (conditions which restrict or contra-indicate treatment):

Are you taking medication: Yes ☐ No ☐ If Yes, please specify _____

Patch test carried out Date: _____ Result: _____

I declare that I have answered all the above questions truthfully

Client signature………………………………… Date…………………………………

When conducting your consultation, ask the following questions and enter the responses onto the record card.

What are your name, address and contact details?
It is important that the client is identified with both their first and family names for insurance purposes. It is also important that you can contact a client should you need to change an appointment. For marketing purposes, the client's details are also useful.

What is your date of birth?
This information allows you to establish your client's stage of life and its hormonal influences; it also further identifies the client. Knowing your client's birthday will allow you to send special birthday greetings and/or offers.

What is your doctor's name and address?
This is important information should you wish to discuss any issues regarding the treatment. (The doctor will not discuss any confidential client information with you unless the client has authorised them to do so.)

Have you had previous sugaring treatment?
This will indicate to you the client's prior knowledge, which will enable you to give the appropriate information. You will also need to be aware of any contra-actions from previous treatments, why the client did not continue and the results of the previous treatment.

On what area/s was your previous sugaring treatment?
This question provides a prompt to ensure that you do not make any assumptions about the area of concern but that you find out from the client which area is to be treated.

Are you using any other temporary methods?
This will help to indicate the current stage of hair growth and establish whether you are seeing the full extent of it. The client's answers will also indicate how the other temporary removal methods have stimulated the growth and allow you to describe fully to the client the probable outcome of sugaring treatment.

> **REMEMBER** !
>
> It is important to inform the client that, if there are hairs just under the skin at the time of treatment, they will quickly appear; this is not re-growth but the growth of hairs not long enough for removal at that time

Pre-treatment precautions

Before commencing a sugaring treatment, examine the condition of skin in the area to be treated. Take note of the general skin condition, paying particular attention to the following as they will restrict or require adaptation of the treatment:

- allergic reactions
- bruising
- cuts and abrasions
- eczema and psoriasis
- heat rash
- skin disorders
- sunburn
- warts and moles

> **PROFESSIONAL TIP** ✔
>
> Recording existing blemishes, scars, pigmentation disorders, etc. prior to commencing treatment, will prevent your client, at a later date, wrongly accusing you of causing them

Sugaring removes dead skins cells from the surface of the skin and as a consequence will lighten natural tans and may completely remove some self tans. You must advise your clients of this effect as they may then choose to delay treatment.

Blemishes

Make a particular note on the record card, and point out to your client, any blemishes, for example scars, pigmentation marks and any other imperfections which are currently present on the proposed treatment area. This will prevent any future misunderstanding should your client only notice them at a later date and attribute them to your sugaring treatment.

Contra-indications/Pre-treatment precautions

While completing the record card, ensure you check the client for all of the contra-indications discussed in Chapter Two. There are also a number of contra-indications specific to sugaring that must be checked:

- *Diabetes*: In some texts it is suggested that a diabetic client is contra-indicated to waxing due to reduced skin healing and even loss of sensation. Whilst there are undoubtedly more considerations when treating a diabetic client, the symptoms are generally controlled by diet and or medication. Every one of your clients should be treated with the same care and precautions, that is: keep the heat levels as low as possible to effectively remove the hairs, use a wax suitable for sensitive skin and take great care of the skin prior to, during and after waxing treatment.

- *Medication*: In particular you need to know about any medication which has an affect on the skin, for example steroid creams, which may have caused skin thinning. If the client is unsure of any skin side effects ask them to check with their GP. Many medications effect hormonal balance and are often listed as precautions to sugaring, for example the contraceptive pill or HRT. Whilst this is important when you are permanently removing hair, hormonal medication has no bearing on temporary methods.

- *Hepatitis* (inflammation of the liver): Hepatitis has many causes, two of which are infection by amoeba (bacteria) and viruses. You should be concerned about hepatitis as it is highly infectious. Hepatitis B is of particular risk to HRPs (hair removal practitioners) as it is extremely easy to contract.

- *Heart conditions*: It is important that you are aware of any heart condition as the client may be on blood thinning medication, which could have an impact upon treatment. If bleeding occurs, the blood flow will take longer than normal to stop. As circulation is affected with heart conditions, the client's healing capacity may be impaired.

- *Epilepsy*: Epilepsy does not necessarily contra-indicate treatment. It is important to find out if a client is epileptic for two reasons:

  1 It may contra-indicate treatment if the stimulus is stress or if you think there is a possibility that you could stimulate a seizure (fit).

HEALTH AND SAFETY ✚

It is recommended that all HRPs be inoculated against hepatitis B

2 It is important that you discuss with your client the frequency and stimulus of attacks in addition to the form the attacks take, as you need to be able to recognise that the client has had a seizure, should it occur in the salon. Not all attacks produce violent seizures and clients are often disorientated following an attack. It may be that the disorientation is the first thing that you notice.

Patch test

If your client has known sensitivities (things she/he is sensitive to) and reactions or has never had a sugaring treatment before, it is advisable to carry out a test patch. To do this, you will need to prepare the area to be tested in the same way as for treatment. All the products that will be used during the treatment – skin sanitiser, wax and after-wax solution – should be applied to an area of approximately 2cm^2, as a control area, and the after-effects noted for a minimum of 24 hours.

Apply a small amount of sugaring product and all other pre- and post-treatment products to be used during treatment to an area of the skin, approximately the size of a 2p piece, which can be covered up in the case of an allergic reaction, for example the inside of the forearm. Remove sugaring product and apply post-treatment products in the normal way. Ask the client to leave the test patch area and return to the salon the next day for you to evaluate the reaction.

Client's signature

Ensure that the client signs and dates the record card to confirm that they have answered all the questions truthfully. In the case of minors, this card must be signed by a parent or guardian.

HEALTH AND SAFETY ✚

Even though a patch test is small, the usual pre- and post-treatment procedures for Health and Safety must be carried out, i.e. wearing PPE

Reverse of Rrecord card

Date	Area	Sugaring method & type	Treatment reactions	Therapist comment & signature	Client signature

Monitoring ongoing treatment

The rear of the card is where details of individual treatments should be recorded.

The following information is recorded in these columns:

- *Date*: To track treatments and ensure the client is receiving regular treatment.
- *Area*: Should another HRP treat your client, they can see which area has been treated. Also records any new areas treated.
- *Sugaring method and type*: For reference and in case of subsequent treatment adjustments, you should record which method of sugaring was used. Also record the type of sugaring product, i.e. sugaring paste, strip sugar, etc.
- *Treatment reactions*: Allows you to record any treatment reactions, good or bad, which will influence your choice of sugaring method and type for subsequent treatments.
- *Therapist comment and signature*: Allows you to record any additional comments on the treatment and the HRP's signature makes it clear exactly who has carried out which treatments.
- *Client signature*: Confirms that the recorded details are correct.

Equipment and materials

As with waxing, you will require the basic equipment of a couch and trolley and these are discussed in greater detail in Chapter Four.

You will also require a standard wax heater to heat the sugar paste; these are available in a variety of different colours, shapes and sizes. Which type of heater is best is often a matter of personal choice; however, they should all:

- be thermostatically controlled
- meet all health and safety requirements and be in good working order
- be wipeable with disinfectant between treatments
- have a lid to keep out airborne particles.

You will also require standard sugaring products which you can buy individually or in the starter kits which most suppliers offer, and which can often be cheaper. However you buy, you must make sure you have the following items as well as the actual sugaring products:

- plastic bed sheet
- gloves
- sanitised wipes
- small bowl
- fabric or paper strip
- powder
- application tool of choice, i.e. spatula

EQUIPMENT LIST

couch
trolley
wax heater
plastic bed sheet
gloves
sanitised wipes
small bowl
fabric or paper strip
powder
application tool
post-treatment soothing lotion
pedal bin with lid
equipment cleaner
clean towels

- post-treatment soothing lotion, oil, gel or cream
- pedal bin with lid – double lined (i.e. with two bin liners)
- equipment cleaner
- clean towels.

PREPARATION OF TREATMENT AREA

TECHNICAL TIP ✔

Sugar paste gets hot very quickly

The preparation required for sugaring is identical to waxing and the steps outlined in Chapter Four should be followed.

In addition, you need to prepare the sugar paste prior to treatment. Sugar paste is heated in a standard thermostatically controlled waxing heater. Place the pot in the heater with the lid on, for 10–20 minutes on a medium setting. You will find that the heater heats the outside of the sugar paste first, leaving the middle still hard. At this point, turn the heater to low as the outer sugar helps to melt the inner sugar. This way it will all reach the correct temperature while avoiding the risk of heating it too much.

Preparation of the therapist

In the same way as when providing waxing treatments, the therapist must present a professional, clean appearance at all times and this is discussed in more detail in Chapter Four.

Treatment preparation

1 Carry out a thorough consultation and note any contra-indications.
2 Turn on the heater – allow sufficient time for the sugaring paste or strip-sugar to heat up and reach the correct temperature/consistency before the client arrives.
3 Prepare the trolley – make sure that all the items needed for the treatment are available.
4 Prepare and protect the couch; use a plastic bed sheet followed by a soft protective paper sheet for the client to rest on.
5 Position the sugar paste; place the heater a safe distance from the client, but near enough to the couch to avoid spillage.
6 Position the client on the couch.
7 Examine the hair and skin in a good light. Note any contra-indications, if present, and also the patterns of hair growth. The record card should be filled in at this stage if it is a new client and any relevant changes noted down for a returning client.
8 Prepare yourself by putting on PPE: disposable gloves (latex or vinyl) and a disposable apron.
9 Prepare the skin by wiping the area to be treated with a sanitiser or pre-treatment wipe, blot dry and sprinkle with powder. Excessively long hairs should be trimmed with scissors that have been disinfected as this will reduce discomfort during the hair removal.

TECHNICAL TIP ✔

Some sugaring experts do not use generic waxing preparation products they prefer to use specific 'sugar wipes' to prepare the skin.

10 Adviseall damp the client about the treatment by explaining what you are going to do, how it will feel and the possible skin reactions.

11 A sm towel or a bowl of water should be on hand to use in case your hand becomes sticky.

TREATMENT APPLICATION

Strip-sugar – method of application on lower legs

Step One: Prepare the skin with antiseptic or a sanitising pre-treatment wipe to ensure the area is free from oils and debris.

Step Two: Powder the area to be treated thoroughly; this is most important because if the hair is not completely dry, it may be difficult to remove.

Step Three: Hold the spatula at a 45° angle. With paste on one side only, spread a very thin layer of strip-sugar in the direction of hair growth covering the front of both legs, as much as you can reach, before using the fabric or paper strip to remove.

Step Four: Apply a fabric or paper strip to the 'sugar' and press firmly up and down the strip two or three times, then holding the skin taut, with a short sharp swing remove the strip against the direction of the hair growth and parallel to the skin (removing the strip parallel to the skin is not of such vital importance with sugaring).

Step Five: If any hairs remain, apply the sugar paste strip against the growth and remove it with or against the direction of growth.

Step Six: Complete the treatment with an application of antiseptic and soothing products – lotion, gel or wipe.

> **PROFESSIONAL TIP**
>
> Experts in the field of sugaring say that one of the great advantages of sugaring is that you can remove hair with or against the direction of growth

Step 1: Preparing the area to be treated

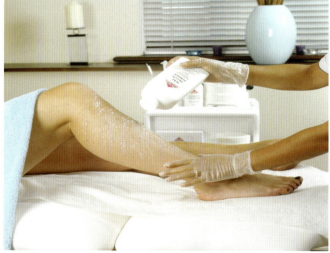

Step 2: Applying powder

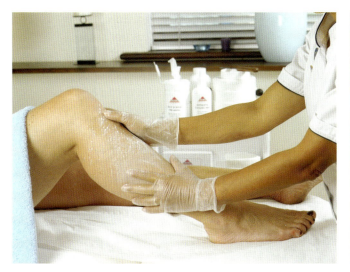

Step 2: Rub in powder

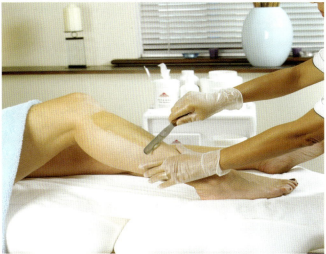

Step 3: Applying sugar wax with spatula

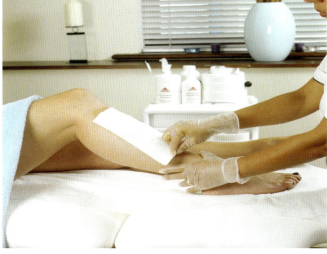

Step 4: Applying strip leaving a small 'grip' area

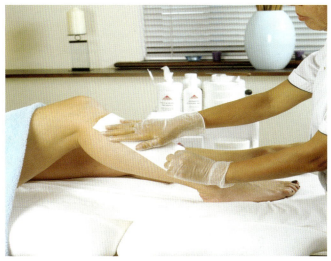

Step 4: Firmly smoothing strip onto wax

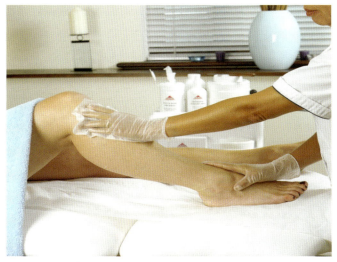

Step 6: Applying antiseptic products

Hand removal method – method of application

It takes longer to become proficient in the hand method of sugaring, and arguably requires more skill. It is a totally different method of application and removal to the sugar strip method, which is just like waxing.

Step One: Prepare the skin with antiseptic or a pre-wipe to ensure the area is free from oils and debris.

Step Two: Powder the area to be treated thoroughly – this is most important because if the hair is not completely dry, it may be difficult to remove.

Step Three: Position yourself at the couch, depending upon the area you are going to treat; make sure your back is always straight. Stand on the right hand side of the client unless you are left handed, in which case you will stand on the left.

Step Four: Remove the required amount of paste. If required, adjust the paste texture (see page 170).

Step Five: Apply hand sugar to the area in a firm downward stroking movement and rub it into the skin.

Step Six: Support the skin to keep it taut, then swing the paste away from you.

Step Seven: Press the area after immediately removal, with the supporting hand, to reduce any stinging.

Step Eight: Apply antiseptic and soothing products to the area.

Step Nine: Remove gloves and apron and dispose of in double lined bin.

Step Ten: Give the client before and after treatment leaflets and explain the aftercare procedure.

Step Eleven: Clean the couch, surfaces and all the product containers with an antiseptic solution and dispose of any waste.

Step Twelve: Ensure the treatment room is clean and tidy, ready for the next client.

TECHNICAL TIP ✔

Keep your client warm. If your client becomes cold, the hair follicle will tighten around the hair, making the treatment more uncomfortable and the hair difficult to remove

---

TECHNICAL TIP ✔

If the hair is difficult to remove, massage the paste two to three times on the skin, making sure to pull back one to two centimetres, release the pressure and then swing

---

Step 1: Preparing the area to be treated

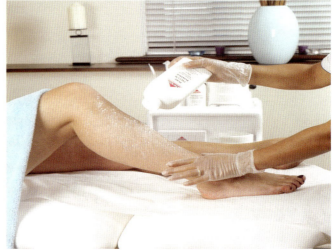

Step 2: Applying powder

Step 2: Rubbing in powder

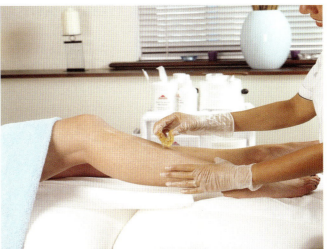

Step 5: Applying sugar paste

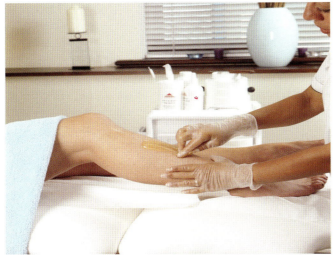

Step 5: Rubbing in the sugar paste

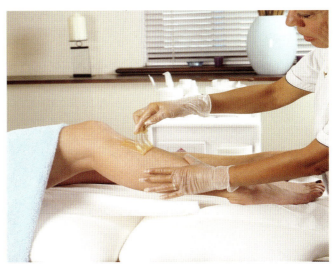

Step 6: Removing the sugar paste

Step 8: Applying antiseptic products

Different ways to swing the paste

1 The fingers can be used to spread the paste, then swing. This method can be used on most parts of the body.

2 The thumb can be used flat, spreading the paste to the folded fingers. This way is mainly used on the thighs and part of the bikini line. This method can also be used on the underarm and, when treating short hair, going with the direction of the hair growth.

These different methods will help you to stand in one position, treating most of the areas by adjusting your wrist. Decide on the best way to remove the paste with full control, without wasting time moving round the couch.

Sugaring paste texture

There are a variety of sugar paste textures, and they all have an effect on the treatment. Being aware of the differences and how to change them is an important part of being a sugaring HRP.

Soft and pliable

Soft, pliable and easy to spread, the softer the paste, the less pressure you apply to the client's skin. The paste will also be more efficient and effective as it sticks to the hair and removes it easily and cleanly.

Too hard

Needs a lot of pressure and is hard to spread. It does not stick to, or remove, the hair and is slower to work with. It can cause bruising and be more painful for clients.

Too soft

Is hard to handle as it sticks to the skin and is difficult to remove.

How to adjust the paste to make it softer

Use strip-sugar paste; apply a small amount of runny strip-sugar to the paste and mix it together between the fingers. Never use too much paste, as it will need more adjusting – a golf ball sized piece is enough to treat half a leg from ankle to knee.

How to harden the paste

If it becomes too soft while using or too difficult to use, throw half of it away and add another small new piece to it as this will harden the paste.

PRACTITIONER PROFILE

Name: Nagwa Stanforth

Bussiness name: Sukar

Nagwa Stanforth started the Sukar business in 1989, but was brought up with sugaring as a child, so for her it was a natural step to take. She was 'trained' at home as a child as she watched her mother and grandmother do sugaring at home. Nagwa brought the idea to the UK from Egypt. As well as having a nursing degree and working in a top hospital in Saudi Arabia, she is an expert in her practice of the sugaring method.

What prompted Nagwa to go into the sugaring business was that on her return to the UK after ten years working in Saudia Arabia as a staff nurse she, and her husband Roger, bought a salon which concentrated mainly on hairdressing and had a staff of fifteen. Nagwa decided she would also carry out hair removal treatments alongside the British professionals and assumed that the waxing products on the market in Britain would be sugar based like the ones she made in Egypt. Nagwa purchased some product (wax) and, in her wisdom, put some in her mouth to taste it – but, not being sugar as she thought, it stuck to her teeth for days!

Nagwa began to make the sugar paste herself and started to offer sugar treatment to her clients. From day one clients loved it – this is how the business 'Sukar' started. (The word *sukar* originates from the Arabic name for sugar which is the base material in the preparation of this product.) Success came quickly, following their first visit to an exhibition in London, after which Peggy Slight from the *LNE* magazine (now *Professional Beauty*) wrote about Sukar. Soon after this, the company started to train people in the UK and then overseas. Sukar is now a well-established company with a highly respected brand of sugaring products.

Nagwa believes that sugaring is kinder to your skin as it only sticks to the hair – not the skin – and she applies it warm, not hot like most waxes. Nagwa believes that sugar has medicinal properties – in fact sugar is used to treat ulcers in hospitals and during the war sugar was used to treat wounds. Sugar has wonderful healing properties as well as being an excellent exfoliator to remove dead skin cells.

Nagwa has travelled widely, demonstrating sugaring, training and promoting its use in the USA, Canada, Russia, Spain, Portugal and Holland, and in Malta she has appeared on radio and TV.

Nagwa has trained many people who have gone on to start up their own businesses. For example, 'Martyn' in London, at the Sugar Shop, looks after male clients in London and has a thriving business.

Assessment of knowledge and understanding

You have now learnt how to conduct sugaring treatments. To test your level of knowledge and understanding, answer the following short questions:

1 Compare and contrast the two different methods of sugaring.

2 Which method would use the most product: strip or hand?

3 Why is it important to make note of any skin blemishes on the client's record card?

4 State the disadvantages of the sugar paste being too soft.

5 Why should talcum powder be used in sugaring treatments?

6 Using Nagwa Stanforth's biography as inspiration, what ways could you or your salon promote sugaring treatments?

7 List two different ways you may 'swing' the paste when using hand sugar.

8 Why is it important to keep the client warm during treatment?

9 How can accidentally spilled sugar paste be removed?

10 Why is it important for the client to sign the record card?

Activities

Conduct the following activities to expand and practise your knowledge of sugaring treatments:

1 Research the history of sugaring.

2 Using your local Yellow Pages, evaluate the proportion of beauty salons advertising sugaring compared to those advertising waxing and produce a chart to illustrate your results.

3 Contact beauty salons to determine which method of sugaring costs more: strip or hand.

Follow up knowledge

To build on the knowledge of sugaring gained in this chapter, complete the following tasks to extend your hair removal skills and understanding:

1 Using the internet and any applicable trade press, research Middle Eastern hair removal treatments and see if you can find any 'recipes' for sugaring.

2 Using the internet, search for the earliest mention of hair removal by sugaring.

Advanced knowledge reference section

Skin cancer

Skin cancer is one of the most common cancers in the UK and the number of people who develop it is increasing. The first visible signs of skin cancer are usually a change in the normal appearance, or feel, of a mole, or a new and unusual skin growth. As an HRP who may see a client regularly, you are in a good position to notice any unusual mole changes or skin growths, particularly those which the client cannot easily observe, for example on the back or back of the legs. Early detection is the key to survival. For this reason it is very important that you are aware of the signs to look for and the best way to tactfully make your client aware of any changes or warning signs that you have noticed.

It is vital to remember that you are not medically qualified to give a diagnosis. However, as an HRP, you have an important role to play in early detection. Always advise your client to seek a medical opinion.

Skin cancer facts

Skin cancer is caused by ultra violet (UV) radiation from the sun. The greater the exposure, the higher the risk. Most skin cancers could be prevented by protecting the skin from excessive exposure to the sun's damaging rays.

What causes skin cancer?

Skin cancer develops when genes in skin cells are damaged by UV radiation. Most skin cancers are the result of excessive exposure to the sun. Many are caused by sun damage in childhood.

Who is most at risk?

People with fair skin that tends to burn or freckle, red or fair hair, or pale eyes are at higher risk. People with black, brown and darker olive complexions have a lower risk of skin cancer.

What are the different types?

There are two main types of skin cancer: malignant melanoma and non-melanoma skin cancer.

Malignant melanoma (also known as melanoma) is the most serious type of skin cancer. It usually develops in cells in the outer layer of the skin but can spread to other parts of the body and may be fatal. It is vital to detect and treat it early. Melanoma can affect young adults as well as older people. It is the second most common cancer in 15–39 year olds.

Signs of melanoma

Alert your client tactfully and advise them to see a doctor immediately if:

- an existing mole or dark patch is getting larger or a new one is growing.

- a mole has a ragged outline (ordinary moles are smooth and regular)

- a mole has a mixture of different shades of brown and black (ordinary moles may be dark brown but are all one shade)

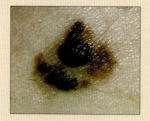

Growing melanoma

Melanoma with an irregular outline

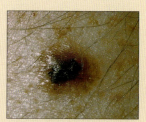

Melanoma with irregular colour shape

The following signs do not necessarily mean that your client has a melanoma, but you should still alert them and advise that they keep an eye on them. If the mole or dark patch does not return to normal within two weeks, they should not ignore it – they should see their doctor as soon as possible, especially if they have:

- an inflamed mole or one with a reddish edge

- a mole that starts to bleed, ooze or crust

- a change in sensation of a mole, like a mild itch

- a mole that is bigger than all their other moles.

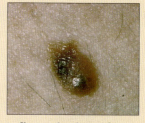

Inflamed edge of a mole melanoma

Non-melanoma skin cancer is the most common and easily treated type of cancer, although treatment can leave scarring. More than nine out of ten skin cancers are of this type. There are over 62,000 new cases registered each year in the UK. There are two main sorts:

- Basal cell cancer is the most common and tends to affect older people. It grows quite slowly and usually starts as a small round or flattened lump that is red, pale or pearly in colour. Sometimes it appears as a scaly, eczema-like patch on the skin. Basal cell cancers usually occur on areas of skin most exposed to the sun such as the head, neck, shoulders and limbs.

Basal cell cancer, showing pearly edge

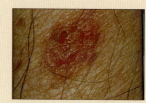

Basal cell cancer, superficial

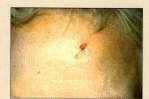

Basal cell cancer, infiltrative

- Squamous cell cancer is more serious than basal cell cancer as it can spread to other parts of the body if left untreated. Squamous cell cancers appear as persistent red scaly spots, lumps, sores or ulcers, which may bleed easily. They also tend to affect older people and occur most often on the head, neck, hands and forearms.

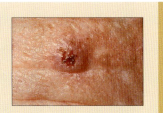

Squamos cell cancer, early ulceration

Signs of non-melanoma skin cancer:

- a new growth or sore that does not heal within four weeks

- a spot or sore that continues to itch, hurt, crust, scab or bleed

- persistent skin ulcers that are not explained by other causes.

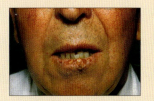

Squamous cell cancer, perilesimal keratoses

For more information see Cancer Research UK's SunSmart website: www.sunsmart.org.uk

skin cancer

How to be sunsmart

...and reduce your risk

CANCER RESEARCH UK

Skin cancer facts

Skin cancer is the most common cancer in the UK and the number of people who get it is increasing. Skin cancer is caused by UV radiation from the sun. The greater your exposure, the higher your risk. Most skin cancers could be prevented by protecting ourselves from the sun's damaging rays.

This leaflet contains information about different types of skin cancer and how you can guard against them.

What causes skin cancer?

Skin cancer develops when genes in skin cells are damaged by ultraviolet radiation. Most skin cancers are the result of excessive exposure to the sun. Many are caused by sun damage in childhood.

Who is most at risk?

People with fair skin that tends to burn or freckle, red or fair hair, or pale eyes are at higher risk. People with black, brown and darker olive complexions have a lower risk of skin cancer.

What are the different types?

There are two main types of skin cancer, malignant melanoma and non-melanoma skin cancer.

Malignant melanoma (also known as melanoma) is the most serious type of skin cancer. It usually develops in cells in the outer layer of the skin but can spread to other parts of the body and may be fatal. It is vital to detect and treat it early. Melanoma can affect young adults as well as older people. It is the third most common cancer in 15-39 year-olds. You can find out much more about it in our leaflet 'Malignant melanoma – be a molewatcher for life'.

Signs of melanoma

See your doctor immediately if...
- an existing mole or dark patch is getting larger or a new one is growing
- a mole has a ragged outline (ordinary moles are smooth and regular)
- a mole has a mixture of different shades of brown and black (ordinary moles may be dark brown but are all one shade)

The following signs do not necessarily mean that you have a melanoma, but you should still look out for them. If your mole or dark patch does not return to normal within two weeks, don't ignore it – see your doctor.
- an inflamed mole or one with a reddish edge
- a mole that starts to bleed, ooze or crust
- a change in sensation of a mole, like a mild itch
- a mole that is bigger than all your other moles

Cancer Research UK leaflet

Reprinted by kind permission of Cancer Research UK

PROFESSIONAL TIP ✔

If you notice a mole or unusual skin growth which you believe is not normal, calmly ask your client if they aware of it and, without causing alarm, tell them that it is salon policy to advise everyone to get a doctor's advice on this type of mole or growth

THREADING

This chapter covers how to provide threading treatments. It describes the competencies required to enable you to:

- **consult with the client**
- **plan the treatment**
- **prepare clients for threading treatments**
- **treat the client using threading techniques.**

INTRODUCTION

KEY TERMS ⭐

Threading: Hair removal method using strands of thread
Folliculitis: A bacterial infection in the hair follicle

Threading has been around for centuries and has been a common technique for temporary hair removal in Asia and the Far East, although it is now also gaining popularity in the West. It is typically used on facial areas – the upper lip, chin and eyebrows – rather than on larger areas such as the legs. Threading can be carried out in a salon as a professional treatment but it can also be used by the client herself, on herself, at home. It is a useful technique that give clean lines and good shape to the eyebrows and also removes hair from the upper lip and other facial areas.

The difference between threading and waxing or sugaring is that the hair is removed without any product coming into contact with the skin. Therefore there is no trauma. However gentle a wax or sugar paste formulation is, however good the quality of the ingredients, however well applied and removed, there is no getting away from the fact that threading does not interfere with the surrounding skin in any way. Clients with sensitive skin may therefore prefer to go to an HRP who offers this technique.

What is threading?

The thread used can be cotton or nylon or a combination of the two. The most commonly used is 100 per cent cotton thread which is twisted and rolled along the surface of the skin, entwining the hair which is then lifted out from the follicle.

As this is primarily a home hair removal technique, there are a variety of applications and techniques which have been passed down through families for generations and, therefore, there is no standardised method. However, the methods discussed here represent the most popular techniques.

Advantages	Disadvantages
✓ Inexpensive compared to other plucking methods. Other than the thread, the only costs are before- and aftercare products.	✗ Threading is a very skilled process for which, at present, there is no formal training available. The skill is something which is passed down from generation to generation and learned from an early age predominantly within the Asian community.
✓ Quick procedure, since many hairs are removed by a single pass of the thread.	✗ Hair removal is not selective and therefore there is often stimulation to vellus growth.
✓ Very well tolerated by sensitive and reactive skins; irritation and skin rashes are rare because no potentially irritating substances are used. The outer layer of dead skin is not stripped off in the treatment process.	✗ Inexperienced practitioners can easily snap of the hairs at the surface of the skin giving poor treatment results and increasing the potential for hairs to become ingrown.
✓ As the treatment is so rapid, it's considered less painful than tweezing.	✗ The mass plucking of hairs can cause irritation and itching.
✓ Good results are achieved for eyebrows and facial hair as the thread quickly catches all the hairs leaving a particularly smooth and neat result.	
✓ Results can last up to two to four weeks.	
✓ Threading can be carried out more frequently than other methods because the hair can be grasped by the thread when it is very short.	

CONSULTATION

As with all hair removal treatments, when providing threading treatments you must follow the general consultation advice and processes discussed in Chapter Two. There are also a number of additional consultation processes specific to threading which must be followed and they are discussed here.

The client's record card plays a key role in threading consultations and you must ensure each stage is completed and entered onto the card. Permanent information is recorded on the front while all current and changeable information (such as treatment progress) should be recorded on the rear of the record card on an on-going basis.

Test patch

It is not always necessary to carry out patch testing prior to a threading treatment as there are very few products used. It is, however, advisable to test the before- and aftercare products you will be using if your client has

Threading Record Card

JAYGEE'S	

Family name:	Date of birth:
First name:	Address:
Home tel:	Doctor's name:
Mobile:	Address:
E-mail:	Tel:

Have you had previous hair removal treatment?: Yes ☐ No ☐

If yes, how many treatments did you have? _____ Over what period? _____

Any skin reactions? _____

When was your last treatment? _____

On what area do you require treatment? _____

☐ Eyebrows

☐ Face

☐ Other

What other temporary measures have you used? _____ Over what period of time?_____

How often? _____ Have you/Do you use a hair growth inhibitor?: _____

Present condition of skin in area to be treated, to include blemishes etc: _____

Related medical information: (conditions which restrict or contra-indicate treatment):

Are you taking medication: Yes ☐ No ☐ If Yes, please specify _____

Patch test carried out Date: _____ Result: _____

I declare that I have answered all the above questions truthfully

Client signature…………………………………… Date…………………………………

known sensitivities (things she/he is sensitive to) and reactions or has never had a previous salon treatment.

All products that will be used during the treatment, – skin sanitiser and soothing aftercare products – should be applied to an area of approximately 2cm², as a control area, and the after effects noted for a minimum of 24 hours. Should no adverse reaction be seen, a full treatment can take place.

Contra-indications

The contra-indications to threading are identical to those for waxing and sugaring. Because threading does not use any product, it may be considered a more suitable treatment for clients with reactive skin.

However, the mass plucking effect from threading can cause the following adverse reactions:

- folliculitis, a bacterial infection in the hair follicle
- excessive skin reddening or puffiness
- in-growing hairs
- changes in skin pigment due to constant plucking of the hairs and trauma to the area.

Equipment and materials

As with waxing, you will require the basic equipment of a couch and trolley and these are discussed in more detail in Chapter Four.

You will also require the following items for a threading treatment:

- skin sanitiser
- cotton wool/tissues in a container with lid
- powder
- thread
- eyebrow brush
- sanitised scissors
- aftercare soothing lotion, oil, gel or cream
- pedal bin with lid – double lined (i.e. with two bin liners)
- clean towels
- disposable gloves (latex or vinyl).

EQUIPMENT LIST
couch
trolley
skin sanitiser
cotton wool/tissues
powder
thread
eyebrow brush
sanitised scissors
aftercare soothing lotion
pedal bin with lid
clean towels
disposable gloves

It is important to wear disposable gloves (latex or vinyl) when carrying out a threading treatment, because the removed hairs may have body fluid on them. During the threading process, the hairs will fly randomly about and could easily attach themselves to your hands and pose a potential cross infection and contamination risk.

Preparation of the therapist

As with waxing treatments, the therapist must present a professional, clean appearance at all times and this is discussed in more detail in Chapter Four.

Treatment preparation

Treatment preparation is an important part of treatment and should be carried out thoroughly. The following will guide you through a typical preparation procedure of yourself and the treatment area prior to conducting a threading treatment:

1 Always confirm the exact area for treatment and discuss carefully with the client the results they wish to achieve.

2 If the client has had a previous treatment with you, before preparing the client and commencing treatment, the client's record card must be retrieved from its confidential and secure storage facility and be on hand in the treatment room.

3 Accompany the client into the treatment room and assist and/or direct the client with the removal of any necessary garments and, if required, help on to the couch.

4 Ascertain from the client any changes which may affect the treatment and its outcomes, using your record card as a point of reference. This should include any reactions or feedback from the last treatment, any changes in medication and health, stress related issues (i.e. work or personal).

5 Once you and your client are happy to continue, prepare the client for treatment.

6 For eyebrow treatment, discuss with and advise the client on the shape they wish to achieve – for more information on eyebrow shaping see page 138. Once the desired eyebrow shape has been agreed with your client, prepare the area for treatment.

7 Ask the client to hold their skin taught during the threading, one of the client's hands should be at the top of the brow and the other over the eye and they should then pull gently apart, if the skin is not properly stretched and taught the thread can cut the skin.

8 Sanitise your hands.

9 Put on single use disposable gloves.

> **TECHNICAL TIP** ✔
>
> When threading the eyebrows, they should be prepared by brushing with an eyebrow brush to ensure the hairs are lying flat and prevent the inadvertent removal of hairs which form the brow. Any long hairs in the brow should be cut with scissors to prevent them being caught in the thread

TREATMENT APPLICATION

The general procedure for a threading treatment is as follows.

1 After completing the preparation steps above, apply skin sanitising product to clean cotton wool and wipe over the area to be treated, in order to sanitise the area and remove any oils or cosmetic products on the skin.

2 Blot treatment area dry with clean tissue.

3 Dispose of cotton wool and tissue in pedal bin (double lined).

4 Apply a light dusting of powder to the area; this will help the thread to slip over the skin.

5 Prepare the thread by looping and twisting into position.

6 Remove the hairs by pulling the loop taught against the direction of growth so that it grasps a number of hairs and provides a multi-plucking effect with the tightened loop. The thread can be used in either two hands, or with one hand and the teeth as described below.

7 Clear the area of hairs in a methodical manner making sure that all hairs are removed.

8 Clear away any removed hairs which are lying on the client's skin with a clean cotton wool pad and dispose of them in a double lined pedal bin.

9 Apply soothing aftercare lotions – oil, gel or cream – to the treated area, blot off any excess with a tissue and dispose of in a double lined pedal bin. Assist the client off the couch and advise on home-care.

ALTERNATIVE THREADING TECHNIQUES

There is no standardised technique for threading and these three techniques are derived from the main technique outlined above.

Technique A

The HRP holds one end of the thread in between their teeth, the other end is placed in either their left or right hand, and the centre of the length of thread is passed through the index and middle fingers of the opposite hand and twisted to form a loop. The free end of the length of thread is then used to pull the loop taut to enable the HRP to grasp a number of hairs and provide a multi-plucking effect with the tightened loop.

Technique B: Teeth threading method

Step One: Preparation of eyebrow area with antiseptic products.

Step Two: Application of powder.

Step Three: Client holds eyebrow area skin taut.

Step Four: Threading applied to the eyebrow area.

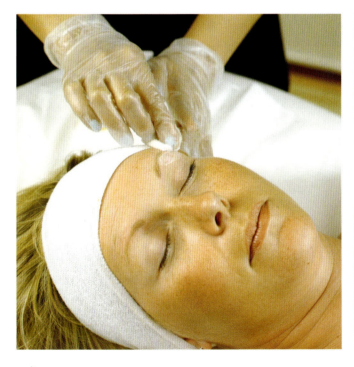

Step 1: Preparing the eyebrow area with antiseptic products

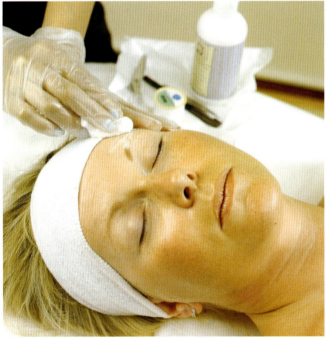

Step 2: Applying powder

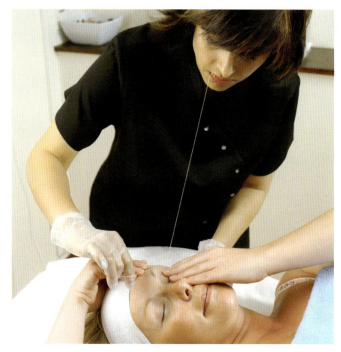

Step 3: Client holding eyebrow area skin taut

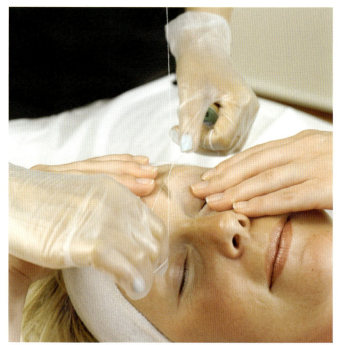

Step 4: Hair is removed

Technique C: Hand only threading method

A piece of thread is tied into a circle and then wrapped around two fingers on both hands (similar to the 'cats cradle' game). The thread is then twisted in such a way that it can be alternately pulled and twisted in opposite directions along the skin using the twist to catch and pull out the hairs. This method is more commonly used when removing your own hair.

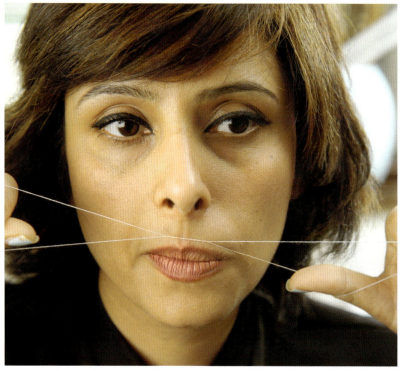

Hand-only method, self-application

JAYGEE'S

Threading home-care

Please read these home-care notes carefully and follow our recommendations. We have taken great care to protect you from infection and in addition, to our normal salon routine, we have applied a soothing antiseptic lotion after your treatment. It is important for you to take extra care of the treated area, especially within the first 2–4 hours. When a large number of hairs have been removed, the area could be prone to infection if not cared for properly.

PLEASE NOTE: If you experience persistent redness or discomfort, contact your hair removal practitioner.

The threading process uses no heat or products and so there are fewer after-effects than for many other hair removal methods. It is, however, advisable to avoid the following for 2–4 hours after treatment:

- perfumed body lotion or creams
- following facial treatment, avoid any application of make-up
- sunbathing and sunbed treatments
- very hot baths
- following body area treatment, avoid friction from tight clothing
- following underarm treatment, avoid deodorants and anti-perspirants.

We recommend that you use a soothing antiseptic lotion daily for 3–4 days after treatment, which should be purchased from your hair removal practitioner.

PRACTITIONER PROFILE

Name: Neenu Batra

Occupation: Beauty therapist

Region: Middlesex

Neenu Batra is an ITEC qualified beauty therapist who also holds professional qualifications in facial electricals and who specialises in model and bridal make-up. She is originally from India where she learnt the art of threading at a young age. This art was passed on to her by her mother.

Neenu's salon is in Wembley, Middlesex, where she runs a hairdressing and beauty salon business with over 3,000 square feet of space. To Neenu the advantage of having both a hair and beauty salon is that clients who come for either service often ask for the other one and also ask for threading to be carried out as an additional treatment.

Neenu always had a passion for making people look and feel beautiful and thus, after having her second child, decided to embark on professional courses with the aim of eventually setting up her own business. In 2001, she established her business which is now enjoying a favourable reputation in the area.

Threading can be performed on any age group – from young teenagers who are conscious of early facial hair to the elderly who want to stay looking hair-free and young. The attraction of this treatment is that there are no side effects. Neenu finds her clientele is 70 per cent from an Asian background and 30 per cent from other ethnic groups.

Neenu has discovered that introducing threading to non-Asian clientele is fascinating for most of them, who find it a new and refreshing experience. When a client sees the results after threading, they are truly exhilarated and can't wait to tell their friends. She has started to cater for the gay community and also many overseas visitors who go back to their home countries with their minds buzzing. Some clients from Paris and Rome have indicated that this phenomenon will take off in their countries.

As well as performing threading Neenu's salon offers other hair removal treatments, ranging from electrolysis using the Apilus computerised epilator to waxing. There are occasions after waxing when some resistant hair has to be removed by threading.

Threading charges range from £5 for a basic eyebrow shaping (both brows) to £30 for a full face threading. The salon at present conducts about 100 threading treatments a week on average, although this figure is rising due to interest from non-Asian clients.

Neenu is now considering offering threading courses in her salon to groups of five people over two days. Neenu's ambition is to create a threading phenomenon throughout the world by opening academies in beauty colleges and then moving this to the commercial world in the form of 'threading bars' which could open in high street shopping centres.

'Threading is a quick, economical and profitable procedure with no equipment or product costs and the results are very pleasing.'

Assessment of knowledge and understanding

You have now learnt how to conduct threading treatments. To test your level of knowledge and understanding, answer the following short questions:

1 What are the benefits of threading over sugaring and waxing?

2 Why is it important to make note of any skin blemishes on the client's record card?

3 What are the two methods of threading?

4 Compare and contrast the three methods of mass plucking.

5 Why is it important to wear disposable gloves when carrying out a threading treatment on a client?

6 List two disadvantages of threading.

7 Why is it important to brush and cut some hairs prior to threading the eyebrows?

8 What areas are most suitable for hair removal by threading?

9 What types of thread should be used for hair removal?

10 List two things which should be avoided by a client following a threading treatment.

Activity

Conduct the following activity to practise your knowledge of threading treatments:

1 In a group, try and make a threading loop and then see if your fingers can create the movement necessary to cause a tweezing action.

Follow up knowledge

To build on the knowledge of threading gained in this chapter, complete the following task to extend your hair removal skills and understanding:

1 Visit the following websites on threading as well as finding your own, to gain further insight into this ancient art of hair removal www. lucidbeauty.com/threading, www.threadingstudio.com

Advanced knowledge reference section

Alternative hair removal products

It is important that, as an HRP, you are aware of all the products which come on to the market. Always keep an open mind and study new products and methods carefully before making a judgement from an educated view point. Try to avoid the 'It will never work' attitude and bear in mind that, as Darwin said, 'It is not the strongest who survive but the most adaptable'.

Hair growth inhibitors

There are a number of these products on the market. They come in many forms – gels, creams and ampoules, etc. – and are usually recommended for use after waxing or other forms of hair removal. The theory behind them is that their active constituent, which is normally an enzyme, enters the follicle once the hair has been removed; the enzyme then retards or restricts new hair growth. Currently the only product of this type which has substantiated its claims is Vaniqa.

Vaniqa

Vaniqa eflornithine 13.9 per cent cream is a prescription cream applied to the skin for the reduction of unwanted facial hair. It is currently only available on prescription.

The cream is not a depilatory, but promising results show that it appears to retard hair growth in some women. Clients need to continue using their usual hair removal method in conjunction with Vaniqa. It will usually take two months of treatment before a result is evident. Vaniqa does not work for everyone.

Vaniqa slows down the rate of hair growth and is effective in up to 70 per cent of cases.[1] It is a topical cream, which is non-hormonal. The active ingredient in Vaniqa is eflornithine hydrochloride, which inhibits an enzyme that affects hair growth, called ornithine decarboxylase (ODC). Clinical data indicates that taking an oral version of the drug can affect hair growth.

[1]Schrode, K. *et al*. 'Randomised, double-blind, vehicle-controlled safety and efficacy evaluation of eflornithine 15 per cent cream in the treatment of women with excessive facial hair.' Presented at 58th Annual Meeting of the Academy of Dermatology 200, 10–15 March. San Francisco, USA, Abstract 291.

Transdermal electrolysis and electric tweezers (non-invasive electrolysis)

In both these methods it is claimed that electricity and in some cases soundwaves are conducted by the hair into the hair follicle to damage the follicle and cause permanent hair removal.

Transdermal methods are often promoted as non-invasive electrolysis. The methods use either a cotton bud or sometimes a conductive plate over a conductive gel on the skin. A current is passed through the plate or cotton bud which the manufacturers claim is attracted to the hair shaft via the gel and conducted by the hair shaft to the follicle where it damages the hair follicle. The tweezer method utilises tweezers that are connected to an electrical current, either high frequency or direct current. The hair is then held with the tweezers above the skin's surface and the current passed for several seconds. The manufacturers claim that the electricity travels down the hair and permanently damages the hair follicle.

These methods were heavily promoted during the 1980s. Some practitioners believed that the methods actually worked and unwittingly took money from clients for ineffective treatments.

The fact is that hair is a very poor conductor of electricity. Skin and the conductive gel are good conductors. Because electricity always follows the path of least resistance, any current passed on to the skin and gel will travel across that gel and skin – it will not pass down the hair. Even if we could use enough current in this way for some of it to pass down the hair shaft, the damage to the surface of the skin would be significant. The same is true of the tweezer method – because the hair is such a poor conductor, it is highly unlikely to pass sufficient current to have any effect on the hair follicle.

None of the claims for permanent hair removal have been substantiated or have any published clinical proof of their claims and none of the methods have FDA (Federal Drug Administration of USA) approval.

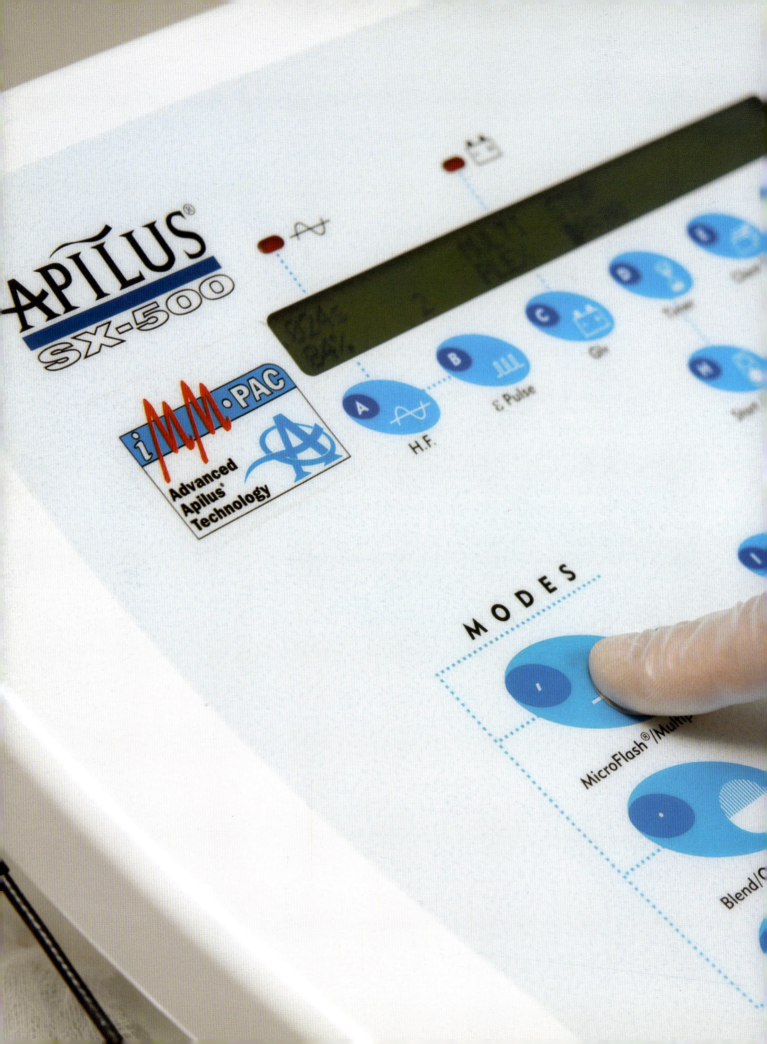

part five

epilation

chapter 7

ELECTROLYSIS

What will I know after reading this chapter?

This chapter covers electrolysis treatments. It describes the competencies required to enable you to:

- **understand what epilation, electrolysis and electro-epilation are and how they work**
- **consult with clients**
- **plan the treatment**
- **prepare for the treatment**
- **treat hair follicles using diathermy, galvanic and blend epilation**
- **complete the treatment.**

BT16: Epilate the hair follicle using diathermy, galvanic and blend techniques

Electrolysis is arguably the most skilled area of beauty therapy, giving unsurpassed emotional and financial rewards to the electrolysis practitioner. Electrolysis/electro-epilation are general terms referring to permanent hair removal, encompassing three methods, techniques or modalities: galvanic, diathermy and blend. All three methods will be discussed in detail throughout this chapter which is divided into four sections:

Section One: Introduction to electrolysis

Section Two: Electrolysis consultation

Section Three: Electricity and electrolysis

Section Four: Best electrolysis practice

SECTION ONE: INTRODUCTION TO ELECTROLYSIS

Electrolysis is defined as the decomposition of an electrolyte by the action of a direct electric current passing through it. Broadly speaking, an electrode the size of the hair (called a needle or probe) is placed into the hair follicle and used to conduct a very low current to the growing portion of the hair follicle. The current disables the growing portion of the follicle leading to its permanent destruction and the inability to produce hair.

Electrolysis is the term used in the hair removal and professional beauty industry, while electro-epilation is the term used, for exactly the same procedure, in education. There is some discussion regarding the term for the person who carries out electrolysis: is someone who studies electrology an electrologist or is someone who carries out electrolysis an electrolosist? Many argue that, as someone in the field of dermatology is a dermatologist, a person in the field of electrolysis should therefore be an electrologist and this is the term used throughout this chapter.

> **KEY TERMS**
>
> **Electrologist**: A person in the field of electrolysis as used throughout this book
> **Epilation**: Permanent removal of unwanted hair

> **KEY TERMS**
>
> To add to the confusion, in colleges electrolysis is often referred to as **electro-epilation**; however, we will not introduce the term electro-epilationists as we believe it would be going too far

THE HISTORY OF ELECTROLYSIS

To understand where electrolysis is now in the field of hair removal we need to understand its history.

1875 — An American ophthalmologist, Dr Charles E. Michel of St Louis, used electrolysis (galvanic current) to remove in-grown eyelashes and wrote a report in 1875 on his findings in the St Louis Medical Record. This report was based on his findings over 6 years. He had been performing electrolysis since 1869. There were other doctors during this time, such as Dr W. A. Hardaway, also in America, who were performing electrolysis.

1880s–1890s — During this time, the first non-medical electrolysis practices were established.

1916 — Prof. Paul M. Kree, of New York, developed the multiple needle galvanic technique, using as many as ten needles simultaneously. Electrolysis spread from the medical profession to the specialist electrologist. His company went on to dominate the practice and teaching of electrolysis in North America until the late 1970s. There were many salons in the UK bearing this famous name, although they were taken over and the name died out in the late 1970s.

1924 — Dr Henri Bordier, of Paris, France, while using the cautery powers of alternating current during micro-surgery, recognised its potential and developed the thermolysis method. This method can also be called diathermy, short-wave diathermy, high frequency (HF) or radio frequency (RF).

1928 — Dr Mildred Trotter published her classic article proving that shaving does not affect hair growth.

1945 — Henri St Pierre, an electrologist, had been working with alternating current and direct current separately and seen the advantages and disadvantages of both. He asked his friend Arthur Hinkel, an engineer with the General Electric Company, to look at the possibility of combining the currents in one epilator. They applied for the patent for the first combined current epilator in 1945, the patent was received in 1948 – and so the blend was born.

1960s — As equipment became more reliable, the treatment became more popular and more manufacturers entered the market, resulting in more choice for electrologists.

1970s — The 1970s saw the introduction of electrolysis training into further education colleges as part of a two-year health and beauty therapy training programme. The vast majority of new electrologists were young women, it having previously only been taught by private tutors.

1980s — The first computerised equipment entered the North American market.

Today — There is a vast array of equipment and manufacturers in the electrolysis market, ranging from basic diathermy only units through to more expensive, advanced, computerised blend and three modalities-in-one equipment for the modern practitioner.

WHY CHOOSE ELECTROLYSIS?

There are new hair removal methods and products appearing on the market almost weekly, often with amazing promises. The potential client needs reassurance that they are choosing the right method.

The box offers a list which could be used in leaflets and on posters, or simply to remind you why!

What electrolysis offers your clients

> - Electrolysis has a safe and proven track record.
> - Electrolysis has been used safely and effectively since 1870.
> - Electrolysis has been proven to be permanent.
> - Electrolysis offers freedom from the constant use of temporary methods of hair removal.
> - Electrolysis allows freedom from the hair growth which causes individuals distress or that they simply don't like the look of.
> - Electrolysis treatment is not restricted to certain hair or skin colours.
> - Electrolysis treatment is easier than you think, with a competent operator.

KEY TERMS ★

Galvanic current: Direct current – the constant flow of electrons along a conductor in one direction with no change of polarity

PROFESSIONAL TIP ✔

It was proven many years ago that shaving doesn't affect hair growth and yet many people believe it does. Part of your role as an Electrologist is to educate clients and addressing this myth is a major issue as it has implications for hair management

PROFESSIONAL TIP ✔

Clients may feel nervous when first receiving electrolysis. Use the facts on what electrolysis offers your clients to help reassure them

SECTION TWO: ELECTROLYSIS CONSULTATION

What will I know after reading this section?

This section covers the specific consultation practices for electrolysis and it will enable you to:

- **know how to carry out an effective electrolysis consultation**
- **appreciate how vital the consultation process is to the success of your treatment**
- **know what to ask, how to ask it and understand why you are asking it.**

The nature of electrolysis means that its consultation is more in-depth than for other hair removal treatments. This is not just because of the more technical practical aspects, but because the potential electrolysis client may have additional emotional requirements. This section discusses in some detail the specific requirements for an electrolysis consultation in addition to the general guidelines for effective consultation outlined in Chapter Two.

INTRODUCTION

Potential electrolysis clients may arrive at your salon for a consultation for a number of reasons, with a variety of needs, a variety of hair growth causes and with a variety of hair growth issues. A thorough consultation is vital to enable the electrologist to make an accurate assessment of the client's needs.

The potential client will often contact you or arrive at your salon because they have been recommended or referred by another party. Referrals may come from a variety of sources, the most common of which are:

- local beauty therapy college
- local beauty salon (which does not offer electrolysis)
- laser operator
- general practitioner (medical doctor or specialist)
- friend.

The potential client may also be aware of your services because of the advertising you have carried out for your business. Advertising can take many forms, for example, awareness adverts that you place regularly and that simply tell potential clients that you exist or specific promotion or events advertising. These adverts can be effectively placed in:

- local newspaper
- local magazine
- local radio
- salon shop front advertising
- Yellow Pages
- leaflet drops to targeted areas.

Whatever the stimulus bringing the potential client to your salon, it is important to remember that first impressions last and, by carefully following the general guidelines for consultation in Chapter Two, the potential client's contact with the salon will always be positive.

Often the potential electrolysis client will see their hair growth as a 'problem'. You should avoid calling their hair growth a problem and remain positive throughout. This will help the potential client to realise she/he has made the right decision by coming to you as you have the ability to permanently remove the hair growth.

THE ELECTROLYSIS CONSULTATION

The consultation must be carried out in total privacy; this is due to the nature of the questions and answers discussed. Privacy is invariably best achieved in a treatment room or cubicle, but the array of equipment and a 'medical' layout can be an overwhelming experience for a potential client.

In some cases, the consultation can be carried out in the reception area, but only if it is large enough for there to be a separate, private area. The discussion can take place at a high table with two chairs or on a low settee by a coffee table.

The main point to be aware of is that not only are potential clients likely to be nervous about the treatment but also it is possibly the first time they have set foot in your, or any, salon or clinic. They may have no idea what you are going to be like and you must develop an ongoing awareness of the client's feelings as this is vital for electrologists.

Consultation positioning

> **PROFESSIONAL TIP** ✔
>
> Never ask the potential client to lie on the couch during the consultation as this leaves them feeling very vulnerable

With experience you will learn to quickly assess your potential client's state of anxiety regarding their hair growth. For potential clients who you feel are very anxious, it is preferable to allow them to have the psychological advantage as far as the seating positioning for consultation is concerned. This is achieved by them sitting higher than you. You can do this quite simply by lowering your stool so that the client is seated slightly higher than you and looking down at you – never have it the other way around.

Also try to ensure the potential client doesn't have to sit opposite you with a barrier in between such as sitting either side of the treatment couch. Ask them to take a seat on the same side of the couch so that you are facing each other without barriers. If space is at a premium, seat the client on the side of the couch looking down at you. Consideration to positioning will help to give them more confidence and open a better flow of communication and give you better quality of information – all of which you need.

It has often been a long road, for the potential client, to reach the stage of asking for help in the form of treatment. It is important that you understand this; put yourself in their shoes and show them empathy and a positive response.

Which area?

Always ask the client which area they require treating, even if you think it is obvious. What you perceive to be excess growth may be perfectly acceptable to the potential client. Both authors, when newly qualified, made an assumption about the hairs to be treated on a client and got it embarrassingly wrong!

Consultation position

The electrolysis consultation process

The electrolysis consultation must be comprehensive. To keep yourself on track and to ensure you don't miss anything out, it is best to follow a set routine. Below is an outline of the recommended eight stages of a comprehensive consultation. It includes an in-depth analysis of why you need to ask the questions and what you will do with the information gathered.

CONSULTATION STAGES
1 Visually assess
2 Question what you see
3 General information gathering
4 Area specific information gathering
5 Skin condition
6 Contra-indications
7 Paperwork
8 Aftercare

First stage – Visually assess

Ask to look at the growth (after the client has told you where it is) and take particular note of the following aspects.

> **REMEMBER** !
>
> Society tells women they should be flawless and having superfluous facial hair growth can leave a woman feeling very masculine and in some cases 'a freak'. Be aware that potential clients may have feelings like this and adapt your consultation style to suit their anxieties

> **REMEMBER** !
>
> Empathy is not sympathy, make sure you know the difference

1 The extent of the growth:
- How much hair is there?
- How dense is it?
- How thick is it?

2 The signs indicating the stage of growth:
- Is the hair shaft pointed?
- Is it just emerging from the follicle?
- Does it look 'new' and glossy?
- Is it long?
- Are there a variety of hairs, some long and some short or any black spots barely visible in the follicle?

3 Signs of previous hair removal methods:
- Is the hair blunt?
- Is there any erythema around the follicles?
- The direction of growth – is it distorted in any way?
- The skin condition – is it sensitised?

Second stage – Question what you see

Once you have made a visual assessment, question the potential client regarding what you see, guiding her or him to give you more information by means of relevant questions.

The site of the unwanted growth should indicate to you the type of question required:

- *Example One*: If the potential client presents with a 'normal' pattern of hair growth (i.e. normal for their age, race or sex), your questions will be designed to discover the type(s) of previous hair removal methods they have tried and consider the effect of these methods on the visible growth.
- *Example Two*: If your potential client presents an 'abnormal' pattern of hair growth (i.e. abnormal for their age, race or sex), your questions will be designed to discover any hormonal imbalance, whether it be normal systemic or abnormal systemic.

The record card is *the* most valuable document you can have of your time with the potential client and it also serves as a record of eventual treatment. Two-way communication is paramount during completion of the record card: maintain eye contact and ensure open gesturing is continued throughout.

The record card will serve as a guide to ensure you conduct a thorough 'investigation' into the causes of the hair growth, the potential client's situation, health and any other factors which will influence your treatment plan. It will also ensure your consultation takes a holistic approach by considering the whole person.

Questions to ask when completing the record card

What you need to know	What the information will tell you
How long has the growth been there and when did they first notice the growth?	It may indicate to you the cause of growth; for example, the potential client may tell you the hair first appeared when she was pregnant.
Notes: Generally potential clients will say things like 'it's always been there'; guide them with appropriate questions with normal systemic causes in mind. Young women: 'Did you first notice them when your periods began?' 'Have you been pregnant; if so, did you first notice the hairs during pregnancy?' Women aged over 30: 'Have you experienced any symptoms of the menopause?'	
What methods of hair removal have been previously used?	This allows you to establish the stage of growth. Advise the client on the effects of the previous hair removal.
Medical history, in particular any: ● hormonal imbalances ● medication ● current health.	These answers will allow you to: ● identify abnormal systemic causes of hair growth and give advice to the client ● establish from the client their current state of health ● identify any contra-indications ● identify any precautions or if medical referral is necessary.

What the potential client needs to know and why

What the potential client needs to know	Why
Effect of previous hair removal.	In order that they can be prepared for the re-growth.
Electrolysis works, it is permanent.	To provide assurance that they are making the right decision.
Electrolysis is progressive.	More than one treatment is necessary – the potential client must be prepared and aware of this.
They must attend regularly, as and when advised by the hair removal practitioner.	Electrolysis is only effective when the hair is in the anagen stage of growth; the client must therefore receive treatment as soon as possible after the hair re-grows.
The client must not use any other method of hair removal between electrolysis treatments, other than shaving or cutting.	Shaving and cutting merely cuts off the hair shaft at the skin surface whereas other methods stimulate or interfere with growth.
The client must follow your aftercare advice and maintain the skin in a good, moist condition. NB See aftercare leaflet below.	Good aftercare procedure will prevent infection and a good moist skin will aid recovery and ensure effective treatment, as it is vital to maintain the skin's moisture levels.
The process of electrolysis, and how the treatment works.	To provide understanding of what will happen to them and an awareness of the process.
What sensation to expect.	In order that they are prepared and reassured.

Electrolysis record card

JAYGEE'S

Family name:	Date of birth:
First name:	Address:
Home Tel:	Doctor's name:
Mobile:	Address:
E-mail:	Tel:

Have you had previous electrolysis treatment? Yes ☐ No ☐

If yes, how many treatments did you have? _____ Over what period? _____

On what area? _____ When was your last treatment? _____

On what area of your face or body do you require treatment? _____

When did you first notice your unwanted hair? _____ years ago

What temporary measures have you used? _____ Over what period? _____

How often? _____ Times per week ☐ month ☐ When did you use it last? _____

Present condition of skin: Oil levels _____ Moisture _____ Blemishes _____

Pigmentation _____ Scarring _____ Sensitivity _____

Medical information _____

Current health: _____

History: _____

Diabetes ☐ Hormonal imbalances ☐ Hepatitis ☐ Heart condition ☐ Pacemaker ☐

Epilepsy ☐ Pregnancies ☐ Nervous disorders ☐ Asthma ☐ Metal implants ☐

Are you taking medication: Yes ☐ No ☐ If Yes, please specify _____

I declare that I have answered all the above questions truthfully

Client signature........................... Date...........................

Third stage – General information gathering

Name, address and contact details

It is important that the client is identified with both their first and family names for insurance purposes. It is also important that you can contact a client should you need to change an appointment. For marketing purposes the client's details are also useful, for example sending a birthday card, special offers, etc. It is increasingly popular for salons to offer a text reminder service, whereby the salon sends a text message to the client either a few hours or the day before their appointment. The clients appreciate the reminder and the salon prevents lost revenue from missed appointments.

Date of birth

This detail allows the electrologist to establish the potential client's stage of life and its hormonal influences; it can also confirm the client's identity should you have more than one with the same name.

You need to know the client's age because:

- If your client is under 18: you will need written permission from a parent or guardian. It could also indicate that the client is still in puberty and may have a temporary hormonal imbalance.

- If the client is 20–40: many factors can come into play during these years which stimulate excess hair growth, for example pregnancy, medication (birth control pills, cortisone, fertility drugs, etc.), medical problems (ovarian cysts, endometriosis, endocrine disorders, etc.).

- If the client is 40–60: the menopause normally occurs between the ages of 35 and 58.

- If the client is 60 or over: the skin is likely to be thin and dry and the healing potential is reduced.

Doctor's name and address

This is important information for you to have, should you need to discuss any issues regarding the treatment with your client's medical practitioner. (NB The doctor will not discuss any confidential client information with you unless the client has authorised them to do so.)

Fourth stage – Area specific information gathering

Have you had previous electrolysis treatment?

This will indicate to you the client's prior knowledge of electrolysis, which will enable you to give the appropriate information. You will also need to be aware of any contra-actions from previous treatments, the results of the previous treatment, and why the client did not continue with it.

On what areas have you previously received treatment?

This question provides a way to ensure you do not make assumptions about the area of concern. This will help you to begin your evaluation of the cause of growth. Remember to guide your client: you know the causes of hair growth, they may not. It is essential that you establish the cause of growth and what it means to the client and treatment.

> **REMEMBER !**
>
> Never simply assume you know which areas require treatment, always ask the client to highlight each area

Temporary methods used?

Understanding when temporary methods were last used, and how often, will help to indicate the current stage of hair growth and establish whether you are seeing the full extent of it. The client's answers will also indicate how the temporary methods have stimulated the growth.

Fifth stage – Skin condition

The condition of the skin is vital to treatment so questions relating to the client's skin condition are a key stage of any electrolysis consultation. In particular, you must check the oil levels of the client's skin as sebum is an insulator and can therefore adversely affect treatment. If appropriate, pre- and post-treatment skin care should be recommended. The client's skin moisture also plays a key role in electrolysis and is vital for effective epilation treatment, regardless of modality. Therefore, pre- and post-treatment skin care, including a well-balanced diet with increased water intake, are vital.

Blemishes

Ask questions regarding vascular or fibrous blemishes, for example telangiectasia (red veins) and skins tags. Use a mirror to point them out to your client, so they are aware that the blemishes were present prior to treatment. Clients often only see the hairs and not the condition of the skin under or around them; once the hairs are removed they see everything. It is like having a spot; your eyes are drawn only to that.

Pigmentation

Some modalities are associated with an increased risk of pigmentation stimulation on susceptible clients; therefore, thorough discussion prior to treatment will ensure you choose the correct modality. Any hypo (whiter than surrounding skin) and hyper (darker than surrounding skin) pigmentation marks on the area to be treated should be noted on the record card and agreed with the client; the record card must also be signed and dated by the client.

Scarring

Any scarring in the area to be treated should be pointed out tactfully to the client and the details recorded on the record card, which should be signed and dated by the client.

Sensitivity

All skins are sensitive to some degree; however, 'reactive' skins will exhibit more effects after treatment and those effects may last longer. Sensitivity may also affect your choice of needle, that is, gold or insulated. It does not, however, affect current levels or needle size.

Sixth stage – Contra-indications

For you to get the most truthful answers from your client, in relation to the following medical section, you should pre-empt your questions by stating that you do need to know the answers to these questions, albeit that you appreciate they are quite personal, as you must accurately establish the reason for their hair growth if you are to give them the best treatment in the long term.

Describe your current state of health

Epilation works best when the body is in good health, therefore the current health of the client needs to be uncovered.

Outline your previous medical history

In particular, you are looking for an indicator of hormonal imbalance and contra-indications to treatment.

KEY TERMS ★

Hypo: Indicates a decrease in or lack of something
Hyper: Indicates an increase in or excess of something

PROFESSIONAL TIP ✔

Recording existing blemishes, scars, pigmentation disorders prior to commencing treatment, will prevent your client wrongly accusing you of causing them at a later date. It is worth nothing, however, if they haven't signed the record card

---

REMEMBER !

You are not a doctor; it is not your job to diagnose

Do you suffer from diabetes?

In some texts it is suggested that a diabetic client is contra-indicated to electrolysis due to inhibited skin healing and even loss of sensation. Whilst there are undoubtedly more considerations when treating a diabetic client, the symptoms are generally controlled by diet and or medication. All of your clients should be treated with the same care and precautions: keep the current levels as low as possible, take great care of the skin prior to, during and post-treatment. There should, therefore, be no need for the common practice of leaving large gaps between the hairs treated on diabetic clients.

Do you suffer from hormonal imbalances?

Androgens are the only hormone which can stimulate hair growth. The hormonal balance in the body is finely tuned and any fluctuations can allow androgens to stimulate hair growth, this is particularly the case with oestrogen and progesterone. It is vital that you are aware of any hormonal imbalances, particularly those which are not controlled medically, as treatment effectiveness may be restricted by constant hormonal stimulation of follicles and therefore hair growth. Also, you must explain in detail, to your client, the likely effects of hormone imbalance on their treatment.

Be aware that the client may not know that she has a hormonal imbalance. However, if she comes to you with an abnormal growth – for example chin or chest hair – you should question the client to establish whether any other possible symptoms are present, in particular irregular menstrual cycle, unexplained weight loss or gain, unexplained emotional problems or skin eruptions. If some or all of these are present, it is advisable to subtly recommend she seeks her doctor's advice regarding a hormone levels test.

> **KEY TERMS** ⭐
>
> **Androgen**: Hormone that stimulates male characteristics
> **Oestrogen and progesterone**: Hormones that stimulate female characteristics

Do you suffer from hepatitis (inflammation of the liver)?

Hepatitis has many causes, two of which are infection by amoeba (bacteria) and viruses. You should be concerned about hepatitis as it is highly infectious. Hepatitis B is a particular risk for electrologists as it is extremely easy to contract.

> **HEALTH AND SAFETY** ✚
>
> It is recommended that all electrologists be inoculated against hepatitis B

Do you have a heart condition?

It is important that the electrologist is aware of any heart condition as the client may be on blood thinning medication. This could have an impact on treatment because, if bleeding occurs, the blood flow may take longer than normal to stop. As circulation is affected with heart conditions, the client's healing capacity may be impaired.

Do you have a pacemaker?

It is essential you find out if your client has a pacemaker as the current may affect it. You should not carry out treatment without a letter from your client's doctor, which should be attached to your clients' record card.

Do you have epilepsy?

Epilepsy does not necessarily contra-indicate treatment. It is important to find out if a client is epileptic for two reasons:

1 It may contra-indicate treatment if the client's stimulus is lights (because of the close proximity of the magnifier light), stress or if there is any possibility that you could stimulate a seizure (fit).

2 It is important that you discuss with your client the frequency and stimulus of attacks in addition to the form the attacks take, as you need to be able to recognise that the client has had a seizure should it occur in the salon. Not all attacks produce violent seizures and clients can sometimes just be disorientated following an attack. It may be that the disorientation is the first thing that you notice and that there is no seizure. If you are in any doubt, seek medical approval.

Pregnancy

As the hormones in pregnancy have a profound effect on hair growth, it is vital that you look into your client's past pregnancies and current pregnancies.

- Current pregnancy: you must find out whether the hair growth started with this pregnancy or before. If the hair growth appeared at the onset of this pregnancy, the chances are that it may well go at the end of the pregnancy. Therefore, you will need to discuss with your client whether or not you should commence treatment. Professional ethics come into play here: do you take money from a client knowing that her unwanted hair may fall out naturally, when the hormone balance is re-established after child birth?

- Treating a pregnant client: pregnant clients can be treated, but only with diathermy and not on the breasts or abdomen areas in the latter stages.

- Past pregnancies: not every pregnancy culminates in the birth of a child. Every pregnancy does, however, have a profound effect on the hormonal balance of the body and as such may be the cause of the hair growth, which is why we need to be aware of past pregnancies. However great care must be taken when pursuing this line of questioning.

PROFESSIONAL TIP ✔

Do not be tempted to take payment for treatment when it is likely that the client's unwanted hair will disappear naturally – in the long run it is your reputation that will suffer

Do you suffer from a nervous disorder?

If you find, during consultation, that the client is very agitated and cannot sit still, you should subtly dissuade them from having treatment. You could cause damage or injury during treatment with the needle through their constant movement.

Do you have asthma?

You need to find out if the client has asthma which is medically controlled, as the medication is normally steroid based which can have an influence on hair growth. There may occasionally be an issue with asthmatic clients preferring to sit more upright during treatment to ease their breathing.

HEALTH AND SAFETY ✚

Do not treat follicles over an area which contains metal with blend or galvanic methods

Metal implants

Clients can have a variety of metal implants – bone pins, dental implants, IUD (inter uterine device), etc., and they will influence your choice of modality. The metal would have an effect on blend and galvanic treatments.

Current medication

It is important to ask the client if they are taking any medication, currently or long term, and its purpose. Make a particular note of medication involving hormonal treatment and anti-coagulants; see the section on 'Heart conditions' above.

Seventh stage – Paperwork

Ensure that the client signs and dates the record card to confirm that they have answered all the questions on the record card truthfully. In the case of minors this card must be signed by a parent or guardian.

The rear of the record card is where details of individual treatments are recorded.

Date: To track treatments and ensure the client is receiving regular treatment.

Area: Should another electrologist treat your client, they can see what area has been previously treated. This can also prevent any embarrassment should they wrongly assume which area the client wants to have treated. Also records any new areas which you have treated.

Needle type and size: Should another electrologist treat your client, they can see the type of needle used and size, this ensures the most suitable needle is used.

Duration, current(s) and intensity(s): Provides a guide as to the progress of treatment and gives an indication of previous treatment levels. The recorded details, however, should not be used as a starting point for the next

Reverse of electrolysis record card

Date	Area	Needle type & size	Duration	Current(s)	Intensity(s)	Treatment reactions & electrologist's signature	Client signature

treatment. Always start as low as possible and increase gradually until the working point is reached. You should expect levels to be slightly different with each treatment as the hair growth diminishes. Also remember the client's skin's moisture and tolerance levels change constantly. In larger salons, the electrologist signs above, or by, these details so a record is also created of which electrologist carried out the treatment.

Treatment reactions: Allows you to record any treatment reactions, good or bad, which will influence your choice of currents and needles for subsequent treatments.

Client signature: Confirms that the recorded details are correct – this is essential!

Informed consent

The record card contains all of the client and treatment information. It is not, however, an agreement between the electrologist and the client. The

Informed consent leaflet

JAYGEE'S

Informed consent for electrolysis treatment

This agreement is in respect of treatment by electrolysis.

.... and .... Thereafter known as 'the client'
   (Electrologist)   (Client's name)

1 The client understands that electrolysis is a progressively permanent treatment and several treatments will be required.

2 Treatments will need to be on a regular basis as directed by the electrologist.

3 The client understands and undertakes to follow all pre- and post-treatment recommendations given verbally and in writing by the electrologist.

4 The client has given clear and accurate answers to the questions during consultation to enable the electrologist to establish the cause of growth and create an effective treatment plan.

5 The client understands that there may be immediate post-treatment reaction, e.g. reddening and slight swelling in the area treated. Providing the area is not interfered with and aftercare instructions are followed, there should be no long-term ill effects.

6 The client agrees to abide by the hair management techniques as discussed and recommended by the electrologist.

7 This agreement will confirm that I have discussed the electrolysis treatment with the undersigned electrologist that I understand that the treatment is progressive and that hair in the area being treated will require additional treatment.

Signature................. ....Electrologist...................................Date

Signature......................................Client ....Date

purpose of 'informed consent' is to confirm that the client understands the treatment fully, what it involves, their role, the likely outcomes of treatment and that they agrees to receive treatment. Before this informed consent can be signed by the client, you must have covered all the points within it. This includes the aftercare procedure.

Stage eight – Aftercare

Aftercare for electrolysis is extremely important, as the client's skin will be prone to infection due to the heat and the tissue destruction caused by the treatment. Keeping the treated area clean should help to prevent infection. It is vital that the electrologist explains to the client all of the aftercare procedures as outlined in the aftercare leaflet.

The following is an example of an aftercare leaflet which should be discussed and given to the client to take away.

JAYGEE'S

Electrolysis home-care

Please read these home-care notes carefully and follow the recommendations. We have taken great care to protect you from infection and, in addition to our normal salon routine, we have applied a soothing antiseptic lotion after your treatment. It is important for you to take extra care of the treated area, especially within the first 24–48 hours. Following electrolysis treatment, the area could be prone to infection if not cared for. It is IMPORTANT that the area is not touched with un-washed hands and the following should be avoided for the first 48 hours following treatment:

- sunbathing and sunbed treatments
- very hot baths (it is fine to have a warm bath or shower)
- friction particularly from tight clothing (wear loose clothing preferably made from natural fibres)
- perfumed body lotion or creams
- deodorants and anti-perspirants for underarm treatment
- following facial treatment; application of make-up (first 4–8 hours only)
- vigorous exercise and swimming in chlorinated water.

We recommend that you use soothing antiseptic aftercare lotion daily for 3–4 days after treatment, which should be purchased from your electrologist.

Normal post treatment reactions are:

- slight redness in the treated area
- slight swelling in the area
- mild heat sensation in the area

- occasional, tiny crusts around the follicle opening particularly after first few treatments.

Please speak to your hair removal practitioner if:

- redness persists for more than 48 hours
- large or honey coloured crusts develop in the area
- pustular spots appear in the area.

Skin and hair management

Remember:

- ✔ Electrolysis works.
- ✔ It is progressive; after each treatment, any hair which re-grows will be sparser, finer and lighter.
- ✔ Hair grows in cycles and only the first cycle provides the results. You should ensure you keep regular appointments as advised by your electrologist.
- ✔ To achieve successful treatment your skin needs to be in good condition and as moist as possible, this is why it is important to eat healthily, drink plenty of water and follow carefully the skin care routines and treatments advised by your electrologist.
- ✔ In between your initial appointments you may need to use some form of hair management at home. Cutting (scissors or razor) is the only method you should use.

If you are concerned or unsure about any aspect of your treatment please contact your electrologist:

Tel: 01234 5678910

E mail: jaygees@hairsolutions.co.uk

There now follow two examples of the kind of dialogue that could take place at a consultation. It won't take you very long to realise that Consultation 1 is an example of a badly conducted consultation, while Consultation 2 illustrates what should have happened.

CONSULTATION 1:   Mrs Jones

The scene: Mrs Jones (Mrs J) has been welcomed into the salon, is sitting in front of the electrologist (ELEC) and now we will 'listen in' to the consultation.

ELEC: I can see a couple of hairs on your chin. Are these the ones that are a problem to you?

Mrs J: Oh yes, they are really obvious aren't they? Can you get rid of them for me?

ELEC: Oh yes. We'll soon get that problem sorted out. I have the latest equipment here and I can promise you the best treatment. How long have you had these hairs?

Mrs J: OK dear. [pause] A long time. Since about the time our Mark was born, now how old is he – oh yes he's 24.

ELEC: Well we'll soon get rid of those for you. You won't have this problem much longer. Would you like to sign this record card?

Treatment begins, lasts 15 minutes, Mrs Jones is helped from the couch and given an aftercare leaflet. The hair removal practitioner advises her to ring for another appointment when the hairs need treating again.

2 weeks later at the client's home: Mrs Jones is very distressed, talking to her daughter.

Mrs J: I can't understand it, she said she'd got the best equipment and I would have the best treatment and I've got lots of hairs. I've never had as many hairs as this, I only had 2. That electrologist has made all these hairs grow; I just don't know what to do now. I thought electrolysis was permanent …

REMEMBER !

An unhappy client tells, on average, 16 people. A happy client, on average tells 3 people. Make sure your client is left happy!

What went wrong?

Not enough information was given and this has resulted in a unhappy and misinformed client who will spread negative information about the electrologist, the business and electrolysis in general, plus the salon has lost a client.

CONSULTATION 2:   Mrs Jones

Setting the scene: Mrs Jones (Mrs J) has been welcomed into the salon, is sitting in front of the electrologist (ELEC) and now we will 'listen in' to the consultation.

ELEC: What's the area that concerns you?

Mrs J: I've just got a couple of hairs on my chin.

ELEC: When did you first notice the growth?

Mrs J: About the time our Mark was born, now how old is he now – Oh yes he's 24.

ELEC: What have you done to them?

> **Mrs J:** Just plucked them occasionally.
>
> **ELEC:** What do you mean by occasionally?
>
> **Mrs J:** Every couple of days.
>
> **ELEC:** By plucking the hairs out on a regular basis, you've not seen the full extent of the hair growth so you will have a lot more than just two and if you were to stop plucking you would find, within a few weeks, that you had lots of hairs in that area.
>
> **Mrs J:** Does that mean everybody will see me with a beard? I'm better off keeping plucking aren't I?
>
> **ELEC:** You're definitely not better off plucking because that's just making it worse. By ripping the hair out from its follicle you are stimulating the blood supply to the hair root which is making them grow back stronger. If you continue to pluck you will be plucking forever.
>
> **Mrs J:** Oh dear …
>
> **ELEC:** Don't worry; you've come to the right place. I'll explain to you what I'm going to do and why and together, over time, we can rid you of these hairs.
>
> The treatment continues, a second appointment is made before Mrs Jones leaves the salon and aftercare advice is given.
>
> *2 weeks later at the client's home*: Mrs Jones is talking to her daughter.
>
> **Mrs J:** I've just got back from my second appointment and I feel so much better. What a lovely girl. I think I'm really going to be free of these hairs at last, if only I'd gone before.

Did you spot the difference? The main lessons to be learnt are:

- don't assume anything
- don't call it a problem
- explain the effects of previous hair removal methods, particularly where plucking is involved.

GENDER DYSPHORIA

Working as a hair removal practitioner and particularly as an electrologist will inevitably bring you into contact with a male to female gender dysphoriac, as one of the key issues is their male pattern hair growth. In order to maintain professional conduct and show empathy with your client, it is important that you understand this medical condition.

Gender dysphoriacs, often known as transsexuals, feel from an early age that they are trapped in the wrong 'gender' or body. In other words they feel they should have been born the opposite sex.

People with this medical condition experience a range of distressing emotions from confusion to extreme loathing about their birth gender and bodies. Many will have 'acted' out much of their lives to fit the gender of the body they were born with, whilst fighting the overwhelming sensation that they are the opposite gender. Males can feel trapped in their feminine body and wish to have a male body, or females can feel trapped in their masculine body and wish to have a female body.

TECHNICAL TIP ✔

Plucking disturbs the hair growth cycle so that it will take some time for the full extent of the hair growth to be evident once the plucking has stopped

PROFESSIONAL TIP ✔

To empathise with these clients just for a moment try and imagine what it would be like to be as you are now, with all the thoughts, desires, likes and dislikes that you have, but when you look in the mirror you see the opposite body to that which you believe you are

REMEMBER !

The distress caused by the condition is so severe that the incidence of self-harm and suicide is very high among people with gender dysphoria

Using appropriate terminology

People with gender dysphoria generally feel very aggrieved about the term 'transsexual' because gender and sex are seen as very separate things, although the terms are often considered interchangeable.

Sex is a physical form and function of the body, whilst gender is the identity of the body and so the dilemma of the person is the difference between sex and gender.

Gender dysphoria is not the same as transvestism, which describes a person who enjoys dressing and acting as the opposite sex.

Treatment – Male to female transition

The first stage of treatment is extensive analysis by psychiatrists and doctors, who decide whether or not the person is suitable for treatment, bearing in mind that the surgery required for gender re-alignment is intensive, difficult and irreversible. Male patients are required to prove their commitment by living as a female for up to three years.

Hormones are prescribed (normally oestrogen and in some cases an additional androgen suppressant) to start the physical transition. The female hormones change the look and feel of the skin, change the curves of the body and cause breasts to grow. Clients will need help with skin treatments to assist with softening and hydrating the skin. Exfoliation and deep hydration treatments are ideal.

Administered hormones suppress the male hormones and therefore some reduction in hair growth is experienced. There will inevitably be some remaining unwanted hair growth, which can easily be treated with electrolysis and light-based treatments. For large areas, it is advisable to treat using laser or light (providing the client is suitable for this method) and the treatment can be concluded with electrolysis.

Gender re-alignment surgery is difficult and usually painful. The male to female surgery removes the male genitals and reshapes the area. Often the person will undergo facial surgery to soften the features.

Electrolysis for the gender dysphoriac client

When treating clients with gender dysphoria, there are a number of important points to remember.

- Be aware of, and prepared for, an emotional client. Remain professional and do not get too involved.
- The actual planning and treatment is exactly the same regardless of the client's gender, the only exception being that male follicles tend to be slightly deeper than those of females.

Assessment of knowledge and understanding

This section has taught you how to conduct an electrolysis consultation. To test your level of knowledge and understanding, answer the following short questions:

1 What are the benefits to a customer of having electrolysis treatment?

2 Give two indicators of the stage of hair growth that are visible above the skin.

3 Define the term transsexual.

4 List two things that a client should avoid following electrolysis treatment.

5 What is the purpose of an informed consent form?

6 Explain why it is important to establish the cause of growth at consultation.

7 For what reasons do we need to know the client's date of birth.

8 Why do electrolysis treatments need to be carried out regularly?

9 List two surface signs which would indicate that a hair is in the anagen stage of growth.

10. State the reason why it is important to seat the client slightly above you during an electrolysis consultation.

Activities

Conduct the following activities to practise your knowledge of electrolysis consultations:

1 Carry out a consultation and decide, based on the information your 'client' has given you, which modality you would chose and why?

2 Design a poster for a salon front window that promotes electrolysis.

3 Carry out a 'mock' consultation with a member of your family or friend, having previously given them a list of hair growth causes to choose from. Tell them NOT to tell you the cause of hair growth they have chosen until you ask the appropriate question(s).

4 Plan an electrolysis treatment for Mrs Kaur who has extensive hair growth on the side of her face:

- she is very concerned because the growth has got much thicker recently

- she has a family wedding to attend in two months' time and would like to be hair free on the day

- the home method she has used for the last 15 years is threading

- she is 52 years of age and currently in good health, but has recently experienced 'hot flushes'.

SECTION THREE: ELECTRICITY AND ELECTROLYSIS

What will I know after reading this section?

This section covers electricity and electrolysis and it will enable you to:

- **have a basic understanding of electrical science**
- **recognise and understand the components of an epilator**
- **understand the three main electrolysis techniques, how they are achieved electrically and their basic methods of application**
- **appreciate alternative epilators and electrolysis equipment.**

Modern electrolysis equipment is standardised and a detailed knowledge of electricity is no longer required for the competent practice of electrolysis, for example how much do you know about the electrical systems of your TV, DVD etc? However, electricity is interesting and the following will give you a better understanding of your equipment and electrolysis in general. It will also allow you to make educated choices when you are buying equipment.

ELECTRICAL SCIENCE

Electricity is the flow of electrons (negatively charged particles) along a conductor, such as an electric cable or an electrolysis needle. Imagine that the electrons represent water flowing in a stream. Electrons (water) flow from an area where there is an excess of electrons (water) to an area where there is less. Electrons flow from negative to positive.

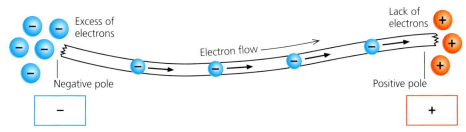

Electrons flow from negative to positive

All matter (every substance in the world) is made of molecules, and the molecule is the smallest part of matter that still maintains its individual physical and chemical characteristics. Molecules are divided into atoms. For example, a molecule of water (H_2O) consists of two atoms of hydrogen and one atom on oxygen.

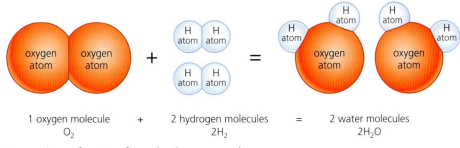

| 1 oxygen molecule | + | 2 hydrogen molecules | = | 2 water molecules |
| O_2 | | $2H_2$ | | $2H_2O$ |

Formation of water from hydrogen and oxygen

The centre of an atom contains a nucleus, consisting of one or more positive protons and a varying number of neutral neutrons. Rotating in orbit around the positive nucleus are the much smaller negative electrons.

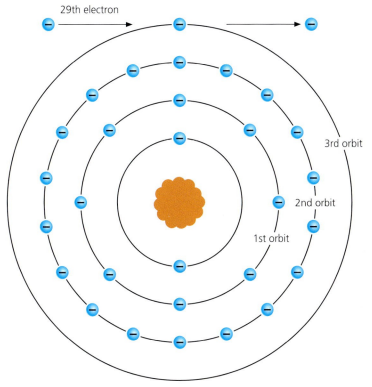

The structure of a copper atom

Sources which generate the flow of electrical current

There is no shortage of electricity; it is abundant. The problem is finding new, practical and non-polluting means of generating it. In order to produce electricity (i.e. move electrons), some form of energy must be used to force the free electrons out of their orbits.

The six basic sources which can be used to produce electricity are:

1 *Friction* – electricity produced by rubbing two materials together.
2 *Pressure* – electricity produced by applying pressure to a crystal of certain materials.
3 *Heat* – electricity produced by heating the junction of a thermo-couple.
4 *Light* – electricity produced by light striking photo-sensitive materials.
5 *Magnetism* – electricity produced by the relative movement of a magnet and a wire that results in cutting through lines of force.
6 *Chemical action* – electricity produced by chemical reactions in an electric cell.

Magnetism and chemical action are currently the two most practical means of generating current flow.

The electric circuit

An electric current is the flow of electricity (the flow of electrons). For a current to keep flowing there must be a continuous path (or circuit) from the generating source of the electricity through all the conductors back to the

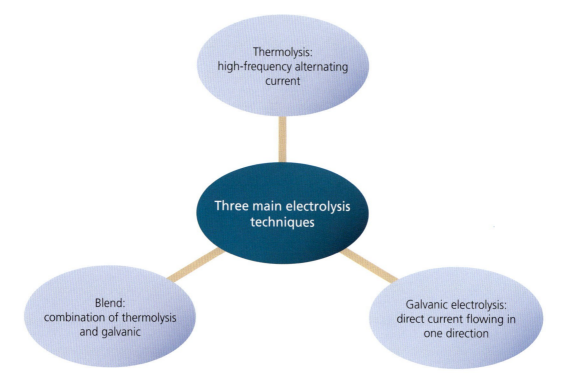

source. Your radio, for example, operates only after you turn on the switch to complete the electrical circuit.

Direct current from batteries

The modern battery is said to have had its origin in 1790 in the kitchen of Mrs Luigi Galvani, who, in the process of preparing frog's leg soup, crossed two dissimilar metallic utensils on a frog's leg and the frog's leg convulsed. When she explained what she had seen to her husband Luigi Galvani, who was a respected professor of anatomy, he could not understand what was taking place. Even while he continued producing this effect, to the amazement of his students, by connecting two dissimilar metals to a frog's leg, he did not comprehend what a fantastic product was about to be born. Although accurate in his facts, Galvani explained the erroneous theory of 'animal electricity'. He, like so many scientists on the brink of a great discovery, prepared the path for others to develop his theory into something of tangible value for all humankind.

An Italian physicist called Alessandro Volta took Galvani's theory and, after much examination and repetition of Galvani's experiments, concluded that it was the moist salty tissue of the frog's leg, which we now know was acting as an electrolyte, combined with the two dissimilar metals, which caused the flow of direct current which caused the convulsing frog's leg. Volta duplicated this effect in 1800 with his invention of an early form of the dry cell battery; this invention was then followed by the first wet cell battery.

Direct current (DC)

In a direct current, the electrons flow continuously in the same direction. In direct current or 'galvanic' electrolysis the electrons flow from the machine source, through the needle holder, and into the electrolysis needle which acts as the negative pole (negative terminal or cathode electrode). From the needle, the electrons flow through the hair follicle, through the body, through the positive electrode (also called positive terminal or anode electrode) and back into the machine. Historically, direct current produced by a battery was known as galvanic current (after Luigi Galvani). Therefore, the words 'direct current' and 'galvanic current' are often used interchangeably. The energy for the first galvanic electrolysis was produced by a large battery.

Alternating current (AC)

In an alternating current, the current flow continuously reverses its direction. The electrons move back and forth along the conductor as each source pole (terminal) rapidly changes its polarity (negative to positive), in cycle with each back and forth movement. You can think of the electrons alternately being pushed and sucked back along the conductor by the machine source. In Europe, the normal household alternating current fluctuates at 50 cycles per second. An electrolysis machine converts our household alternating

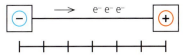

Direct current flows only in one direction

REMEMBER

Electron flow is always negative to positive

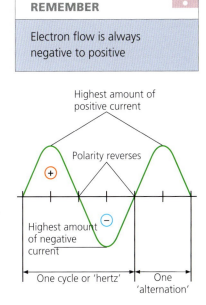

Alternating current

current to the direct current required for galvanic electrolysis by means of a rectifier and filter circuit.

High-frequency alternating current

The high-frequency alternating current required for the thermolysis modality (also called diathermy, shortwave diathermy, radio frequency (RF) or just high frequency (HF) is produced by an oscillator. An oscillator increases the frequency of our household alternating current to the millions of cycles per second required for thermolysis.

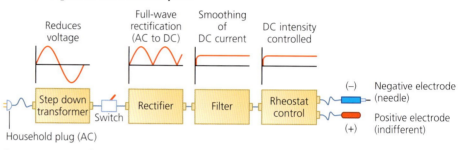

The anatomy of a thermolysis machine

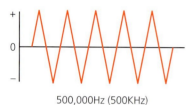

500,000Hz (500KHz)

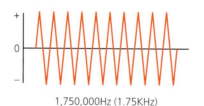

1,750,000Hz (1.75KHz)

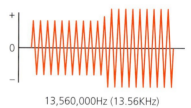

13,560,000Hz (13.56KHz)

The alternating current frequencies used in thermolysis

Friction

These frequencies are in the range of radio waves, but machine frequencies are regulated in order that there is no conflict with radio wave transmission, although with older equipment there may be some interference. Some computerised equipment is in the high-frequency range.

The thermolysis machine is giving and taking away electrical energy almost simultaneously. Some of the electrical energy is lost to the surrounding air and furniture. The rapid high-frequency to and from movement of the electrical energy focusing in the 'tiny' electrolysis needle stimulates the adjacent moisture molecules in the hair follicle to vibrate, which results in friction causing destructive heat energy.

Friction from vibration can be likened to the heat generated by rubbing sticks together to start a fire.

Electrical measurements

Electrical measurements are easier to understand if, once again, current flow is compared with water flowing along a stream.

Ampere (amount)

The ampere is the unit of measurement for the amount of current flow through a conductor (the total amount of water passing any given point in a stream). Galvanic electrolysis uses the measurement of *milli*amperes (1/1000 of an ampere, since an ampere is too large an amount). A range of 0 to 1.0 milliampere is used in galvanic electrolysis and the blend, with the most common being 0.3 to 0.7 milliampere. Household fuses are most frequently 13 ampere fuses.

Thermolysis uses megahertz (1,000,000Hz). The range of megahertz used in thermolysis is from 0 up to as much as 27MHz on some computerised machines.

Volt (pressure)

The volt is a measurement of electrical pressure. It is the force that pushes the electrical current along a conductor. A comparison would be a pump pushing water along a stream, or the more natural occurrence of stream water falling down a hill from a higher area to a lower area. Household current in the UK is 240 volts.

Ohm (resistance)

An ohm is the unit of measurement of electrical resistance. When the pressure of volts pushes the amp of electrons along the conducting wire, they meet resistance. Think of water running into obstacles, such as boulders in a stream. One ohm is equal to the resistance of a circuit in which a force of one volt maintains a current flow of one ampere. Conductors, such as copper or stainless steel, offer little resistance, whereas plastic and rubber offer great resistance. Dry skin is a bad conductor, but wet skin is a good conductor.

> #### Ohm's law
>
> It takes a pressure of ONE VOLT to push a current of one AMPERE through a resistance of ONE OHM.

Watt (work or power)

The watt is the unit of electrical work or power. Watts equal amperes times volts (W = A × V). Household light bulbs ordinarily require 60–100 watts, and 746 watts are roughly equivalent to one horsepower. Your household electricity bill is charged in kilowatt hours: 100-watt light bulb burning for 10 hours equals one kilowatt hour. Electrolysis machines are economical to operate, requiring about 35 watts of power.

Electrodes and completing the circuit

In galvanic electrolysis, a complete circuit is required. The electrolysis needle acts as the negative electrode (cathode) and is connected to the negative terminal or outlet point. The indifferent plate or bar acts as the positive electrode (anode) and is connected to the positive terminal or outlet point.

TECHNICAL TIP

A fuse is made of material which is melted from excessive current, leaving a gap across which the current cannot flow

TECHNICAL TIP

AVOW is a mnemonic to help people remember electrical units of measurement: Ampere, Volts, Ohm and Watts. NB: To avow is to make a promise, so you 'avow' to remember this

TECHNICAL TIP

The positive electrode is also known as the indifferent electrode because its action is of no consequence i.e. is indifferent, in galvanic electrolysis, other than completing the electrical circuit

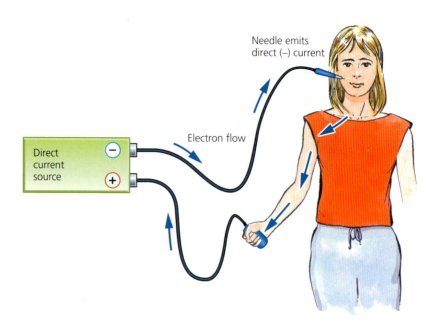

Needle emits
direct (−) current

Electron flow

Direct
current
source

−

+

Galvanic flow: negatively
charged electrons flow from
the negative pole to the
positive pole

Like flowing water, the electrical current or electrons always take the easiest route. They flow from the machine (power source) through the needle holder to the needle. Then they pass from the needle through the conducting salt water tissue fluid in the hair follicle, taking the shortest route through the body (generally the skin) to the positive electrode (metal plate or bar) and back into the machine.

Don't be concerned about clients wearing rings. Rings touching the positive electrode do not present a big problem because the ring becomes part of the positive electrode; however the current may cause some discolouration of certain jewellery and will detract the current flow. It is usual practice to cover the bar by wrapping it with a flat sponge, damp gauze, tissue or disposable wipe.

In thermolysis, the alternating current produces a high-frequency electromagnetic field around the needle, stimulating the water molecules in the hair follicle to vibrate, which produces heat. The actual high-frequency current is largely dissipated, some of the current goes through the body into space, and some returns to the machine. In thermolysis, therefore, you do not need a positive (indifferent) electrode to complete the circuit.

Conductors and insulators

Electric currents (like water in a river) like to take the easiest path. Conductors permit electric current (electrons) to flow through them easily.

Examples of good conductors are copper wire, stainless steel needles, salt solutions (found throughout the human body) and wet skin. Poor conductors or insulators resist or stop the flow of electric current. Examples of insulators are rubber, sebum and dehydrated skin.

Everyone is familiar with copper conducting electric wires being wrapped with rubber or plastic insulators. If we were holding on to a live wire, but

PROFESSIONAL TIP ✔

The more you understand about how electricity works, the less apprehensive you will be about it and the more able you will be to make sound judgements about equipment and its practical use, particularly when faced with a 'pushy' salesperson

were wearing thick rubber-soled shoes, the rubber would resist the flow of current through our bodies. The rubber in the shoes acts as a dam, stopping the continuing flow of the current, so very little passes through us. However, if we were standing in water, the current would continue to flow through us, since water is a good conductor.

'Ground wires' conduct electricity to the earth, and are excellent conductors. They act as a safety feature, removing unwanted electricity flow. In a household, the ground circuits are connected to metal pipes which go from your house into the ground, or to wires, which lead to metal rods buried in the ground.

TYPES OF ELECTROLYSIS

There are three main electrolysis techniques:

1 galvanic electrolysis

2 thermolysis

3 blend.

Comparison of electrolysis, thermolysis and blend

	Electrolysis	*Thermolysis*	*Blend*
Alternative names	True electrolysis Galvanic DC	Radio frequency RF high frequency HF shortwave diathermy	Combined current
Current type	Direct current	Oscillating (alternating) current	Direct current combined (with alternating) current
Type of destruction resulting	Chemical Sodium hydroxide (Lye)	Heat destruction Desiccation Coagulation/cauterisation	Warmed Chemical (Lye)
Length of time current supplied	10 seconds minimum	1000th second–3 seconds	4–8 seconds
Advantages	Effective on deep and distorted follicles Less discomfort for the client	Quick treatment of each follicle It can sometimes be used where direct current is contra-indicated Larger areas can be cleared in one sitting	Combined benefits of the two currents, speed of the thermolysis combined with the effectiveness of the galvanic Quicker conclusion to treatment due to enhanced effectiveness
Disadvantages	Slow process – longer time needed per follicle	Not effective on deep and distorted follicles, therefore reduces chance of permanent removal More discomfort for the client	Skill required in balancing currents and time, except with pre-set or computerised machines

GALVANIC ELECTROLYSIS

In galvanic electrolysis, the needle acts as the negative electrode (cathode), conducting the direct electrical current (flow of electrons) into the hair follicle. The galvanic current flows evenly from all parts of the needle. When the current passes through a conducting electrolysis needle into the conductive salt and water tissue fluid in a hair follicle, the direct current causes the water and salt to break up into its component parts to form ions (charged particles). These free ions recombine at the needle cathode (negative electrode) in a different manner to form hydrogen gas, chlorine gas and sodium hydroxide or lye. Lye is caustic and briefly remains in the hair follicle where it destroys the cells in the bottom regions of the hair follicle.

Action of galvanic current during electrolysis

This chemical action is not instantaneous, but takes time to develop in the follicle. It does not stop when the current ceases to be applied, it continues for a very short time afterwards.

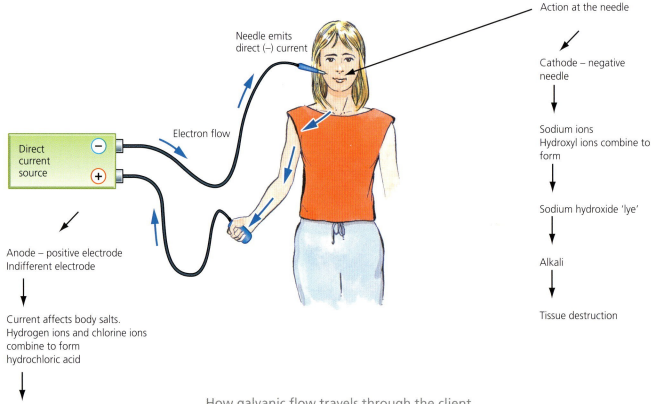

How galvanic flow travels through the client

The amount of lye produced depends upon:

- the amount of *moisture* present in the follicle being treated
- the *intensity* (amount) of current being used
- the *length* of time for which current flows.

The current is available the whole length of the needle, but affects tissue only where moisture is available.

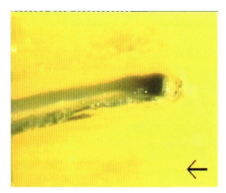

Production of lye around the needle in the follicle

Galvanic action at tip of the needle

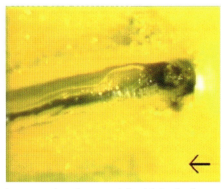

Lye production and 'bubbles' of hydrogen gas

Photos courtesy of Dr James Shuster

The upper portion of the follicle is less moist, and additionally, the sebum (oil) produced by the sebaceous gland (oil gland) at the top portion of the follicle is a poor conductor, so it acts as something of an insulator to protect the skin against the galvanic electrolysis at the top of the needle. More lye will be produced if either the intensity or the duration is increased. The hydrogen gas evaporates out of the hair follicle. Water is continually ionising so there is always easily available OH⁻ in solution to combine with the sodium.

$$2NaCl \text{ (salt)} + 2H_2O \text{ (water)} + \text{direct current electrical energy} = H_2 \text{ (hydrogen gas)} + 2NaOH \text{ (lye-sodium hydroxide)} + Cl_2 \text{ (chlorine gas)}$$

At the opposite pole (the positive anode, which is known as the indifferent electrode, the pad or bar which the client holds) chlorine gas is formed. Some of this combines with water in the skin to form hydrochloric acid. Only a small amount is formed, and only rarely is this irritating to the skin. When the chlorine gas joins with water, there is also some release of oxygen.

Units of lye

The quantity of lye we produce in the follicle can be calculated using Faradays Law, a method made popular by Arthur Hinkel (one of the inventors of blend electrolysis). The law uses the term 'unit of lye' or UL value. It states that one unit of lye is produced if 0.1 milliamp intensity of current flows for one second.

UNITS OF LYE CHART
0.1 milliamp of current flowing for one second produces one unit of lye
0.1 milliamp of current flowing for two seconds produces two units of lye
0.1 milliamp of current flowing for three seconds produces three units of lye
0.2 milliamps of current flowing for one second produces two units of lye
0.2 milliamps of current flowing for two seconds produced four units of lye
1.0 milliamp of current flowing for five seconds produces fifty units of lye

In galvanic electrolysis, if the intensity or the duration are increased, then the amount of lye produced will be increased. In other words:

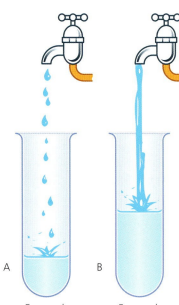

Filling follicles: Time and intensity

A   B
5 seconds   5 seconds

EQUIPMENT LIST
couch
trolley
stool
galvanic epilator
magnifying lamp
chuck cap
needle holder
gloves
needles (1- or 2-piece)
sterilised scissors
towels/pillows
eye shields
cotton wool/tissues
aftercare soothing lotion
skin sanitiser
sharps box
tweezers

REMEMBER

This is a guide only, always follow manufacturer's instructions

---

PRODUCTION OF LYE
INTENSITY × DURATION = UNITS OF LYE PRODUCED Increased INTENSITY × (or) increased DURATION = MORE UNITS OF LYE which is greater TREATMENT ENERGY

This means that, when using galvanic current, hair can be efficiently removed by using a higher current for shorter periods of time or a lower current for longer periods of time.

Imagine the follicle as a test tube which you want to fill with water. You can fill your test tube under a gushing tap very quickly. You can also fill your test tube under a dripping tap; you would simply have to stay there for longer:

● The gushing tap represents a high current passed for a short period

● The dripping tap represents a low current passed for a longer period of time.

Units of lye: Amount for specific locations

Hair type	Usual location	Units of lye
Shallow – vellus	Side face, lip, eyebrows	8–15
Medium – terminal	Face, chin, neck, arms, chest	35–45
Thick deep – terminal	Face, legs, back, bikini line	45–60
Very deep – terminal	Face, legs, back, bikini line	60–80

The galvanic treatment technique

Before conducting this treatment, ensure you have followed the pre-treatment procedures discussed in Section Four. The steps outlined here are general ones and electrologists should always follow the manufacturer's recommendations for their particular epilator.

1 Prepare yourself, the client and treatment area, as previously described.

2 Set the timer to 5 – following manufacturer's instructions

3 Set the galvanic to minimum – following manufacturer's instructions.

4 Treat a hair follicle that is representative of those to be treated. See if the hair will release, if yes – you have found the working point, if no – go to next step.

5 Ascertain from the client their level of comfort.

6 Treating a different hair follicle each time, gradually increase the galvanic from minimum until the working point is reached, checking with the client after each increase to ascertain their level of comfort. If the client is comfortable, you may continue increasing the current until the hair removes without traction.

7 Optional step. If the client reports discomfort, decrease the galvanic intensity to the level they did find comfortable and increase the time until the hair releases without traction.

THERMOLYSIS

Heinrich Hertz is considered the first scientist to have demonstrated the existence of high frequency waves in 1888. High frequency current did not become popular as a method of hair removal until the 1920s when this new method became known as 'thermolysis' because it destroyed tissue by heat (thermal) action.

When the alternating high-frequency current is passed down the electrolysis needle, it stimulates (by creating a high-frequency, electromagnetic field) the water molecules of the moist follicle tissue to vibrate, and this vibration produces heat.

KEY TERMS ★

Thermolysis: Derived from the Greek words 'thermo' (heat) and 'ysis' (to dissolve); the treatment is also sometimes called 'diathermy', 'high frequency' or 'shortwave'

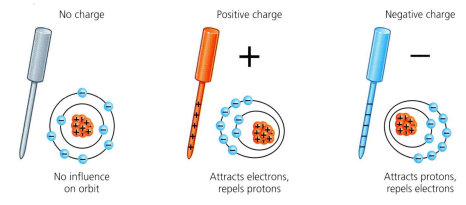

The heating action of high-frequency current

The needle itself is not hot in the beginning, but can heat up after a prolonged period of time due to the friction it has stimulated in the adjacent water fluid. The heat is greatest in the moist areas, and therefore more heat is produced in the lower portions of the follicle.

Types of destruction

Alternating current frequencies used for thermolysis

Class	Abbreviation	Range
Low frequency	LF	30–300 kiloHertz
Medium frequency	MF	300–3000 kiloHertz
High frequency	HF	3–30 megaHertz
Very high frequency	VHF	30–300 megaHertz

The way tissue is destroyed by high frequency depends upon the amount of heat generated by the action of the current.

Very high frequency (VHF) and high frequency (HF) currents produce electro-desiccation or drying of the tissue.

Medium or low frequencies produce electro-coagulation or a cooking (congealing) action.

There are many theories regarding which is the most beneficial, however both methods have their place and each can be useful for treating different follicles.

Electro-coagulation converts fluid into a thickened mass as in boiling an egg. This method is relatively slower than desiccation, it may however allow a wider spread of destruction and therefore produce better results in deeper follicles with larger dermal papillae.

Electro-desiccation deprives the tissue of moisture and causes it to dry up as in grilling. This effect happens at high intensity and fast speeds. For this reason, it is known as the flash technique, and it may therefore produce better results on straight follicles, as the area affected around the needle is small because the duration of current flow is very fast and the current effect will not reach larger dermal papillae or curved follicles.

Heat pattern

Heat pattern is the term used to describe the shape and size of the heat formed around the tip of the needle when passing an alternating current. During thermolysis treatment, the greatest concentration of high-frequency energy is at the needle tip where the needle offers least resistance to the current. This is known as the point effect.

The heat production begins at the needle tip first, and therefore acts there the longest. Heat production rises up in a pear or tear-drop shape towards the skin surface. This means that the deeper parts of the follicles receive heat more intensely and for a longer period of time than the higher portions of the follicle.

> **PROFESSIONAL TIP** ✔
>
> The flash technique can be highly effective, however it should only be conducted using computerised machines

> **PROFESSIONAL TIP** ✔
>
> Understanding how the heat is formed and the pattern it takes around the needle helps you to imagine what is happening in the follicle

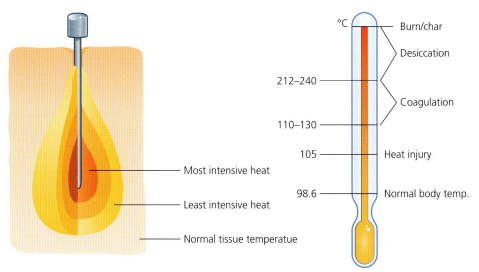

Heat pattern of thermolysis

Heat levels and tissue damage

°C
Burn/char
Desiccation
212–240
Coagulation
110–130
105 — Heat injury
98.6 — Normal body temp.

Most intensive heat
Least intensive heat
Normal tissue temperatue

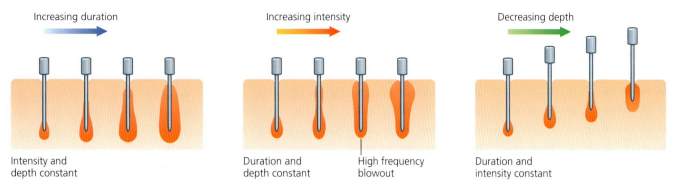

Increasing duration

Increasing intensity

Decreasing depth

Intensity and
depth constant

Duration and
depth constant

High frequency
blowout

Duration and
intensity constant

Effect of duration, intensity and depth on heating patterns of thermolysis

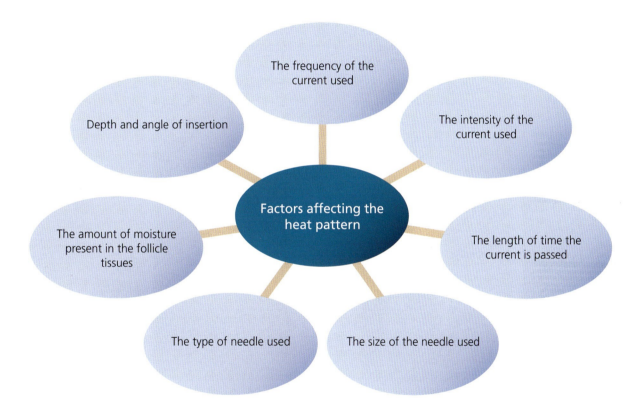

The frequency of the current used

The intensity of the current used

Depth and angle of insertion

Factors affecting the heat pattern

The length of time the current is passed

The amount of moisture present in the follicle tissues

The type of needle used

The size of the needle used

The heat pattern formed will vary according to a number of factors and you must understand all of them in order to provide successful treatment.

- *The frequency of the current used*: affects the heat pattern because higher frequencies generate faster movement to and fro of the positive and negative atoms; higher frequencies produce more heat.

- *The intensity of the current used*: the intensity of the current is the amount of current used. The precise amount of the current delivered is dependent upon frequency, moisture and duration.

- *The length of time the current is passed*: the length of time the current is passed directly affects the heat pattern:
  (a) when using a low intensity and longer period of time (1–3 seconds), the heat pattern will spread from the tip of the needle upwards and out-wards from the point.

(b) when using a high intensity current for a shorter period of time, the heat pattern does not spread up the needle but is more intensified at the tip.

- *The size of needle used*: the needle size refers to the diameter of the needle. A larger diameter allows a larger area of current flow; a smaller diameter intensifies the same amount of energy into a concentrated area.

- *The type of needle used*: the type of needle directly affects the heat pattern in several ways. Gold is a very effective conductor. Current intensity should be marginally reduced when using a gold plated needle to achieve the same effects as slightly higher currents when using standard stainless steel needles.

Insulated probes direct the current to the tip of the needle and are therefore only suitable for thermolysis current. As the current can only be emitted from the tip of the needle it becomes more intense and therefore, should be used at lower intensity than when using a stainless steel or gold plated needle.

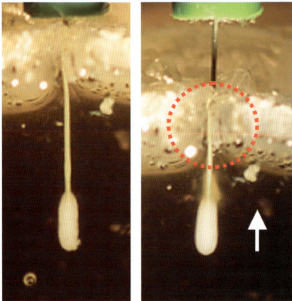 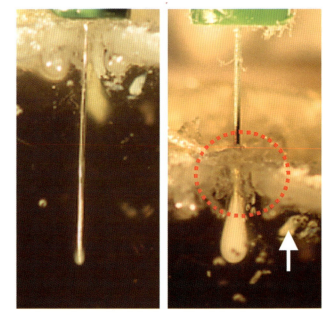

Effects of insulated needle on heating patterns

© Dectro International

In this experiment, egg whites are coagulated with an insulated needle (the two images on the left) and a non-insulated needle (the two images on the right). The coagulation pattern at the tip of the insulated needle is identical, regardless of the depth of insertion, as opposed to the non-insulated needle, where the coagulated area (white mass) widens when the needle is moved towards the surface of the skin.

- *The amount of moisture present in the follicle tissues*: moisture is vital for effective electrolysis treatment. In order to generate heat, the moisture molecules must vibrate and cause friction. Therefore, if the amount of moisture is limited the heat will also be limited.

- *Depth and angle of insertion*: the deeper the insertion, i.e. in an anagen follicle, the more moisture there will be, resulting in a more effective treatment. Treatment of shallow follicles, i.e. in catagen or telogen follicles, will be ineffective. However, should treatment be carried out on these follicles, care will need to be taken as the needle tip will still generate heat, which may lead to upper skin damage.

If the intensity is too high, then the tissue fluid may boil, which produces steam. This effect is often indicated by a crackling sound and excess sticking of tissue debris to the electrolysis needle. It can be prevented by reducing intensities and/or durations. High intensities should be used only with very short durations (flash technique).

Thermolysis treatment techniques

Destruction in the follicle caused by thermolysis

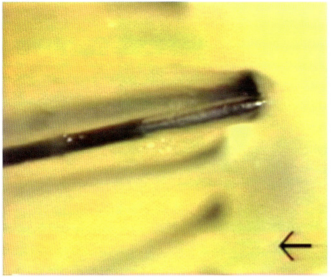

Insulated needle inserted

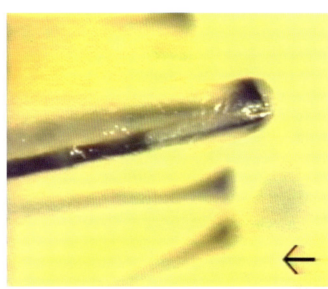

Current passed

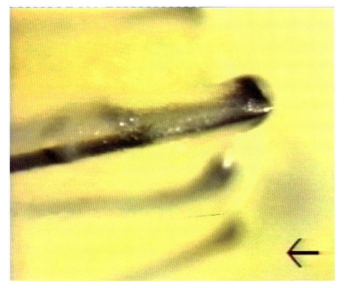

Heat starts to coagulate

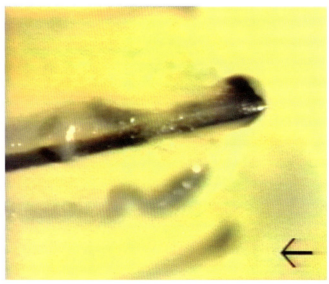

Further coagulation

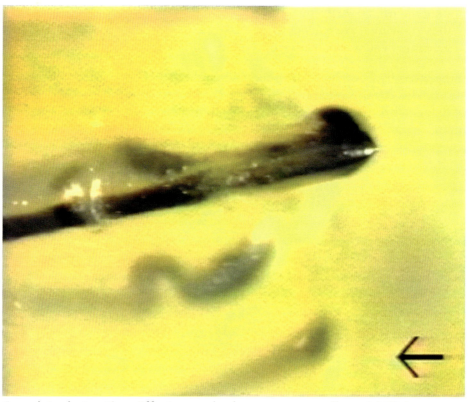

Complete destruction. Effects can also be seen on an adjacent follicle.

Photos courtesy of Dr James Shuster

EQUIPMENT LIST
couch
trolley
stool
thermolysis epilator
magnifying lamp
chuck cap
needle holder
gloves
needles (1- or 2-piece)
sterilised scissors
towels/pillows
eye shields
cotton wool/tissues
aftercare soothing lotion
skin sanitiser
sharps box
tweezers

Traditional (European) thermolysis technique

Before conducting this treatment ensure you have followed the pre-treatment procedures discussed in Section Four. The steps outlined here are general ones and electrologists should always follow the manufacturer's recommendations for their particular epilator.

Step One: Prepare yourself, the client and treatment area.

Step Two: Put on appropriate personal protection equipment.

Step Three: Sanitise the area to be treated.

Step Four: Aseptically load the needle.

Step Five: Switch on the epilator.

Step Six: Choose a hair follicle representative of those to be treated.

Step Seven: Starting with the lowest possible current level, insert your needle into the follicle and pass the current. After the timer has gone off or you have come to the end of your manual count, stop the current flow and withdraw the needle.

Step Eight: Try the hair with your tweezers to see if it will release without traction (plucking), if not then gradually increase the current, a follicle at a time, until the hair releases easily with your tweezers, again without traction. Check with the client after each increase to find out their level of comfort. If the client is comfortable you may continue with the treatment. If the client is finding the treatment too uncomfortable you may need to adapt your method – try a higher current for less time or a lower current for longer. Alternatively you could change modality.

Step Nine: Remove the hair from the treated follicle, ensuring that it released without traction.

Step Ten: Dispose of the hair carefully on to a conveniently placed piece of cotton wool or tissue.

Step Eleven: Discharge used needle aseptically into sharps box.

Step Twelve: When the area is cleared according to the agreed treatment plan, carry out cataphoresis treatment, if available.

Step Thirteen: Apply the chosen aftercare solution and ensure your client is aware of the home-care procedure.

> **TECHNICAL TIP** ✔
>
> Keep touching, fiddling and wiping to a minimum; although you may need to occasionally wipe the treatment area with antiseptic during the treatment, you should only do so when necessary and in moderation. Constant wiping of the skin increases the risk of infection, wastes time and can be irritating to the client

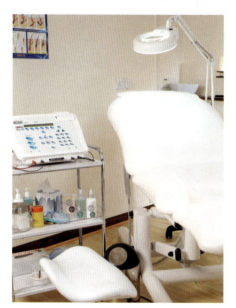

Step 2: Put on appropriate PPE

Step 3: Sanitise the area to be treated

Step 1: Prepare the treatment area

Step 4: Aseptically load the needle – one piece

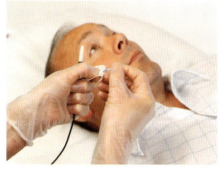

Step 4: Aseptically load the needle – two piece

Step 5: Switch on the epilator

Step 6: Choose a hair follicle

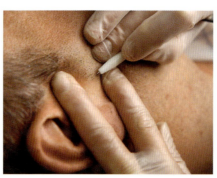

Step 7: With the lowest possible current, insert the needle into the follicle and pass the current

Step 8: Using tweezers, try to remove the hair without traction. Repeat with increased current if necessary

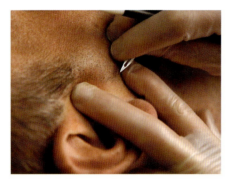

Step 9: Remove hair without traction

Step 10: Dispose of hair carefully

Step 11: Discharge needle to sharps box

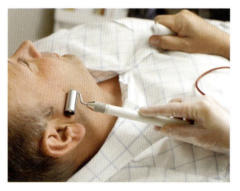

Step 12: Carry out cataphoresis treatment

Step 13: Apply aftercare

Alternative methods of treatment with thermolysis

Flash

The flash technique utilises very high intensities for very short periods of time. Although the flash method is used by some practitioners using conventional equipment, there is a high risk of heat overspill from the follicle as there may be variations in current output and length of time for which the current is passed. It can only safely be used on computerised equipment where intensity, current and timings are more effectively controlled than with manual operation.

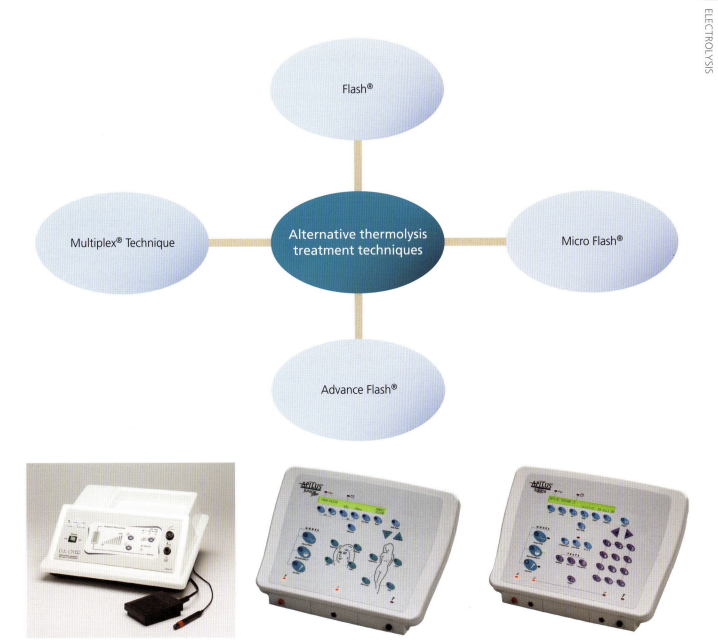

Flash®

Multiplex® Technique

Alternative thermolysis treatment techniques

Micro Flash®

Advance Flash®

Computerised epilators
Dectro International

'Micro' flash®

This is a method which is only available on computerised machines. The computer controls the output and the timing very precisely, allowing a powerful high intensity, high frequency current to be passed for very short periods of time (some units, for example the Apilus SX500, operate at speeds of one thousandth of a second). This method is suitable for straight follicles as the heat pattern is intense and precise at the tip of the needle. The sensation from this current is less than with other methods; this is because the current passes for such a short period of time that the heat nerve receptors do not have time to notice the sensation.

Advance flash

This method too is only available when using a computerised machine. It is possible to use a technique referred to as the P&B technique (or retraction insertion), because is treats both the papilla and bulge during the insertion. It should only be used by experienced electrologists, as it requires movement within the follicle.

Procedure for advance flash:

1 The needle is inserted into the follicle as usual in preparation for the emission of two high pulses of current.

2 For the release of the first pulse the needle is positioned at the base of the follicle, at the papilla.

3 Then the needle is retracted (moved upwards) in a controlled and timed manner so that the second pulse is released further up the follicle at the bulge area.

The epilator's computer controls the output of the current, it also allows the operator to adjust the time between the two pulses according to their speed and experience. Some computerised epilators, the Apilus senior 11 for example, automatically and proportionally reduces the power of the second pulse to ensure that it does not overspill the follicle.

Multiplex® technique

This method is patented to Dectro, manufacturers of 'Apilus', a computerised epilator.

Procedure for the Multiplex technique:

1 A low-intensity high-frequency current is passed for around 1 second; this pre-warms the follicle.

2 An automatic high-intensity micro flash of high frequency is then passed for a fraction of a second. This allows the heat pattern to spread slightly further away from the needle than with standard computerised flash.

This method is ideal for hairs which are very slightly distorted as it allows this type of hair to be treated quickly and efficiently and provides a stepping stone from thermolysis to blend epilation.

Simple experiments to observe electrolysis energy

Consolidate your electrolysis techniques by completing the following simple experiments.

Galvanic experiment on a piece of meat or fish

Place a piece of moist meat or fish on top of a sheet of aluminium foil, which is on top of the indifferent electrode. Lay your needle lengthways on top of the meat or fish so you can observe the destruction by the lye which dissolves the meat or fish.

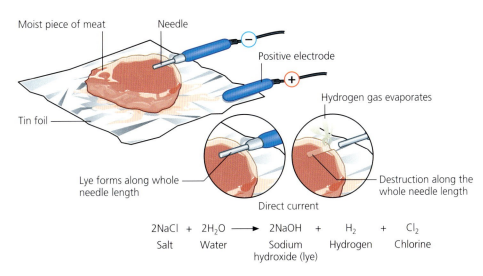

$$2NaCl \ + \ 2H_2O \longrightarrow 2NaOH \ + \ H_2 \ + \ Cl_2$$

| Salt | Water | Sodium hydroxide (lye) | Hydrogen | Chlorine |

Demonstration of the action of lye using a piece of meat

Thermolysis experiment on egg whites

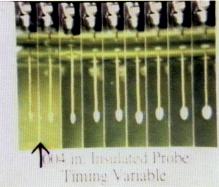

Variable timings with insulated needles

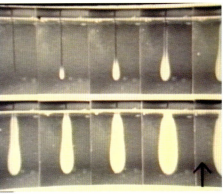

Variable timing with non-insulated needles

Pictures courtesy of Dr James Shuster

Place the egg white in a cup containing a strip of foil or lined with, or made of aluminium foil. Observe the different patterns of coagulation of the egg white that occur around the needle with various intensities and needle coatings.

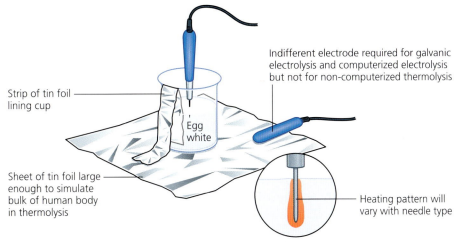

Demonstration of the action of lye using egg white

Moisture test

If your computerised epilator is equipped with a moisture sensor, use it to assess the moisture at different depths of the follicles in various regions of the body. You will notice that electricity is more easily conducted in the depth of the follicle than it is in the epidermis. Repeat the test in a moist area, such as the perspiring axillae (under arm) and in a dry area such as the knee.

THE BLEND TECHNIQUE

History

The blend method was developed in order to address the shortcomings of both galvanic (its slowness) and thermolysis (its inefficiency on distorted follicles) methods. In the late 1930s, an American electrologist, Henri St Pierre and his GEC engineer friend, Arthur Hinkel, began to experiment with combining the two currents as they realised the limitation of each individual modality and therefore the benefits of combining the two.

In 1945 the first patent for a combined current epilator was granted to St Pierre and Hinkel. Today their original concept has been further developed and new technology gives the field of professional electrolysis a range of equipment and operator choice, for example basic manual or single modality, through to computerised pre-set treatment techniques.

Arthur Hinkel

Courtesy: *International Hair Route Magazine.* Photo: Alfred and Fabris Studios

What is the blend technique?

In the blend technique, both the galvanic direct current and the thermolysis high-frequency alternating current are passed down the same needle at the same time. This combination of galvanic electrolysis and thermolysis (DC+RF) gives the benefits of both modalities – the speed of the heat in thermolysis combined with the efficiency of the chemical action of galvanic. These combined qualities have made the blend especially effective in treating the deep bulbous terminal hairs and curved follicles which have proven too difficult for high-frequency current alone.

In the blend method the thermolysis warms the lye and warmed lye is much more effective in destroying tissue. Additionally, the damaged tissue around the base of the follicle produced by the thermolysis permits the lye to spread out through the tissues more easily and more rapidly.

Hinkel's research showed that the blend only requires a quarter to a half of the time normally needed for galvanic electrolysis when used on its own. Therefore, in the blend, galvanic electrolysis settings are established at a quarter to a half of their usual time for galvanic alone. This time works out to be just slightly more than the duration of thermolysis for a similar hair's working point, but the treatment benefits are greatly increased. Imagine a test tube full of a chemical. The chemical is having a gradual destructive effect. Now add heat from a Bunsen burner and the chemical effect happens more rapidly. For each 6°C increase in temperature, the speed of the chemical reaction doubles, therefore heated lye can be up to six times more caustic than lye at body temperature.

The destruction in the follicle

Start of blend current release | Lye forming in follicle

Destruction of the follicle

Photos courtesy of Dr James Shuster

Two currents, one needle, how is it possible?

The blend epilator combines the currents so that they pass down the needle simultaneously. This is possible due to the nature of the electrons. The direct current is a linear (straight line) passage of electrons from atom to atom through a conductive solution. Radio frequency (RF) is a rapid transfer of electrons backwards and forwards between positive and negative atoms. To explain how one electron performs both actions, Hinkel asks us to envisage a train travelling along a track, inside which someone is playing table tennis. The ball, whilst passing back and forth over the table (RF), is, at the same time, still travelling forward in the train (DC).

While the electrons bounce back and forth, they still move towards the positive

Even though the two currents are together, they maintain their own treatment characteristics and effect in the follicle as if they were working independently. The destruction is more efficient, and faster, as the heat from the thermolysis warms the sodium hydroxide or lye.

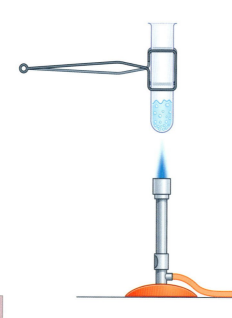

Lye working in the follicle

Picture courtesy of Dr James Shuster

Heat increases the action of lye

REMEMBER !

You have more choice of current settings and timings when using the blend modality so you can more easily adapt the treatment to suit your client's needs, whilst successfully treating follicles

EQUIPMENT LIST

couch

trolley

stool

blend epilator

magnifying lamp

chuck cap

needle holder

gloves

needles (1- or 2-piece)

sterilised scissors

towels/pillows

eye shields

cotton wool/tissues

aftercare soothing lotion

skin sanitiser

sharps box

tweezers

Benefits of blend

There are two main benefits for clients provided by the blend technique.

1 The blend method offers a choice of treatment techniques which can be adapted to each client, based on their pain threshold and length of time available for treatment. A lower current passed for a longer time can provide greater levels of comfort but will take more time per follicle, so less hair will be removed per session. This method is often referred to as 'lower for longer'. Lower for longer is often preferred on areas where comfort is more of an issue.

2 When high current levels are passed for shorter periods of time it may not provide as much comfort. It will, however, result in a shorter overall treatment time and more hairs removed per session. This method is often referred to as 'higher for shorter'. Many electrologists find their clients prefer this technique on the face as it treats the most follicles, and therefore gets rid of the most hairs, per session.

The blend treatment technique

Before conducting this treatment, ensure you have followed the pre-treatment procedures discussed in Section Four. The steps outlined here are general ones and electrologists should always follow the manufacturer's recommendations for their particular epilator.

1 Prepare yourself, the client and treatment area, as previously described.

2 Set the RF level for blend (normally minimum).

3 Set the timer to 5 and set the galvanic to minimum.

4 Treat a representative hair follicle of those to be treated. See if the hair will release, if yes – you have found the working point, if no – go to next step.

5 Find out from your client their level of comfort.

6 Treating a different hair follicle each time, gradually increase the galvanic until the working point is reached, checking with the client after each increase to find out their level of comfort. If the client is comfortable, you may continue increasing the current until the hair removes without traction.

7 If the client reports discomfort, decrease the galvanic intensity to the level they did find comfortable and increase the time until the hair releases without traction.

8 Remove the hair from the treated follicle with tweezers, ensuring that it releases without traction, then dispose of it carefully on to a conveniently placed cotton wool or tissue.

9 When the area is cleared according to the agreed treatment plan, carry out cataphoresis, if available.

10 Apply the chosen aftercare solution and ensure your client is aware of the home-care procedure.

The Carlton Group

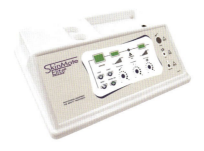

Silhouette International

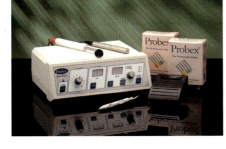

House of Famuir Ltd www.hofbeauty.co.uk

House of Famuir Ltd www.hofbeauty.co.uk

Non-computerised blend epilators

Sterex Electrolysis

Alternative blend treatment techniques

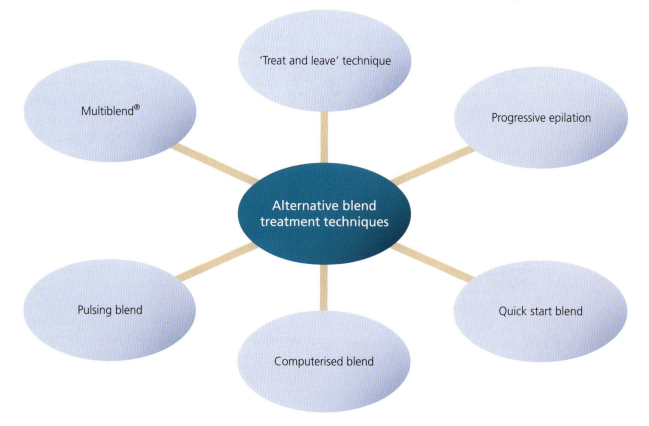

Treat and leave technique

To help speed up the treatment process, you can adopt the 'treat and leave' technique. This technique involves treating a group of hair follicles but not immediately removing the hairs, then treating another group, again not removing the hairs but going back to the first group of hairs and removing them with tweezers, and then removing those from the second group. This speeds up the process by removing the hairs all together as opposed to after each insertion. In a salon situation, one side of the upper lip, for example, would be treated, then the other side, and then the hairs from both sides removed.

Progressive epilation

This method is rarely used but is helpful for clients with a low tolerance to the currents and utilises the absolute minimum levels of both galvanic and RF. Insert into the follicle and, whilst continually passing both currents at minimum levels, occasionally test the hair's resistance by applying tension to the hair with tweezers. When the hair releases smoothly, the hair follicle has been successfully treated. Keep the needle inserted with the currents flowing for a further 5 seconds, in order to flood the empty follicle with warmed lye. The time taken for this technique is measured in minutes not seconds!

Quick start blend

Some blend units are available with a 'Quick start'. The high frequency current is passed for a short burst at the beginning of the current's flow; it then reduces to an absolute minimum and passes simultaneously with the galvanic current for the remainder of the time. This short initial burst anaesthetises the follicle by over-stimulating the sensory receptors. The remainder of the current's flow feels much more comfortable as a consequence.

Computerised blend

The use of computer software in epilation machines has made possible a number of advances and options in the use and application of currents.

Micro-processors control the current, ensure consistent output, and allow more controlled flow in addition to a wider range of application possibilities. The order of current flow may be changed, that is the galvanic may begin before the RF or vice versa.

Computerised blend epilators

© Dectro International

Pulsing blend

During this method, the high frequency current is applied in a series of pulses during the constant flow of the galvanic current. This method is designed to increase comfort levels as a smaller amount of high frequency is used. It is also suggested that this method is more suitable for less moist skin as less high frequency is used. The galvanic current is applied for slightly longer to produce more lye, as opposed to using more heat which can dry out the follicle.

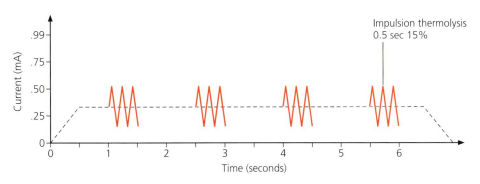

Pulsing blend

Multiblend®

This method is patented to Dectro (the manufacturers of Apilus) and is only available on an Apilus machine. Both high frequency and galvanic are applied to the follicle simultaneously (as in standard blend). This generates 'warm lye' in the follicle; a high powered 'flash' of high frequency is then delivered for a fraction of a second. This high and quick burst of energy 'charges' the warm lye and makes it highly destructive. This method is ideal for deep follicles and very distorted growth.

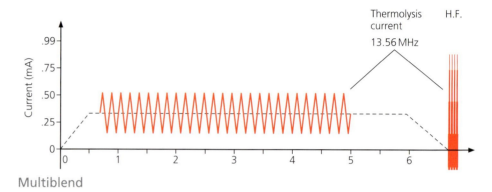

Multiblend

Multiple needle epilation

Developed in 1916 by Prof. Paul Kree, this method, as the name suggests, uses not one needle but between 12 and 16. This is not as widely used as the single needle method, but it is worthy of note. It is a method known to be fast and effective in experienced hands as it treats multiple follicles at the same time.

The needle-holders are totally different as they are not held by hand but are suspended from a 'rack' to keep them separated from each other and support the needles once they have been loaded and inserted into the follicles. The needle-holders are colour coded at both ends so you can see which needle is where.

Multiple needle epilators: Shirley Hurtubise and husband Dan demonstrate multi-needle depilation at the American Electrology Convention, Las Vegas, Nevada, October 2004

Courtesy: *International Hair Route Magazine*; Photo: Karen V. Vickers

Modern day multiple needle machines are computerised in order to maintain control over the timing of the insertions and current flow. The computer allows for pre-setting of the current levels and duration of time for each outlet, when the time is completed the current is discontinued and there is normally an audible 'bleep' and a visual sign – invariably an indicator light which goes off when the needle is no longer passing current.

Multiple needle electrolysis (MNE) has historically been used for galvanic treatments only, however, they are also being used now for blend treatments.

The advantage is that 12–16 follicles are treated at a time, the disadvantage is that it can be 'finicky' and, as it is totally different to single needle application, takes some getting used to.

Standard multiple needle electrolysis treatment technique

Before conducting this treatment, ensure you have followed the pre-treatment procedures discussed in Section Four. The steps outlined here are general ones and electrologists should always follow the manufacturer's recommendations for their particular epilator.

1 Switch the multi-needle epilator machine on.
2 Insert needles into 'needle-holders' and ensure 'needle-holders' are in the correct order.
3 Attach the positive electrode to the client.
4 Set insertion delay (normally 2–3 seconds). This is the time allowed from when the needle is inserted to when the current starts flowing.
5 Set the duration of current flow for each needle (each needle delivers the same current intensity for the same duration).
6 Adjust the intensity, depending on the client's tolerance of the current.
7 Prepare the skin.
8 Lift the 'needle-holders', one at a time, from the rack.
9 Insert one needle into one follicle (a visual indicator tells you when the current is flowing and goes out when the current ceases. The average hair requires 180–300 seconds).
10 Continue to insert your needles in a memorable order.
11 By the time you have completed your last insertion, the current flow may have ceased in your first follicle. You should now remove the needle, remove the hair and insert the needle into an adjacent follicle.

Differences in treatment to single needle electrolysis

1 All the follicles must be the same type and depth.
2 The needle needs to be positioned so that the shank does not touch the surrounding skin – the preferred angle is 45°.
3 Some electrologists find that the use of a magnifying lamp is difficult as it gets in the way of the MNE needle rack.

EQUIPMENT LIST
couch
trolley
stool
multi-needle epilator
magnifying lamp
chuck cap
needle holder
gloves
needles (1- or 2-piece)
sterilised scissors
towels/pillows
eye shields
cotton wool/tissues
aftercare soothing lotion
skin sanitiser
sharps box
tweezers

REMEMBER !

The standard MNE treatment outlined here is a guide only, always follow manufacturer's instructions

4 This treatment method uses a lower current than single needle electrolysis.

5 The client needs to remain still during treatment so as not to dislodge any of the 12–16 needles.

6 Careful positioning is essential in certain areas, i.e. under the chin, to ensure the needles stay in the correct position.

7 As the treatment uses 12–16 needles, this additional cost should be passed on to the client.

EQUIPMENT

Epilators

Epilators
© Sterex Electrolysis

The epilator unit is the most vital piece of equipment. Carefully assess your requirements and select your machine after taking into consideration the following factors.

- Does the unit offer thermolysis, galvanic and/or blend?
- Does the epilator provide a choice of control – finger button, foot or computer controlled automatic current release?
- What are the guarantee and servicing agreements?
- What technical support is available?
- What introductory training is offered and what additional courses are available?
- What additional/advanced features, e.g. computerisation, hair counter, moisture sensor, cataphoresis/anaphoresis, facility to treat minor skin blemishes (skin tags) and telangiectasia (dilated capillaries) does the machine have?
- Consider the machine's ease of use.
- Cost – consider your budget and evaluate that against the features and benefits of each machine.
- Think about the size and appearance of the unit, and whether it will fit easily into your working area.
- Don't forget to take into account any promotional materials and products offered with the epilator.

When purchasing an epilator, you will find there are a wide variety of machines available and you must choose between a 'standard' or 'computerised' model:

- Standard epilators tend to be available in a choice of thermolysis only and blend machines. Look for features such as an integrated timer, digital controls and optional foot pedal operation.
- Computerised machines offer a very wide range of options in modalities. In addition, some offer the option of a setting which allows an automatic discharge of the current once the needle is in the follicle and after a pre-set safety delay. In order for the computer to detect the insertion, a positive (indifferent) electrode is required to provide a complete circuit. This is the only occasion when a positive electrode is required for thermolysis.

Couches

The treatment couch must not only offer comfort for your client, it must also provide accessibility for them and for you. Because of these access issues and the age ranges of possible clients, the electrolysis couch must have easy access for the electrologist however the client is positioned, for example the electrologist needs to be able to sit down comfortably with knees under the couch.

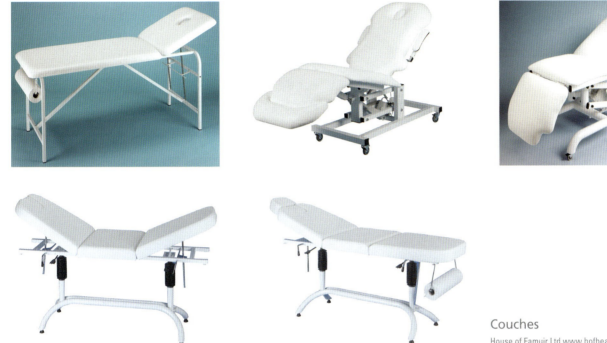

Couches

House of Famuir Ltd www.hofbeauty.co.uk

Some clients may not be able to climb up onto the couch. The ideal solution would be to have either an electric or hydraulic couch, which can be lowered sufficiently to allow disabled or elderly clients to get on. However, if finances will not allow you to buy an electric couch, you will need a sturdy foot stool or step to assist clients onto a basic couch.

Stools

As you will spend a significant amount of your working day seated, the seat should be wide enough to support your bottom and deep enough to be comfortable. To help with the significant amount of movement you will be required to make during an electrolysis treatment, the stool should have castors.

The stool should be fully adjustable with either a screw lift or, preferably, gas lift. Height adjustment is often required during treatment and a gas lift will allow the electrologist to do this promptly and without having to get up. Stools are available with or without backrests.

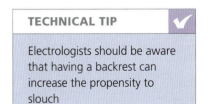

TECHNICAL TIP ✔

Electrologists should be aware that having a backrest can increase the propensity to slouch

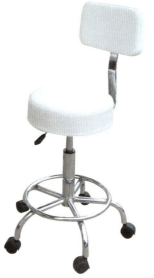

Stools

House of Famuir Ltd www.hofbeauty.co.uk

Trolley

The trolley should have enough shelving and storage capacity to hold all the equipment, consumables and spare accessories for the treatment. It is recommended that the trolley should have two or three shelves and preferably one drawer.

Trolleys

House of Famuir Ltd www.hofbeauty.co.uk

It is highly recommended that a double socket power pack is attached to the side of the trolley, so that the epilator and magnifier lamp can be plugged into it, leaving only one lead going to the wall.

Magnifier lamp

This is a vital piece of equipment because it serves two key roles:

- to illuminate the treatment area
- to magnify the treatment area.

Magnifiers come in a variety of shapes and sizes and costs. The most popular are round magnifying lenses with a circular fluorescent tube. Others are rectangular with two fluorescent straight tubes on either side, which can be

HEALTH AND SAFETY ⭐

When using a magnifying lamp which is fixed on to a rolling base, take care not to pull the head of the lamp out so far from the base that it can easily unbalance and topple over on to the client. Always move both the base and lamp together

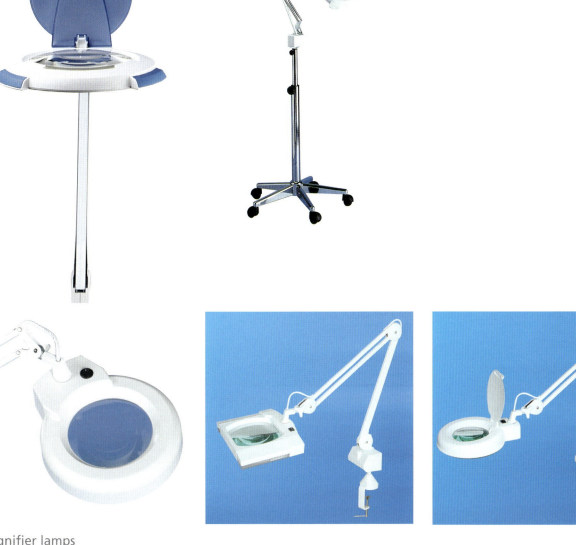

Magnifier lamps
House of Famuir Ltd www.hofbeauty.co.uk

operated independently, this can be of great assistance when treating fair and fine hairs, as when one tube is switched off it creates a shadow on the hair allowing you to see it better.

A lamp with a larger glass lens provides a larger viewing area, which means you can treat more follicles before having to move the lamp, which saves time. Lamp magnification is measured in 'diopters' and 3 is a good level of magnification for electrolysis. This magnifies the area by 1.75 times (× 1.75). Also available are 5 diopter lenses which magnify by × 2.25, this strength of magnification is generally only required if you have poor eyesight.

Lamps are normally provided with a 'G' clamp in order to attach them to a trolley, couch or other surface. It is preferable, however, to attach the lamp either to a rolling base for ease of positioning or into a holder on the trolley, as already discussed. Also available are wall fixing brackets, which is probably the least desirable option. It is very difficult to position the lamp successfully and the probability of the lamp falling off the wall, when it is fully extended, is unacceptably high, increasing the risk of injury to yourself and your client. In some countries magnification and illumination is achieved by the use of specially made glasses.

Needle-holder

There are two main types of needle-holder:

- switched
- unswitched.

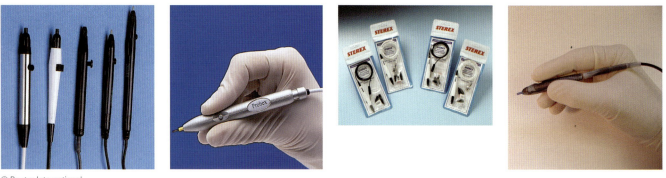

© Dectro International

Sterex Electrolysis

Needle-holders

Switched needle-holders are normally wide to facilitate the button and internal electronic switch. The switched needle-holder is used without a foot pedal – most epilators have the option of using either a finger button (switched) or foot pedal. If you choose to use a foot pedal, you will use an unswitched needle-holder.

Unswitched needle-holders, although often the same width as the switched (due to the same tooling used to make both) can be much thinner as there is no switch. North American needle-holder manufacturers, for example, mainly produce unswitched holders, so they are very narrow. European and particularly British manufacturers, although offering both, produce units that are the same thickness and length. Some needle-holders have integral cables and others are supplied with detachable ones; detachable cables are useful because the needle-holders do not have to be replaced if it is just the cable that is broken.

Some needle-holders have an ejector button which allows for safe and easy loading and unloading of the needle.

The length of the needle-holder (not including the cable) varies from 60 mm to 130 mm. There is no 'correct' length or width, but choose a size to fit your hand and that you feel comfortable with. It is advisable, however, to use a smaller size wherever possible as it will allow easier access to difficult areas, under the chin and in the bikini line for example, where space is restricted.

Detachable cables for needle-holders

Chuck caps

Chuck caps go on the end of the needle-holder; in fact they screw onto the 'chuck', which is the part of the needle-holder which holds the needle. The chuck cap, when screwed on, tightens the chuck onto the needle and keeps it in position during treatment. There are large and small chuck caps available, depending on the make of needle holder. There is a tendency nowadays for some new brands of needles to have colour coded (for size) and integral chuck caps.

Colour-coded, integral chuck caps

© Dectro International

Needles

Electrolysis needles are made from stainless steel and are available in stainless steel only or with gold and insulated coatings. There are two types of needle construction: one-piece and two-piece.

HEALTH AND SAFETY ✚

You should always have spare chuck caps available. This will enable you to disinfect them between clients. If they become contaminated by body fluids they should be sterilised

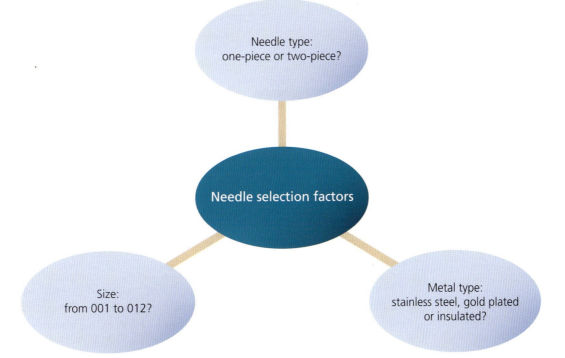

Needle type:
one-piece or two-piece?

Needle selection factors

Size:
from 001 to 012?

Metal type:
stainless steel, gold plated
or insulated?

One-piece needle

Sterex Electrolysis

One-piece

A one-piece needle is constructed from one piece of metal which tapers towards the tip. As the needles are made from one piece of metal they are more 'rigid' than two-piece needles and some electrologists find them less likely to bend upon insertion.

Two-piece

A two-piece needle is constructed of two pieces of metal. The two parts are the shank, which is the part fitted into the needle holder, and the wire needle part (the shaft), which is inserted into the follicle. The two pieces are crimped together. As the needles are made from two pieces they are more flexible than one-piece needles and some electrologists find them more likely to bend upon insertion.

Both one- and two-piece needles are available in three types:

- stainless steel
- gold plated
- insulated.

PROFESSIONAL TIP ✔

Use of one-piece or two-piece needles is very much a matter of choice and you should ideally have a selection of both types

---

Dectro International

Sterex Electrolysis

A selection of 2-piece needles

Gold is a more efficient conductor than stainless steel and so current levels may be reduced very slightly when using gold needles. Gold has properties that allow it to tone skin and it is therefore more suitable for sensitive or reactive skins.

Gold needles can be difficult to use on clients with red or light brown hairs as it can be difficult to distinguish between the hair and the needle. The same problem can occur with grey or blond hairs when using a stainless steel needle.

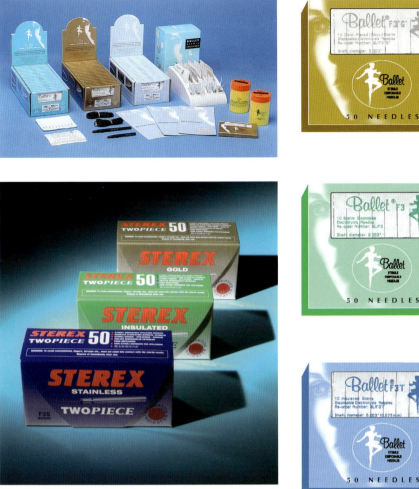

A selection of gold, insulated and stainless needles

Insulated needles are made from stainless steel and are covered in a medical grade insulating material, leaving only the tip exposed. This targets the current to the tip of the needles which means that the heat pattern is more intense. The insulation provides a reduction in surface erythema as the current is targeted to the tip of the needle and therefore to the base of the follicle.

Insulation also provides a reduction in treatment discomfort. As the current is only emitted at the tip of the needle, and it is correctly inserted, it means that many of the pain receptors, which are located in the upper level of the follicle, are by-passed. As a result of the concentrated current, the electrologist can use lower current levels when treating with insulated needles.

Needle size

Needles are available in a variety of sizes from 001 to 012. These measurements refer to the diameter of the needle. The number is pre-fixed with an 'F' or a 'K' (this letter refers to the shank size). Most British and North American needle-holders are made to fit 'F' shank needles; some European needles are 'K' shank which are thinner.

The diameter of the needle should match the diameter of the hair. A smaller diameter needle concentrates the current. A larger diameter, therefore,

REMEMBER	!

When it comes to needles, size matters!

TECHNICAL TIP	✔

Use the largest needle that will comfortably fit into the follicle

allows a wider flow of current. The effect is similar to a garden hose pipe: if the size of the opening is reduced, the water is forced out in an intense and small jet, just as current is with a small diameter needle. When the garden hose pipe opening is widened, the jet of water becomes more widely spread and more gentle, and it is the same with a large diameter needle.

A larger needle will therefore allow a larger flow of current and a larger affected area. If, however, the needle is too large, it may rupture and damage the follicle during insertion and cause bruising if forced into the follicle.

Using a needle which is too small will intensify the current and make the heat pattern too narrow, therefore missing target areas of the follicle.

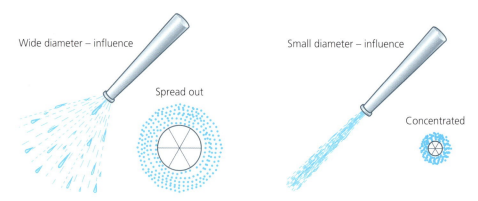

The effect of needle size treatment

Packaging

It is important to understand the two ways needles are commonly packaged by manufacturers, as you will frequently need to unpack them at short notice during treatments.

- One-piece needles are generally packed in a vacuum formed plastic pocket which encapsulates the needle in a sterile environment and protects the shaft of the needle. The individual pockets are normally connected in a row of ten needles. Remove a one-piece needle by peeling the protective paper from the 'blister pack' packaging, like a banana, whilst holding the shaft. Insert the needle shank into a loosened chuck cap, tighten to hold the needle in position, and remove packaging to expose shaft.
- Two-piece needles are generally packed in individual sachets with a hard plastic sheath encasing the shaft part of the needle to protect it from damage, which also acts as a positioning tool. Remove a two-piece needle from its individual wrapper by holding it by its plastic positioning cap. Insert the shank into a loosened chuck cap, tighten to hold the needle in position, and remove the plastic cap to expose the shaft.

> **TECHNICAL TIP** ✔
>
> Always ensure you have a full selection of needle sizes and types available to ensure effective treatment

Assessment of knowledge and understanding

This section has described electricity and electrolysis. To test your level of knowledge and understanding, answer the following short questions:

1 Describe what the following are and what role they play in electricity:

   a ampere

   b volt

   c ohm

   d watt.

2 What are the chemical steps in the change from saline to lye?

3 Identify which diameter of needle would produce a more intense heating pattern – a 002 or 005 – and state the reasons why.

4 What are the options when working with blend if the hairs do not remove without traction and:

   a the client is quite comfortable with the level of current

   b the client is uncomfortable with the level of current.

5 In what case would you use the multiple needle method and why?

6 What methods of blend are available?

7 List two examples of materials which are insulators and two which are conductors.

8 List two factors which should be considered when purchasing an electrolysis machine.

9 Give an alternative name for sodium hydroxide.

10 What is the purpose of an indifferent electrode?

Activities

Conduct the following activities to practise your knowledge of electricity and electrolysis:

1 Find and visit the websites of manufacturers and suppliers of epilators to gather information about their epilators. Then create a chart highlighting the main differences between at least four brands.

2 Look through suppliers' brochures and catalogues and choose a couch and a stool specifically for you to carry out electrolysis; the couch must be comfortable for both you and your clients.

3 Research supply companies and discover the various costs and types of epilators, equipment and treatment furniture for the above area.

4 Using diagrams to illustrate, design an electrolysis treatment area to include the required equipment.

To build on the knowledge of electricity and electrolysis gained in this section, complete the following tasks to extend your hair removal skills and understanding:

1 Visit the Dectro website at www.dectro.com

2 Visit Ballet's website at www.ballet.com

3 Visit Sterex's website www.sterex-electrolysis-int.co.uk

4 Investigate other hair removal suppliers via www.salonwebshop. co.uk. Click onto 'Beauty' then 'Hair Removal Room' from the Beauty home page.

Further reading

Electrolysis Thermolysis and the Blend, A. R. Hinkel and R. W. Lind, Arroway California, 1968.

SECTION FOUR: BEST ELECTROLYSIS PRACTICE

What will I know after reading this section?

This section covers best electrolysis practice and it will enable you to:

- **perform the correct treatment procedure**
- **understand the essentials of best practice**
- **correctly position the client for treatment.**

ESSENTIALS OF BEST PRACTICE

Technique

There are essentially two techniques generally adopted by electrolysis practitioners: the one-handed technique and the two-handed technique.

As the name implies, in the one-handed technique, the needle-holder and the tweezers are held in the same hand. In the two-handed technique, the needle-holder is held in one hand and the tweezers in the other.

Both techniques have advantages and disadvantages and the method you adopt is a matter of personal preference.

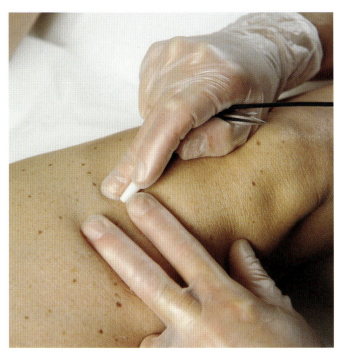

One-handed technique

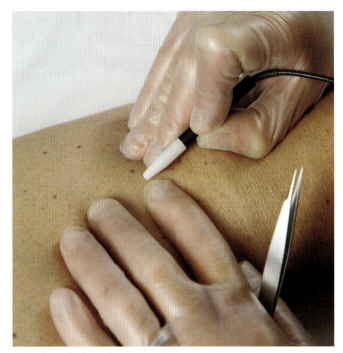

Two-handed technique

Advantages and disadvantages of the one-handed technique

Advantages	Disadvantages
✓ Quicker way of working.	✗ Prevents the needle-holder hand from being really flat so insertions will always be at an angle which is not suitable on all areas, i.e. the legs and bikini.
✓ Allows the other hand to 'stretch' or support the skin of the treatment area in different ways.	✗ Takes a little getting used to.

PROFESSIONAL TIP ✔

It is important to be aware that you cannot achieve an accurate and fast working technique unless you persevere and put in a lot of effort. Education is not received; it is achieved! Every client that you treat will bring you closer to a professional technique

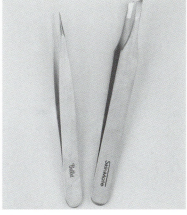

Electrolysis tweezers

Tweezers

There are numerous different types of tweezers, which vary in length, weight and tip shape. There is not right or wrong tweezer, it is more a case of what 'feels' right in your hand. Experiment to see what type of tweezer feels comfortable and secure in your hand when carrying out a treatment.

Tweezers with pointed tips are more commonly used for epilation treatments, as they are more precise and help to prevent the electrologist from pulling hairs surrounding the treated one, therefore avoiding accidental plucking.

TECHNICAL TIP ✔

Take good care of your tweezers, they are vital tools which can be delicate, particularly the ones with pointed tips. Where possible keep a protective cover over the tips. If the tweezers are dropped without protection they can easily 'splay out' which will render them useless for gripping hairs

'Stretch'

The stretch is one of the most important things to get right. It is what facilitates your needle access into the follicle. If you do not 'open' the follicle sufficiently, needle access will inevitably be restricted or at best difficult.

The skin around the follicles to be treated should be supported by the hand not holding the needle-holder, this makes the client feel secure and it helps to aid insertions when a slight stretch is used.

The follicle opening is generally speaking circular and if you apply pressure top and bottom of it, it will elongate the opening but will make it very thin, like a slit, which makes it is difficult to insert the needle into the follicle.

Some hair removal practitioners, in their attempts to insert, then stretch harder making the thin 'slit' even thinner, making insertion impossible. The best way to support and offer some stretch is to do it in three directions. This 'opens' the circle to become a bigger circle.

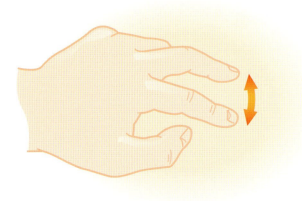

Two-finger stretch

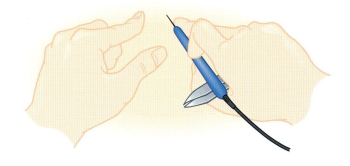

Three-finger stretch

Skin manipulation with stretching

You will often be required to use the stretch to gently manipulate the skin into a position to assist insertion. For example, along the mandible gentle manipulation allows you to lift the skin over the bone, giving easier access to the follicle. Also, by putting more pressure on the upper fingers, the hair is lifted up.

Perfect insertions

The most important aspect of achieving a successful electrolysis technique is to carry out perfect insertions. This is not difficult, but it can take a little time to become proficient. To make perfect insertions and carry out effective electrolysis treatment you need to do the following two key things:

1 choose the correct amount of current
2 discharge it in the correct place.

To discharge the current into the correct place requires you to do three things with the needle correctly: insert it in the right direction, at the right angle and to the right depth. Mastering these three stages takes practice. Don't worry about getting hairs out to start with, just concentrate on getting the insertion right.

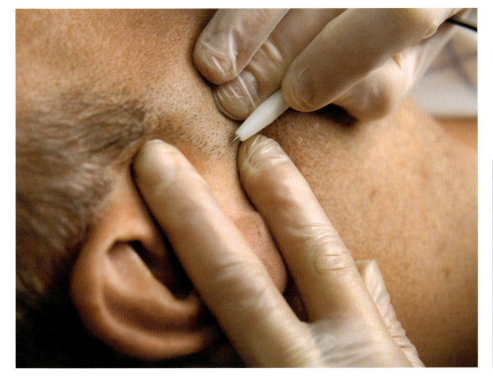

Skin manipulation

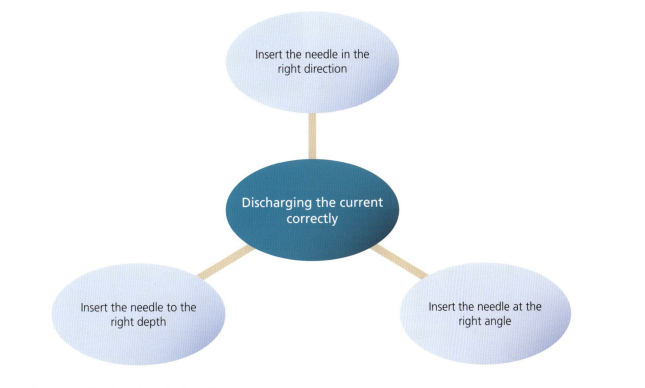

Insert the needle in the right direction

To achieve the right direction of insertion you must ensure that your body and the client are correctly positioned.

At all times, you should position your body so that, where possible, your needle-holder, wrist and elbow are in the direction of the hair growth.

EPILATION

As a general rule, the electrologist should try to be seated so that, when viewed from the back, their shoulders and spine should form the shape of a capital 'T'.

Therapist's posture

This positioning will not only protect the hair removal practitioner's posture and prevent muscular aches and pains; it will also prevent putting unnecessary weight on to the client.

The position of the electrologist is paramount, but so is the positioning of the client. The aim should be to keep the client as comfortable as possible, but the primary objective must always be to position the client so that you have the best possible chance to insert the needle in the correct direction.

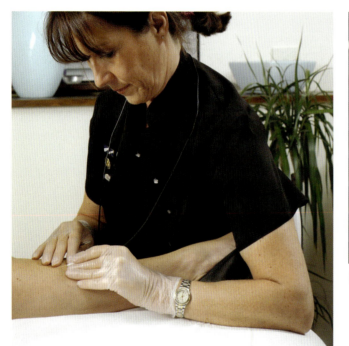

Left-handed practitioner

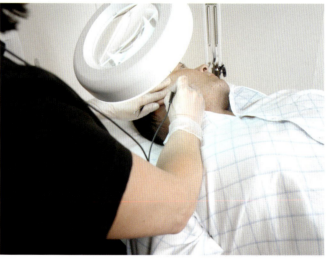

Right-handed practitioner

Electrologist posture

TECHNICAL TIP ✔

The right direction is important because if you try to insert the needle in the wrong direction, you will not discharge the current in the right place, i.e. in the target area

HEALTH AND SAFETY ✚

Your back is at risk if you do not position yourself correctly. Ensure you maintain the correct working posture i.e. the 'T'

REMEMBER !

You and your client will change position continually throughout the treatment in order to be in the correct position for each follicle. It is for this reason that your stool must have castors

'Hand, wrist and elbow line'

The start point when trying to position your body is that your hand, wrist and elbow are in line with the direction of hair growth. When working on the face, in order to achieve this position and therefore a perfect insertion, it is often necessary to turn the client's head slightly away from you, so you are working in a less cramped way, thereby giving your fingers more room to move.

In order to achieve the best insertions, your wrist must be very flexible. It is important to strengthen and increase the flexibility of your wrist by carrying out regular wrist exercises.

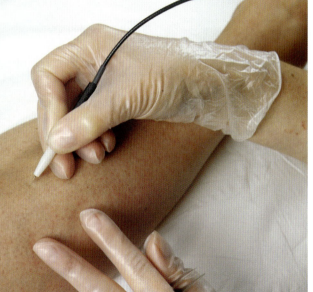

Correct positioning

Incorrect positioning

The forearm and wrist should be supported so that your muscles are not holding the weight of your arm or wrist, upon insertion. If the wrist and arm are not fully supported, there will not be enough control over the needle-holder – the arm will tire very easily, which will cause shaking and wobbling and lead to incorrect insertions.

PROFESSIONAL TIP ✔

The client may not know which way to turn when you ask them to, so physically guide them, gently, to the position you require

Rotate wrists clockwise then anti-clockwise to loosen the wrists

With backs of hands facing, clench the fingers together. Pull fingers apart, nut maintain contact

Rotate fists in a circular motion

Finger-pad resistance – press against each other one by one

Place palm together and apply slight pressure, maintaining contact

Place alternate fingers down on a hard surface, as if playing the piano

Positioning of the client

Hairline

Before work commences on the hairline, it is important to discuss carefully with the client their desired outcome in terms of shape. After discussion, and with the client in an upright position, use a mirror and draw a line with an eyebrow pencil (this can also be useful to help the client visualise how it will look on completion) to find out and agree the line required.

The best technique to use on this area is thinning, as this avoids harsh lines which can look unnatural.

Eyebrows

First find out exactly the shape the client requires in the same way as described for eyebrow waxing in Chapter Four.

To treat follicles under the arch of the eyebrow, position yourself and client in a similar way to that described above in treating the hairline. Turn the client's head away from you in order to gain best access to the hairs nearest to your body. Gradually turn the client's head towards you as you work across towards the nose.

In order to be in the correct position for the side opposite you (the client's left if you are right handed and right if you are left handed) where space in your work area allows, move to the opposite side of the couch and repeat the positioning and procedure. If you cannot gain access to the opposite side of the couch, it will be necessary to ask your client to turn onto her or his side and turn the client's head as far towards you as possible. Holding your needle-holder as normal, turn your hand 180° so that the back of your hand is on the client and continue with insertions. We will refer to this method as 'reverse insertion'.

Continue treating the follicles working towards you, gradually turning the client's head as required.

PROFESSIONAL TIP ✔

The method of working with the back of your hand on the client (reverse insertion) requires practice, but will allow accurate insertions in any position. However, it is not recommended for prolonged treatment as it can causes stress on the wrist which can lead to RSI (repetitive strain injury). Wrist exercises can be found above and on previous page

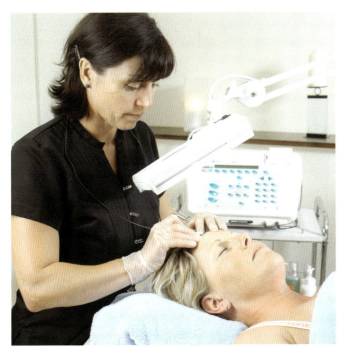

Hairline position

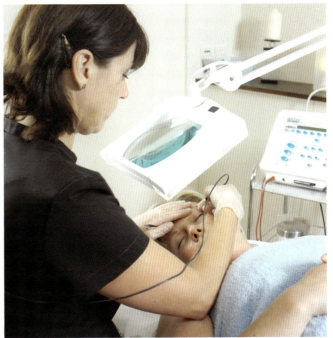

Eyebrow position and 'reverse insertion'

Lip – upper and lower

When working on the upper lip, it is important to carefully discuss possible outcomes with the client. It is never advisable to totally remove all the hairs from the upper lip as it leaves a very unnatural 'shiny' appearance. For this reason it is best to remove the darker, thicker more obvious hairs and use the thinning technique on the remainder.

Start on the side nearest to you. Ask your client to turn their head away from you and to tilt their head back slightly until you have good access to the hairs. Work from outside to inside, turning your client's head towards you and dropping the chin slightly and gradually as you work towards the centre line. Do not cross the centre line. Then begin on the opposite side by turning the client's head as far towards you as possible and again tilting the head slightly upwards. Work from outside to inside.

Ideally you will work with your arm rested across the client's shoulder. In some cases, however, it may be necessary to work with your arm across the client's chest in order to be in the correct position for insertions. In the case of a female client, try to position your arm in between the breasts. If you feel this may cause embarrassment to the client, place a rolled up towel on the area for you to lean on. It may also be necessary to use the reverse insertion technique, being aware not to apply this technique for too long.

There is often a small area of hair growth just below the lower lip. Position yourself so that hand, wrist and elbow are in line with the hairs and work from the outside to the inside. Do not cross the centre line.

PROFESSIONAL TIP

During upper lip treatment, some electrologists ask their clients to pull their upper lip tightly over their teeth or push their tongue into the area being treated. Often, however, this merely hinders the insertion by distorting the follicle openings. Always control the stretch yourself

PROFESSIONAL TIP ✔

It should be noted that hairs on the lower lip can often have very shallow follicles

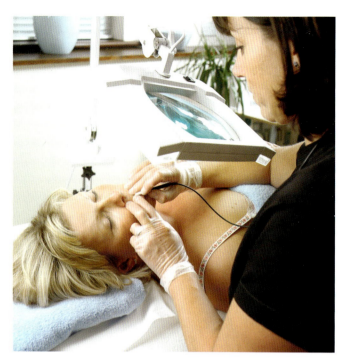

Upper lip positioning

Lower lip positioning

Chin/male beard pattern growth

The normal rules apply of positioning yourself so your wrist and elbow are in line with the direction of hair growth. Begin by working on the hairs opposite you; turn the client's head towards you until you have a good position for access to the follicles. Work from the outside (ear) to the inside (centre point of the chin).

To work on the side nearest to you, you may need to position yourself slightly further down the couch, towards the client's feet and work from the outside (ear) to the inside (centre point of the chin). When working across the jaw-line, it is often necessary to ask the client to tilt their chin upwards in order to gain access to the follicles.

Neck

In order to gain access to hairs on the neck it is often necessary to tilt the client's head back as far possible. In this situation, you should ask the client to move up the couch as far as possible so that her or his head is almost falling back. Place a small rolled up hand towel under the back of the client's neck in order to provide support. By doing this it allows you more room to gain access to the follicle openings and provide room to ensure insertions are made at the correct angle. These hairs can often be the most problematic: move yourself as much as is necessary to achieve the best position. You may have to move behind the client's head for hairs which are growing upwards, towards the chin, and you may also have to adopt the 'reverse insertion' method.

Nape of neck

At the back of the neck the hairs tend to grow from outside to inside. Begin by working on the hairs opposite you. Work from the outside (ear) to the inside (centre point neck). To work on the side nearest you, position

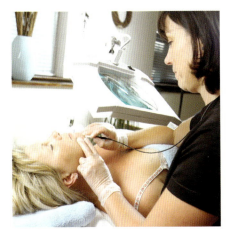

Chin position

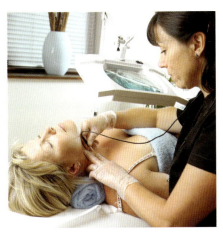

Neck position

Nape of neck position

yourself for wrist and elbow positioning, which may be slightly further down the couch, towards the client's feet and then work from the outside (ear) to the inside (centre point of the neck). When the hairs are growing in a upwards direction, towards the head, you may need to move to the top of the couch or adopt the 'reverse insertion' technique.

Chest/back

Position yourself roughly in line with the client's lower abdomen. Begin by treating the hairs opposite you and work from outside to inside, continually adjusting your position as dictated by the hairs being treated, as described previously for other areas. You may ask your client to sit up or tilt their body towards you as required. Remember to always provide support to the client's body using rolled up towels or other support cushions.

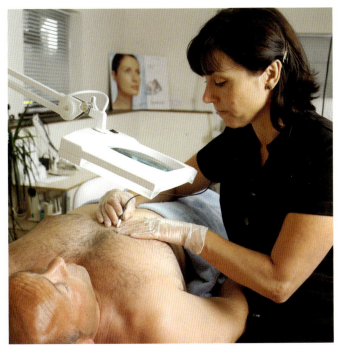

Chest position

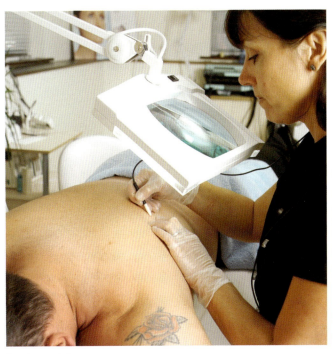

Back position

Breasts

The direction of growth of breast hairs tends to be circular around the outer edge of the pigmented ring surrounding the nipple (areola mammae). Growth is also often found in the centre line between the breasts where the hairs mainly grow in two directions from a parting line. To treat hairs around the nipple, ask the client to tilt their body towards you, supporting where required. Take care not to over-stretch the skin, as this may cause discomfort for the client as well as distort the follicle opening. In order to prevent over-tightening of the skin, avoid touching the nipple itself, cover with a tissue throughout the treatment. To treat hairs in the centre line, move up the couch towards the client's head or work from the top of the couch, moving to the opposite side where necessary or adopt the 'reverse insertion' technique.

Underarms

Ask the client to lift their arm above their head. To provide a more comfortable position for the client, place a rolled hand towel under the elbow of the raised arm (where there is a gap between their arm and the couch for support). You may need to move behind the client, to the opposite side or adopt the reverse insertion technique in order to maintain accurate insertions.

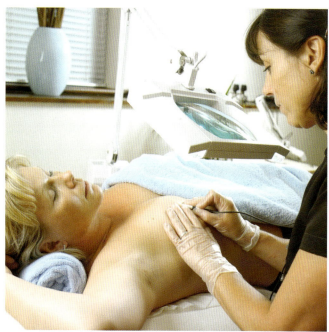

Breast position

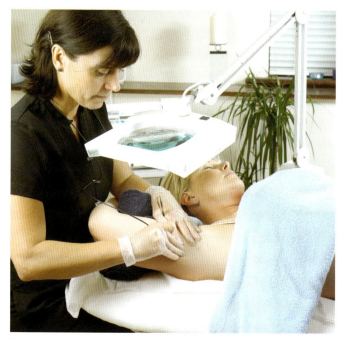

Underarm position

Forearms

With the client in a seated position on the coach, supported by the upright couch back, place their arm onto a pillow or support that is covered with disposable paper. Move the client's arm and yourself until you are in the correct position. Alternatively, you may ask the client to sit on a stool or chair at the opposite side of the couch from you and then position their arm on the couch accordingly.

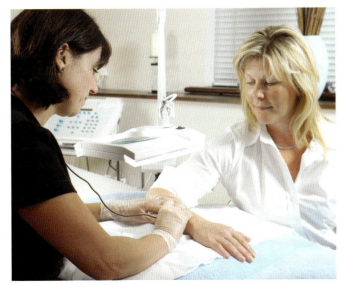

Forearm position – across the couch

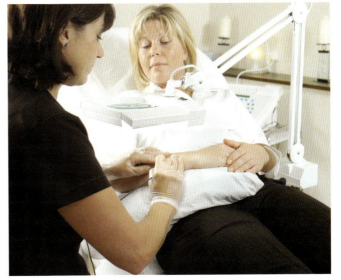

Forearm position - sitting on the couch

Fingers

The positioning for finger treatment is the same as for forearms. Ask the client to spread out their fingers and keep their hand as still and relaxed as possible.

Abdomen

Line your hand, wrist and elbow with the hairs as normal. You may need to position yourself with your back to the client, facing their toes in order to be in the correct position for hairs which grow up towards the chest. You may also need to move to the opposite side of the couch or adopt the reverse insertion technique.

Bikini line

The client may be lying flat, or slightly raised. Work on the opposite side to where you are seated first. Ask the client to bend their leg at the knee and

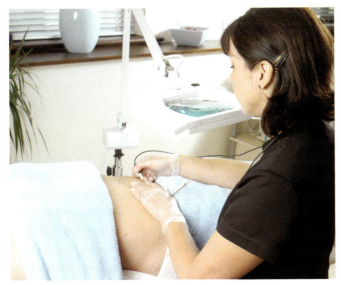

Abdomen position

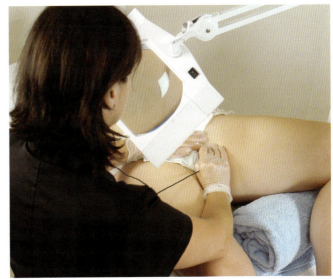

Bikini position – normal

open the leg outwards; support the bent knee with a rolled up large towel or pillow. In order to treat hairs on the side furthest away from you, bend the leg as previously described and either move to the opposite side of the couch, or if that is not possible use the reverse insertion technique. Alternatively, ask the client to turn towards you and tilt the leg out further. In order to treat hairs which are underneath the leg, ask the client to pull their leg with knee bent towards their chest and turn their body until you have access. It is sometimes necessary to turn the client over, so that they are lying on their stomach, and access the hairs from that position.

Legs

Position yourself at the lower end of the couch and turn and support the client's legs as required. In order to treat hairs on the inner thigh, you will need to ask the client to adopt the bent knee position as described in the bikini line positioning. When treating hairs on the backs of the legs, turn the client over, so that they are lying on their stomach, then depending upon the direction of growth you may need to move to the opposite side of the couch or use the reverse insertion technique.

Feet and toes

Ask the client to place their foot flat on the couch and turn the foot in order to position your hand, wrist and elbow in line with the hairs.

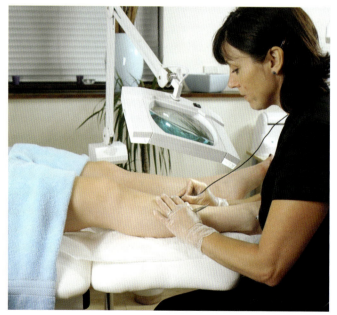

Leg position

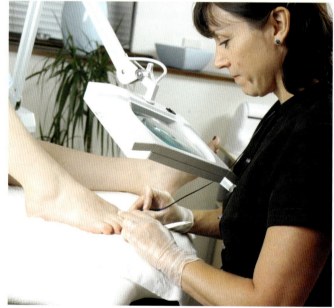

Feet and toe position

Angle of insertion

Once you have established the direction of growth and you and your client are in the correct position, the next consideration is the angle of insertion. This is the angle of the insertion in relation to the skin surface and it is dictated by the angle at which the hair emerges from the follicle.

Hairs can grow from any angle. The hairs which are most difficult to assess and insert into are those which grow from distorted follicles.

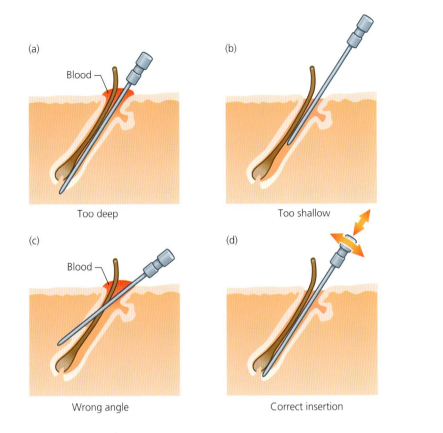

(a)

Blood

Too deep

(b)

Too shallow

(c)

Blood

Wrong angle

(d)

Correct insertion

Insertion angles – Correct and Incorrect

How distorted hairs affect the angle

Follicles are distorted for many reasons. They may naturally grow distorted as curly hair or through mechanical interference, for example plucking or prolonged friction (on the part of the legs that rub when crossed).

Distorted hair follicles

L-shaped   U-shaped   S-shaped   Corkscrew

Distorted follicles

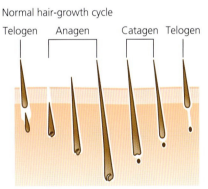

Normal hair-growth cycle

Telogen   Anagen   Catagen   Telogen

Follicle lengths – normal

When inserting into a distorted follicle of any shape, be aware that your insertion depth will be restricted by the bend of the follicle. The current will therefore not be discharged to the target area. For this reason, galvanic or blended currents are the only effective methods.

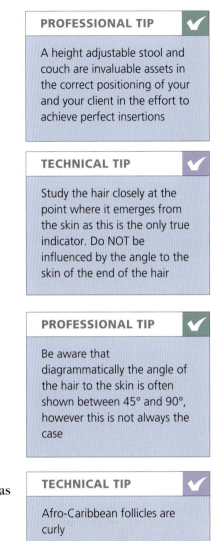

PROFESSIONAL TIP ✓

A height adjustable stool and couch are invaluable assets in the correct positioning of your and your client in the effort to achieve perfect insertions

TECHNICAL TIP ✓

Study the hair closely at the point where it emerges from the skin as this is the only true indicator. Do NOT be influenced by the angle to the skin of the end of the hair

PROFESSIONAL TIP ✓

Be aware that diagrammatically the angle of the hair to the skin is often shown between 45° and 90°, however this is not always the case

TECHNICAL TIP ✓

Afro-Caribbean follicles are curly

TECHNICAL TIP ✓

Thermolysis is not suitable for distorted follicles

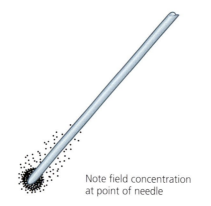

Note field concentration
at point of needle

Thermolysis in the follicle

Galvanic electrolysis in the follicle

Hand positioning

Having discussed distorted hair follicles, it should be noted that an undisturbed follicle, that is one where there has been no plucking, etc. will, generally speaking, produce a hair which will lay flatter to the skin. Your insertion, therefore, must be very flat. To make your insertion as flat as possible, ensure you do not rest the needle-holder on the fingers of the stretching hand (if using the two-handed technique) or tuck fingers of the hand holding the needle-holder underneath, as both these actions lift up the angle of the needle-holder so you won't be able to insert your needle at the correct angle.

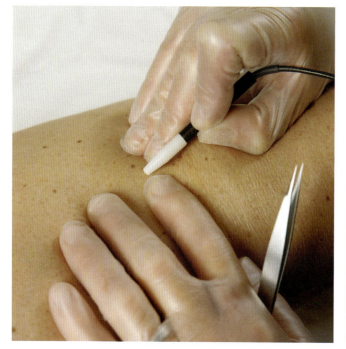

Holding the needle-holder flat

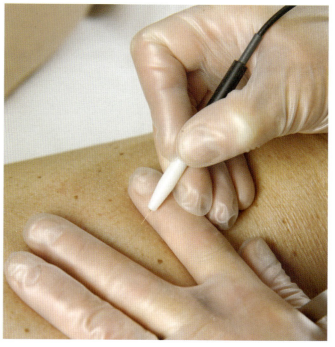

Holding the needle-holder too upright

Tombstone hairs

Towards the completion of a successful series of treatments, you may encounter 'tombstone hairs'. These are dull, thick, dark and disfigured in appearance. They are brittle and break off easily. Tombstones are the remains of an early forming anagen hair in a follicle from which a catagen or telogen hair was treated. They appear rumpled and disfigured due to the current they were exposed to in their early, vulnerable stage. They work their way out just like a splinter, and are signs of a departed follicle. There is no need to treat tombstone hairs, just lift them out.

Insert the needle to the right depth

The right direction and the right angle on their own is not enough: the current must be discharged at the correct depth, that is at the target area. Follicles vary significantly in depth from area to area; upper lip follicles for example are shallower than those on the chin. The colour of the hair can give some indication of the depth of the follicle, although this, strictly speaking, is only true on virgin hairs (hairs which have not been treated in any way). For instance, a client with dark hair will have hairs of varying shades of colour from black-black to brown. In almost every case, the darker colour hairs have deeper follicles; the same is true with shades of blonde hair. Grey hair is the exception to the rule as it always has deeper follicles.

The target area of the follicle lies in the dermal or subcutis layer. Dr Christian Barnard, when asked what was the most difficult part of a heart transplant operation, replied 'when I am working blind'. As you can't see the target area and depth of follicle, you are also working blind, so you need to look for other indicators of correct depth. These depth indicators are referred to as 'follicle feedback'. It is vital to take note of follicle feedback indicators. You should also be aware that the follicle is not composed of elastic tissue and therefore the needle will not 'spring' back once the bottom of the follicle is reached: this is a common misconception.

> **PROFESSIONAL TIP** ✔
>
> Once the needle is inserted in the follicle, keep it as still as possible. Moving the needle up and down or in a circular fashion is very poor and is used in compensation of bad insertion technique. Maintain accurate insertions and when the current is activated, hold the needle as steady as possible

> **TECHNICAL TIP** ✔
>
> Never enter or leave the follicle whilst the current is flowing, as this can cause superficial skin damage. This is another reason for your insertions to be slowed right down

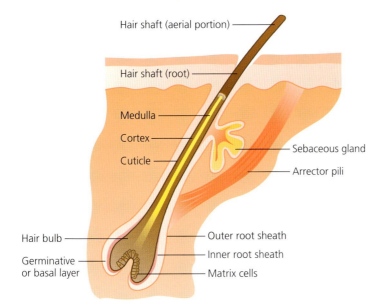

The target area of the follicle

If the needle is not inserted correctly, there are indicators above the skin that show you it is incorrect – but you need to know what to look for. One sign is dimpling or puckering around the skin. Another sign is if the needle bends, as this demonstrates it has met resistance (insertion being either too long or at the wrong angle). The bend itself can be seen or it may appear as a change in the light reflected from the needle. To ensure you have time to see the above indicators, your insertion should be controlled and not rushed. This is where the electrologist needs to 'feel their way' into the follicle and then down to the target area.

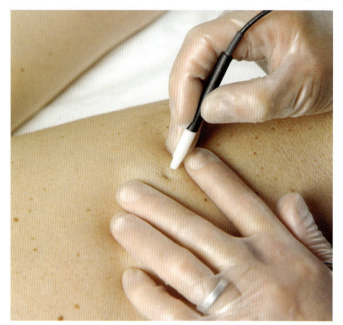

Signs to watch for – skin dimpling

Signs to watch for – light reflection and needle bend

Client reaction

If the client shows a pain response, for example moving away or flinching, you must have pierced the follicle at some point. The follicle is a pocket in the skin and provided your needle is within that follicle, your client will feel very little sensation.

TECHNICAL TIP ✔

A strange phenomenon can occur when a grey hair is just emerging from the follicle in early anagen. It can often be the original colour of the surrounding hairs, then, as it grows longer and the root grows deeper, it loses its pigment

PROFESSIONAL TIP ✔

'Feel' your way into the follicle, do not rush! You need to be effective and that does not necessarily mean being quick. Good electrologists are often slow at inserting but very effective at treatment

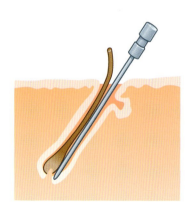

Correct depth of needle insertion

Incorrect depth of needle insertion

Hair growth cycle

To ensure that the needle is inserted to the right depth, you also need to understand the three stages of the hair growth cycle: (1) anagen; (2) catagen; (3) telogen. The three stages of hair growth are described in detail in Chapter

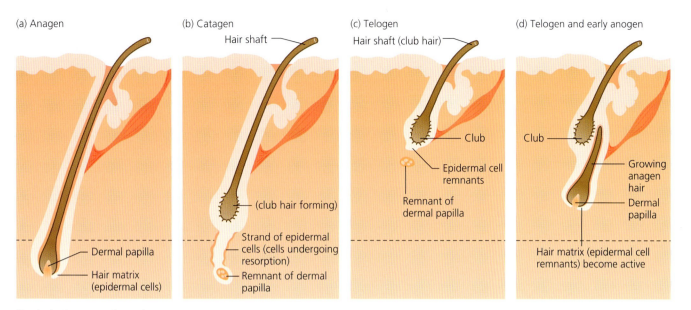

(a) Anagen   (b) Catagen   (c) Telogen   (d) Telogen and early anogen

Hair shaft —

Hair shaft (club hair) —

Club —

Club —

Epidermal cell remnants

Growing anagen hair

(club hair forming) —

Remnant of dermal papilla

Dermal papilla

Dermal papilla —

Strand of epidermal cells (cells undergoing resorption)

Hair matrix (epidermal cell remnants) become active

Hair matrix (epidermal cells) —

Remnant of dermal papilla —

Basic hair growth cycle

Three and histological images can be seen in the reference section, however, the following is a brief summary:

- Anagen is the growing stage and is the only stage where the follicle and the hair are fully formed. It is the most desirable stage for permanent hair removal.

- Catagen is the transition stage where the hair detaches from the base of the follicle. The follicle gradually degenerates, moving upwards towards the surface of the skin. The hair itself dehydrates and forms what is known as a 'club' hair.

- Telogen is the resting stage where the lower part of the follicle (under the sebaceous gland) has completely degenerated and the dermal papilla has shrunk and separated from the hair but remains connected by a tiny strand of epidermal cells. The hair normally remains in the follicle, eventually falling away naturally. Often a new anagen hair is forming underneath the telogen hair which pushes the telogen hair out.

Having studied, in detail, the hair growth cycle in the anatomy and physiology section, it should be clear that anagen is the only stage at which permanent hair removal can be achieved. With the degeneration of the follicle at the catagen and telogen stages making it impossible to access and therefore damage the stem cells, it is vital for successful treatment that your client visits on a regular basis, in order to ensure you are treating anagen follicles. If the follicles are not at the anagen stage, treatment results will be at best limited and at worst totally ineffective.

At initial treatments, you will also need to be aware of indicators above the skin surface of the stage of hair growth:

- Anagen – hairs appear glossy, healthy and have a pointed tip.
- Catagen – hairs have a duller appearance, tend to be longer and begin to take on a dry appearance.
- Telogen – hairs are very dehydrated, lack lustre and are sometimes crinkled.

PROFESSIONAL TIP ✔

The depth of insertion will guide you as to the stage of hair growth; a full length insertion for example will be an anagen stage hair

PROFESSIONAL TIP ✔

At last it is becoming more popular in the UK for electrologists to recommend that their clients pre-shave 3 or 4 days prior to treatment to ensure only hairs from anagen follicles are present at the time of treatment

PRE-TREATMENT CONSIDERATIONS

Sensations

The sensations experienced by clients during treatment will vary from area to area, treatment to treatment and client to client. Not only is every person's pain threshold different, their threshold will vary from day to day, minute to minute, and from one body area to another. It is important to instil confidence in the client. Always speak and act confidently and be calm and positive, even if that is not how you are feeling. If the client trusts you, it will make them relax and therefore the treatment will be more comfortable.

Localised sensations

Unorganised, basket-like meshes of nerves encircle and penetrate the connective tissue sheath just below the level of the sebaceous glands. Some follicles have fewer nerves than others. This accounts for variations in pain response from follicle to follicle.

The deeper the insertion, the greater the current that can be induced before the nerve responds; this allows thorough action with minimum discomfort. This is another reason for always inserting the needle to the full anagen depth. Any conscious sensation of pain in the treatment area will be determined by the number of nerve fibrils activated, and by the frequency and total number of impulses being sent along the neural communication links. The sensation will be more intense over bony areas such as eyebrows. The centre line areas, for example the centre upper lip, where the pain receptors overlap, should not be worked across due to the increased and intense levels of sensation. Instead you should work from each side towards the centre to avoid crossing the centre line. Working in an area where nerve endings overlap (such as the centre of the upper lip) produces a message of double intensity to the brain, since many nerves are reporting the 'pain factor' to the brain.

The objective is to work as close to the client's pain/sensation threshold as possible, employing the maximum amount of current that the client can tolerate. We must also be aware that the 'pain threshold' refers to the degree of pain sensation beyond which the intensity of that pain becomes consciously uncomfortable or intolerable. There are two factors which affect the threshold: the chemical composition of the synapses (nerve junctions) and the conscious focus of the client. If nerve messages are sent repeatedly through a synapse, it begins to relay its messages more slowly. You can observe this when getting into a hot bath: when you first get in, it seems very hot, but eventually the water becomes tolerable, not because it has cooled to any great degree, but because the synapses have tired of relaying the message of 'hot water'.

Take advantage of synapse fatigue by treating follicles in a localised area. Avoid skipping around; although there are situations when you need to spread treatment, generally speaking, it is best to confine treatment to a localised area, which would be served by a single nerve, thus allowing the synapses to send weaker pain messages as your work area gradually spreads.

Treating sensitive clients

At certain times you will notice that your client will be more sensitive than at other times. This can be for physical reasons, for example before and during menstruation, or for emotional reasons, for example when under stress or pressure. Adrenaline and tension can make the pain seem worse. It is important to try and keep the client calm and relaxed prior to and during treatment.

Encourage the client to relax, they may wish to take off their shoes. Encourage them to wear loose clothes. The more comfortable they are, the more relaxed they will be. If they are too hot or cold, it may also affect their levels of tolerance.

Stimulants, especially caffeine and sugar, may make the client more sensitive to pain. Advise them to try and avoid these substances before treatment.

Topical anaesthetics

Some topical anaesthetics are available on prescription. These can be useful for clients who cannot easily tolerate the electrolysis treatment. The most commonly used is EMLA brand topical cream (this stands for Eutectic Mixture of Local Anaesthetics). The drawbacks include the inconvenience of having to apply the cream 30–90 minutes prior to treatment. For the best effect, the anaesthetised area should be covered with an airtight dressing such as cling film. The client must also obtain the prescription from their GP.

> **REMEMBER** !
>
> There are more pain receptors located nearer the surface of the skin; the client will therefore feel more sensation from shallower insertions and less sensation from deeper insertions

> **TECHNICAL TIP** ✔
>
> Adapting current modalities and the use of computerised epilators can reduce treatment discomfort considerably

> **TECHNICAL TIP** ✔
>
> When touching a dehydrated skin, the suppleness which is felt is due to the good balance of sebum in the skin

Skin types

Entire body systems and function, the general health and wellbeing of the client and, in particular, the client's skin condition, all have a major effect on the outcomes of electrolysis. Each skin type will have an influence on the pre-treatment and post-treatment care of the skin. The skin must be carefully considered and treated appropriately pre- and post-treatment, as well as during treatment. The hair is not a stand-alone structure, it is an integral part of the skin, which is the largest organ of the body, and therefore directly impacted upon by internal and external factors.

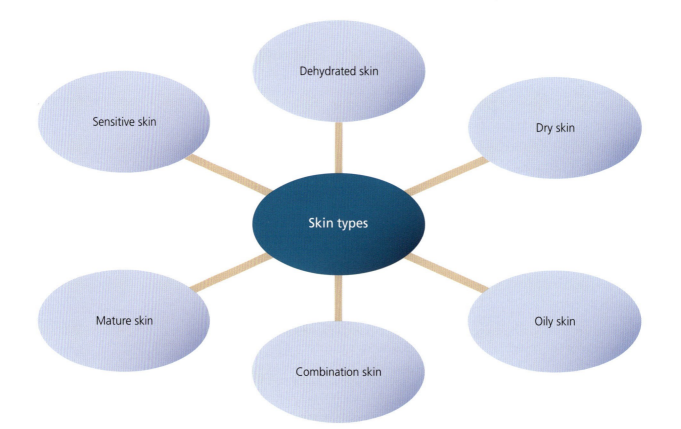

DEHYDRATED SKIN

Description: The skin lacks moisture; this is mainly caused by external factors, for example: the sun; central heating; air conditioning; poor diet; alcohol; smoking; poor skin care or previous bad electrolysis treatments. It is the most commonly seen skin type.

How it can be recognised: The skin has dull appearance, the stratum corneum is thickened, the surface may be slightly scaly and horizontal lines may be present. The pore size is generally medium. The skin will feel slightly rough on the surface but supple to the touch.

Effects on current: Lack of moisture inhibits the heat action of thermolysis and reduces the production of sodium hydroxide/lye when working with galvanic or blend. It also inhibits the healing potential of the skin.

Pre-treatment: Moisture is an essential element for epilation. A dehydrated skin is lacking in moisture and therefore, it is vital to rebalance the moisture levels in the skin by intensive moisturising facials, intensive moisturising products for home use and regular exfoliation. It is also possible to carry out anaphoresis – using negatively active polarity on a naturally positively charged skin. This will have the effect of vasodilation – relaxing of the follicles and encouraging blood flow to the area.

Post-treatment: It is important that the client maintains good moisturisation of the skin at home; that they reconsider their diet; increase water intake and decrease any diuretics, for example alcohol or coffee. Iontophoresis may be used with ionised products in order to enhance the product moisturisation effects by attracting them more deeply into the skin.

KEY TERMS ⭐

Iontophoresis: Introduction of ionised products into the deeper layers of the skin

DRY SKIN

Description: The skin is lacking in sebum; this is caused by internal factors, for example, the individual is genetically pre-disposed to dry skin; hormonal influences, particularly at menopause; illness and medication which may affect hormonal balance. It cannot be externally caused.

How it can be recognised: The skin has a fine, thin, papery appearance. The pore size is small. The skin may be slightly flaky on the surface. It is often sensitised due to its fineness. There are often milia around the eye and cheek area. The client may complain of tightness of the skin and premature wrinkling is often prevalent.

Effects on current: There is a higher possibility of sensitivity on dry skin. There may be an increase in erythema, caused by the treatment which may last longer than on other skin types.

Pre-treatment: Moisture is an essential element for epilation. A dry skin is often lacking in moisture as well as sebum and, therefore, it is vital to rebalance the moisture levels in the skin by intensive moisturising facials, intensive moisturising products for home use and regular exfoliation. Rebalancing and nourishing products to restore the acid mantle are very important, in order to ensure that the skin is protected from the entry of bacteria. When hormones are influencing the skin, clients should be advised to seek medical opinion regarding balancing hormones.

Post-treatment: It is important that the client continues with regular exfoliation and nourishing treatments of the skin at home; that they reconsider their diet, increase water intake and decrease any diuretics, for example alcohol or coffee. Iontophoresis may be used on ionised products in order to enhance the product moisturisation effects by attracting them deeper into the skin.

OILY SKIN

Description: This is skin with excess sebum which is caused, mainly, by internal factors, for example the individual is genetically pre-disposed to oily skin; hormone imbalance and medications. The oiliness can be exacerbated by harsh surface treatment, for example harsh cleansing routines.

How it can be recognised: The excess sebum causes the skin to appear shiny. The pore size is large. Often the skin is over-keratinised and therefore may appear thicker. The excess sebum causes an imbalance in the acid mantle and changes the skin's pH which allows bacteria to enter into the skin, resulting in pustules. Papules and comedones are also symptoms of over-active sebaceous glands.

Effects on current: Sebum acts as an insulator and can restrict the current flow to a degree. Oily skin is often dehydrated and, therefore, the action of the current is diminished.

Pre-treatment: Regular exfoliation is essential to combat over-keratinisation which leads to blocked pores and follicles which can in turn cause in-growing hairs. It is vital to rebalance the moisture levels in the skin by intensive moisturising facials, and using intensive moisturising products at home. It is possible to carry out desincrustation immediately prior to epilation treatment in order to remove the excess sebum on the skin surface and unblock pores and follicles.

Post-treatment: It is important that the client maintains good moisturisation of the skin at home; that they reconsider their diet; increase water intake and decrease any diuretics, for example alcohol or coffee. Iontophoresis may be used on ionised products in order to enhance the product moisturisation effects by attracting them deeper into the skin.

COMBINATION SKIN

Description: This is skin which combines two different skin types – the most common being an oily T-zone and general dehydration. The skin will often be dull overall, have shiny patches, possible comedones and occasional pustules. This type of combination skin often starts as severe dehydrated skin all over the face, which is often caused by harsh treatment with aggressive/astringent products or is skin which has been left untreated. There are naturally more oil glands in the T-zone which begin to over-produce sebum as a consequence of the thickening and over-treatment of the skin.

How it can be recognised: Skin texture is different on two or more areas of the face. The difference can be seen in pore size, texture, luminosity and lustre.

Effects on current: See discussion of individual skin types. You must be aware when moving from one skin type to another on the same client, that you may need to adjust settings accordingly.

Pre-treatment: See discussion of individual skin types. Be aware that the different areas of skin will require different products and treatment. When carrying out epilation the key is the skin moisture balance. Desincrustation will be beneficial on oily areas either immediately prior to epilation treatment or in the week previous to treatment.

Post-treatment: When carrying out epilation the key is the skin moisture balance. It is important that the client maintains good moisturisation of the skin at home; that they reconsider their diet; increase water intake and decrease any diuretics, for example alcohol or coffee. Iontophoresis may be used on ionised products in order to enhance the product moisturisation effects by attracting them deeper into the skin.

MATURE SKIN

Description: During the natural ageing process, cellular activity decreases which can be recognised by wrinkling and loss of plumpness. As a consequence of the reduced mitotic (cellular renewal) activity, the dead skin cells are shed less readily and the skin becomes dehydrated and thickened on the surface. There is also loss of skin tone, particularly noticeable around the cheek, jaw and nasolabial fold.

How it can be recognised: The most obvious sign of ageing is wrinkling – this may be superficial or appear as deep lines, generated first around the eyes and neck areas. The skin is often dry and dehydrated and feels thickened to the touch. Pigmentation marks are often visible as are vascular legions, for example spider naevi.

Effects on current: The insertion depth will invariably be shallower. This is because the collagen in the dermis has reduced, which leads to a reduction in depth of the dermal layer. Even though the epidermal layer is thicker, with the dermal layer being thinner, the insertion depth is shallower.

Pre-treatment: Anti-ageing and moisturising treatments, including intensive pure collagen film, are advised on a regular basis and in addition to daily care of the skin, body and wellbeing.

Post treatment: Anti-ageing and moisturising treatments, including intensive pure collagen film, are advised on a regular basis and in addition to daily care of the skin, body and wellbeing. Iontophoresis may be used on ionised products in order to enhance the product moisturisation effects by attracting them deeper into the skin.

SENSITIVE SKIN

Description: Sensitive is not technically a skin type: it is a condition which may be present on any skin type. Skin may be sensitised due to external and internal factors: external factors such as the sun and abrasive cleansing products; internal factors such as medications and hormone changes. Allergic reactions may also leave skin sensitised. Skin sensitivity can be recognised by a number of factors; extreme erythema, oedema, and over-reaction to even mild stimulus, for example cleansing. A sensitive skin should not be confused with a reactive skin. A reactive skin has a specific reaction to a specific stimulus; however, a sensitive skin has a general sensitivity to a variety of stimuli, for example urticaria.

How it can be recognised: The skin is easily irritated and erythema is readily induced. The degree of sensitivity will affect the amount and length of time it takes for erythema to diminish. The skin may be very warm to the touch due to increased blood flow.

Effects on current: Contrary to popular belief, the current should not be turned down, as the current needs to be at the correct level to treat the follicle. However, using lower current for longer, particularly in blend methods, can assist in reducing the overall erythema.

Pre-treatment: Gentle moisturising products should be used to maintain skin moisture. The client should be particularly advised to avoid any skin stimulation immediately prior to treatment. The client should be calm and relaxed prior and during the treatment, to avoid excess redness.

Post-treatment: Soothing products should be applied immediately post-treatment. This can be refrigerated soothing gel, applied on a cold compress directly to the skin, pure collagen film to reduce redness and induce hydration and, of course, cataphoresis (see later in this chapter). Iontophoresis may be used on ionised products in order to enhance the product moisturisation effects by attracting them deeper into the skin.

TECHNICAL TIP

For an immediate intensive rehydration, you may wish to use pure collagen film just prior to epilation. It can also provide a valuable aftercare treatment

TECHNICAL TIP

Post-treatment – galvanic current using the cataphoresis technique: i.e. a positive active electrode used directly on the skin which is naturally positively charged, will provide vaso-constriction, therefore reducing redness, reducing swelling and soothing the skin

Black skin

When treating black or highly pigmented skin types, the following points should be taken into consideration.

- The stratum corneum is thicker in black skin than in white skin. Pigmentation is present in the dead and flaking skin cells and so may appear as dark scales on the needle.
- It is difficult to detect erythema when treating a black skin; you will need to be extra vigilant to ensure that you do not over-treat, particularly as the skin is often very heat sensitive.
- There are more numerous sebaceous glands present and a greater number of them open directly onto the skin's surface. As sebum is an insulator, the current flow can be restricted.
- The actual number of melanocytes is not larger than in white skin; the melanin granules which it secretes however are significantly larger. There is a great risk of hyper pigmentation if high frequency is used at high levels.
- Black skin contains more collagen fibres than white skin, which makes the skin age less quickly; it does however make the skin more prone to keloid scarring.

EPILATION

● The hair follicles on black skin are usually curved, so, with this fact in mind and considering the fact that excessive heat can easily cause hyper pigmentation, blend is the most suitable electrolysis method to use for black skin.

Asian skin

Asian skin has essentially the same characteristics as white skin other than the colour; there are wide variations in the colour of Asian skin from light to very dark brown. As is the case with black skin, great care should be taken not to use excessive high-frequency currents as there is an increased risk of hyper pigmentation.

TREATMENT PLANNING

It is vital that clients attend for treatment on a regular basis. As previously discussed, it is of paramount importance that the hair is in the anagen stage of growth. The treatments should be booked to coincide with the anagen cycle and the anagen growth varies from area to area. As a general rule, clients are booked in, initially, for appointments at weekly or fortnightly intervals; this ensures the visible hairs are in anagen. As the treatment progresses and the hair growth diminishes, treatment sessions will be of a

TECHNICAL TIP ✔

'Tidy up' refers to the occasional treatment appointments to remove one or two odd stray hairs

REMEMBER !

Electrolysis is permanent. Results are achieved progressively with the client seeing a continual improvement

Hair growth table

Body area	Percent resting hairs telogen	Percent growing hairs anagen	Percent catagen	Percent dystrophic or uncertain	Duration of telogen	Duration of anagen	No. follicles per sq. cm	Daily growth rate	Total no. of follicles	Approx. depth of terminal anagen follicle
Scalp	13	85	1–2	1–2	3–4 months	2–6 years	350	0.35mm		3–5mm
Eyebrows	90	10			3 months	4–8 weeks		0.16mm	1 million total for all of head and scalp	2–2.5mm
Ear	85	15			3 months	4–8 weeks				
Cheeks	30–50	50–70					880	0.32mm		2–4mm
Beard (chin)	30	70			10 weeks	1 year	500	0.38mm		2–4mm
	35	65			6 weeks	16 weeks	500			1–2.5mm
Axillae	70	30			3 months	4 months	65	0.3mm		3.5–4.5mm
Trunk							70	0.3mm	425,000	2–4.5mm
Pubic area	70	30			2 weeks	months	70			3.5–4.75mm
Arms	80	20			18 weeks	13 weeks	80	0.3mm	220,000	
Legs and thighs	80	20			24 weeks	16 weeks	60	0.21mm	370,000	2.5–4mm
Breasts	70	30					65	0.35mm		3–4.5mm

Note: Many factors affect these figures but they do serve as a useful guide. Early research indicates that the percentage of telogen hairs on the cheeks, beard (chin) and moustache (upper lip) may be much higher than indicated on the table by some of the other earlier investigators. More research is required.

shorter duration and a longer period of time in between, until eventually, clients are coming at most once or twice a year for a 'tidy up', as any new hairs appear.

Your primary concern is the stage of hair growth but there are other factors that need to be taken into account, for example, the client's social calendar; her/his outings, special occasions; holidays; client's work calendar: exhibitions, meetings, appointments with important clients. To ensure the skin is in the best condition possible, with the least amount of hair for any of the above events, these details must be gone through at the consultation stage and on an ongoing basis.

Client responsibility within the treatment plan

The electrologist needs to be aware that clients can be challenging! For example, some clients may not turn up for appointments, may pluck the

Dear _____

We hope that your last treatment was effective and satisfactory.

If, however, you experienced any difficulties or have any questions, we are always available to give help and advice face to face or by phone: 01234 5678910 or via e-mail: jaygees@hairsolutions.co.uk.

We would like to remind you that electrolysis will give you a progressive and ultimately permanent removal of your hair growth; however, it does require regular treatments and you should not wait too long between visits. It is to your advantage for me to remove any 're-growth' or new growth before it has time to become fully developed.

We look forward to seeing you soon.

Yours sincerely,

Your signature

Your printed name

Template of a letter to a lapsed client

occasional hair, do not follow the aftercare procedures and may blame you. This is why you should lay down the ground rules at the consultation, by explaining clearly that their positive participation is vital to the success of the treatment.

Non-returning clients

Regular treatment is vital if there is to be a successful outcome. Certain clients may not have understood this point at initial treatments or may have become discouraged for other reasons. It is important for your business that you encourage all clients to continue with treatment and to speak to you if they have any doubts or problems. Ideally, you should make contact with the client via the telephone, try to establish the reason why they have not returned, answer any questions, reassure them and schedule an appointment for them. If it is not possible to contact them on the telephone, a template of a letter is included here. This could be sent to try and encourage the client to contact you.

HEALTH AND SAFETY

Hairs need to be disposed of hygienically as they retain body fluids, which pose a potential risk of cross-infection

PROFESSIONAL TIP

Try to not to pause between insertions as it is a great waste of your client's time. If you find you are stopping after each epilation, check to make sure that you are comfortable. Is your client properly positioned? Learn to anticipate your next insertion. Develop a consistent pace and move from follicle to follicle with a smooth rhythm of movement

Methodical working practice

Treatment plans are many and varied and range from clearing hairs section by section, to clearing the whole area, to thinning. The technique used will depend on the information gained at consultation, that is: hair growth, client need, client tolerance and area of concern.

Methodical working practices

	When	*Why*
Clearing the whole area	Whenever client time and finances allow, also giving consideration to skin sensitivity	Gives clients days or weeks of total freedom from hair growth and ensures all growth is anagen on their next visit. This method will achieve the fastest results.
Section by section	If client time and and/or finances are restricted	Clearing of the whole of one pre-determined section at a time, allowing the client to cut or shave in between treatments to maintain aesthetic appearance
Thinning	Dense, downy growth, i.e. sides of the face and upper lip	A certain amount of downy growth is natural and acceptable in most cultures, therefore removing an entire growth can make the skin appear unnatural

Whichever method is agreed between yourself and the client, it is important to work methodically through the pre-determined areas. We have previously discussed that insertions should not be rushed, however, for commercial acceptability, total treatment time should be kept to a minimum. This can be achieved without compromising your insertion accuracy by working methodically, that is to say, working in a set pattern and not dotting around the area. You also need to develop a good technique and dispose of the removed hairs efficiently and hygienically.

ELECTROLYSIS AFTERCARE

Post-treatment cleaning of the skin is necessary to remove any body fluids which have been drawn out of the follicle during treatment. This will reduce the likelihood of infection. Wipe over the treatment area with a very small amount of antiseptic product on a clean, dry piece of cotton wool, but don't use too much as it may sting. Blot dry with a clean tissue, and apply the selected aftercare product.

It is important that, on the aftercare leaflet, you emphasise that the client has a responsible role in the aftercare procedure. Electrolysis causes a controlled amount of trauma to the treated area. The skin will also have some retained heat post-treatment. Consequently it is important that the client avoids trauma in the first few days following treatment.

- The client should avoid sunbathing and sunbeds as the skin already has retained heat and because the skin may be more prone to pigmentation immediately following treatment.
- Hot baths and showers are a further source of heat which should be avoided immediately following treatment.
- Advising the client to wear loose fitting clothing made from natural fibres will avoid friction to the area and reduce the risk of irritation.
- Perfumed products often contain alcohol which can cause stinging on the treated area. Perfume has a high potential to cause irritation to the treated skin, which is also the case for deodorants and antiperspirants following underarm treatment.
- Following facial treatments, many clients will not feel comfortable, unless they can apply make-up. Check their skin is not broken or over-treated and advise them on how to apply make-up gently without excessive irritation to the skin. Advise them to use clean make-up, that is either a new pot or from a tube or pump dispenser, not from a previously used pot in which they have put their fingers.
- Vigorous exercise causes the body temperature to rise; it will therefore cause a further rise in temperature to the treated area. Swimming pool water contains chlorine, which can easily irritate sensitised skin; these activities should therefore be avoided for 48 hours following treatment.
- By prescribing aftercare carefully, the electrologist can ensure that the client is taking the appropriate care of the treated area.

Make sure the client is fully aware of what a normal reaction is and how to recognise any potential adverse reactions. Also ensure that your client fully understands what to do should they be concerned and that they know how to contact you. It is far better that they contact you should they have any problems rather than someone else.

Aftercare products

There is a vast range of aftercare products available. There is no such thing as a best product or a worst product, this is more a matter or personal choice. However, the cheapest is normally not the best. Some electrologists prefer a cooling gel formulation while others prefer a lotion. The choice from the range is wide:

- antiseptic powder
- milks, lotions, creams
- gels
- essential oil blends.

As well as the traditional aftercare products above, there are two other options that are becoming increasingly popular, and are seen to be particularly in line with holistic treatment and being mindful of clients' skin conditions. The first is cataphoresis, which utilises the electrolysis machine, and the second is the application of pure collagen to the skin.

Cataphoresis

Cataphoresis is a technique used after epilation treatment to reduce inflammation, tighten the pores and reduce reddening on the skin. It also has a germicidal effect.

By using a positive polarity on a naturally positively charged skin, a vaso-constricting action is achieved, thereby reducing redness in the area. The positive polarity is also anti-oedemic (reduces swelling) and helps to restore the skin's natural pH balance in addition to its natural germicidal effect. The negative polarity reduces the skins natural pH by breaking down the sebum present on the skin surface. Removing sebum is a big advantage for the epilation process, because sebum acts as an insulator which can inhibit the action of thermolysis and reduce the production of the galvanic lye.

Using an electrolysis machine with an anaphoresis/cataphoresis facility, select the cataphoresis setting and apply the active electrode – the roller, wand, etc. – over the treatment area, moving continuously in a sweeping motion, whilst gradually increasing the current. The client should feel a mild tingling sensation. Once a sensation has been felt, stop increasing the current but continue to move over the area for 1–2 minutes or until the client reports increased sensation. A standard facial galvanic machine can also be used. Following the instructions above, select positive–active and negative–indifferent for cataphoresis and vice versa for anaphoresis. Anaphoresis describes the use of a galvanic current, where the active electrode has a negative polarity it is carried out prior to electrolysis. Cataphoresis describes the use of a galvanic current, where the active electrode has a positive polarity it is carried out after electrolysis.

Collagen

The use of pure collagen bio-matrix as an aftercare procedure has the benefit of reducing erythema, soothing the skin and providing intensive re-hydration, by replacing lost moisture via an osmotic action which swells the cells with moisture and thereby aids repair.

TECHNICAL TIP ✔

Anaphoresis is used as a preparatory treatment. Using a negative electrode on a naturally positively charged skin has a vaso-dilation action which brings blood, fluid and nutrients to the upper layers of the skin, thereby relaxing the pores and follicles; it also softens the skin thereby aiding insertion, particularly on a dehydrated skin

Collagen sheets

Client home-care

Client aftercare at home is particularly important for electrolysis treatments and, in addition to the standard aftercare procedures described in Chapter Two, you must reaffirm the specific electrolysis procedures after each treatment:

- keep the area clean
- use aftercare products as advised
- only use the hair management method advised (cutting with scissors or razor).

In order to achieve a more effective treatment result, holistic care of the skin is required, which means:

- regular exfoliation
- an efficient skin care regime to maintain and improve hydration levels – in addition, the electrologist removal practitioner should recommend facial treatments to reinforce the home-care regime
- a good diet with recommended daily amounts (RDA) of water, fruit and vegetables with the avoidance of alcohol
- a healthy lifestyle – regular exercise, good sleeping pattern and avoidance of primary and secondary smoking.

CONTRA-ACTIONS

These are effects which may arise following treatment, particularly if the treated area is delicate or the therapist's technique is incorrect. After each treatment there will be some after-effects, electrolysis is after all a 'selective destruction' treatment, but it does cause destruction of tissue nevertheless and consequently there will be some reaction. The table describes some common contra-actions.

> **REMEMBER** !
>
> Always re-affirm with your client the home aftercare procedures that she/he needs to carry out

> **REMEMBER** !
>
> Good skin care, particularly moisturising and re-hydration, are vital to achieve success with epilation

Contra-action	Cause	Action
Erythema (redness)	Some redness is inevitable during treatment, however if the skin becomes excessively red or swollen this may indicate over-treatment.	Discontinue treatment if severe. The treatment plan and modality chosen should be reviewed and adapted to suit the circumstances.
Profuse sweating	Typically affects very nervous or hot clients.	If this cannot be controlled by changing the temperature in the room and/or wiping the skin, the treatment should be discontinued as too much moisture can cause superficial skin damage. Treatment should also be discontinued if the client is experiencing palpitations.
Blanching or whitening of the epidermis	Excessive use of current during treatment, forcing the skin to dry too quickly.	Apply soothing compress and ensure current is restricted in future treatments.
Weeping follicle	Excessive galvanic current overworking the skin.	A strong indication that you should stop the treatment. Otherwise, you could move to a new area of skin and, at the same time, re-evaluate your technique.
Crusts	When electrolysis is performed correctly, crusts will rarely develop. However, in a small percentage of cases, and particularly on body areas such as bikini line, abdomen and breast, small crusts may appear following treatment.	The client's skin should gradually adjust to the treatment but, if severe, advise the client to apply an antiseptic cream as the skin heals. Ensure your treatments are at the right depth and keep the current low.
Inflammation	Mild inflammation occurs in most treatments, particularly following blend treatment.	Standard post-treatment care, in particular cataphoresis, is advised to reduce the swelling.
Hyper pigmentation	May occur in dark-skinned clients.	Current levels should be re-assessed and, where possible, blend or galvanic methods used. Hyper pigmentation will normally fade within a few weeks or months.
Scarring	Poor treatment and therefore should not occur! However, scarring can also occur from aggressive plucking, when the skin is pinched, and your client picking any little scabs, either before or after treatment.	Reassess all processes, in particular, check your insertion depth and current levels. Check that your client fully understands and is following the aftercare procedure.

Contra-action	Cause	Action
Hypo pigmentation	When the right amount of current is discharged too near the surface of the skin in the follicle or too high a level of current is discharged anywhere in the follicle, even in the correct place.	Ensure you are treating at the correct depth and keep the current low.

If contra-actions persist and cannot be rectified, treatment will have to be discontinued and discussions regarding alternative methods of hair removal, for example light treatments or mass plucking (waxing), should take place.

> **HEALTH AND SAFETY** ✚
>
> The heat generated by thermolysis could be a cause of intensifying pigment in dark skins

In-growing hairs

In-growing hairs grow just under the surface of the skin. A hair becomes in-growing when it cannot emerge from the follicle opening so it travels along just under the skin. If the hair is dark and straight it looks like a thin thread.

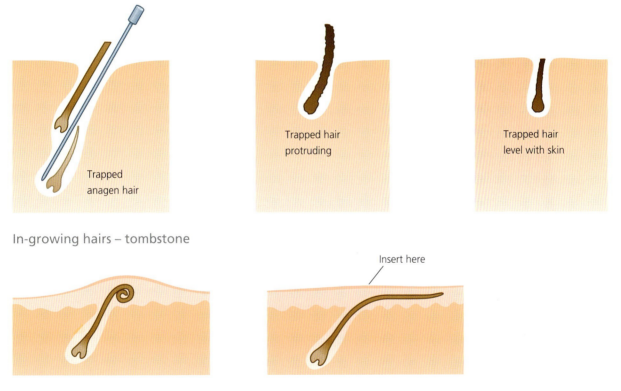

Trapped anagen hair

Trapped hair protruding

Trapped hair level with skin

In-growing hairs – tombstone

Insert here

In-growing hairs – embedded

In-growing hairs can also be seen when they turn back on themselves into the follicle (especially if the hair is curly). They are then treated as foreign bodies and infection can sometimes occur leading to boil-like eruptions. The hair, when eventually removed, is often extremely tightly coiled. There are cases where in-growing hairs have required medical surgical intervention to

TECHNICAL TIP ✔

Over-keratinisation of the skin and therefore the follicle opening, plus poor skin care are undoubted causes of in-growing hairs

REMEMBER !

It is the responsibility of the Electrologist to ensure correct skin care is carried out at home and in-growing hairs are just one indication of the effects of poor skin care

remove them, specifically when they in-grow around the anus; they can become extremely painful and infected.

Treating in-growing hairs that do not require surgical intervention should only be carried out once the hair has been released from the follicle, but not removed, and the surrounding skin has healed. The surrounding skin will invariably be broken due to the technique required to release the hair; a large sterile needle (size 6 or above, i.e. 10 or 12 which are used for the removal of fibrous blemishes) or a microlance is used to pierce the skin. Remove any pus and manipulate the skin until you can see the hair, then put the needle or microlance underneath the hair and hook it out. The hair will invariably be curly and difficult to control but the aim is to release the end of the hair onto the skin and allow the skin to heal around it, when the skin has healed (at least a week) you can then treat it as a normal hair and follicle. It is important that you don't pull the hair out at this stage, otherwise the skin may again grow over the follicle opening and the whole process will start once more.

Re-growth

There will always be a certain amount of re-growth after initial electrolysis treatments, even when they are performed by a skilled operator. Whilst opinions differ as to what is an acceptable percentage, most experienced practitioners estimate that for a treatment to be considered effective, at least 40–50 per cent of the hairs should be permanently removed with each treatment. The average is (or should be) 50–60 per cent with 60–75 per cent being roughly the highest level possible. Experts cannot give a definitive figure because there are so many variables which affect outcomes. The electrologist's skill in working with these variables will determine the percentage of permanency for each individual treatment. Don't get discouraged; practise to increase your skills and always try to treat follicles in the anagen stage. Also ensure your client attends for treatment regularly. These practices will ensure you get the most positive results.

Over-treatment

In order to avoid over-treatment you must continually monitor the treatment area, looking for telltale indications that the skin is being over-treated. If the area looks blanched (having lost its normal colour), clammy or sweaty, or the client feels little sensation, there is a strong chance the skin has been overworked. Move to another area or terminate the treatment. Remember that over-treatment is usually caused by one or all of the following: working too high in the follicle, working for too long, discharging current at too shallow a depth or working in follicles that are too close together. As you become more experienced, you can use the knowledge of issues you have encountered before to anticipate most problems.

THE COMPLETE TREATMENT

Using all of the elements of best practice and the electrolysis skills described in the sections of this chapter should mean you are now better able to provide a complete treatment.

1 Discuss with existing clients any changes in circumstances, health and skin reaction since their last treatment, as these will all affect the treatment you perform on this occasion. Record any changes on the client's record card. If it is a first treatment you will carry out this treatment immediately after consultation and will have all the relevant information.

2 Guide the client to the treatment area and position her or him correctly for treatment.

3 Position trolley so that equipment is within comfortable reach and ensure equipment is turned on at the power supply.

4 Manoeuvre the magnifying lamp into initial position.

5 Place eye pads onto the client's eyes if they are light sensitive. The pads may be useful and requested by the client for other reasons, i.e. headache.

6 Put on appropriate PPE: gloves, disposable surgical mask.

7 Visually access the hairs to be removed and select an appropriate needle size and type.

8 Aseptically load the needle-holder.

9 Plan and mentally visualise how you will proceed with the treatment, i.e. where you will start, where you will finish, what area is to be covered, etc.

10 Sanitise the area.

11 Select a hair representative of those to be treated, insert the needle into that follicle using the lowest possible level of current. Gradually increase the current each time you insert into a different follicle, continuing until the hair releases without traction.

12 Work methodically to clear the area, adjusting current levels and timings where necessary and modalities where appropriate.

13 Dispose of hairs aseptically throughout.

14 Carry out in-salon aftercare procedures, reminding the client of their home-care responsibilities.

15 Accompany the client to reception, book the next appointment, take payment and ensure they have the required home-care products.

> **TECHNICAL TIP** ✔
>
> More accurate insertions require less current

> **PROFESSIONAL TIP** ✔
>
> If treating an existing client, remember that the previously recorded current levels are a guide only and not a start point. This is because the growth will have improved and the skin will have changed since the last treatment

Summary

A good general treatment procedure and a good treatment technique are not something an electrologist is born with. These skills are learnt through practice, as with other skills.

The most important thing you can do to improve your insertion skills is to be honest with yourself. By this we mean that if you feel you are 'pushing' the needle into the follicle, it is clearly not right, so be honest, re-assess the situation, consider all your options and don't give in! No points are scored by forcing the needle into the skin and practising insertions on yourself every now and then is the best way to know if you are doing it right.

Always take the time to make your client feel appreciated and special. With so much to think about, this may be difficult at first, but gradually it will become a habit. You can help yourself to develop the habit by asking yourself, about five minutes before the end of each treatment: 'Have I said something during this treatment to let this person know that she or he is important to me?' These are the clients who will recognise you as a professional. They will recommend you to their friends, thus becoming in effect, walking-talking advertisements for your services.

ELECTROLYSIS CASE STUDY 1

Age: 32

Skin type: Slightly dehydrated.

Hair growth: Strong dark terminal hair on chin, two dense patches at either side of the point of the chin. Dark hairs scattered along the remainder of the jaw line.

Previous treatment: Waxing for two years (at home) every 1–2 weeks until 3 months ago then began shaving daily.

Situation: The client was very aggressive and uncooperative at the consultation and during the first few treatments. The hair had been getting worse over the last few years and she had recently started to shave as she could not stand to let the re-growth grow long enough to wait for the next waxing session. She later revealed that she no longer had a social life, refused to have a relationship with a man and was missing significant time from work because of the hairs she felt everyone could see.

Treatment: The initial treatment session was for over two hours in order to remove the dense growth. The client's skin tolerated the treatment well. Following the first treatment, the client needed to shave three times before the second treatment which was planned for two weeks later. A combination of thermolysis for speed and blend for the more distorted hairs was used.

The treatment progressed at twice-weekly intervals and was progressively reduced from two hours to 20 minute sessions within 12 treatments. As the hair growth improved, so did the client's manner. She was finally persuaded to seek medical advice and later revealed that she also had hairs on her breasts and chest, which were subsequently treated.

After many tests it was revealed that she had a large cyst on her ovary which was later removed. The hair growths were successfully treated over a period of 32 months, the later treatments were spaced at 4–6-weekly intervals. Having appeared as a very disagreeable character initially, as the hairs were removed so her true personality was revealed. The electrologist was invited to her wedding one year after the end of the treatment!

ELECTROLYSIS CASE STUDY 2

Age: 53

Skin type: Mature and sensitised.

Hair growth: A dense growth on the upper lip; the hair is a mixture of dark and grey in colour.

Previous treatment: Depilatory cream twice weekly for the past five years, also has occasionally plucked out a few at the outer edge of the upper lip.

Situation: This client has noticed the hairs getting worse over the years. They began to be obvious around the time of the menopause, but she describes herself as always having been hairy. She has decided to try electrolysis because the skin on her upper lip is starting to react to the constant application of the depilatory cream.

Treatment mode: Thermolysis was used throughout treatment. The stronger more obvious hairs were removed and the remainder thinned rather than cleared in order to avoid over-treatment and an unnaturally bare lip. Fifteen-minute sessions were carried out at fortnightly intervals for 18 sessions. The client returned for tidy up sessions at approximately 8–10-week intervals. The client had regular soothing and hydrating treatments throughout the course of electrolysis in order to repair the damage done from the excessive use of depilatory cream.

ELECTROLYSIS CASE STUDY 3

Age: 19

Skin type: Asian and prone to hyper pigmentation.

Hair growth: Fine dark hairs on the chin and upper lip and sides of the face up to the ears. The growth is a natural distribution for the client's age, sex and race with some stimulation from threading.

Treatment: The hairs were not distorted, because there had been minimal disturbance to the growth, the client having only previously had threading treatment once or twice.

Mode: The blend method was used. The client's skin was prone to hyper pigmentation and therefore the use of thermolysis had to be kept to an absolute minimum. The restricted use of thermolysis meant an increase in treatment time in order to generate sufficient lye. One-hour treatment sessions were carried out at 14-day intervals. The hairs which were treated were spread out over the area in a thinning procedure in order to avoid a build up of heat. A total of 36 treatments were given until the client was satisfied with the results.

ELECTROLYSIS CASE STUDY 4

Age: 41

Skin type: Devitalised and dehydrated with some scarring along the chin from acne.

Hair growth: The client wanted treatment for a low hairline on the forehead. The hairs were fine and dense with shallow follicles, the growth extended from the hairline down to the top of the brow. The hairs were denser at the hairline and extended in points towards the brow.

Treatment: The client had a course of three facials with Pure collagen matrix and used exfoliator 3 times a week for 3 weeks prior to starting the electrolysis treatment as her skin was not previously in a moist enough state to achieve successful treatment.

Treatment: Thermolysis was used and 20-minute sessions were agreed at weekly intervals. The treatment was progressive, beginning from the top of the brow and working in sections up towards the hairline.

The skin reacted quite severely after the first session; the area was red, bumpy and swollen for two days. Because the follicles were shallow, the needle was changed to insulated which allowed more targeted and lower intensity currents and cataphoresis was carried out post-treatment which resolved the reaction problem. Treatment continued for 11 sessions at weekly intervals, the sessions were then spaced to fortnightly and, after a further 12 sessions, the treatment was concluded.

Assessment of knowledge and understanding

This section has taught you how to conduct a best practice electrolysis treatment. To test your level of knowledge and understanding, answer the following short questions:

1 What three things do you have to carry out correctly to make a perfect insertion and why are they essential?

2 Why should you position your wrist and elbow in line with the follicle and how does that assist in making perfect insertions?

3 Describe two different skin types and how you might advise the clients regarding a home skin care regime and explain why improved skin care has a positive effect on electrolysis treatments.

4 When might you use iontophoresis and desincrustation and what benefits would you expect with each?

5 What is meant by 'the stretch' and why is it important to successful treatment?

6 What is a distorted follicle and how does it affect insertions?

7 Describe how the electrologist can take advantage of synapse fatigue when carrying out treatment.

8 At what stage of the treatment would cataphoresis be carried out and what will its actions be on the skin?

9 Why are easily adjusted couches and stools important when carrying out electrolysis?

10 Which is the only stage of hair growth at which total destruction of the follicle's target zone is possible?

Activities

Conduct the following activities to practise your knowledge of electrolysis best practice:

1 Carry out treatments working with the one-handed and two-handed techniques and count how many hairs you remove with each technique within the same time frame, e.g. 10 minutes.

2 Get a colleague to act as a client and move yourself around the couch on a stool so you can position your wrist and elbow in the correct way to access all areas of the body and different hair directions.

3 Insert very slowly into several follicles to enable you to see and feel 'follicle feedback'.

4 Practise the three-way stretch and note if your insertions are easier, the same or worse as with the traditional two-way stretch.

Follow-up knowledge

To build on the knowledge of electrolysis best practice gained in this section, complete the following tasks to extend your hair removal skills and understanding:

1 An excellent, specific, magazine just for electrolysis, called *Hair Route*, can be found at www.hairroute.com

2 Search the American internet for electrolysis magnifying glasses and weigh up the advantages and disadvantages.

3 Visit www.wrope.com The Worldwide Registry of Professional Electrologists and see how many British electrologists are registered.

4 Visit, read about and try to understand the distress caused by polycystic ovaries www.pcosupport.org (Polycystic Ovarian Support Group) or the self-help group for PCOS sufferers www.verity-pcos.org.uk

5 For information regarding electrolysis in America visit www.electrology.com the website of the American Electrolysis Association.

6 Information on diabetes and how it can affect your clients can be found at www.diabetes.org.uk

7 Information on the British Institute and Association of Electrolysis can be found at www.electrolysis.co.uk

Advanced knowledge reference section
Charles J. Doillon and Clément Beaumont

'A bit of science': Bulge versus bulb

Controversy has persisted for some time now over the very existence of an area termed 'bulge', located in the hair follicle, and for which electro-epilation techniques may be adapted to become even more effective.

However, the existence of this area was scientifically demonstrated and advanced research has provided new insight on the hair follicle regeneration process over the course of a growth cycle. Based on this new data, studies were undertaken in a research centre in Québec, in order to observe microscopic lesions on human follicles following electro-epilation.

The controversial area was discovered by observing the growth cycle of hairs. Each hair on the human body follows a regular growth cycle consisting of three phases: anagen, catagen and telogen. The bulge is located at the boundary between the permanent and transient hair, that is near the sebaceous gland and the junction with the arrector pili muscle.

Recently, the bulge has been the focus of advanced studies by scientific experts, since it was believed to host the stem cells* and progenitor cells* of the epidermis and skin appendages (hair follicle, sebaceous and sudoriferous glands). These cells were found to occur in the outer root sheath within the bulge area.

During the follicle growth cycle, the stimulation of stem cells in the bulge leads to the differentiation* and migration of progenitor cells towards the epidermis, including keratinocytes*, and the skin appendages, among which, interestingly, is the bulb of the hair follicle. Thus, they differentiate into a variety of epidermal cells, and namely form the cells of the bulb in the newly formed follicle in the anagen phase. The bulge therefore plays a key role in the life cycle of the hair follicle, when the conditions are suitable.

This scientific knowledge is extremely relevant to adapt electrolysis techniques. Based on this new data, we are now better able to permanently destroy the cells in the hair follicle and prevent their reproduction.

* see Glossary terms on p. 290

Logically, two areas of the hair follicle should therefore be targeted: the bulb and the bulge. But there is a problem: the stem cells at rest in the bulge area are more heat-resistant than progenitor cells, and are therefore harder to destroy. It would be more appropriate to target migrating progenitor cells [moving down the outer root sheath], located between the bulge and the bulb, as well as progenitor cells located in the bulb itself [in the inner sheath]. The reproduction and differentiation of these cells is very active in these two locations. Unfortunately, the heat that reaches outer root sheath may be reduced, and the destruction of the latter may consequently be limited. Cellular growth (hair cycle) may therefore either perpetuate or be inadequate (e.g. produce thin and curved hair, which would be harder to treat a second time). Targeting only the outer root sheath area would most likely prove ineffective. It therefore becomes essential to target both the area along the hair shaft to the bulge as well as the bulb area.

It is possible to achieve this using Apilus computerised epilators and blend technique (on hair follicles in the anagen phase for better conductivity). Another alternative would be to use an insulated probe with two pulses of thermolysis (MicroFlash®) to be delivered in two different locations, in order to target the bulge area then move towards the bulb area to apply the second pulse (or vice versa). Thanks to its configuration, the insulated probe may be moved within the follicle without risk of epidermal damage, as long as it remains within the lower two-thirds of the follicle. This type of procedure would not be possible with a non-insulated probe, since the area warmed by the latter increases when it is moved closer to the skin surface, thereby increasing the risk of superficial epidermis burns.

For the other phases of the hair cycle, the application of this new data appears to differ. Thus, thermolysis (MicroFlash®) applied to a hair follicle in the telogen phase will directly target the stem cells and progenitor cells, but may require a greater amount of energy (considering their resistance to heat) which can be provided by an insulated probe (heat concentration at the tip). On the other hand, it is difficult to determine if a follicle in the catagen phase would be easy to destroy, given the presence of two types of cells: those in a catabolic state* (which will be destroyed since they cannot withstand heat) and the stem cells at rest in the bulge (which will be heat-resistant).

We are now better able to understand, thanks to this new data, what can, in conjunction with other factors, improve or not electro-epilation treatments. It is still difficult, however, to predict with any certainty if a hair follicle will regenerate or not after treatment. But ongoing research is well underway, and these latest results already represent an exceptional breakthrough in terms of insertion techniques.

How is cellular migration observed?

The demonstration was made possible thanks to genetically engineered rodents, in which a fluorescent (green) probe was introduced into the genetic material of most cells, then transferred by hair follicle transplant into non-fluorescent animals. Thus, it was observed that fluorescent cells are concentrated in the bulge area during the telogen and early anagen phases. Then, in the late anagen phase, the fluorescence is concentrated in the bulb. Stem cells in the bulge area are normally resting during the catagen, telogen and most of the anagen phase, but they multiply briefly and rapidly at the onset of the anagen phase. Thus, we can see the pluripotent character of these stem cells emerging from the bulge. In the bulge, the progenitor cells migrate at the onset of the anagen phase, and their proliferation is intensely stimulated (the highest proliferation rate of any mammalian tissue). The bulge most likely supplies (?) the life cycle of the hair follicle. However, this phenomenon requires the presence of connective tissue cells (mesenchymal cells in the dermis near the hair follicle) and the formation of capillaries or microvessels by endothelial cells (i.e. angiogenesis). These two types of external cells set off the reproduction of progenitor cells and their differentiation into specialised cells to form the new bulb and thus regenerate the lower follicle (i.e. the transient portion) at the onset of a new follicular cycle in adults.

Glossary

Stem cell – A stem cell is an *undifferentiated progenitor cell* which, on the one hand, can replicate itself as it reproduces, and on the other hand, can produce most cell types in the tissue to which it is attached.

Progenitor cell – The progeny of stem cells becomes the progenitor cells. A progenitor cell is somewhat more specialised than a stem cell, but can still change its outcome based on surrounding conditions.

Keratinocyte – Any cell in the epidermis, from the basal layer to the uppermost layers, which evolves towards keratosic maturation, resulting in the thickening of the stratum corneum of the epidermis.

Differentiation – Progressive loss of characteristics and acquisition of others in the process of becoming an adult ('mature') cell, related to specialisation.

Catabolic state – Degenerative state.

Arthur Hinkel (1916–1993), Father of the blend

While working for the General Electric Company's medical division in the 1930s, Arthur Hinkel met Henri St Pierre, a practising electrologist with offices in northern and southern California. At Henri's request, Arthur began modifying existing medical equipment to enable it to remove hair using high-frequency current. Henri had been using galvanic current and was interested in the work or Dr Bordier of France who held high esteem for the speed of the high-frequency process. After years of

Courtesy: International Hair Route Magazine; Photo: Alfred and Fabris Studio

tinkering with high-frequency equipment and finding the re-growth to be much higher than Henri had been accustomed to with galvanic current, Henri convinced Arthur to design a piece of equipment that would 'blend' galvanic and high frequency current together at the needle at the same time. In 1948, Henri St Pierre received a patent approval for the 'Blend' epilator.

Arthur received his California electrology licence in 1947 and spent the next 35 years operating the Wilshire School of Electrology at Wester and Wilshire Blvd in Los Angeles and at another location in Orange County. He owned a chain of electrolysis salons under the name 'Arroway Labs' in southern California and also had concessions with the Broadway and Buffums department stores for whom he provided equipment and electrologists who worked in the beauty salon areas of these stores. At one time, he employed 40 electrologists for these operations. The A.R. Hinkel Company was a one-room operation at the Wilshire and Western address that made equipment solely for his operations and graduates from the Wilshire School. As he grew toward retirement age, he began spinning off parts of his business to his employees.

Daniel J. Mahler (1860–1934)

Founder of D.J. Mahler Inc. and The Instantron Company

It was the 1880s and a time for invention, growth and action. It was also a carefree time and the country was filled with optimism which preceded the 'Gay Nineties' era. Daniel J. Mahler lived, worked hard and fashioned a good life for himself through his own intense motivations. He educated himself with extension courses at Brown University and opened a beauty parlour in downtown providence, Rhode Island. By 1888 he was treating patients for permanent hair removal with galvanic electrolysis only 12 years after the procedure was developed. My father was a man of perhaps 5' 6" or so in height and a springy 130 pounds ... he was impressive, serious, intellectual, dedicated and a good businessman. The business prospered and as a matter of fact, we still have some of his early price lists, diaries and other mementos in our files – a priceless heritage of the electrolysis industry today.

My fondest recollections of him are of the time when he was 63 or 64, a well-dressed, mustachioed elder who kept me busy around the shop as well as eight or ten other employees working in the office. Both he and Mom were among the very few practising electrologists in the area. There may have been others, but the professional electrologist was rare in those days. For most people, electrolysis treatments meant Boston or New York City. At that time I was just doing shop and clerical work in the office, learning a few fundamentals about how a business operates internally and externally. Looking back on that period which was around 1925, I recall how archaic and primitive the equipment, accessories and supplies were compared to today's modern shortwave epilators and supplies. I marvel at the technological achievements and recognition of the industry from the original concept Dr Michel developed so long ago to destroy the hair roots of inverted eyelashes.

My father's character and professionalism are readily apparent from the language used in a 1900 product catalogue. In it he stated:
'Of all facial blemishes with which womanhood is embarrassed, there is none so annoying as a growth of unwanted hair on the face, neck or arms. The features of many an otherwise beautiful woman are made unattractive by such disfigurement. It is to such women that this booklet is addressed, showing them that there is one method by which they can gain positive, permanent relief and still have a perfect complexion when the treatments are completed. During my more than twenty years of experience as a hair specialist, it has been my pleasure to be the means of relieving the suffering of many ladies afflicted with superfluous hair growth.'

Elsewhere he said, 'I have every confidence that electrolysis is the only positive and permanent way to remove unwanted hair forever and that the integrity of the treatment depends entirely upon the skill and expertise of the electrologist.' Such is the legacy my father left us when he died in 1934, and we have sustained his business on that premise ever since.

By capitalising on technological changes and expanding our product lines, we have been successful in increasing our size and volume every year. As the recognised leader in equipment innovation, styling and performance, we are one of the best sources for information, equipment, education, and supplies for the professional electrologist – and we owe it all to the basic business principles established almost one hundred years ago by D. J. Mahler. I am sure he would be proud to see how greatly this industry has developed from the rudimentary origins he was part of during the latter 1880s. About 1955, the electrolysis industry began to blossom from a narrowly defined and fuzzy image industry to one which, every year, brings more people into the business, more people teaching, better training, more sophistiction and more seminars and conventions which are perfect exchanges for educational information to benefit the credibility and respect of all professional electrologists. We, as a company, have always tried to encourage the organisations who are responsible for these changing conditions, with sizeable conditions, with sizeable contributions given to support this work every year.

After Dad passed away, my mother carried on the company affairs for several years along with my brothers, Dan and Harold, and myself. In 1936 the company evolved into D. J. Mahler, Inc., and in 1969 it was formally changed to Instantron to reflect the changes in our presentation to the practising electrologist. We had been using the INSTANTRON name since 1946 because this has always been the name of our shortwave epilator. As far as I know, we are the oldest manufacturers, instructors and practising electrologists in a continuous family owned and directed electrolysis business.

Instantron is what it is today because a young man with little formal education recognised a need of his time and through his own efforts gained the knowledge, experience and expertise to satisfy that need. In conjunction with that innovation, he also developed the necessary marketing, merchandising and advertising skills to propel this business into the twentieth century and beyond.

Charles J. Doillon, Doctor at the CHUL research center, and Clément Beaumont, President, Dectro International

chapter 8

LASER AND INTENSE PULSED LIGHT

What will I know after reading this chapter?

This chapter covers laser and intense pulsed light (IPL) hair removal treatments. It describes the core competencies required to enable you to:

- understand how light-based hair removal systems operate
- recognise the differences between laser and IPL
- plan light-based hair removal treatments
- prepare clients for light-based hair removal treatments
- conduct light-based hair removal treatments
- complete the treatment.

BT37 Remove hair using light or laser systems

LIGHT AND LASER SYSTEMS

The use of light-based hair removal systems has burst on to the professional hair removal market over a relatively short period of time. The high volume turnover for the companies involved has meant that a vast array of systems have become available with a considerable difference in cost from one system to another. Some of these companies make extravagant, sometimes unsubstantiated marketing claims.

What are light-based hair removal systems?

KEY TERMS ★
Light systems: Any system which emits light energy, e.g. laser or intense pulsed light

Laser and light hair removal systems aim to damage the hair follicle by heating the hair shaft sufficiently in order for the heat to diffuse from the hair shaft to the follicle and damage the follicle, thus retarding growth.

There are essentially two main light systems used in hair removal; they are laser and flash lamp or as they are more commonly called 'intense pulsed light' or IPL. Both involve the use of laser light to damage hair and/or hair follicles and rely on the melanin in the hair to generate destructive heat.

LASER SCIENCE

The commonly used word 'Laser' is an acronym for:

Light
Amplification *by*
Stimulated
Emission *of*
Radiation

The first concept of the laser was suggested by Albert Einstein as long ago as 1917. The first working laser was not available until 1960. They were initially developed simply to prove Einstein's theory – at this stage they had no specific use. The ruby laser was the first laser to be demonstrated in 1960. Although some early studies looked at using lasers on the skin to remove tattoos, it wasn't until 1996 that Grossman *et al*. found that the ruby laser could be used for successful long-term hair reduction.

Albert Einstein
Bettman/CORBIS

Laser light

Laser and flash lamp systems are a complex system of radiant energy. The laser medium – which can be gas, crystal or liquid, depending upon the type of laser – is charged with energy, which then releases small 'energy bundles' (photons) in the form of laser light.

Laser light has several special qualities:

- it only emits one colour (different lasers emit different colours)
- it is a thin beam
- it can be very intense
- it can be focused on a tiny spot.

Laser ∿∿∿∿∿∿∿

Laser light:
- emits a coherent beam of waves
  that travel in step or in phase

Laser beam

> ### KEY TERMS ★
>
> **Monochromatic**: All the photons of light are the same colour (wavelength)
> **Coherent**: All the photons of light are in phase (synchronised) with each other. A common analogy is a platoon of soldiers marching in step, compared with a group of pedestrians in a busy shopping street who are moving in lots of different directions. The soldiers are said to moving in a coherent manner, whereas the pedestrians' movement is random
> **Collimated**: In light which is generated by lasers, the light waves are parallel. This highly ordered pattern of the light allows the beam to pass across long distances, e.g. along optical fibres, and it means that the laser light can be very well controlled and focused down to very small and accurate spot sizes (the size of the emitted beam)

How laser light is generated

Energy from a flash lamp, electrical source or other source, such as gas, is pumped into a material called the active medium, which is contained in the laser cavity.

⬇

The active medium determines the wavelength (colour) of the laser radiation. The active medium also gives the laser its name, e.g. ruby.

⬇

As this energy is absorbed, the individual atoms in the active medium move into an 'excited' state.

⬇

The energy is re-emitted from the excited active medium as optical radiation.

⬇

Mirrors are placed at either end of the cavity to reflect the radiation back into the active medium. This stimulates the active medium into producing more radiation, called laser radiation.

⬇

The laser radiation is amplified by the process of stimulation. If one of the mirrors is partially transmitting, some of the laser radiation will be emitted as the laser beam.

The following shows an example of one type of laser and how the beam of light is generated.

Step One: A ruby laser consists of a flash tube, a ruby rod and two mirrors (one half-silvered). The ruby rod is the lasing medium and the flash tube pumps it.

Step Two: The flash tube fires and injects energy into the ruby rod. The light energy excites or stimulates atoms in the ruby.

Step Three: The stimulation causes some of these atoms to emit photons.

Step Four: Some of these photons run in a direction parallel to the ruby's axis, they then bounce back and forth off the mirrors at either end. As they pass through the crystal, they stimulate emission in other atoms.

Step Five: Monochromatic, single-phase, light leaves through the half-silvered mirror – this is the laser light.

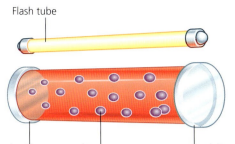

Flash tube

Mirrored surface   Atoms   Partially mirrored surface

Step 1: The laser in its non-lasing state

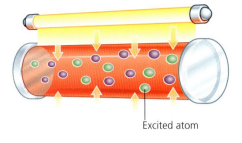

Excited atom

Step 2: The flash tube fires and injects light (energy) into the ruby rod. The light energy excites or stimulates atoms in the ruby

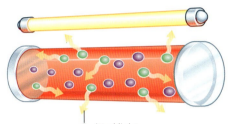

Emitted light

Step 3: The stimulation causes some of these atoms to emit photons

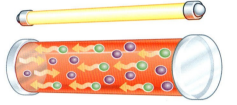

Step 4: Some of these photons run in a direction parallel to the ruby's axis; they then bounce back and forth off the mirrors at either end. As they pass through the crystal, they stimulate emission in other atoms

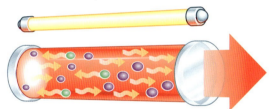

Step 5: Monochromatic, single-phase light leaves through the half-silvered mirror – this is the laser light

Wavelength

What gives laser light its impact is the fact that the photons are all the same wavelength: they all travel in one direction and are in step with each other. Wavelength is the term used to describe the 'length' of a light wave typically quoted in nanometres (nm). The wavelength determines the colour of the beam and the type of interaction with different materials, for example blood, melanin, water.

Certain targets in the skin, known as chromophores (an object which will absorb the light energy and so be destroyed), are known to absorb energy of particular wavelengths. In other words, different wavelengths affect different chromophores. In the 400–590nm range, for example, when laser light is applied to the skin there is strong absorption by superficial melanin and blood vessels, which prevent this particular wavelength from penetrating deeply enough into the skin to treat a follicle.

In hair treatment one of the primary requirements of wavelength is that the light must penetrate deeply enough to reach the base of the follicle. Selecting the correct wavelength is crucial in order to achieve effective treatment on hair follicles whilst avoiding undesirable effects on the surrounding tissue. Current research says that the ideal wavelength for hair removal is between

KEY TERMS ★

Chromophore: Anything which absorbs light. The target chromophore for hair removal is melanin. Each chromophore absorbs light at varying wavelengths

600 and 1100nm and all laser and light source technology used for hair removal is in the visible and near infra-red electromagnetic spectrum.

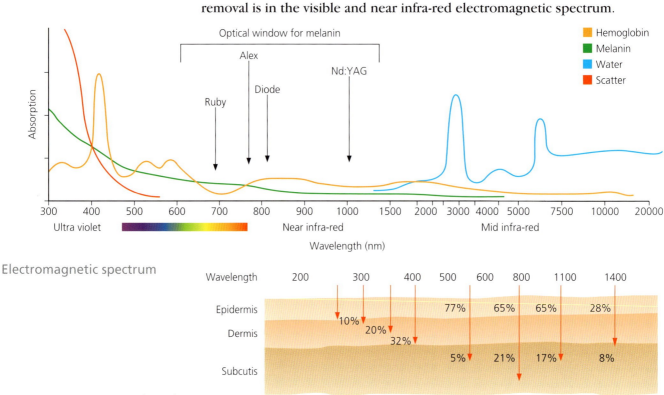

Electromagnetic spectrum

Wavelengths

% absorption in skin at varying wavelengths

This process of limiting the transfer of laser energy to a particular site because of the selective absorption of a chromophore at that site is known as selective photothermolysis.

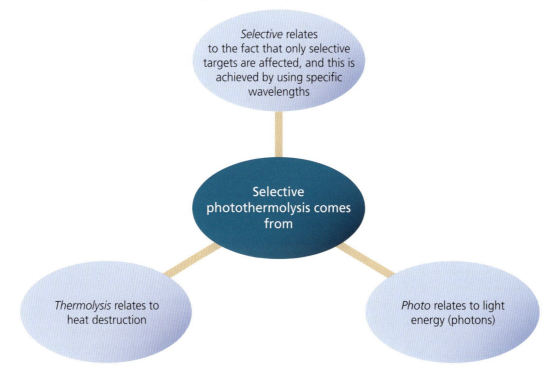

Selective relates to the fact that only selective targets are affected, and this is achieved by using specific wavelengths

Selective photothermolysis comes from

Thermolysis relates to heat destruction

Photo relates to light energy (photons)

Light source hair removal summarised

Light source hair removal works by the process of selective photothermolysis. Hair in the early anagen growth phase is most susceptible to permanent damage.

⬇

Laser or intense pulsed light source of the correct wavelength is absorbed by the melanin in the hair shaft, the base of the hair follicle lies between 2mm and 5mm into the skin.

⬇

This IPL or laser light causes the hair to heat rapidly; the heat is conducted from the hair shaft to the follicle leading to destruction of the cells.

⬇

The cells responsible for re-growth of the hair are heated above 70°C and destroyed.

⬇

New hair growth appears as hairs enter the anagen phase.

⬇

New hair growth can be treated again and the percentage of re-growth decreases with each subsequent treatment.

PROFESSIONAL TIP ✔

Light based hair removal has *not* been proven to result in permanent hair removal

---

Thermal relaxation time (TRT)

Thermal relaxation time is the period of time the target structure takes to lose a given percentage of the heat generated by the absorption of light energy, that is to cool down. Once heated, objects lose heat at varying rates, for example large objects lose heat much more slowly than small objects.

The length of time for which a laser beam is emitted is critical in achieving hair follicle damage. In order to achieve heat destruction of the hair and follicle, they must be heated for an equal or slightly shorter time than its thermal relaxation time. This is because the heat destruction should be limited to the target areas. In this way excessive thermal diffusion (skin damage by burning) can be avoided.

Laser energy

Watts

Watts are the amount of output power that the laser unit is capable of generating. When more watts are available, the laser will be capable of more energy density – in laser terminology 'fluence'.

Fluence

Fluence is the energy density generated by the laser, that is the amount of light energy delivered over a given treatment area. It is measured in joules per cm^2.

Fluence is a function of:

- the laser light power
- the area covered by the spot size
- the time the skin is exposed to the laser light.

The fluence calculation is based on the formula:

$$\frac{\text{Laser output (watts)} \times \text{Laser exposure time (seconds)}}{\text{Area of delivered laser beam (cm}^2)} = \text{Energy fluence (Jcm}^2)$$

Laser classifications

Lasers are classified into four broad areas (two of which are subdivided again) depending on their potential for causing biological damage. All lasers should be labelled with one of these class designations:

- Class I – These lasers cannot emit laser radiation at known hazard levels.
- Class IA – This is a special designation that applies only to lasers that are 'not intended for viewing', such as a supermarket laser scanner.
- Class II – These are low-power visible lasers that emit above Class I levels but at a radiant power not above 1 watt. The concept is that the human aversion reaction to bright light will protect a person.
- Class IIIA – These are intermediate-power lasers which are hazardous only for intrabeam viewing. Most pen-like pointing lasers are in this class.
- Class IIIB – These are moderate-power lasers.
- Class IV – These are high-power lasers, which are hazardous to view under any condition (directly or diffusely scattered), and are a potential fire and skin hazard. Significant controls are required of Class IV laser facilities.

LASERS USED IN THE HAIR REMOVAL PROCESS

In terms of hair removal, lasers are used to cause:

- selective damage and destruction of the anagen hair follicle through the principle of selective photothermolysis

PROFESSIONAL TIP ✔

It should be noted that contrary to some laser and light marketing messages; both epilation and laser and light rely very much on the skill and knowledge of the operator. Laser and light treatments are not an easy treatment option and shouldn't be regarded as such

- significant and stable loss of hair for a period longer than the complete natural hair growth cycle. (R.Rox Anderson, MD)

During the process of epilation we utilise a tiny needle to direct destructive heat and or chemical to the follicle. Laser and light treatments utilise the hair shaft, or more precisely the melanin in the hair shaft to 'conduct' or 'transmit' sufficient heat to the follicle in order to damage or destroy it.

It could be argued that laser and light energy is more problematic than electrolysis to use accurately and consistently. Laser and light energy is a relatively new method of hair removal treatment and it will still be a matter of time before the complexities are fully understood.

When a pulse of laser light at the correct wavelength is delivered to the skin it should ideally penetrate approximately 5mm into the skin.

- The energy of the light is absorbed by the melanin in the hair shaft and transformed into heat.
- The heat increases the temperature in the hair follicle to 60–75°C, causing the hair and follicle to be damaged. Surrounding tissue should be unaffected by the laser light, if it has been correctly applied.

Spot size and pulse width

Spot size refers to the width of the emitted beam used for treatment. The size of the spot is quoted in millimetres (mm). The use of a larger spot size will allow deeper penetration of light energy into the skin and will enable faster treatment times.

The spot size plays an important role in the efficacy of the treatment, it is very important that it is sufficiently big to reach the target area and so ensure the treatment objectives are achieved. In other words it must be big enough to reach the base of the follicle.

The diagram shows the effect of the spot size on the penetration depth of the beam.

In order to achieve an effective hair removal treatment, the spot size must be a minimum of 3–5mm if it is to reach the maximal depth of laser light penetration, and cause sufficient damage to the base of the follicle.

The spot size also has an impact on the speed of treatment. In order to achieve rapid treatment rates, it is desirable to operate at the largest possible spot size. Achieving high fluence levels in large spot sizes is dependent upon the ability of the laser to produce enough energy. For example, a 400nm laser will not penetrate the skin deeply, no matter how large the spot size.

Short and long pulse width

The pulse width is one of the main parameters which will determine the effects of the treatment at a given energy level. If the pulse width is too short, it will not target the follicle effectively and, potentially, will cause damage to surrounding skin and smaller structures. If it is too long, the follicle will not get hot enough to cause sufficient damage. Some lasers offer very long pulse

PROFESSIONAL TIP ✔

The key advantage that lasers and IPLs offer over electrolysis is the ability to treat large areas quickly

TECHNICAL TIP ✔

Larger spot sizes give deeper penetration of the light into the follicle

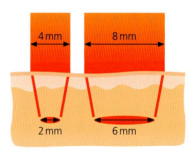

Spot size and penetration depth

KEY TERMS ★

Fluence: The energy density generated by the laser

TECHNICAL TIP ✔

The area of the spot size is used in the calculation of fluence (energy density)

widths in order to prevent skin damage, particularly on darker skin types, and still successfully damage the hair follicle. These lasers require much higher fluence levels, which increases the overall energy input into the skin.

It is desirable to have the facility to adjust the selected pulse width for individual skin types, as not all clients are the same.

The key considerations of pulse duration are as follows:

- pulse duration and TRT are very closely linked, as the pulse duration is selected according to the TRT of the target
- long pulse duration allows heat to be diffused and is therefore suitable for darker skin types where more melanin is present
- shorter pulse duration concentrates the heat and gives more destructive power; shorter pulse durations are only suitable for lighter skin colours.

Skin cooling

It is vital to protect and avoid damage to the epidermis and tissue surrounding the hair follicle during the treatment. Since the target chromophore (melanin) is present in both the hair and the skin, it is essential to prevent too much thermal diffusion and keep the skin cool.

The process of selective photothermolysis inevitably generates a certain amount of heat in the skin, which is why it is beneficial, and in most cases essential, to provide some kind of cooling pre-, during and post-laser treatment in order to counteract the build-up of heat in the skin. Preventing or counteracting this build-up of heat helps to prevent adverse reactions such as burning. Skin cooling is also useful and usually required in order to maintain client comfort.

Effective pre-cooling of the skin can provide an analgesic effect. Cooling helps to detract from the heat sensation that is inevitably experienced by clients, particularly in areas of dense hair growth and in sensitive areas such as the bikini line.

There are various methods of skin cooling, but the most popular methods today are the following.

1 *Cold air or cryogen spray*: Cold air is generated and directed onto the treatment area either by the laser operator or occasionally the client is asked to direct the air if they feel discomfort, both pre- and post-treatment. This method means that the cool air can be precisely directed to the required area. Cryogen cooling is built into some laser systems – they use a cryogen spray which is timed to be delivered just prior to a laser pulse.

2 *Simultaneous contact cooling*: This system is available on lasers which operate through a scanner – a device which speeds treatment time by allowing a series of laser pulses to be emitted in quick succession and in a controlled area of approximately $3 \times 3cm^2$. The laser beam is emitted through a sapphire (glass) window, which provides a vehicle for cooled water, this facilitates easy pre- and post-treatment cooling as well as simultaneous cooling with the lasing.

3 *Ice packs*: Cooling with ice packs is an economical method. Ice packs can be applied to the treatment area, pre- and post-treatment. They cannot however be used simultaneously with the lasing. Great care should be taken not to apply ice packs directly to the skin as this could cause an 'ice burn': packs should be wrapped in a disposable thin covering such as a couch roll.

4 *Cooling gel*: Water-based gels are applied to the skin pre-treatment, and if necessary after treatment. The gel cools the skin by evaporation.

Types of laser used in hair removal

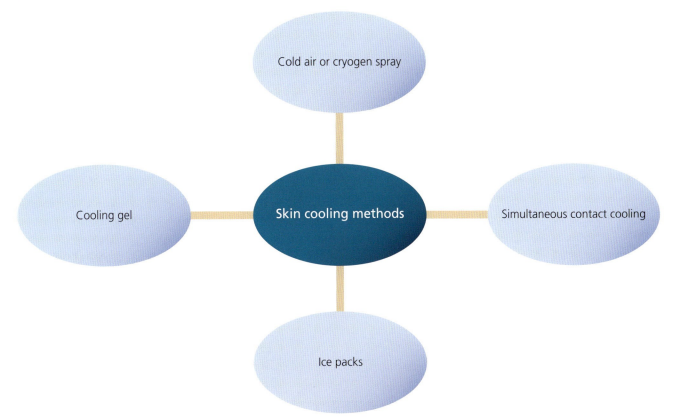

There are four main types of laser used in the hair removal process:

1 Alexandrite – a type of laser which emits 755nm visible light/near infra-red wavelength. This wavelength is absorbed strongly by melanin and so has an increased risk of pigmentary changes. More cooling and long pulse durations are required.

2 Ruby – a type of laser which emits 694nm visible light wavelength. This wavelength is absorbed strongly by melanin and so there is an increased risk of pigmentary changes. More cooling and long pulse durations are required.

3 Diode – a type of laser which emits 800nm near infra-red wavelength, this wavelength is absorbed strongly by melanin and so there is an increased risk of pigmentary changes. More cooling and long pulse durations are required. A diode is a semi-conductive material which mainly lets energy travel in one direction and not in the other. You will be familiar with light-

Laser systems – Polaris

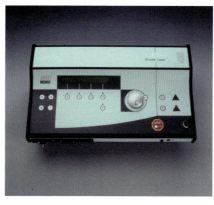

Laser systems – Diode

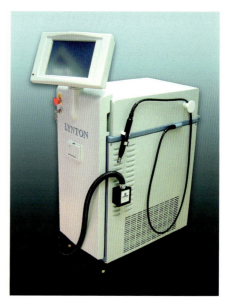

Laser systems – Lumina

Lynton Lasers Ltd UK

emitting diodes (LEDs) as they are used for the numeric displays on microwaves and VCRs as well as for lasers.

4 Nd: YAG – a type of laser which emits 1064nm infra-red wavelength. At this wavelength there is much less absorption by melanin than with visible light wavelengths, which reduces the risk of post-inflammatory and pigmentary changes.

FLASH LAMP SYSTEMS

Flash lamp systems are more commonly known as IPL systems.

What does IPL stand for?

Intense
Pulsed
Light

TECHNICAL TIP ✔

Both laser and intense pulsed light involve the use of light to destroy hairs and hair follicles

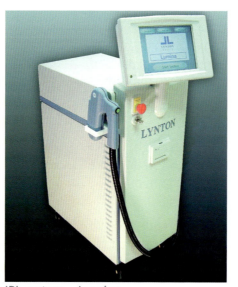

IPL system – Lumina

Lynton Lasers Ltd UK

History of intense pulsed light

Intense pulsed light (IPL) systems have been developed using the principle of selective photothermolysis that also applies to laser technology.

As is the case with lasers, flash lamps were first developed for medical purposes in the 1960s.

The Xenon flash lamp, which was first developed as an energy source for activating lasers was the first light source to be used therapeutically for hair removal with direct applications of its energy.

Xenon is commonly used as a light source because of the brilliant, full spectrum illumination it provides when exposed to energy. It is also used for items such as the flashes in photographic equipment and in surgical lighting equipment.

Studies of flash lamp (IPL) systems began in the 1970s and by the mid-1990s; researchers were exploring the use of flash lamps for treating vascular lesions. In the process of the studies, one researcher noted that hair loss was a side effect of treatment. Other research papers also indicated promising results, prompting one manufacturer to apply for and receive Food and Drug Administration (FDA) clearance for hair removal in 1997. In 2000, the FDA began allowing some brands to claim permanent hair reduction in most skin types. The darkest skin type was not included in this clearance.

> **KEY TERMS** ★
>
> **FDA** (Food and Drug Administration): An American body with responsibility for protecting the public health by assuring safety, efficacy and security of human and veterinary drugs, biological products, medical devices, food supply, cosmetics and products that emit radiation. The FDA is also responsible for advancing the public health by helping to speed innovations that make medicines and foods more effective, safer and more affordable; and helping the public get the accurate, science-based information they need to use medicines and foods to improve their health

Intense pulsed light science

IPL is a non-laser source. IPL has the full spectrum of light; it is broadband or white light. IPL is non-coherent which means all the photons of light are moving randomly and are not in phase.

How IPL works

The theory of intense pulsed light hair removal is very similar to laser. It uses different wavelengths of light to deliver energy and heat to varying depths of the skin, specifically targeting melanin in the follicle.

When light enters the skin, the majority of it will be absorbed by blood, melanin and water. Different wavelengths of light (different colours) will be absorbed by different chromophores; for example the wavelength 577nm (yellow) light is heavily absorbed in the blood. It is important to note that melanin is a good absorber of most wavelengths, which is why melanin is the

White light or intense pulsed light emits a non-coherent beam

Lumina filters

Lynton Lasers Ltd UK

skin's natural defence against harmful sunrays. Water is a relatively poor absorber of visible light but has a strong absorption at longer wavelengths (2000nm) such as infra-red.

IPL systems release light in a broad spectrum; the light is polychromatic, which means it has many (poly) wavelengths (colours). Unfiltered IPL systems emit every wavelength of light in the visible spectrum from about 400 to 1100 nanometres, and some systems in the band of infra-red radiation emit up to about 1200 nanometres.

IPLs use filters to block out the unwanted, hazardous wavelengths, and 'select' the appropriate wavelength for the treatment. These filters discolour with each shot, affecting the performance and therefore the treatment. Most systems will filter out the shorter wavelengths, which are heavily absorbed by the epidermal melanin and superficial blood vessels. For hair removal, the wavelengths emitted typically start around 600nm. The light is focused by a reflector and transmitted through a set of filters which will determine its characteristics.

This non-coherent, polychromatic light source can be filtered to allow only a specified range of wavelengths; and 'tuned' to provide a variety of fluences and pulse durations. The filter is selected by the laser operator and attached to a handpiece. The filtered light is delivered from the handpiece into the skin. The light is delivered in millisecond pulses separated by short thermal relaxation intervals.

IPL systems emit a beam which covers a larger area than lasers as the latter do not have a scanner. Some IPL systems have a rectangular spot, rather than the round type that is usually standard on lasers.

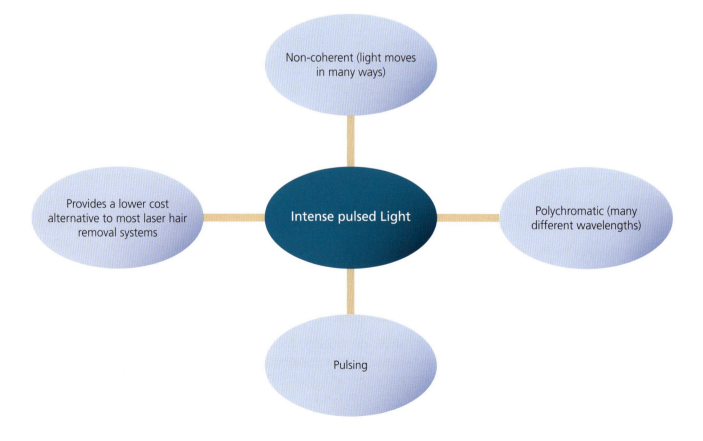

Spot size and repetition rate

IPL systems deliver the light in pulses which are separated by thermal relaxation intervals. The speed at which the system is able to deliver the pulses is critical to treatment outcome and treatment time.

The theory of TRT is exactly the same for both laser and IPL.

The length of time for which the pulse is emitted is critical in achieving hair follicle damage. In order to achieve heat destruction of the hair and follicle, they must be heated for an equal or slightly shorter time than its TRT. The pulses of light must be spaced to prevent too much cooling of the hair.

A large spot size and high repetition rate are important factors. Some IPLs only produce one pulse every 3–4 seconds, making the treatment very slow.

The operator must select all the parameters, in other words select the wavelength, pulse duration, pulse delay, etc. The operator must therefore be highly trained and competent in order to make the correct judgements and ultimately the correct treatments.

LASER SAFETY

Registration

Currently all establishments in the UK that provide light heat energy treatment must register with the Healthcare Commission under the Care Standards Act 2000, as amended by the Health and Social Care (Community Health and Standards) Act 2003. This includes hair removal procedures and skin therapies. These treatments fall within the definition of intense pulsed light, as defined in the Private and Voluntary Healthcare (England) Regulations 2001, PART 1, regulation 3(1) (b).

The Healthcare Commission assesses the suitability or 'fitness' of people, services and organisations to provide services. The commission will check:

- fitness of premises
- fitness of persons
- fitness of services.

The registration process usually takes in the region of three months, but there are often delays. At the time of writing, a non-refundable registration and annual fee are payable.

Registration is generally in two phases, application and inspection.

The application form requires in-depth information which includes:

- machine specification
- treatment details
- protocols which must be produced by a medical or dental practitioner
- details of your registration with a fully accredited laser protection advisor
- safety procedures
- business plan

HEALTH AND SAFETY

Some IPL systems produce significant energy at lower wavelengths and, if not successfully filtered, can cause burning. Water absorption starts to play a part at approx 1300nm. Some IPL systems produce significant energy at this wavelength and, if not successfully filtered, can cause burning

HEALTH AND SAFETY

Because there are a number of variations and choices of delivered energy and wavelength when using an IPL system, the process can become quite complex and, if used by untrained or incompetent operators, may cause inconsistency in efficacy and, potentially, damage to other structures in the skin

- statement of purpose, which includes:
  - aims and objectives of the business
  - name and address of business and responsible person and manager
  - relevant qualifications of service providers
  - number of staff with their relevant qualifications and experience
  - organisational structure
  - treatments and services available
  - consultation arrangements
  - complaints policy
  - privacy arrangements for clients
- policies and procedures
- verification of insurance
- financial information including 2 years of accounts
- copy of business lease and site plan.

All staff must have relevant training and qualifications and must be checked with the Criminal Records Bureau (CRB), an executive agency of the Home Office that has been appointed by government to carry out Police, Department of Health and Department for Education and Skills checks. Anyone who owns, manages or works in a service dealing with children or vulnerable adults has to undergo a CRB check. This includes all of the independent healthcare services regulated by the Healthcare Commission.

All applications for registration as a manager, a provider or a responsible individual on behalf of an organisation require you to have a satisfactory CRB check at enhanced level.

PREPARATION OF THE TREATMENT AREA

The controlled area

The 'controlled area' is the commonly used term for the room where the laser or light treatment takes place. In order to ensure the controlled area is safe and that the requirements which apply to the laser environment are met, in addition to your normal health and safety standards, the room should meet the following criteria.

- The room should be dedicated to light treatments, it should not be used for any other purpose, and only those authorised to do so should have access.
- There should be no more than one laser or IPL source operating in a room at the same time.
- All lasers and intense light sources must have labels identifying them, their wavelength or range of wavelengths, and maximum output power of radiation emitted.
- Warning signs must be displayed on the equipment and on the outside of doors to the controlled area (laser/light room). On or over the outside of

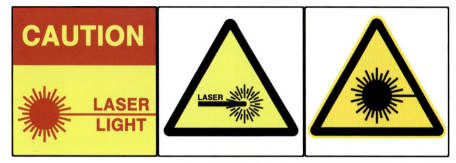

Standard laser radiation warning signs

these doors there must be a red light that is switched on when the laser is in use.

Laser radiation

- Protective eyewear must be worn by everyone in the controlled area whenever there is a risk of exposure to hazardous levels of laser or intense light radiation. The protective eyewear requirements are normally glasses or goggles that are made from plastic or glass. They must be specifically made to filter out the wavelength and output of the particular laser or light system in use.

- All windows must be covered by blinds or shutters during treatments in order to prevent the laser light passing through the glass and potentially causing damage if the radiation reaches unprotected eyes.

- Surfaces should ideally be non-reflective, particularly around the treatment area, because if the laser beam were to be inadvertently fired towards a reflective object it would be deflected and could potentially cause damage, for example if it were directed towards a person whose eyes were uncovered.

- Doors should be lockable or interlocked with the light source so that the machine automatically switches off if the door is accidentally opened.

- No flammable materials should be stored in the controlled area.

- Local rules should be displayed near the light source, and read and signed by all operators.

Local rules are the written rules and procedures that must be followed when working with light systems in the salon. They should include:

- equipment procedures: how to turn on, off, operate safely and maintain the equipment

- safety: what are the hazards, checks, who is responsible, how to prevent use by unauthorised persons and adverse incident procedures

- controlled area procedures and access

- the PPE required.

Protocols

Protocols are a precise and detailed plan which should be followed when carrying out a treatment. They should be written by a medical or dental practitioner. Most laser manufacturers supply a user manual, which should state the required procedure for:

- pre-treatment consultation and tests
- the settings to use and the permitted parameters for the system's variable settings
- the procedure to be followed if anything goes wrong with the treatment
- the procedure if the equipment should fail to operate
- post-treatment care
- treatment techniques, and when to stop treatment
- identification of contra-indications
- identification of treatment-related problems.

PRE-TREATMENT CONSIDERATIONS

Treatment planning is vital for any treatment; when providing laser or light treatment there are a number of additional considerations. During the process of electrolysis we are able to treat any hair and skin type presented to us with the exception of clients with contra-indications. This is not the case with laser and light.

The use of lasers and IPL sources to remove hair relies on the absorption of light by the melanin contained in the hair shaft in preference to absorption

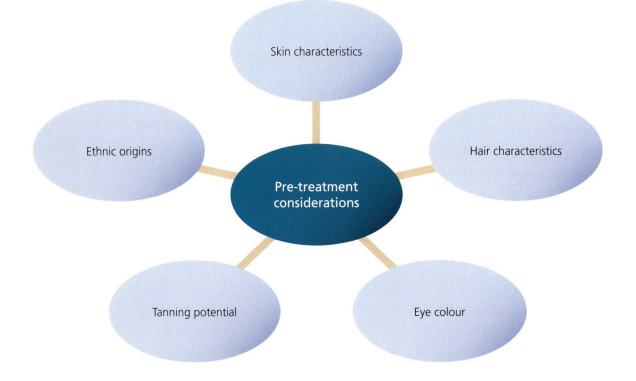

Skin characteristics

Ethnic origins

Hair characteristics

Pre-treatment considerations

Tanning potential

Eye colour

by melanin in the skin. As melanin is present in the epidermis and the dermis, as well as within the hair, it is essential that the hair is darker than the skin in order for preferential absorption to occur. The best results are achieved for clients with dark hair and fair skin.

Skin characteristics

In order to assess a client's suitability for treatment and to select the correct parameters for treatment, it is important to evaluate the skin and hair type. The evaluation of skin pigment – the amount and type of melanin in the skin – is vital pre-treatment information. We are not so concerned with skin type or condition, as we are with electrolysis, although that is also a consideration.

Skin classification

The Fitzpatrick skin classification system is the most commonly used method by HRPs to determine a client's suitability for laser treatment. The Fitzpatrick classification was developed to assist in the prediction of the skin's pigmentary responsiveness and the person's lifetime risk of developing skin cancer. The Fitzpatrick Scale is a guide that is based on how your client's skin reacts in the sun without protection. There are six skin types, which are defined as shown in the table.

It is sometimes difficult to decide between Skin Types II and III. If you are not sure, then look at the client's eyes carefully. Most Skin Type IIs will have blue/green eyes and Skin Type IIIs will have brown/hazel eyes. This is not always the case, but it acts as a useful guideline.

Even though Skin Type VI is on the scale, most light systems treat up to Skin Type V only as the skin needs to be lighter than the colour of the hair.

The Fitzpatrick Scale (adapted to include ethnic skin type)

Skin type	Ethnic skin type	Typical colour*	Pigmentation response
I	Caucasian	Blond/white hair Very pale skin with no pigment Pale eye colour	Always burns Never tans
II	Caucasian	Blond hair Pale eye colour White skin, with slight pigment	Always burns Sometimes tans or tans eventually
III	Caucasian	Medium hair colour Medium eye colour Pale skin with medium pigment	Sometimes burns Always tans
IV	Hispanic, light Asian	Moderately pigmented Dark eyes and hair	Occasionally burns Always tans
V	Dark Asian	Very dark skin Dark hair and eyes	Never burns Always tans
VI	Afro-Caribbean	Black skin Dark hair and eyes	Rarely burns

* Typical colour: note lighter skin types do not necessarily have light colour hair. You should always consider all the factors.

The higher up the scale and the more pigment there is in the skin, the more care must be taken when selecting the treatment parameters.

Ethnic skin type

The Fitzpatrick Scale should not be used as the only guideline; ethnic skin type should also be assessed. The client's parent's and grandparent's ethnic origin should be considered as an influencing factor in order to avoid over treatment.

<table>
<tr><td>

TECHNICAL TIP ✔

It is not possible to treat un-pigmented hair with a laser or light source

</td></tr>
</table>

SKIN TYPE CLASSIFICATION EXAMPLE

For example, two fair-skinned, blue-eyed women, both 35 and non-smokers in good health, are treated on identical settings for Skin Type II.

Client A has no reaction; client B, however, has prolonged reddening and irregular pigmentation. Her paternal grandfather is of Native American origin, therefore she has more melanin; her skin classification is actually a III.

Treatment is faster and more successful, the darker the hair and the paler the skin. It is possible to treat paler hair and darker skin, providing the equipment is versatile.

The melanin in Skin Types I–III is less dense in the skin than in the hair follicles. Most of the light is therefore directed at the melanin in the hair and not in the skin. The light therefore safely disables the hair follicles to impair growth without damaging the surrounding skin.

Hair characteristics

Once the skin type has been taken into consideration the following hair characteristics should be evaluated in order to select the correct treatment parameters according to your protocol.

- The colour of the hair; as we have seen, darker hair will give better results, providing the skin is lighter in colour. Often there will be variations in shades of colour throughout the proposed treatment area; in this case the client should be warned of the possibility that the lighter hairs will not respond well to treatment.

- The thickness of the hair will affect the parameter setting. Because larger objects lose heat more slowly than smaller ones, the TRT for a large, thick hair will therefore be marginally longer than for a fine, thin hair.

Anatomical site:

- The location of the hair to be treated should be considered prior to treatment because the hair growth cycle varies from area to area and so will affect the timings of treatment.

- Hair density; the treatment is likely to be more uncomfortable on bony areas and areas where the hair growth is more dense.

The combination of the above factors will help to determine the treatment parameters.

PRECAUTIONS AND CONTRA-INDICATIONS

The following are specific contra-indications and precautions to light-based hair removal treatment. You should also be aware of the standard contra-indications for waxing and electrolysis described in Chapters Four and Seven.

- The client's current health. If the client is not in good health, the skin's healing potential is likely to be reduced, and they are likely to be taking medication. Do not begin treatment until the client is in good health; in cases where a course of treatment has already begun, treatment may have to be deferred.
- The treatment should not be carried out in areas of broken skin or active eczema, dermatitis, psoriasis or acne.
- Heart conditions – clients with medically controlled blood pressure problems may be treated; care should be taken with blood pressure clients when they sit up following treatment as they can feel dizzy and faint if they get up too quickly. Clients with heart conditions should not be treated.
- Allergies – if a client has recently experienced an allergic reaction to a substance unrelated to the treatment, their skin may be over-sensitised and treatment should be delayed until the body has completely recovered. Allergies to products used during treatment will contra-indicate treatment unless substitute products can be found.
- Epilepsy (doctor's referral is required) – once medical clearance is attained you should check with the client that their condition is well controlled and establish what form their seizures (fits) take and what you should do if a seizure occurs during their time in the salon.
- Medication, current and long term – in particular photo-sensitising drugs, certain antibacterial, antibiotics, antifungal, non-steroidal anti-inflammatories, cardio-vascular drugs, some anti-depressants and hormonal medication (this also includes herbal remedies particularly St Johns Wort).
- Post-sun exposure – suntanned skin cannot be treated until at least two weeks after the tan has completely faded due to the increased level of melanin.
- Artificial tans – clients can only be treated once the product has completely faded from the skin.
- Pigmentary conditions, for example vitiligo or melasma, cannot be treated.
- Avoid treating any moles on the skin.
- Pregnancy – there are many hormonal and pigmentary changes during pregnancy which increase the risk of hypo or hyper pigmentation due to treatment. It is also advisable to delay treatment until after the baby is born, as some hair growths diminish or disappear once the pregnancy hormones have settled.

- Diabetes – as skin healing may be impaired (for insulin dependent clients, a doctor's referral is recommended as the symptoms may be more profound).

- Skins prone to keloid scarring are contra-indicated, as they are more at risk from skin damage.

- Steroid-based treatments thin the skin and, therefore, any client currently taking steroids should not have treatment.

- Photo therapy – light-based hair removal treatment should not be carried out as there is a greater risk of pigmentation changes and the possibility that it could interfere with the effectiveness of the photo therapy.

- Herpes simplex (cold sore) – light-based treatments are known triggers of the herpes virus; clients who regularly suffer from cold sores should be recommended to use anti-viral products before and during the treatment to control any outbreaks. If a client has an active herpes infection, the area should be avoided during treatment.

- Tattoos and permanent make-up – it is not possible to carry out treatment on hair which grows in the area of tattoos or permanent make-up. The pigmentation would cause adverse reactions such as burning, and there is also the possibility of the removal of pigment from the tattoo.

- General skin condition and hydration levels – it is important that the skin is in good condition, in particular that the skin is well hydrated, as the skin's healing potential will then be optimised.

CONSULTATION

The consultation is a critical part of a successful laser treatment and should allow you to determine whether the client is suitable for treatment. In addition to following the standard hair removal consultation processes described in Chapter Two, you must make sure the client understands the following factors unique to laser treatments before treatment begins:

- There is a heightened public awareness of laser and light hair removal treatments thanks to intense advertising and marketing. Prices of treatment are relatively high; both these factors mean that client expectations are also high. Client expectations should be thoroughly assessed to ensure they are realistic. Always be realistic and tell the truth about expected outcomes.

- More than one treatment is invariably necessary, the number of treatments will vary according to hair, skin type, stage of growth, etc.

- The treatment is not without discomfort. The sensation should be discussed with the client prior to treatment; it is often described by clients as being similar to the flick of an elastic band on the skin or hot water being sprinkled. The sensation will be more intense over bony areas. At certain times the client will be more sensitive than at others, this can be for physical reasons, e.g. before and during menstruation, or for emotional reasons, e.g. increased stress or pressure. Adrenaline and tension can exacerbate the pain. It is important to try and keep the client calm and relaxed prior to and during treatment. Encourage the client to relax. They

TECHNICAL TIP ✔

Laser and light treatment rely on the melanin in the hair shaft to generate heat. For this reason it is incorrect procedure to remove the hair from the follicle by waxing or plucking prior to treatment

may wish to take off their shoes; encourage them to wear loose clothes. The more comfortable they are, the more relaxed they will be.

- The client must not wax or have electrolysis on the treatment area during the course of the treatment; the hair shaft must be present in the follicle in order for treatment to be effective.

- The hair will appear to be growing in the days following treatment. These are known as hair casts and are the treated hair shafts, which are carbonised by the laser and are being shed from the follicle. They will fall out between 2 days to 2 weeks post-treatment. Emphasise to your client that the hairs will be there for a few days post-treatment and will then begin to fall out.

- The client must carefully follow aftercare procedures.

- The hair should be visible prior to treatment and will be shaved by the operator immediately before the treatment. The hairs must be shaved in order to prevent the thermal energy which will be built up in the hair shaft from conducting on to the skin; this would happen if the hair was long and lying on the skin during light treatment. Shaving will also reduce the odour which comes from the heated hair.

The client's record card plays a key role in laser treatment consultations and you must ensure each stage is completed and entered onto the card. Permanent information is recorded on the front while all current and changeable information (such as treatment progress) should be recorded on the rear of the record card on an ongoing basis.

TECHNICAL TIP ✔

Electrolysis may be carried out on very light or unpigmented hairs

---

PROFESSIONAL TIP ✔

Gentle exfoliation will encourage the treated hairs to fall out more quickly. This should only be carried out if the skin is fully recovered and there are no contra-actions

Consultation record/treatment plan

JAYGEE'S

Laser/Light Hair Reduction

Name: ....

Address:...

Tel: Home .... Mobile: .... Email: ....

Source:...

Area/s to be treated:...

Previous hair removal history

What: .... How often: ....

For how long: .... Last treatment: ....

Type and likely stage of hair growth: ....

Lifestyle

Diet/eating pattern...

....

Alcohol yes/no   Average units per week.................. Smoker yes/no   Number per day ....

Sun exposure .... Outdoor activities ....

Occupation .... Frequent flyer yes/no

Sleep pattern ....

Sporting activities/exercise ....

Skin care routine ....

Products currently used ....

Medical condition at present (incl. pregnancy) ....

Dr .... Surgery...

Telephone .... Allergies: ....

Previous treatments

Strong (glycolic or other) peels; microdermabrasion; laser resurfacing; cosmetic surgery; botox; sclerotherapy; laser hair removal; electrolysis.

Please list any side effects or adverse reactions to previous treatments:

....

Skin: Fitzpatrick classification

I Always burns, never tans	☐	IV Never burns, always tans	☐
II Always burns, sometimes tans	☐	V Moderately pigmented	☐
III Sometimes burns, always tans	☐	VI Black skin	☐

Skin condition including type, pigmentation marks, scar tissue, muscle tone, texture

....

Medical expert's referral/Comments: ....

....

Laser operator's signature: ....

Client's signature: ....

Treatment record card

JAYGEE'S

Treatment Record Card

Date	Laser operator	Area	Watts	Fluence	Pulse	Shots	Reactions	Operator signature	Client signature

Please attach all photographic evidence and aftercare procedure

JAYGEE'S

Medical History Questionnaire

Name: .... Consultation date:...........................

Address...

.... D.O.B....................

Are you?	Yes	No	Details
1. Receiving medical treatment at present?			
2. Taking any prescribed medication?			
3. Taking any herbal remedies i.e. St Johns Wort?			
4. Allergic to medicines or other substances?			
5. Pregnant?			
6. Diabetic?			
7. Have you been diagnosed with epilepsy?			
8. Please list any admissions to hospital/surgical operations			
9. Do you have any heart disorders?			
10. Have you ever had raised blood pressure?			
11. Have you ever had hepatitis, jaundice?			
12. Have you been diagnosed as HIV positive?			
13. Are you currently undergoing photo therapy?			
14. Do you have asthma?			
15. Have you ever had any endocrine or hormonal problems?			
16. Do you ever suffer from cold sores?			
17. Do you suffer from varicose veins?			
18. How does your skin heal after injury or surgery?			
19. Are you prone to the development of keloid scars?			

I confirm to the best of my knowledge, that the above answers are correct and that I have not withheld any information that may be relevant to my treatment.

I acknowledge that... (Salon) cannot be held responsible for side effects or problems occurring that arise as a result of information that has been withheld. I understand the benefits cannot be guaranteed.

Signed: .... (Client)   Date: ....

Informed consent

The record card contains all of the client and treatment information. It is not, however, an agreement between yourself and the client. The purpose of 'informed consent' is to confirm that the client understands the treatment fully, what it involves, the risks, their role and likely outcomes and agrees to receive treatment.

Informed consent form

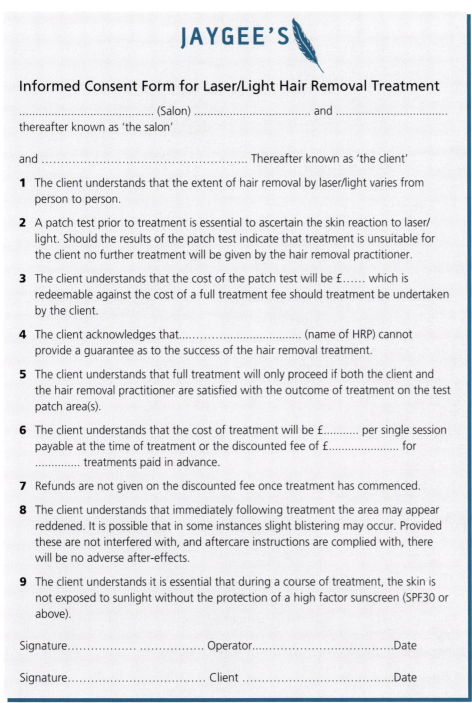

JAYGEE'S

Informed Consent Form for Laser/Light Hair Removal Treatment

.... (Salon) .... and ....
thereafter known as 'the salon'

and .... Thereafter known as 'the client'

1 The client understands that the extent of hair removal by laser/light varies from person to person.

2 A patch test prior to treatment is essential to ascertain the skin reaction to laser/light. Should the results of the patch test indicate that treatment is unsuitable for the client no further treatment will be given by the hair removal practitioner.

3 The client understands that the cost of the patch test will be £...... which is redeemable against the cost of a full treatment fee should treatment be undertaken by the client.

4 The client acknowledges that....................................... (name of HRP) cannot provide a guarantee as to the success of the hair removal treatment.

5 The client understands that full treatment will only proceed if both the client and the hair removal practitioner are satisfied with the outcome of treatment on the test patch area(s).

6 The client understands that the cost of treatment will be £........... per single session payable at the time of treatment or the discounted fee of £...................... for .... treatments paid in advance.

7 Refunds are not given on the discounted fee once treatment has commenced.

8 The client understands that immediately following treatment the area may appear reddened. It is possible that in some instances slight blistering may occur. Provided these are not interfered with, and aftercare instructions are complied with, there will be no adverse after-effects.

9 The client understands it is essential that during a course of treatment, the skin is not exposed to sunlight without the protection of a high factor sunscreen (SPF30 or above).

Signature................. .... Operator..Date

Signature.................................... Client ....…..Date

REMEMBER

When a client is very concerned about a hair growth, they will only see the hair. Once you succesfully remove the hair, the client will then begin to notice other imperfections in the area. A good quality photograph will assist you by proving that the imperfections were there before the treatment started

Photographs

It is good practice to take photographs of the area to be treated at consultation before the treatment commences and immediately after treatments. The photographs should be taken because:

- they provide an invaluable record of the growth prior to treatment
- they allow you and your client to monitor the treatment's progress
- the condition of the skin prior to treatment can be accurately recorded to avoid any misunderstandings after the treatment
- any adverse reactions can be recorded and monitored.

The photographs should be:

- attatched to or stored with the client's record card
- safely and securely stored in accordance with the Data Protection Act 1998.

You should have a written policy for the salon's procedure for creating, storing and disposing of the images.

The camera

The ideal camera is a digital one because the image can be immediately viewed and adapted and re-taken if necessary. In order to get the best possible images, the camera should:

- be of good quality with flash facilities
- ideally have advanced close-up settings.

There should be a label on or near to the treatment area which will appear on the photograph. It should be clearly labelled with:

- the date and treatment sequence number
- the area of the body treated
- client name or confidential number code to identify them.

REMEMBER

You may need to use the photographs to show the treatment results, after-effects and your competence should your client complain about your treatment. Make sure you photograph every stage which may help to illustrate this

Patch tests

Patch testing prior to treatment is vital for all laser and light treatments.

A patch test is a small trial area which will help you to assess

- the skin's reactions
- the client's reaction
- the hair growth's response to the light energy.

The results of the patch test will help you to determine:

- if treatment is possible
- the correct treatment parameters.

The patch test should preferably be carried out in the area to be treated, as this will give the truest indication of the reactions. If this is not possible, a discreet area with similar hair and skin to the proposed treatment area should be selected.

The area chosen should be small and one or two pulses of energy should be released into the area. Take photographs immediately before and after the test.

In order to gauge immediate and longer-term response, the client should be asked to return to the salon 48 hours after treatment for monitoring. If no adverse reactions are visible an initial treatment should be booked for the following week. For darker skins and those clients with pigmentation problems, at least two weeks should be left between patch test and initial treatment, because pigmentation reactions can take some time to become obvious.

The ideal outcome of a patch test is that the skin and hair will respond 'normally' – in other words there will be no excessive erythema, blistering, swelling or pigmentation changes. A percentage of the hair should be destroyed.

It is important to make clear and accurate notes on the record card detailing the parameters used and the reactions which occur, just as you would for a complete treatment. Always ask the client to sign the treatment record.

TREATMENT APPLICATION

Treatment procedures vary from system to system. The following guidelines offer a brief outline of procedures. Always follow the manufacturer's instructions and the salon's protocols.

> **REMEMBER**
>
> Treatment can only begin following consultation, completion of record card, informed consent and a normal patch test response

1 Discuss with an existing client any changes in circumstances, such as health and skin reaction since the last treatment, as these will all affect your treatment. Record any changes on the client's record card.

2 Guide the client to the treatment room and position her or him correctly for treatment.

3 Ensure the client is comfortable and all safety precautions have been followed before commencing treatment.

4 Photograph the areas on which you are intending to carry out treatment, taking care to label the area correctly.

5 Position equipment so that it is within easy reach and ensure equipment is turned on at the power supply.

6 Put on appropriate PPE e.g. disposable gloves, disposable surgical mask.

HEALTH AND SAFETY

If you intend to carry out treatment on more than one area, you must carry out a patch test on each of the proposed treatment sites. A bikini line may react completely differently to the chin, for example, because of the difference in hair density, skin type and amount of UV exposure

REMEMBER

You should not carry out a patch test until you have carried out a thorough consultation and the client has signed the informed consent

EQUIPMENT LIST

couch
trolley
stool
magnifying lamp
laser device
camera
gloves
sterilised scissors
towels/pillows
eye shields
cotton wool/tissues
aftercare soothing lotion
skin sanitiser
sharps box
tweezers
gel or cooling spray

HEALTH AND SAFETY ✚

If the client is already too hot, the sensation will be intensified as you are inducing further heat into the skin with the light source. Wait until the client is both calm and cool before you begin treatment

HEALTH AND SAFETY ✚

Razors used during treatment should be disposed of in a sharps disposal box immediately after use

HEALTH AND SAFETY ✚

Remember, not all protective glasses or goggles offer protection at all wavelengths. It is essential that the correct eye wear is provided for the wavelength/s of the light or laser system being used

TECHNICAL TIP ✔

Some operators find it difficult to visualise the treatment area. If this is the case, the treatment area can be marked with a white pencil

HEALTH AND SAFETY ✚

You must not use a coloured pencil for marking the area as the dark pigments may cause burning

REMEMBER !

Throughout the treatment check that the client is comfortable. Adjust the parameters where possible and increase cooling if the client is experiencing too much discomfort

7   Visually access the hairs to be removed and pre-cleanse and shave the area to be treated. Dispose of razors in a sharps box.

8   The client and operator should put on the appropriate protective eyewear (goggles or glasses) before commencing treatment. The eyewear should be kept on while the laser or light system is in stand by mode or is operating.

9   Set the treatment parameters. When using an IPL system, the operator should select the appropriate IPL handpiece.

10 Mentally visualise how you will proceed with the treatment, i.e. where you will start, where you will finish, which area is to be covered, etc.

11 Cool the area thoroughly immediately prior to treatment. When using an IPL system, this is normally achieved by applying a thin layer (1–2mm) of cold, clear gel to the skin. When using a laser, cooling can be achieved by gel, cooling spray, ice packs, etc.

12 Work methodically to cover the area, adjusting parameters where necessary. Constantly monitor the client's skin reaction and stop treatment immediately if any adverse reactions such as excessive erythema, any sign of blistering or bruising occur.

13 Carry out in-salon aftercare procedures, reminding the client of their home-care responsibilities.

14 Details of the treatment should be accurately recorded on the client's record card; the treatment record should be signed and dated by the client and operator.

15 The next treatment should be booked before the client leaves the salon.

PROFESSIONAL TIP ✔

The parameters may be set individually and might include fluence, watts, number of pulses, pulse delay, spot size, dwell time and, when appropriate, scan delay. Some systems will automatically set some of the parameters, according to the joules selected or information entered into the system's computer. Remember to always follow protocols

HEALTH AND SAFETY ✚

The treatment area should be cooled before, during and after treatment to improve client comfort, reduce erythema and allow the use of higher fluences. Clear gel should be kept in the fridge if possible so that it is cool and ready to use

Put on appropriate PPE

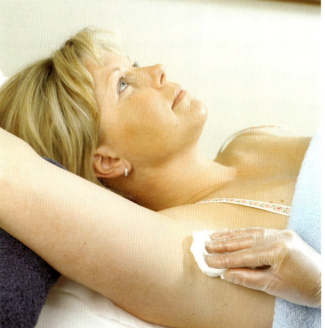

Pre-cleanse the area to be treated

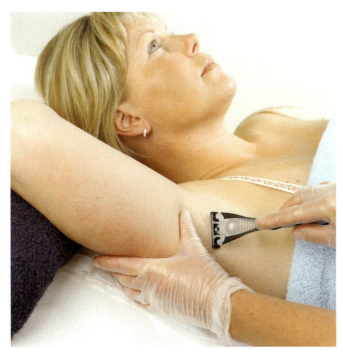

Shave the area to be treated

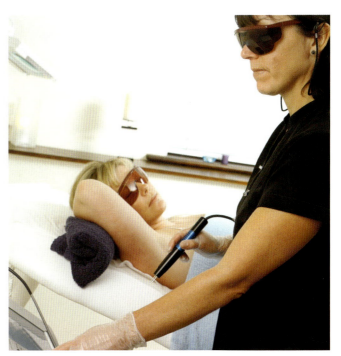

Both client and electrologist should wear
protective eyewear throughtout the treatment

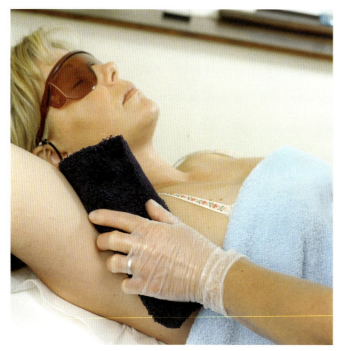

Cool the area thoroughly

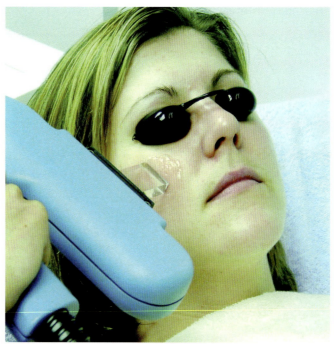

Cooling using gel

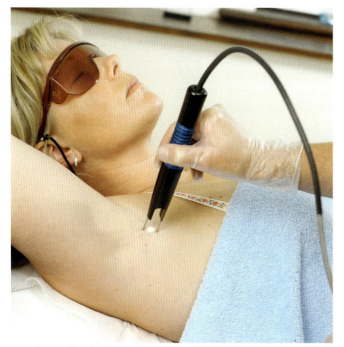

Work methodically over the area

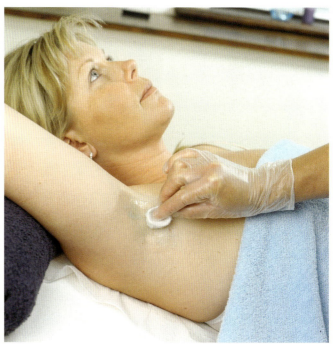

Apply aftercare products

Treatment intervals

It is important to ensure that subsequent treatments are given at regular intervals. This is because the hair needs to be in the anagen stage of growth in order to achieve optimum results. The chart shows a guide to the approximate time in weeks which should be left between laser or light treatments on various areas.

Treatment intervals

Area	Re-treatment in weeks
Eyebrows	5–7
Chin	3–5
Upper lip	4–6
Armpits	6–8
Bikini line	6–8
Arms	8–10
Legs	6–12

Laser and light treatment results

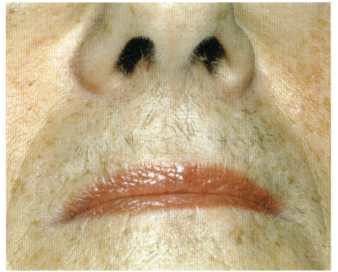

Back before ASAH

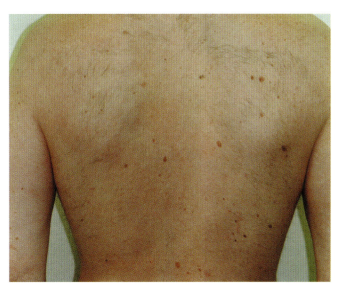

Back after ASAH

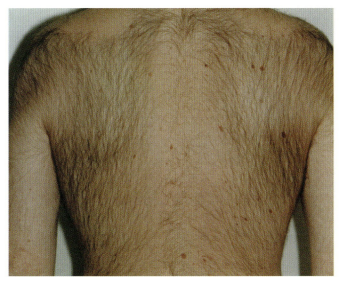

Upper lip before ASAH

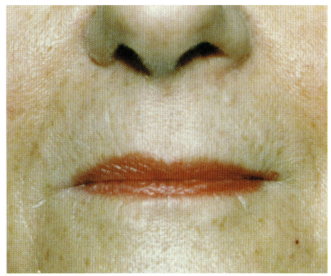

Upper lip after ASAH

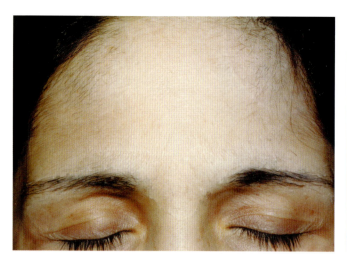

Forehead before ASAH

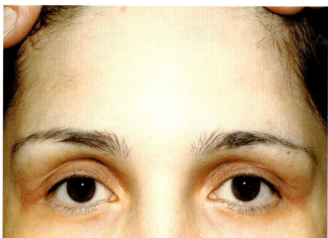

Forehead after ASAH

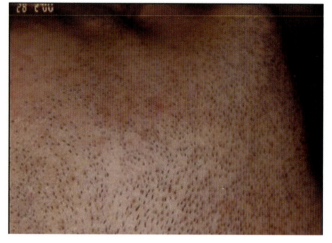

Male beard before
Lumina ASAH

Lynton Laser Ltd UK

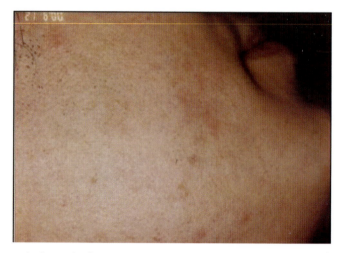

Male beard after Lumina
ASAH

AFTERCARE

Aftercare for laser treatments is vital and it is important that the following key features of laser aftercare are explained fully to the client.

- Following light-based treatment, there will be increased heat in the treated area and a degree of trauma to the follicle. This is why it is important for the client to avoid additional trauma in the first few days following treatment.

- As previously mentioned, following light-based treatment, there will be increased heat in the area, therefore the client should avoid any additional activities or situations which may stimulate further heat.

- Because laser and light treatments have the potential to affect the melanin in the skin, it is important that any form of exposure to UV radiation is avoided throughout the treatment course.

JAYGEE'S

Home care procedures post laser hair removal

Please read these home-care notes carefully and follow our recommendations.

We have taken great care to provide the best treatment. It is important for you to take extra care of the treated area, especially within the first 24–48 hours. Following laser/light treatment, the area will be heat and light sensitive. It is IMPORTANT that the area is kept away from, heat, friction and UV light, particularly for the first 48 hours following treatment:

1. Care should be taken to prevent trauma and friction to the treated area for the first 4–5 days following treatment.
2. Excessive heat should be avoided for the first 48 hours following treatment, e.g. saunas, steam rooms, vigorous exercise, night clubs (acceptable providing you are not dancing all night), heat treatments in salons, etc.
3. Sunscreen should be used to avoid exposure to sunlight during the treatment period. Suntanning activates the melanin in the skin which could result in pigmentation marks. Sunbed sessions should not be taken for the duration of the treatment course.
4. Self-tanning products should not be used for 7–10 days prior to hair removal by laser treatment.
5. If the skin is tender or warm apply a cool compress, e.g. cotton wool or gauze soaked in cold water. Do not put ice directly onto the skin's surface or a freezer burn may occur.
6. Make-up may be applied as long as the skin's surface is not broken.
7. Avoid applying perfumed products or aftershave to the treatment area for 4–5 days.

NB If you are concerned or unsure about any aspect of your treatment please contact your hair removal practitioner:

Tel: 01324 67543890

E mail: jaygees@hairsolutions.co.uk

8. Apply aftercare lotion/gel as recommended by your hair removal practitioner for one week after treatment, morning and night, more frequently if necessary.
9. Avoid swimming for 48 hours.
10. Avoid vigorous exercise for 48 hours.
11. Loose clothing should be worn to avoid friction on treated areas such as bikini line, legs, arms, chest, abdomen etc.
12. It is recommended that the treatment area should not be immersed in a hot bath for 4–5 days. Cool/warm showers are recommended as an alternative.

Skin and hair management during your laser/light treatment programme

Remember:

✔ Please inform your hair removal practitioner of any change in your medical condition or medication, or if you could have become pregnant, before commencing future treatments.
✔ Hair grows in cycles and results are only achievable in the first cycle. You should ensure you keep regular appointments as advised by your hair removal practitioner.
✔ To achieve successful treatment, your skin needs to be in good condition and as moist as possible, this is why it is important to eat healthily, drink plenty of water and follow carefully the skin care routines and treatments advised by your hair removal practitioner.
✔ Do not expose the skin to UV (sun exposure or tanning beds) for at least 4 weeks following treatment. Use a sunblock with SPF of 30+.
✔ Don't use bleaching creams or perfumed products for 24 hours.
✔ If blistering or crusting occurs, do not pick or scratch the treated area as this could result in scar tissue formation.
✔ In between your initial appointments, you may need to use some form of hair management at home. Cutting (scissors or razor) is the only method you should use.

Salon home-care leaflet

- Self-tanning lotions often contain a pigment to change the colour of the skin, the actions of the light-based treatments could potentially be intensified by those pigments and possibly cause burning or pigmentation.
- It is important that the client has the information required to deal with any after-effects from treatment.
- Following facial treatments, many clients will not feel comfortable unless they can apply make-up. Check that their skin is not broken or over-treated and advise them on how to apply make-up gently without excessive irritation to the skin.
- Perfumed products often contain alcohol which can cause stinging on the treated area. Perfume also has the potential to cause irritation to the skin and so should be avoided.

- Applying the aftercare prescribed by the hair removal practitioner will ensure that the client is taking appropriate care of the treated area.

- Swimming pool water contains chlorine, which can easily irritate sensitised skin. Pools should therefore be avoided for 48 hours following treatment.

- Vigorous exercise causes the body temperature to rise; it will therefore cause a further rise in temperature to the treated area, and should be avoided for the first 48 hours.

- Advising the client to wear loose fitting clothing will avoid friction to the area and reduce the risk of irritation.

- Hot baths and showers are a further source of heat which should also be avoided following treatment.

Always make sure that your client fully understands what to do and also how to contact you should they have any concerns. It is far better that they contact you than someone else.

An aftercare leaflet, such as the one illustrated, should be discussed and given to the client to take away.

PROFILE OF A LASER SPECIALIST

Name: Samantha Hills

Occupation: Laser specialist

Dr Samantha Hills is the clinical development manager at Lynton Lasers who are a leading UK company manufacturing lasers and intense pulsed light systems for medical and cosmetic surgery. Before joining Lynton, Sam completed a degree in physics and then obtained a PhD in physics and pharmaceutical sciences, working in the field of light responsive drug delivery. After graduation, Sam continued to work at the university, carrying out research into various aspects of lasers and light.

Sam joined Lynton Lasers in 2001 and used her previous research experience to develop a clinical research programme which uniquely combines the laser expertise at Lynton with the medical understanding of plastic surgeons, dermatologists and leading therapists from all over the UK. The wide variety of clinical trials currently being undertaken include everything from using intense pulsed light for hair removal and skin rejuvenation, to treating dermatological conditions such as acne, port wine stains, and pre-cancerous skin lesions. Alongside implementing clinical trials, Sam has developed an in-depth training programme for new customers acknowledged as being amongst the most informative, thorough and enjoyable currently on offer in the UK.

An important part of Sam's work is providing ongoing clinical support and feedback to customers using Lynton products. Travelling to meet customers and attending conferences is an essential part of the job and in the last 12 months Sam has been lucky enough to travel all over the world, including such exotic locations as Florida, Hong Kong, Turkey and Lithuania!

LASER CASE STUDY 1

Unwanted hair removal: The Lumina

Age: 44 years old

Gender: Female

Treatment area: 'Sideburn' area of face

Treatment parameters: Lumina Medical Flashlamp System

Fluence range: 18–22 J/cm²

Hair colour: Dark brown

Skin type: III

Treatments: 5

Number of pulses: 4 with 40ms delay

Patient comments: 'After years of painful waxing, this gentle treatment has been wonderful; and there has been no re-growth for six months now!'

Lynton Lasers Ltd 2002

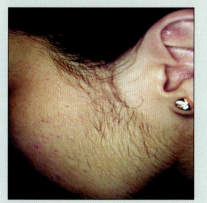

Sideburns before Lumina treatment

Courtesy of Dr Patrick Bowler

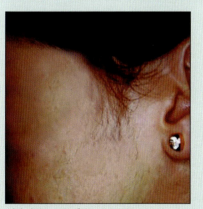

Sideburns after Lumina treatment

Courtesy of Dr Patrick Bowler

LASER CASE STUDY 2

Gender: Female

Age: 37 years old

Treatment area: Face and neck

Medical background: Polycystic ovaries

Treatment parameters: Lumina Medical Flashlamp System

Fluence range: 16–24 J/cm^2

Hair colour: Black

Skin type: IV

Treatments: 4

Number of pulses: 4 with 40ms delay

Lynton Lasers Ltd 2003

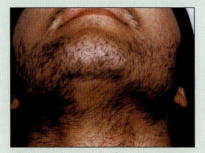

Chin and neck before Lumina
treatment

Courtesy of The Iranian Laser Centre

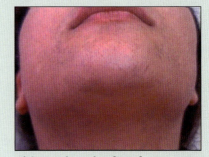

Chin and neck after four
Lumina treatments

Courtesy of The Iranian Laser Centre

LASER CASE STUDY 3

Unwanted hair removal: Lumina

Gender: Female

Age: 30 years old

Treatment area: Upper lip

Treatment parameters: Lumina Medical Flashlamp System

Fluence range: 16–20 J/cm^2

Hair colour: Dark brown

Skin type: V

Treatments: 4

Number of pulses: 4 with 40ms delay

Patient comments: 'I feel so much more feminine, I am so happy with the results.'

Lynton Lasers Ltd 2002

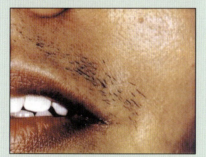

Upper lip before Lumina
treatment

Courtesy of Seema Health & Beauty

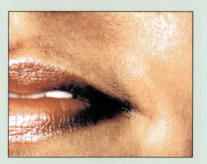

Upper lip after three Lumina
treatments

Courtesy of Seema Health & Beauty

LASER CASE STUDY 4

Unwanted hair removal: Lumina 650 handpiece

Gender: Female

Age: 32 years old

Treatment area: Underarm

Treatment parameters: 650 Lumina handpiece

Fluence range: 22–28 J/cm^2

Hair colour: Dark brown

Skin type: II

Treatments: 5

Number of pulses: 3 with 35ms delay

Lynton Lasers Ltd 2002

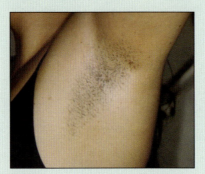

Underarm before Lumina treatment

Courtesy of Dr Patrick Bowler

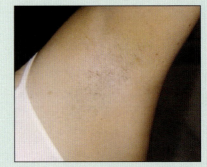

Underarm after five Lumina treatments

Courtesy of Dr Patrick Bowler

Assessment of knowledge and understanding

You have now learnt how to conduct laser treatments. To test your level of knowledge and understanding, answer the following short questions:

1 Name the two types of light systems used for hair removal.

2 List two special qualities of laser light.

3 What is the term used to describe the length of a specific light wave?

4 Define photothermolysis.

5 What is the target chromophore for hair removal using light systems?

6 What are the ideal wavelengths for hair removal?

7 Define fluence and state the units used to measure it.

8 List two methods of skin cooling when carrying out photothermolysis.

9 What is the purpose of a filter on an intense pulsed light system?

10 Describe in detail how laser and light sources affect the hair and follicle.

11 State when a patch test should be carried out.

12 What is the purpose of informed consent?

Activities

Conduct the following activities to practise your knowledge of laser treatments:

1 Study carefully the differences between intense pulsed light systems and lasers. Then compose a comparison chart to include the advantages and disadvantages of each.

2 Prepare a presentation which summarises how laser and light source works and what outcomes might be anticipated. Your audience is a women's group.

3 Carry out a mock consultation and prepare a treatment plan for a client as follows:
   - Name: Mrs B
   - Age: 35
   - Skin Type: III
   - Ethnic origin: European
   - Previous hair removal: Waxing every 8 weeks for 17 years
   - Hair texture: Fine

- Hair colour: Medium/dark brown
- Good health, no medication
- Large number of freckles and moles on body.

4 Contact several laser manufacturers and distributors and compile a list of each system's features. Using your knowledge list the benefits (if any) of each feature.

Follow-up knowledge

To build on the knowledge of laser treatments gained in this chapter, complete the following tasks to extend your hair removal skills and understanding:

1 Visit www.healthcarecommission.org.uk and review the latest guidelines and regulations.

2 Visit www.lasertraining.com and study their library of medical papers about laser hair removal.

Further reading

M. C. Grossman, C. Dierickx, W. Farinelli, T. Flotte and R. R Anderson 'Damage to hair follicles by normal-mode ruby laser pulses' *Journal of the American Academy of Dermatologists* 35, 889, 1996.

Advanced knowledge reference section

Focus on hair removal

Gill Mann

This is an exciting time for beauty therapy related to laser and intense pulsed light treatments, with new equipment and techniques being continually developed. Laser and Intense pulsed light or IPL hair removal systems are becoming more and more popular.

There is always confusion among therapists as to whether these treatments are permanent. Some companies still advertise them as 'permanent'. Most will say 'permanent hair reduction' or 'long-term removal'. Clinical research and studies have proved that laser and IPL treatments can significantly reduce hair growth compared to other methods such as shaving or waxing.

Laser hair removal systems have been around approximately 30 years and IPLs for approximately 10 years and they have proven to be very successful. I myself had treatment over 7 years ago and am only just starting to notice some re-growth on my bikini and underarms. For this reason, I believe these treatments can be described as either 'permanent hair reduction' or 'long-term removal'.

Light-based treatments are still relatively new procedures compared to electrolysis, which is the only method we can truly say is permanent due to the fact it has been around since 1875 and has been proven.

Whether the method you use is laser, IPL or electrolysis, it is not instant and the time it takes for successful completion depends on a number of factors:

- the cause of the hair growth, i.e. puberty, pregnancy, menopause, certain medications, genetic factors
- whether the body is still producing more hair
- the quantity of hair to be treated
- any underlying medical condition, i.e. polycystic ovaries syndrome which keeps producing more hair
- previous temporary methods of hair removal used (some can encourage hair growth, e.g. plucking)
- stage of hair growth, i.e. active, transitional or dormant.

Even if you do not want to offer this advanced technology, it is extremely important that you understand how it works, as your clients may be interested and you will be the first person they will turn to for advice.

Laser and intense pulsed light systems

These systems work by introducing light into the hair follicle where it will destroy hairs in such a way as to inhibit their regrowth for as long as possible. First, a clear cool gel is applied to the skin and then the light is delivered in a pulse, or several pulses, through the gel into the skin, where the energy is absorbed by the pigment within the hair follicle. The sensation felt by the client is that of a very quick splash of hot fat which is instantaneous and lasts for micro seconds. When the light is introduced into the hair follicle, the temperature of the follicle is raised, destroying the lower part of the follicle. When using IPL systems and some of the newer laser systems, the light is introduced in several pulses to gradually build up the heat within the hair follicle without overheating the skin's surface.

In order to understand this process, it is important to understand the normal hair growth cycle which occurs in three distinct phases. The hair follicle goes through a continuous cycle of:

1 active growth

2 transitional stage

3 dormant or resting stage.

During the first (growing) stage of development, the follicle is actively producing a hair and the pigment content within the follicle is at its highest level. This is the most responsive stage at which to treat unwanted hair. After a period of time, the follicle goes into a transitional stage where it begins to shrink and the hair starts to move up the follicle. Follicles treated at this stage will require further treatment but re-growth will be finer. The final phase is the dormant, resting stage where there is no hair present in the follicle, and therefore no pigment. Treatment on these follicles will not work.

It is because of the hair growth cycle that more than one treatment will be necessary in order to achieve long-term results. The number of treatment sessions will vary between 6 and 12, depending on the area of the body being treated and whether there is an underlying medical condition. We only know a minimal amount about the hair growth cycle, but most companies recommend treatment spacing as follows:

- facial areas – every 3 to 4 weeks
- bikini line, underarms, chest, stomach – every 4 to 6 weeks
- legs and backs – every 6 to 8 weeks.

These intervals are only a guide. As the hair re-growth becomes slower, treatments should be spaced further apart.

These versatile light-based treatments are effective on a wide range of hair textures and colours and are suitable for the majority of skin types and colours. However, due to the nature of the treatment, – light being absorbed by the pigment in the hair – it is not possible to remove white/ blonde hairs successfully. The colour of the hair must always be darker than the colour of the skin.

Although most clients will react differently, a number of post-treatment reactions are commonly seen.

- An initial erythema of the treated area is the first sign of a positive reaction.
- The skin may be warm and feel tender to the touch; this should disappear within a few hours.
- A slight swelling may be present around the follicles; this will subside within a short period of time.

Aloe vera gel or an equivalent aftercare lotion should be applied to the treated area to help protect the skin immediately after treatment and for a few days afterwards. There are very few side effects; however, there are a few points that should be discussed with the client and a consent form signed before treatment commences. Some loss of pigment (hypo pigmentation) or excess pigment (hyper pigmentation) may occur from time to time but this usually fades within 6 months. Small blisters rarely occur, but, provided these are not interfered with, they will cause no adverse after-effects.

It is essential that, during a course of treatment, the skin is not exposed to sunlight without the protection of a high factor sunscreen. If any excess tan is present, do not treat for a minimum of 28 days or longer if your client keeps his or her tan for longer. If you are not sure if the skin has faded back to its natural colour, then don't treat. It is better to be safe than sorry. If you do treat, then active melanin will be absorbed and the skin will burn, leading to blistering and possible scarring.

Electrolysis

We know that lasers and IPLs only treat pigmented hairs. So what happens if your client has white/blond or grey hairs? A lot of people think electrolysis is time consuming and tedious. However, there is still a need for it and a shortage of electrolysists out there in the industry. Once the pigmented hairs have been treated, your client is still left with the white or grey hairs and, for some, this can still be very embarrassing.

So what do we know about 'electrolysis'? This term has come to be used for all types of hair removal by electrical means.

There are, however, three main types of hair removal with electrolysis:

1 shortwave diathermy

2 galvanic

3 blend (a combination of short wave diathermy and galvanic).

The aim is to coagulate the base of the growing hair in order to cut off the blood supply and nutrition to the hair, preventing any new growth from developing.

Shortwave diathermy does this by heat and the galvanic method creates a chemical reaction. Blend combines the two properties of each current. The type used will depend on the client's skin type, the strength and density of the hair and the area to be treated.

With electrolysis, a fine sterile needle is inserted into the follicle and heat applied to the base to coagulate the cells which produce the new hair. The hair is then lifted out with tweezers. Treatment sessions take 15–60 minutes per visit, depending upon the extent of hair growth present and the size of area to be treated. Appointments may be booked weekly or fortnightly, with the length of time between treatments increasing as the problem improves.

Galvanic hair removal started in 1875 when Dr Charles E. Michel, an ophthalmologist, used galvanic current to remove in-grown eyelashes and found that they did not grow back. This method, however, was very slow and it could take up to 20 seconds for the chemical reaction to take place.

In 1924, Dr Henri Bordier of France developed the thermolysis method, which is also known as shortwave diathermy or high frequency. This was much faster than galvanic but not effective on deep, distorted follicles, for example those resulting from previously plucked hairs.

In 1945, Arthur Hinkel and Henri St Pierre applied for the patent of the first blend epilator combining galvanic and shortwave currents. The patent was received in 1948. The action from both was found to be more successful in treating curved and distorted follicles and the treatment time was speeded up significantly. Shortwave diathermy and blend are the two most popular methods used today.

The results

Lasers/IPLs can cover a larger area during a treatment session and are fast and effective. They are excellent for treating large areas, for example legs, back and arms and up to 80 per cent clearance can be seen over a course of 6–12 treatments, depending on the underlying cause. Electrolysis is still very effective and suitable for smaller areas such as the upper lip or chin. However, it does need to be carried out on a more regular basis.

The future

Technology is moving forward all the time and lasers and IPLs are here to stay. Electrolysis has been proven in the past, is here in the present and is definitely still needed in the future. By offering both methods, a hair removal practitioner can cover all his or her clients' hair removal needs.

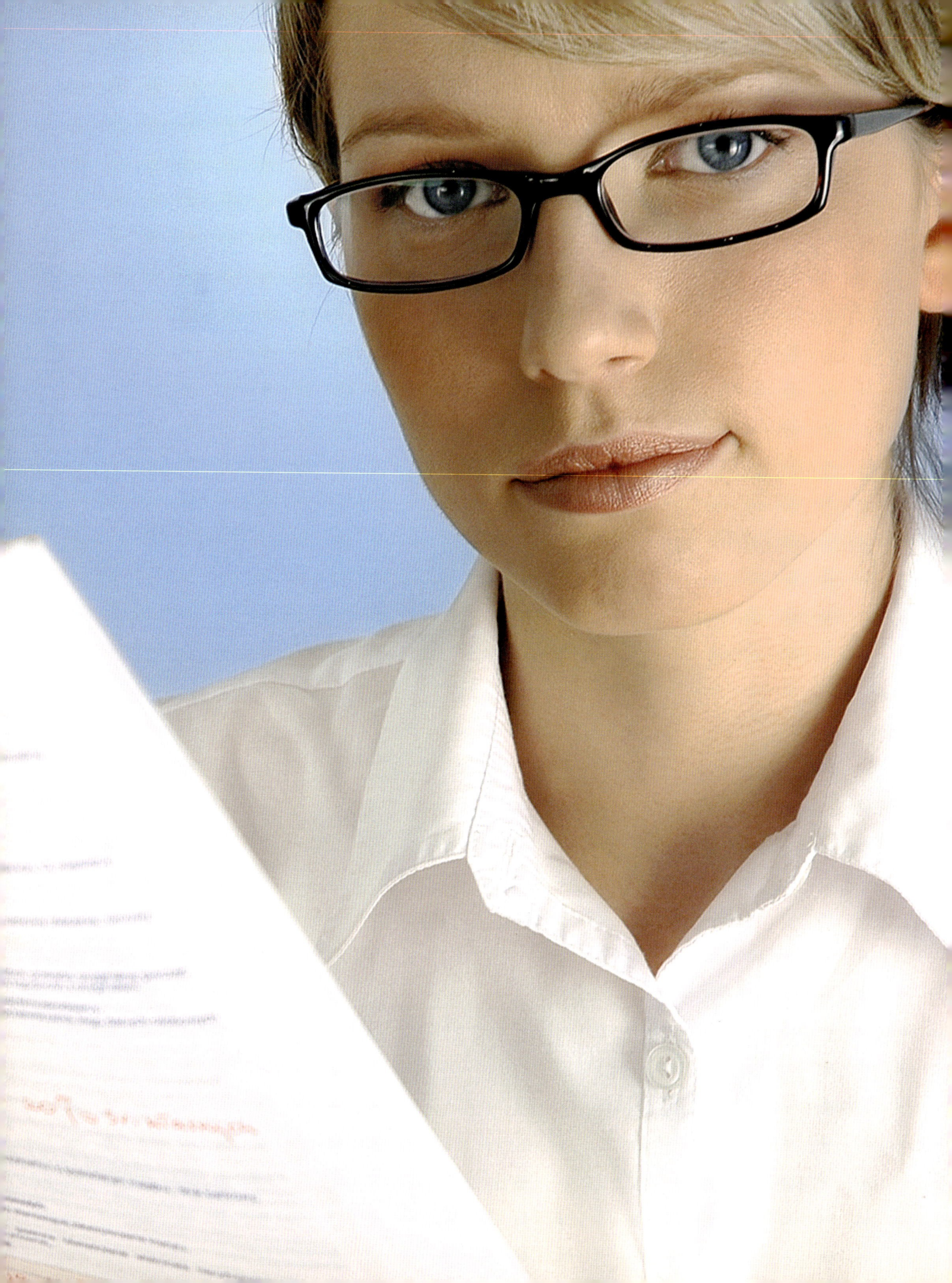

part six

business basics

chapter 9

BUSINESS SUCCESS

What will I know after reading this chapter?

This chapter covers the basics of working within and operating a successful hair removal business. It describes the competencies required to enable you to:

- **understand how to start a hair removal business**
- **understand what human resources is**
- **contribute to successful working relationships**
- **identify and purchase the correct equipment.**

G11 Contribute to the financial effectiveness of the business and G6 Promote additional products or services to clients

PROFESSIONAL TIP ✔
Think of yourself as a business person who works in the field of hair removal

PROFESSIONAL TIP ✔
If you fail to plan, you plan to fail

INTRODUCTION

Hair removal is an exciting and worthwhile career which will give you not only great satisfaction but also a healthy bank balance, if you plan it correctly! This section is arguably the most important, as there is no point in being the best hair removal practitioner (HRP) in the world if no one knows about you, so this business aspect is absolutely vital to your future financial success. Although you are training to be an HRP (or you are already an HRP), you are primarily a business person.

Even if your ultimate aim is to have your own business – a salon of your own or as a self-employed person renting space in a 'host' business – it is recommended that you work for an established business first to learn the ropes, not just from the treatment side but from the business side too.

When you have some experience under your belt, you may wish to consider starting your own business. However, rather than rush straight into it, you must first plan ahead and do some considerable research, culminating in the production of a Business Plan.

THE BUSINESS PLAN

Your Business Plan will fall into a variety of sections, each one covering a vital business area. Illustrated here is a typical contents page for a Business Plan. They are all different and there is no set way to lay one out, as long as the items listed on this contents page are included:

Good business organisation is crucial

Graphic Business Plan

Contents

Executive Summary

Section 1: Company Objectives

1.1   Goals & Objectives

1.2   Mission Statement

1.3   Critical Success Factors

Section 2: The Company

2.1   History & Background

2.2   Directors & Officers

Section 3: Description of Services

3.1   Facilities/Premises

3.2   Provision of Services

3.3   Future Plans & Opportunities

Section 4: Market Analysis & Marketing Plan

4.1   Background to 'Hair Today Gone Tomorrow'

4.2   Industry Analysis

4.3   Target Market

4.4   Market Share & Competition

4.5   Competitive Strategy

4.6   Sales Strategy

4.7   Sales Forecast

4.8   Staff

4.9   Equipment, products and suppliers

Section 5: Management Organisation

5.1   Management Structure

5.2   Additional Staff

5.3   Salary Background

Section 6: Financial Plan

6.1   Financial Summary

6.2   Break-Even Analysis

6.3   Start-Up Requirements

6.4   Projected Profit & Loss

6.5   Projected Cash Flow

6.6   Projected Balance Sheet

Section 7: Appendix

> **REMEMBER** !
>
> The Business Plan is a major document which will become your guide to business success – DON'T SKIMP and DON'T RUSH!

The executive summary

The executive summary is at the beginning of the plan, but it is the last thing you write as it is a summary of all the research and financial information you have gathered. This is the part where you have to grasp the attention of the reader – who may be your bank manager, from whom you may be hoping to get a loan to start the business – so you need to ensure he or she has all the vital information in no more than two pages, as he or she may well lose interest if there is excessive amounts of information to wade through to get to the main points.

Section One: Company objectives

The first main section after the executive summary deals with your company objectives, in other words what you intend to achieve. You also itemise here the main issues that will help or hinder your progress and what it is that your company offers. The description of your 'offering' is normally presented over a few sentences or a short paragraph and it is referred to as the Mission Statement.

Section Two: The company

The next section is about the company and the type of company you are considering setting up, for example sole trader, partnership or limited company. It also includes the people involved and the roles they will play – investor, receptionist, therapist, etc. Some background on yourself is important at this stage so that any reader can get a feel for who you are, what drives you, what you are passionate about and why you want to set up this business.

Section Three: Description of services

The description of services is exactly as its name implies: it defines what treatments you intend to offer, why you have chosen those particular ones, how you intend to offer them, when and where. You should itemise any other individuals that will assist in the delivery of these services: who they are, whether they are full time or part time, self-employed or employed; experienced or novices. You may also wish to detail your hopes and objectives and explain where you see the business in the future.

Section Four: Market analysis and Marketing Plan

The Marketing Plan is an integral part of the Business Plan: it is a plan within a plan, detailing information about your prior research for the business, the area, the property, the potential clients, why you will be different to all the other businesses serving hair removal (you need to be thinking NOW about why a client would want to come to your business and not to the business of the person studying or working next to you – after all you have all been trained in the same way, how are you going to be different?). This is also where you detail how you will market your business, your projected set-up and ongoing costs and projected sales forecast.

PROFESSIONAL TIP ✔

Plans and budgets are often thought of as boring but planning your business success is vital

Section Five: Management organisation

The management organisation section comes here and details the hierarchy of the business, who reports to whom, areas of responsibility, wages, etc.

Section Six: Financial Plan

The Financial Plan can often be the first section that a bank manager may turn to after reading the executive summary. It must be in a format that is easy for the reader to follow and a spreadsheet is the obvious choice. You may need more than one spreadsheet but ensure each one has a title for easy access to your information. The first spreadsheet should always be a summary of the rest of the information, so the reader can see on one sheet all the main pieces of information. The remaining spreadsheets give the body of the information by including all the detail and specific breakdowns and any assumptions that you have made, for example the number of clients in year 1.

REMEMBER !

The money in the till at the end of each week is not profit

Profit and loss must be worked out and is normally stated in a spreadsheet format. In this section you should state the profit you believe your company will make whilst also stating the losses, or costs, that you will incur. For example a month's takings may be many £1,000s but you must consider what the costs of getting that money will be, for example fixed costs and variable costs. You must attempt to project your profit and loss (or P&L as it is often referred to), as it will form the basis of other financial plans.

You will need to work out the number of clients that you expect to treat over the period of the plan (usually 1–3 years), what treatments they will have, how often, the costs associated with these treatments (variable costs) and the fixed costs associated with the building and salaries, etc. which you need to pay from the profit left over from those treatments.

Computer balance sheet

A projected cash flow is another plan or budget that helps with your finances. Projecting your cash flow allows you to plan for spending and being thrifty by highlighting when you think you will be busy and therefore earning the most money and when you think you will be quiet and have to keep spending to a minimum. Other issues like a training budget will be formulated based on the financial projections of the cash flow.

The projected balance sheet is a financial tool which helps you. At its most basic it is a piece of paper (or more likely a computer spreadsheet) with your costs on one side and your income on the other. It must be your aim to 'balance' the income and expenditure so that at the end of the year they are the same, with the profit for the business built in. Further financial information can be found in 'accounts'.

The appendix

The appendix is the last section. It should include any additional information which supports your case, but which you felt it was not necessary to include in the main body of the plan. The appendix should have its own contents page and if you refer to any of its contents in the rest of the plan you would add 'See Appendix page xx' so the reader can easily find it should they wish to find out additional information.

Good parking is important
when selecting premises

PREMISES

Location is vital and the research you will have carried out for the business plan will be invaluable. There is a great deal of information which you will need to discover and a commercial agent (an estate agent who deals with commercial properties) will be able to supply you with much of it. However, it will not be specific information relating to a service business – this information you will need to research. Don't forget that you will need to consider the needs of potential clients as well as your own. The two lists which follow include a number of suggestions of factors for you to consider, but they are not definitive. Issues for clients include:

- parking
- bus routes
- taxi rank
- payment terms
- cancellation policies
- vouchers
- treatment choice
- prices
- opening times.

Premise issues for the business include:

- rent
- rates
- square footage required
- whather the is area suitable for target market
- access to building for equipment i.e. sun showers
- special requirements: 3-phase electricity, reinforced floors, rooms without windows
- parking for clients and staff
- disabled access
- lease issues
- refurbishment
- décor.

Promotion and marketing issues include:

- pricing structure
- sales strategy
- promotional plan, publicity plan
- product choice
- equipment choice
- staff
- tangible evidence which underlines the quality of the business.

HUMAN RESOURCES

The most important asset of any business is its human resources: the people employed in the business utilising all of their skills and qualifications. Maintaining professional working relationships throughout the business, particularly between employers and employees, is vital and is achieved through an understanding of the following six areas:

1   terms of employment (contract)
2   employment legislation
3   staff training
4   grievance procedures
5   salon rules
6   communication systems.

Terms of employment (contract)

Contract

A contract of employment (required by the Employment Rights Act 1996) is essential and must include the following:

- name of employer
- name of employee
- start date
- job title
- place of work
- remuneration
- hours of work
- holidays
- sick pay arrangements
- disciplinary and grievance procedure
- pension arrangements
- notice requirements.

You might also include any specific requirements such as:

- recovery of overpayments
- a facility to relocate staff to other sites
- a demanding probationary period
- restrictive covenant (to prevent the employee leaving and setting up close to the employer; it can also include certain treatments)
- a right to search staff
- a facility to recover training costs if staff leave (this is a very popular addition as the employer often wants to recoup a percentage of training costs if the employee leaves within a stated and agreed timescale).

A contract for every employee is required by the Employment Rights Act 1996

All of the above are perfectly acceptable if they are part of your offer of employment which the employee accepts upon appointment. The contract of employment is absolutely key for the employer, but it must be clearly written and unambiguous.

Employee rights

Aside from the rights expressly stated in their contract, an employee also has a number of other rights including the following:

- The right to receive a written contract of employment within 8 weeks of taking up a post.
- The right not to be discriminated against, either at recruitment stage (i.e. they do not even have to be an employee) or during employment, on the grounds of sex, marital status, race, colour, ethnic origin, disability, religion and religious belief, sexual orientation, trade union membership/ non-membership.
- Employees on fixed term or temporary contracts and part-time staff should have the same benefits as full-time staff.
- The right not to be unfairly selected for redundancy.
- Rights under the Working Time Regulations: e.g. 4 weeks' paid leave, 20 minutes' break after 6 hours and a 48-hour maximum working week (there are several others in addition).
- The right, subject to service, of up to 52 weeks' maternity leave.
- The right to 2 weeks' paid paternity leave.
- The right to equal pay for work of equal value.
- The right to receive the minimm wage for their age group: i.e. 16–17, 18–21 and the adult wage at 22 years.
- The right to a safe working environment.
- The right to receive a risk assessment. There are additional rights for pregnant workers.
- The right to transfer all terms and conditions when a business is sold TUPE (i.e. under the Transfer of Undertakings Regulations).
- The right not to be dismissed until the written disciplinary procedure, which must meet the statutory 3 stage requirements, has been followed.
- The right, subject to one years continuous service (except in cases of discrimination) to go to an employment tribunal.

Employer rights

Employers have many legal rights and the employee has numerous obligations to their employer. In Common Law, the employee is still classed as the employer's servant and is expected to work loyally for you.

- Even without specific rules, the employee is expected to work in your best interests and to carry out to the best of their ability their duties and responsibilities.
- The employee is also expected to follow safe working practices in accordance with your instructions.
- Failure to meet these requirements allows the employer to terminate their employee's employment.

Employment legislation

Working Time Directive 1998

The Working Time Directive aims to ensure that employees are protected against adverse conditions with regard to their health and safety caused by excessively long working hours with inadequate rest or disrupted work patterns.

The working time directive provides for:

- a maximum 48-hour working week
- a minimum daily rest period of 11 hours
- a rest break where the working day is longer than 6 hours
- a minimum rest period of 1 day per week
- night work on average must not exceed 8 hours.

Equal opportunities

Discrimination based on race, sex, disability, marital status or union membership is against the law.

Race Relations Act 1976

This Act prevents discrimination on the basis of colour, race, ethnic or national origin. The Commission for Racial Equality has produced a code of conduct to eradicate racial discrimination practice.

Disability Discrimination Act 1995

This Act was introduced to prohibit disabled persons from being discriminated against during both recruitment and employment. Employers must remove physical barriers and adjust working conditions to prevent discrimination on the basis of having a disability.

Sex Discrimination Acts 1975 and 1985 and the Equal Pay Act 1970

These Acts were designed to prevent discrimination or less favourable treatment of a man or a woman on the basis of gender. These Acts cover pay and conditions as well as promotion and equal opportunities.

Trade Union and Labour Relations (Consolidation) Act 1992

This legislation prevents trade union members being treated less favourably than non-members and vice versa. If penalised, the employee can complain to an employment tribunal.

Staff training

Staff training is important. If staff are not sufficiently trained, it will affect their ability to effectively carry out treatments. This will result in client dissatisfaction and the potential loss of clientele. It is likewise important to make sure staff have good product knowledge to enable them to give informed advice and maximixe product sales. Investing in staff training and enabling staff to provide a good quality service will result in good client relations and make it more likely that a client will return for future treatments, which will be financially beneficial of the business.

Grievance procedures

The disciplinary procedure is another invaluable tool for employers. In this document the employer lists their expectations. It is important that this is also drafted to reflect the specific business needs; for example, all disciplinary procedures will specify that staff will be dismissed for theft, harassment or discrimination. However, in a salon you will have further expectations, for example client confidentiality issues and restrictions on poaching clients from the salon to be treated elsewhere.

When internal procedures fail, the dispute is usually taken to the employment tribunal. Employees, including temporary staff and those on fixed term contracts, can go to a tribunal to claim unfair dismissal after 12 months' service. Employees, even applicants for jobs, do not require any length of service to go to a tribunal if they can claim to have been subject to any form of discrimination. For example, a therapist who feels she failed her probationary period because the salon owner became aware that she was pregnant could claim sex discrimination.

Salon rules

It is excellent practice for the employer to have their own written salon rules. These can supplement the contract of employment and disciplinary procedures. Listed below are just some of the areas that might be included.

- Arrangements for booking holidays and even determining when some holidays must be taken.
- A requirement for attending training and retraining.
- Requirements for recording client consultation and treatment records.
- Your requirements for sickness reporting arrangements.
- Your dress code, and supply of uniforms.
- Grooming, i.e. make-up and hair.
- Detailed arrangements for the calculation and payment of commission.
- Opening and closing procedures.
- Your rules regarding concessionary or free treatments for staff and family.
- Banking and access to the till.
- Loss and damage of products and equipment.

- Rules about special leave/medical appointments.
- Use of salon equipment such as telephone and computers.
- Rules for reporting adverse incidents.

Communication systems

In a modern employment relationship it is important that the employee is absolutely clear of their employer's expectations – otherwise how can the employee fulfil them? There can often be a breakdown in communications between employer and employee and frequently this is due to miscommunication or no communication at all, each party feeling the other doesn't understand their situation or viewpoint.

Good working relationships between colleagues are essential. Every member of staff, or the *team*, plays a different role, each ensuring the success of the business. Poor working relationships create an unpleasant environment for both staff and clients. Good communication systems are important, especially when staff responsibilities are shared.

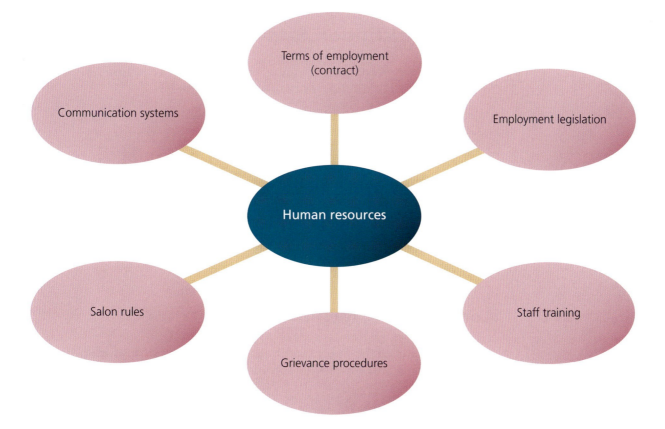

CONSUMER PROTECTION LEGISLATION

When delivering hair removal products and services to clients (consumers) you must meet the requirements of all of the following pieces of consumer protection legislation.

Sales and Supply of Goods Act 1994

Under this Act all goods must be as described, fit for their intended purpose and of merchantable quality. It also covers the processes under which consumers can return goods and replaced the 1982 Act, to include service standards requirements.

Resale Prices Act 1964 and 1976

According to these Acts, manufacturers can provide a recommended retail price (RRP) with their product, but the seller is not obliged to sell to consumers at the recommended price.

Prices Act 1974

This Act requires all product prices to be clearly displayed in order to prevent the consumer being misled.

Trades Description Acts 1968 and 1972

These two Acts prevent manufacturers, retailers or service industry providers from using false descriptions for their goods and services.

Hair removal businesses and their employees must not:

- provide false descriptions of products
- supply misleading information
- make false statements to consumers
- provide misleading price comparisons, particularly between past and present prices
- only offer products at a 'reduced' price if the full price quoted has been in effect for a minimum of 28 days.

Consumer Protection Act 1987

This Act introduced the European Community (EC) directive which protects the consumer against services and products which are deemed unsafe.

Consumer Safety Act 1978

This Act is designed to reduce the risk to consumer from potentially dangerous products.

Consumer Protection (Distance Selling) Regulations 2000

Derived from an EC directive, this legislation regulates the supply of goods and services between suppliers acting in a commercial capacity and consumers. All purchases made by telephone, fax, internet, digital television, and mail order (including catalogue shopping) are subject to these regulations and when making such purchases consumers must receive:

- clear information on goods and services including supplier details, payment and delivery arrangements
- consumer cancellation rights which should be provided in writing
- a seven working day 'cooling off' period during which they may cancel their purchase.

SETTING UP YOUR BUSINESS

Equipment and suppliers

As part of your business plan you must research the market for suppliers, that is the companies you will deal with who will supply you with all your goods so you can run your business.

It is important that you very carefully select your suppliers, as they will play an important role in the success of your business. Although getting value for money is an important business issue, it is not about buying the cheapest goods – couch, epilator, wax pot stool, etc. – because when the goods break down, or collapse, or fail to work, it costs you to replace or repair and possibly also costs you money from disappointed clients who couldn't have their treatment. Clients are very unforgiving about broken equipment or missing goods which mean they forgo their appointment, and they have long memories – it is best to ensure those memories are good ones!

So what does value for money mean? It means being cost effective, which in turn means giving you the best return on that money: if you buy a cheap couch that lasts you for 3 years instead of a more expensive one that lasts for 15 years, which is the most cost effective? It is usually the more 'expensive' one, but the lesson here is that cheap and expensive are words without meaning unless you look at the whole picture.

For basic salon equipment such as the following it is worth spending more initially as you will save in the long term:

- quality couch – which is multi-positional and preferably height adjustable
- sturdy trolley – preferably with one or two drawers and a side panel with two electric sockets and a magnifying lamp holder
- magnifying lamp – which is easily adjustable and has a large magnification area
- practitioner stool – there is no price on your comfort
- sterilising system.

PROFESSIONAL TIP ✔

The cheapest option can often be the most expensive in the long term, don't be fooled into buying cheap equipment and products!

Which suppliers are the best?

Your first research step for suppliers will probably be the trade press. These magazines are for the professional beauty industry only and they are a good source of articles and adverts, so you'll find plenty of information. Examples of trade press publications are:

Health & Beauty Salon
Guild News
Professional Beauty
Vitality.

It is also worth trying membership magazines such as:

Guild Gazette (Guild of Professional Beauty Therapists)
International Therapist (Federation of Holistic Therapists)
Embody (International Therapy Exam Council)
Vitality (BABTAC).

Another good source of information which won't cost you anything are trade websites. However, ensure you are searching non-company specific sites, otherwise you will get biased information. Some publications have websites and a good generic one designed for students is www.salonwebshop.co.uk.

Meeting suppliers face to face is a good idea so you can gauge for yourself how they might be to deal with. A cost effective method of seeing lots of suppliers at the same time is trade shows and exhibitions. These are normally held in February, May, September and October, the main ones are Edinburgh, Manchester, Birmingham and London. Some exhibitions are for specialist areas and others are more general. They are generally organised by trade publications or membership associations.

Always ask people in industry whom they buy from and their opinions; ask your college who supplies them and how they find them to deal with; also ask any salons that are not or will not be your competitors for their feedback.

Many supplies are sold on a cash and carry basis, where you go to the supplier's premises and buy from a warehouse. An alternative method is through mail order, where you order by phone or online and your goods are delivered to you. Some companies have both methods of supply. It is usual when buying equipment to initially set up a salon for you to visit an equipment showroom or warehouse and try the equipment yourself – there is not a brochure in existence that can tell you how comfortable a couch is, you just have to try it yourself. This is another good reason for going to trade shows, although they do get very busy and you won't get the personal attention you may need. They are great for research though.

Once you have all your large equipment, you will need to buy the 'tools of your trade' – the equipment, products and consumables specific to the treatment you intend to carry out. These items have been highlighted in earlier chapters and you will need to make a list, like a normal shopping list, of your requirements. Remember you need to buy not just enough to start with, but to sustain your business through the first 6–9 months; also give consideration to training. Training needs are equipment, product and business based, that is, you will need to know how to use the specific equipment to give your clients the most effective treatment as well as how to

PROFESSIONAL TIP ✔

What do industry colleagues say about the supplier you are thinking of going to?

Trade shows are a great way to meet suppliers

Photo courtesy of Trades Exhibitions Professional Beauty 2006, Excel, London

make the most out of the products and consumables. Don't forget business training: it is no good being the best practitioner if you don't have the business skills and acumen that will enable you to grow and employ others. Research training companies in the same way as other suppliers. They are often at exhibitions giving lectures and talks, and that is an ideal way to see them and to judge whether you like what they say and how they say it.

Funding

There are a number of government-run funding schemes for which you may meet the criteria. Some are specifically for young business people, while there are others for 'returners to work' or the long-term unemployed. A good first point of contact is Business Link which is run by local area Chambers of Commerce, and they work by putting people in touch with other organisations – in other words they 'link' you with those who are best positioned to help you, be it for finance, employment or marketing issues.

The normal route, however, to funding a new business is through family members or banks and for these, as with any of the 'funding' organisations above, the Business Plan as already discussed is a vital document. It assists investors and lenders to see the essence of the business and the direction it will be going in, as well as the set-up and ongoing costs.

> **REMEMBER** !
>
> Borrowing money is easy, but ensure you have a plan to pay it back

BASIC BUSINESS STRATEGIES

Accounts

It is simple to see what is coming into your business by looking in the till, but it's not as straightforward to see what is going out: all monies have to be accounted for.

Costs

In general terms there are two types of costs:

1 fixed
2 variable.

Fixed costs are those costs which you have to pay regardless of whether you have any clients coming into the salon or not – in other words they stay the same, for example rent, rates, loan repayments, insurances, etc.

Variable costs are those costs which change depending on the number of clients you have. Examples are products and consumables, but salaries and commissions, etc. are also variable costs.

You will need to find out how much it costs you to run your business as this will help when it comes to pricing your treatments. For example, if it costs you £20 an hour to be in your premises, you must charge more than that to make any profit – and you'll need to alter that figure to take into account your variable or changeable costs.

Work out what your costs per annum are for one year or your projected (or estimated), costs if you are not in business yet. Divide that figure by the number of hours you intend to open for business. That will tell you what you need to take in the till before you start to make any money. Be thorough when compiling your list: forgetting little things which add up over the year can make for a very costly mistake. This exercise will also help you to decide which premises may be suitable and which may not – it's no good having great premises if your charges to recoup the money are not realistic.

You may find it helpful to employ a book keeper to keep your accounts up to date and the 'books' in order. 'Books' refers to an era when all accounts were kept in different books, each book recording different information, for example invoices and Value Added Tax (VAT) paid, plus sales and VAT charged. Nowadays most businesses have accountancy software and do their accounts on the computer; a common accountancy package is SAGE which offers a variety of packages to suit small businesses. You may still find it useful to designate the job of keeping the accounts up to date to one member of staff.

You will also need the services of an accountant each year, to check that all your records are correct and assess your tax liability (what your business has to pay). This person will be in a position to guide you financially through the often cloudy and changing waters of financial legislation. Your accountant may also deal with your personal tax liability as it makes sense for the same person to do this since he or she has all the relevant information at their fingertips.

Choosing an accountant or book keeper should not just be a question of trawling through the classified adverts under accountancy services. You should enquire of other people, in similar businesses, whom they use and whom they can recommend. Also, for reasons of confidentiality, consider that it may be better to have someone who is not a friend.

Assessment of knowledge and understanding

You have now learnt the business basics for hair removal. To test your level of knowledge and understanding, answer the following short questions:

1 Why do you need to know about business to be successful as HRP?

2 Why isn't the money in the till at the end of the week your profit?

3 What is the difference between gross and net profit?

4 What is the difference between fixed and variable costs?

5 What are the benefits of a Business Plan?

6 Why do Business Plans change?

7 Why do you need to set targets/goal/objectives?

8 What is networking and why should you do it?

Activities

Conduct the following activities to practise your knowledge of hair removal business basics:

1 Create a basic Business Plan using the headings in this chapter.

2 Create a folder of information regarding business training based on duration and cost.

3 Search the internet for basic general business training.

4 Search trade magazines and internet sites i.e. www.salonwebshop. co.uk for trade related business training.

5 Go to the library and look for business books relating to service industries.

Follow-up knowledge

To build on the knowledge of business basics gained in this chapter, complete the following tasks to extend your business skills and understanding:

1 Visit www.companieshouse.gov.uk for in-depth advice on forming a company.

2 Visit www.thegmtgroup.co.uk for business training designed for this industry.

3 Visit www.businesslink.gov.uk as they have lots of helpful advice and links to other organisations.

4 Visit www.britishchambers.org.uk another organisation which gives help and advice and is also a good networking tool.

5 Visit www.business.barclays.co.uk as they offer a system of home learning through their Clearly Business programme; visit other bank websites too to see what they offer.

 Advanced knowledge reference section

Employment tribunals don't happen in the health and beauty industry ... do they?

David Wright

Last year 176,000 employees took their employer to Tribunal. I am dealing with five cases at the moment from the beauty sector, and almost universally employers tell me that they cannot believe that their employee, whom they have treated so well, has rewarded them by going to employment tribunal. You must remember that an employee will often have an entirely different perspective to you, the salon owner, and believe that they are only pursuing their rights. If they have lost their job or wages, there is even less reason to retain any loyalty. The beauty industry has no special reason to be exempt from tribunal cases. In fact it is largely made up of small employers with limited knowledge of personnel practice. Many staff do not have contracts of employment and/or disciplinary procedures, and, of greatest significance, the workforce is largely young and female.

The Law

All employees including temporary and those on fixed term contracts can go to tribunal to claim unfair dismissal after 12 months' service.

Employees, even applicants for jobs, do not need any length of service to go to tribunal if they claim to have been subject to any form of discrimination. For example a therapist who feels she failed her probationary period because the salon owner became aware that she was pregnant could claim sex discrimination.

Helpful hints

It may seem obvious, but do not make decisions about your staff based on what you feel is right, or even fair. The legislation gives employees basic rights but the employer is still free, in many areas, to decide their terms and conditions for their business. I have written many times that most employers lose because they do not have good quality documentation. Even more frequently their rules and procedures aren't written.

In short you should:

- have a contract of employment that both you and your staff understand
- have a disciplinary and grievance procedure which is right for your salon
- have written salon rules
- recruit and select staff using objective criteria and keep a record of your decision.

Tribunal cases in the beauty industry

1 A salon was failing to achieve its targets and the owner felt that they could no longer afford to keep the manager, who did not carry out treatments. This was a reasonable conclusion. The manager was advised of the decision and this was confirmed in writing. However, legislation requires that employees have a right of appeal against decisions to dismiss. This is a clear example where the failing was only one of process. Recent legislation allows tribunals to award an additional 50 per cent when employers haven't followed the three stage disciplinary procedure. The former employee is claiming £10,000 at tribunal.

2 After a very heated arguement, which involved a therapist verbally abusing the salon manager and a client, the therapist was told to leave and not come back. The following day, after she had taken advice, the manager invited the therapist to attend a disciplinary hearing. However, it was too late. The therapist realised the likely outcome of employment tribunal would be dismissal. She, therefore, wrote to the manager indicating that she had already been dismissed (unfairly as there had been no disciplinary hearing) and would take the case to tribunal.

3 A therapist resigned and gave a week's notice. The employer recovered a week's leave which the employee had taken and £400 training costs from the final salary. The employee, at tribunal, argued that they were owed 'lieu' time and that they had never signed their contract. The tribunal rejected the lieu time argument as this was quite separate from holiday pay. They were also unimpressed that the employee hadn't signed their contract. If an employee has received it and is accepting all the benefits of it she has therefore implicitly accepted it. However, the sticking point was that the contract only gave a right to recover training costs, it did not specify 'from your final salary'. The tribunal ruled that the employer's actions represented an unlawful deduction of pay.

Consider the time, money and anxiety that you would face if you were taken to tribunal. In all of these cases it could have been avoided if the employer had processes, policies and procedures in place which worked for them or, having processed them, sought advice straight away.

David Wright, reproduced courtesy of *Health & Beauty Salon*.

chapter 10

HEALTH, HYGIENE AND SAFETY

What will I know after reading this chapter?

This chapter introduces you to the standards of best practice with regard to health, hygiene and safety which should be carried out by professional hair removal practitioners. It describes the competencies required to ensure that:

- **your own actions do not create any health and safety risks**
- **you do not ignore significant risks in your workplace**
- **you take sensible action to maintain a safe working environment**
- **you understand bacteriology**
- **you recognise all relevant legislation.**

G1 Ensure your own actions reduce risks to health and safety

The importance of salon hygiene cannot be overstated

As a hair removal practitioner you are legally obliged to provide a safe and hygienic environment. It is particularly important to have a basic understanding of bacteriology in order to appreciate the reasons for stringent hygiene procedures.

BACTERIOLOGY

Bacteriology is the branch of biology that deals with the study of micro organisms. In order to understand the importance of hygiene and sterilisation, HRPs should understand how the spread of disease can be prevented and be aware of the precautions which should be taken to protect your own, as well as your client's health. You should understand the relationship of bacteria to the procedures necessary to maintain salon cleanliness and prevent cross-infection.

Contagious diseases and skin infections are caused either by the passing of infectious material directly from one person to another, or by unsterilised implements which have been used first on an infected person and then used on someone else. Other sources of contagion are dirty hands and fingernails, contaminated containers and unsanitary facilities.

Bacteria

Bacteria are minute, one-celled micro organisms that are found nearly everywhere. They are especially numerous in dust, dirt, refuse and diseased tissue. Bacteria are also known as germs or microbes, they are especially numerous on the skin and in water, air, decayed matter, bodily secretions, clothing, and under the free edge of the nails.

Bacteria are not visible except with the aid of a microscope: 1,500 rod-shaped bacteria will barely reach across the head of a pin.

Types of bacteria

There are hundreds of different kinds of bacteria. These are generally classified into two types:

1 *Non-pathogenic organisms*: Beneficial or harmless types of bacteria which perform many useful functions such as decomposing, reusing and improving the fertility of the soil. Non-pathogenic organisms are far more numerous than pathogenic (harmful) bacteria.

2 *Pathogenic organisms*: Disease producing or the harmful type, although they are in the minority, they cause considerable damage when they invade plant or animal tissue. Pathogenic bacteria are harmful because they produce disease. Parasites which require living matter for their growth belong to this group.

Pathogenic bacteria

Because they are harmful and disease causing, we are concerned with pathogenic bacteria, which are classified as follows:

1 **Cocci** – round-shaped organisms which appear singly or in groups. Those which form in groups include:

a **Staphylococci** – pus-forming organisms which grow in a bunch or clusters; they are present in abscesses, pustules and boils

b **Streptococci** – pus-forming organisms which grow in chains

c **Diplococci** which grow in pairs; they cause pneumonia.

2 **Bacilli** are rod-shaped organisms which are short, and may have either a thin or thick structure. Bacilli are the most common and produce such diseases as tetanus, influenza, typhoid fever, tuberculosis and diphtheria. Many bacilli are spore forming.

3 **Spirilla** are curved or corkscrew-shaped organisms.

TECHNICAL TIP

Individual bacteria have distinct forms or shape which aid in their identification

Bacterial growth and reproduction

Bacteria are composed of an outer cell membrane and internal protoplasm. They manufacture their own food from the surrounding environment, give off waste products, grow and reproduce. Bacteria exhibit two distinct phases in their life cycle: the active or vegetative stage and the inactive or spore-forming stage.

Active or vegetative bacteria

Bacteria

During the active stage, bacteria grow and reproduce. Micro organisms multiply best in warm, dark, damp, dirty places, where sufficient food is present. When conditions are favourable, bacteria reproduce very quickly. As food is absorbed, the bacterial cell divides crosswise into halves, thereby forming two daughter cells. From one original bacterium, as many as 16 million germs may develop in half a day. When favourable conditions cease to exist, bacteria either die or become inactive.

Inactive or spore-forming bacteria

Certain bacteria (such as the anthrax and tetanus bacilli) form spores in order to withstand periods of famine, drought and unsuitable temperature. In this stage, spores can be blown about in the dust and not be harmed by disinfectants, heat or cold. When favourable conditions are restored, the spores enter the active or vegetative stage, and start to grow and reproduce.

Movement of bacteria

For the most part, only the bacilli and spirilla are able to move about. The cocci rarely show mobility. Bacteria move by means of hair-like projections, known as flagella or cilia. The movement of these hairs propels the bacteria about in liquid.

Bacterial infections

When pathogenic bacteria invade the body, an infection will occur if the body is unable to cope with the bacteria and the harmful toxins they produce.

A local infection is indicated by a boil or a pimple containing pus.

A general infection results when the blood stream carries the bacteria and their toxins to all parts of the body, as in blood poisoning.

Pus

The presence of pus is a sign of infection. Staphylococci are the most common pus-forming bacteria; pus is a combination of bacteria, waste matter, decayed tissue, body cells and blood cells.

Contagious disease

A disease which is spread from one person to another by contact is known as contagious. Some of the more common contagious diseases which would prevent an HRP from treating a client are tuberculosis, ringworm, scabies, lice, viral infections and any type of skin disease.

Sources of infection

The main sources of infection are unclean hands and instruments, open sores, mouth and nose discharges and the common use of drinking cups and towels. Coughing, sneezing and spitting also spread germs.

Bacterial entry

There can be no infection without the presence of an entry site. Pathogenic bacteria can enter the body through:

- a break in the skin, such as a cut, pimple or scratch
- breathing (air) or swallowing (water or food)
- the nose (air)
- the eyes or ears (dirt)
- sexual contact.

Cuts must be covered with a waterproof plaster

HEALTH AND SAFETY ✚

Cuts left open and unprotected provide an easy target for pathogenic bacteria and may cause infection

Other infectious agents

Filterable viruses are living organisms so small that they will pass through the pores of a porcelain filter. They cause the common cold and other respiratory and gastrointestinal infections.

Parasites are plants or animals that live upon other living organisms without giving anything in return.

Plant parasites or fungi, such as moulds, mildews and yeasts, can produce contagious diseases such as ringworm. Animal parasites, certain insects and pediculosis are caused by lice.

Immunity

Immunity is the ability of the body to resist invasion by bacteria or to destroy bacteria after entry. Immunity to disease is a sign of good health and it may be natural or acquired. Natural immunity means resistance to disease from birth, which can then be maximised by hygienic living. Acquired immunity occurs after the body has overcome diseases, or after it has received vaccinations.

Acquired Immune Deficiency Syndrome

Acquired Immune Deficiency Syndrome (AIDS) should not cause excessive concern to the HRP, providing stringent hygiene and sterilisation procedures are followed and disposable needles are used and carefully disposed of.

Human disease carrier

A human disease carrier is a person who is immune to a disease, and yet carries germs which can infect other people. Typhoid fever and diphtheria may be transmitted in this manner.

Destruction of bacteria

Bacteria may be destroyed by exposure to intense heat. This can be produced by an autoclave, a glass bead steriliser or chemical sterilising solutions.

Vaccinations

Vaccinations are effective against such diseases as polio, typhoid fever, chicken pox, smallpox, whooping cough, measles, tetanus, hepatitis and various other diseases.

Antibiotics

Antibiotics are substances which destroy an organism or inhibit its growth. Antibiotics are produced by various micro organisms and fungi. They have the power to slow growth and to destroy other micro organisms. Penicillin is an antibiotic produced in several forms for the treatment of a wide variety of bacterial infections.

Body defences

The body is constantly defending itself against invasion by disease. The body's defences are categorised as first-line, second-line and third-line defences.

First-line defences

Bacteria can enter the body through any opening, such as the mouth or nose. Bacteria are taken into the body in food and liquids, or can enter by way of breaks, cuts or punctures in the skin.

Healthy skin is one of the body's most important defences against disease. The acid mantle helps the skin to act as a barrier by resisting the penetration of harmful bacteria.

Autoclave

House of Famuir www.hofbeauty.co.uk

The nose has mucus and fine hairs that serve as protection against bacteria. A sneeze or cough, for example, is the body protecting itself against bacteria. Other barriers are created by mucus membranes in the mouth, gastric juices in the stomach, and organisms within the intestines and other areas of the body. Tears in the eyes also serve to flush out harmful bacteria and foreign objects.

Second-line defences

The body also defends itself from harmful bacteria by producing inflammation. Redness and swelling indicate an increase in temperature and metabolic activity, the inflamed area will be sensitive to the touch. The white corpuscles in the blood cells go into action to destroy harmful micro organisms in the bloodstream so that healing can take place.

Third-line defences

The body can produce substances which inhibit or destroy harmful bacteria. These protective substances are called anti-bodies or anti-toxins.

HEALTH AND SAFETY BEST PRACTICE

One named person in a hair removal business must be responsible for compiling details and writing procedures for best practice. This person is the 'responsible person'.

Each business should have a 'responsible person' who should be aged over 18 years old and nominated in writing by the business operator. This person is responsible for the implementation of best practice and is in charge of the business premises. The responsible person should be available on the premises whenever the business is open and have adequate assistance by suitable persons (aged 18 or over) to ensure supervision when they are unavailable. They must ensure they are available by not engaging in other duties which will prevent them from exercising general supervision.

Responsibilities

The responsible person should ensure:

- all reasonable precautions are taken for the safety of all persons using the premises
- compliance with the Health and Safety at Work Act (1974)
- they complete a risk assessment of the business in compliance with the management of Health and Safety at Work Regulations 1999.

Staff

All staff carrying out hair removal treatments should be competent and have recognised qualifications, and in addition:

- have documented evidence of their success

- be fully trained in the safe use of salon equipment
- be fully and regularly trained in health and safety procedures
- be given regular and relevant up-to-date training
- have suitable protective wear available.

All staff should be provided with:

- a safe storage place for outdoor wear and personal belongings
- adequate toilet and sanitary disposal facilities
- rest areas.

Personal hygiene

During the course of your work as an HRP you will regularly make close contact with your clients. In order to influence the client's perception of your standards and professionalism and, critically, to prevent cross-infection, it is vital that your standards of personal presentation and hygiene are constantly kept to the highest standards.

All practitioners must:

- wear clean, washable clothing
- wear disposable gloves for hair removal treatments and change them for each client
- cover any open wounds or open skin with a waterproof dressing
- ensure their hands are kept scrupulously clean and washed immediately prior to and immediately after any treatment
- refrain from smoking, drinking or eating during treatments
- not be under the influence of alcohol or drugs when carrying out treatment
- not carry out treatment if suffering from an acute respiratory infection and wear a disposable face mask when suffering from a mild infection such as a common cold
- keep their hair clean and secured away from the face to prevent it from restricting vision or trailing on the client
- wear low heeled, supportive and fully enclosed footwear, in order to provide comfort, help maintain good posture and protect feet from injury.

Finally, hair removal practitioners should be all vaccinated against hepatitis B to remove the risk of contracting this disease. This is because there is a relatively high risk of HRPs coming into contact with body fluids.

Standards for hand washing and the use of gloves

Hand washing is the single most important procedure for preventing cross-infection and is, generally, a brief rubbing together of the hands with soap followed by rinsing under a steam of water.

Although various products are available, hand washing can be classified simply by whether plain soap or antibacterial products are used. Hand

> **REMEMBER** !
>
> Smoking, eating and drinking during the course of a treatment allows close contact with the mouth, transferring micro organisms to the hand, which can then spread to the client

washing with plain soaps (in bar, granule, leaflet or liquid form) suspends micro organisms and allows them to be rinsed off. This process is often referred to as the mechanical removal of micro organisms. Hand washing with antibacterial products kills or inhibits the growth of micro organisms. This process is often referred to as the chemical removal of micro organisms.

Because of the potential for the HRP's hands to come into contact with a client's body fluids or blood, a fresh pair of disposable gloves (latex or vinyl) should be worn for each client. The consistent wearing of gloves will also protect the client from potential exposure to micro organisms from the HRP, particularly where there are cuts or abrasions on the practitioner's hands.

Procedure for hand washing and the use of disposable gloves

The ideal duration of hand washing is not known, but washing times of 15– 30 seconds have been reported as effective in removing most transient contaminants from the skin.

Hand washing

- A sink with hot and cold running water should be located in each treatment room. The taps should ideally be wrist or foot operated. If the taps are hand operated a disposable paper handwipe should be used to turn the taps on and off.
- Hands should be washed:
  1 before and after treatment of each client
  2 before putting on gloves and immediately after gloves are removed
  3 all the way up to the elbow.
- Soaps should ideally be antibacterial:
  1 Bar soaps are not recommended as they may harbour micro organisms.
  2 Liquid soap containers should be disposable; or reusable containers should be cleaned and refilled with fresh soap at least once month.
- Hand washing technique should include:
  1 applying 3–5ml of antibacterial soap
  2 rubbing hands vigorously together, covering all surfaces of hands, wrists and lower arms, especially between the fingers and fingernail area, for at least 10 seconds
  3 rinsing thoroughly under a stream of water
  4 drying hands, wrists and arms thoroughly with a clean disposable paper towel, then turning the tap off using the paper towel.

Use of gloves

- A fresh pair of disposable examination gloves (latex or vinyl) should be worn during the treatment of each client.
- Hands should be washed in accordance with the hand washing procedure before putting on the gloves and immediately after the gloves are removed.
- Low-powdered gloves should be worn and/or excess exterior powder should be removed with a clean disposable paper towel moistened with

Wash hands thoroughly using soap and plenty of running water

TECHNICAL TIP ✔

When washing your hands do not use too much soap as excess can cause a build-up on the skin and increase the risk of skin irritation

tap water and dried gently with a clean disposable paper towel to prevent powder from contacting client's skin during treatment.

- When a treatment session is interrupted:

  1 a protective covering should be used over the gloved hand or hands before touching anything else, for example the telephone; or

  2 gloves should be removed and discarded.

- When gloves are removed during a treatment session, hands should be washed and a fresh pair of gloves used.

- Gloves should be worn during the procedures of removing the used needle from the needle-holder in electrolysis treatment and the cleaning, rinsing, and drying of tweezers for both electrolysis and waxing, and when cleaning used wax applicators.

- Torn or perforated gloves should be removed immediately, and hands should be washed after gloves are removed. The gloves should then be replaced with a new pair.

SALON HYGIENE

Key hygiene terms

Sterilisation

Sterilisation is the absolute destruction of all forms of microbial life, including spores. A sterile object is free from all living organisms. You cannot sterilise your hands or a client.

> **REMEMBER** !
>
> Always follow manufacturer's instructions when using sterilisation equipment

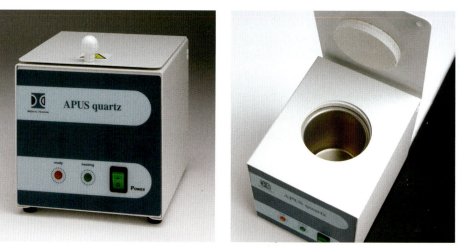

Glass bead steriliser

House of Famuir Ltd www.hofbeauty.co.uk

Disinfection

Disinfection is the destruction of the growing forms of infection and infectious microbes, but not spores. When the disinfection effect wears off, the organism re-grows. Disinfectants should not be used on the skin; they are for inanimate objects only. Examples include Barbicide or a UV cabinet.

UV cabinet

House of Famuir www.hofbeauty.co.uk

Antiseptic

Antiseptics are similar to disinfectant and safe to use on living tissues. They kill bacteria and fungi completely, but not spores. Antiseptic is ideal for use on the skin. In addition to labelling the bottles of antiseptics with the expiry date, it is useful to have a date chart on the wall in the sterilisation area, which clearly indicates the date which the antiseptic solution was mixed (diluted) and the date when it expires and needs replacing. This helps to avoid confusion and prevents the accidental use of inactive solutions. An example is Hibitaine.

Sanitiser

The use of a sanitiser reduces microbes to a level considered safe by the public health administration. Disinfectants and antiseptics are sanitisers.

Bacteriostatic

A substance which is said to be bacteriostatic creates an environment in which growing forms of bacteria are temporarily inhibited.

Bactericidal

A substance which is bactericidal is one in which growing forms of bacteria are killed. It is essential to use, for example, a bactericidal hand cleanser prior to and after treating a client.

Sepsis

This term refers to the state of being infected with pus producing micro organisms.

Asepsis

Asepsis is the opposite of sepsis and refers to the state of being free from pathogenic organisms and so free from infection.

Aseptic

The term aseptic refers to the prevention of sepsis by the process of attempting to eliminate bacteria. All electrolysis procedures must be aseptic. This means the HRP must be wearing disposable gloves, have washed their hands, and it includes the safe disposal of sharps, contaminated cotton wool, tissues, etc.

Methods of sterilisation

There are various methods of sterilisation and the list given in the illustration is not exhaustive. It does, however, cover the methods you are likely to use or need to be aware of as an HRP.

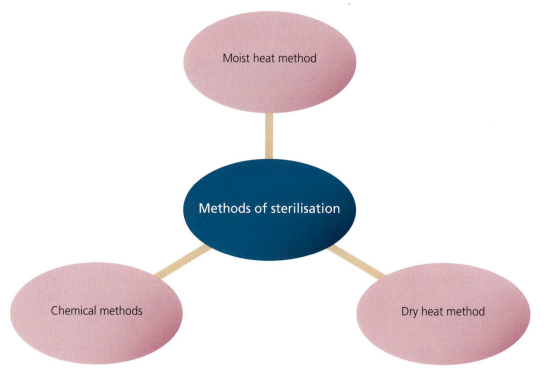

Moist heat method

The autoclave is the most commonly used method of sterilisation. The process is quick and efficient and uses steam under pressure. It is economical to use compared to the regular purchase of chemical sterilising solutions. Make sure the autoclave is CE marked, as this indicates that it is of the required standard.

Systems vary and you should always follow the manufacturer's instructions carefully. In most cases a specified amount of distilled water is poured into the sterilising chamber, the lid securely closed and any pressure release valves closed. The cycle is then initiated by pressing the start switch. The autoclave will begin the sterilising sequence by heating the water to between 121° and 134°C to generate the pressurised steam. This temperature is maintained for the duration of the sterilising cycle – approximately 15 minutes – however, the complete procedure takes 20–30 minutes, which allows the autoclave to de-pressurise and cool. The stages of the process are usually indicated by a series of indicator lights on the front or top of the autoclave. Indicator tape can also be used, this is placed inside the autoclave and changes colour to confirm that sterilisation has been achieved.

Dry heat method

The glass bead steriliser is the main system of dry heat sterilisation. This method is only suitable for small objects such as tweezers. Tiny glass beads are heated in a chamber to approximately 250°C, and the glass beads then conduct the heat to the items being sterilised. The process takes approximately 30 minutes, and at least another 20 minutes is allowed for the sterilised objects to cool. The disadvantage of this method is that tweezers cannot be fully inserted into the beads, although the majority of the surface is sterilised the upper portion is left unsterilised.

Chemical methods

Specific chemicals can be utilised to reduce or destroy pathogenic micro organisms on items which are immersed in them or wiped with them.

The cleaning of equipment and the working environment is essential and must be carried out prior to sterilising or disinfecting objects, particularly as some disinfectants are inactivated by organic material, such as skin or dirt. They may also be inactivated by detergents and soap, which is why rinsing is important.

Disinfectants are generally classified according to their main active ingredients.

Aldehydes

Gluteraldehyde, Cidex and Sporicidin are brands of gluteraldehyde which have, until recently, been extensively used in hair removal practices. Recent guidance however strongly discourages their use due to their potential as a skin irritant and a carcinogen.

Halogens

Chlorine and iodine are halogens. Chlorines can be used for cleaning work surfaces, trolleys, stools and floors and other non-metallic objects. Hypochlorite (bleach) solutions are recommended for disinfecting work surfaces and general equipment. An effective dilution is 1:100 dilution of household bleach in water. For clearing any body fluid spillage, a dilution of 1:10 should be used. Remember that brands may vary in strength and may deteriorate with lengthy storage. Chlorine is corrosive to metals and discolours paints and fabric, so should be used with care. Make up a dilution daily and dilute to 70 per cent bleach/30 per cent water. Iodine can be used on skin tissues, but is not generally used in hair removal practices.

Diguanides

The best known member of this group is chlorhexidine (Hibitaine) which is widely used for skin disinfection. A similar product (Hibiscrub) is used for hand cleansing. The incidence of skin irritation with these products is low.

Alcohol

Isopropyl alcohol (70 per cent) and surgical spirit are the two most commonly used alcohols. They can be used for cleaning debris from tweezers and wax dispensers; they can also be used sparingly to clean the skin. Isopropyl 70 per cent is the main ingredient in medi swabs. Care should be taken not to use too much alcohol on the skin as it can have a drying effect if overused. The smell can also be over-powering when too much is used near to the client's nose. When using surgical spirit, use only one or two drops on a clean piece of cotton wool or gauze.

HEALTH AND SAFETY ✚

Do not use Gluteraldehyde, Cidex and Sporicidin brands of gluteraldehyde for sterilisation as they are potential skin irritants and carcinogenic

---

PROFESSIONAL TIP ✔

Hibitaine tends to bind to the skin, which provides a longer lasting effect, it can also, however, cause a tacky sensation on the skin and in some cases restrict access to the follicle; this is particularly the case on dehydrated skins, as the product tends to cling to the dead skin cells

---

HEALTH AND SAFETY ★

Alcohols are not kind to equipment, laminated or painted surfaces as they tend to have a stripping effect over time

REMEMBER !

It is important to ensure that manufacturer's instructions are closely followed, and that care is taken to store chemicals safely away from direct sunlight or hot environments. The regulations under the legislation Control of Substances Hazardous to Health Regulations 1990 (COSHH) must be strictly adhered to

HEALTH AND SAFETY ✚

Used and contaminated sharps (i.e. electrolysis needles and razors) are a real danger. Check sharps boxes regularly to ensure that the lid is closed and secure and that it is not overfilled

HEALTH AND SAFETY ✚

A sharps box is a specific receptacle for the safe storage prior to disposal of sharp waste, for example, electrolysis needles and razors

Phenols

Dettox and Dettol are phenols; these cannot be used on the skin. They are very useful for cleaning equipment and work surfaces, lamps, etc. as they do not have the stripping effects of alcohols.

Radiation and gas

Electrolysis needles are pre-sterilised and packed in medical grade packaging. They are generally sterilised by either gamma irradiation or ethylene oxide gas.

SALON HYGIENE PROCEDURES

In addition to personal hygiene, every HRP has a moral and legal obligation to ensure that their working environment and procedures are hygienic and safe as follows:

- all treatment couches, seats and chairs should be covered with disposable paper sheet, which must be changed for each client
- a 'no smoking' notice should be displayed
- all materials and equipment used on the premises must be cleaned, disinfected and/or sterilised to the appropriate standard
- For each client only single use sterile needles are used and these are disposed of immediately after each treatment into a 'sharps box'. Razors used on clients pre-light treatment should be disposed of in a sharps box.

Re-usable equipment (e.g. tweezers) should be sterilised by:

- cleaning thoroughly in water and detergent to remove organic materials such as skin hair and grease
- rinsing thoroughly
- sterilising in an autoclave ensuring the equipment does not overlap each other.

Once sterilised, store items in sterile conditions, for example a UV cabinet, ready for use. If the items are not used within 3 hours, they should be re-sterilised.

Hard surfaces, including equipment lamps and the trolley, should be disinfected before and after each client.

Waxing applicators should also be cleaned and disinfected. Roller tops and applicators for waxing should be changed before every client. To clean the applicators:

- remove roller and clean away all residue wax, using wax removing solution
- wash thoroughly in water and detergent
- soak in disinfecting solution, such as hypochlorite (bleach) 70 per cent and 30 per cent water
- rinse and dry thoroughly
- store in clean environment ready for use, e.g. a UV cabinet.

Waste disposal

- The Environmental Protection Regulations 1991 state that producers of waste must ensure that all refuse – in particular clinical waste, i.e. electrolysis needles, swabs and used wax strips – is collected and disposed of by a registered waste carrier.
- Sharps boxes must not be allowed to become over-filled. They must be stored safely and collected and disposed of regularly.
- Clinical waste should be stored in yellow waste bags and disposed of regularly.
- Rubbish should always be stored in covered receptacles.

Sharps box

Needle-stick injuries

If a needle-stick injury occurs with an electrolysis needle, the following procedure should be followed:

- Encourage bleeding in the wound to 'flush' the area.
- Rinse under running water without soap.
- Cover with a dry dressing.
- Seek medical advice as soon as possible (within 1 hour). The hospital accident and emergency department will give a protective injection against hepatitis B. This injection should be administered within 48 hours of the injury. The employer must investigate the incident to analyse and reduce any future risk and all details must be recorded.
- If infection occurs as a result of the incident, it should be reported to the Local Environmental Health Officer under the Reporting of Injuries and Diseases and Dangerous Occurrences Regulations (RIDDOR) 1995.

> **HEALTH AND SAFETY** ✚
>
> If you intend to assist a person who has sustained a needle-stick injury, in order to protect yourself, make sure you put on protective, disposable (latex or vinyl) gloves prior to giving assistance

Hepatitis B

Hepatitis B is a serious infection of the liver and other bodily systems caused by the hepatitis B virus.

Acute hepatitis B causes jaundice (yellowing of the skin), extreme loss of appetite, severe malaise (feeling very ill) and other symptoms which may last for weeks or months. Recovery from acute hepatitis B is usual, but it can be fatal. An infection without symptoms may occur and these patients are more likely to become chronic carriers of hepatitis B. Many of these non-symptomatic patients develop chronic progressive liver disease which may lead to cirrhosis, liver failure or cancer.

The source of hepatitis B infection is a person suffering from acute hepatitis B, someone in the later stages of incubating hepatitis (i.e. 1–2 weeks before symptoms show) or a carrier. Like HIV, hepatitis B can be transmitted by various bodily fluids, but the most important of these for the therapist is blood or serum. The disease is one of the most highly infectious; it only requires minute amounts of blood or serum, invisible to the naked eye, to cause infection. For this reason, any object that has pierced a person's skin always needs to be sterilised before it can be re-used on another person.

> **REMEMBER** !
>
> Since hepatitis B is easily contracted through small amounts of body fluid, HRPs are at real risk, which is why it is so important to wear disposable gloves (latex or vinyl)

HEALTH AND SAFETY ✚

Because it is not possible to spot a carrier, it is important to be inoculated against hepatitis B in order to protect yourself from accidental infection

TECHNICAL TIP ✔

People do not have to have clinical AIDS to be infectious

It is not possible to spot a carrier of hepatitis B, or someone who is incubating the disease. A history of jaundice is not helpful, because jaundice can have many causes and those who become carriers are less likely to have had a history of jaundice. The professional HRP should treat each and every customer equally, secure in the knowledge that the hygienic procedures employed should ensure that infection cannot be transmitted within the salon from one person to another by contaminated, inadequately sterilised equipment.

AIDS

AIDS is a serious infection caused by the Human Immunodeficiency Virus (HIV). The word AIDS should only be applied to those who develop certain defined clinical features as a result of the HIV infection. AIDS is fatal. This single fact if the most important determining factor in formulating the amount of care that needs to be taken. For every patient with AIDS there are many others with HIV infection who have no symptoms (carriers). We do not know how many of these peole will develop AIDS, and the incubation period – that is, the time between acquisition of infection and the development of symptoms – may be many years.

HIV has been found to be present in other bodily secretions of patients and carriers, besides blood, semen and cervical secretions. The sources most likely to be of importance to HRPs and beauty therapists are blood, saliva and tears. However, transmission causing definite infection from saliva or tears has not been documented. Nevertheless, care should be exercised when working round the eyes or mouth.

The amount of blood required for transmission of HIV infection is a complicated question. A single small 'pinhead' injected dose of infected blood is generally considered to be associated with a very small risk. Nevertheless, it is also known that much depends on the stage of the disease in the carrier from whom the blood was derived. AIDS/HIV infection is now known to have been transmitted by acupuncture, so that any skin piercing activity carried out by beauty therapists should be considered as a risk factor.

The remarks about the impossibility of 'spotting' hepatitis B carriers apply equally to HIV carriers.

Although the AIDS virus is said not to survive for long periods on inanimate surfaces, the time required is in fact quite variable, depending as it does on factors such as dose, temperature, light, relative humidity, etc., and it is insufficient to rely on this in beauty therapy. Professional beauty therapists need to take more active measures to destroy the AIDS virus: hepatitis B is, in any case, much more resistant and may survive for a considerable period of time.

Health and safety in your treatment area

In order to conform with health and safety regulations and create a safe and comfortable environment, the following rules should be applied to all treatment areas.

- There should be a minimum of 5m² of floor space for each operator.

- The internal walls, partitions, floors and windows should be in good repair in order that they be kept clean.
- The floor of the treatment area should be smooth, even and easily cleaned.
- All furniture and fittings in the treatment area should have a smooth impervious surface so that it is easily cleaned.
- There should be an easily accessible wash basin with hot and cold water, sanitising soap and disposable towels available.
- Taps should ideally be wrist or foot operated.
- The temperature of the room should be easily controlled (a temperature of at least 16°C should be maintained) and the room should be adequately ventilated.
- All items being used in treatment should be disinfected or sterilised as appropriate and stored in clean and suitable storage to avoid contamination.
- Suitable screening to provide privacy for the client must be available.
- Fire precautions: all fire exits must be kept with free access, unobstructed and clearly signed. All other requirements of the fire authority, particularly The Fire Precautions Act 1971 and The Fire Precautions (Workplace) Regulations 1997 should be followed strictly.

RELEVANT LEGISLATION

It is vital that you and your salon comply with all applicable health and safety legislation, as harming your client or placing them at risk makes you liable for prosecution.

Due to the large amount of legislation, it is recommended that you contact your local Health and Safety Executive office and ask for a pack of all relevant health and safety information.

The Health and Safety at Work Act 1974

This is the central piece of legislation. It requires employers and self-employed people to ensure the health and safety and welfare of anyone attending their business. The employer is legally responsible for implementing the Act and for ensuring they make every reasonable effort to manage the health and safety at work of the people for whom they are responsible and of those who may be affected by the work they do.

Control of Substances Hazardous to Health (COSHH) Regulations 1998 (consolidated 2002)

This legislation covers the use, storage, risk assessment and general safe working practices in relation to chemicals and biohazard substances. All hazardous substances in the workplace must be identified and rated in writing by the employer. All staff must then be trained in safety procedures which address any identified hazards.

COSHH RISK ASSESSMENT					
Staff member responsible:		Date:		Review date:	
Hazard	What is the risk?	Who is at risk?	Risk rating High/Med/Low	Safety procedure required to address risk	

Controlled Waste Regulations 1992

This legislation requires all clinical waste (used needles, used swabs, used waxing strips, etc.) to be disposed of separately and collected by a licensed contractor.

Reporting of Injuries, Diseases and Dangerous Occurrences Regulations 1995 (RIDDOR)

This legislation requires employers to report certain workplace accidents, incidents and infections which result from a work activity.

Electricity at Work Regulations 1989

This legislation requires all portable (moveable) electrical appliances used in the workplace to be regularly maintained. Every piece of electrical equipment in the workplace must be tested every 12 months by a qualified electrician.

Management of Health and Safety at Work Regulations 1999

These regulations require any business operator to carry out a risk assessment of the business; the outcomes of the assessment should be utilised to implement safe working practices.

Provision and Use of Work Equipment Regulations 1989

This legislation states that work equipment must be suitable for its intended use, safe for use and only used by trained, informed people accompanied by appropriate safety measures. Powered equipment must have CE markings.

Disability Discrimination Act 1995

This Act states that access and facilities for disabled people should be provided at the premises.

The Personal Protective Equipment at Work Regulations 1992

Under these regulations workplace managers must identify, through a risk assessment, those activities or processes which require special protective clothing or equipment. Employees must then be supplied with and use this clothing and equipment.

Workplace (Health, Safety and Welfare) Regulations 1992

These regulations require both employers and employees to maintain the cleanliness, safety and security of the workplace.

Fire Precautions Act 1971

This Act requires all staff to be trained in fire and emergency evacuation procedures for their workplace.

The Fire Precautions (Workplace) Regulations 1997

In accordance with the Management of Health and Safety Regulations 1999, every employer must carry out a risk assessment for their workplace which ensures:

- the workplace is equipped with adequate fire detection equipment
- all obstacles which may obstruct evacuation are identified and removed
- escape routes are clearly marked and equipped with emergency lighting
- an adequate fire warning system is in place
- suitable fire-fighting equipment is in place and is maintained
- fire evacuation procedures are consistently reviewed with alarms tested once a week and at least one drill conducted each year.

Disabled parking sign

Assessment of knowledge and understanding

You have now learnt about health and safety for hair removal. To test your level of knowledge and understanding, answer the following short questions:

1 Name two ways in which disease can be spread.
2 Name two types of bacteria.
3 State two ways which bacteria can enter the body.
4 Describe the body's natural defences against disease.
5 State why it is important for an HRP to have high standards of personal hygiene.
6 When is it necessary to change disposable gloves?
7 State two methods of sterilisation and one method of disinfection.
8 If a pair of tweezers become contaminated with blood do they need to be disinfected?
9 What is a sharps box used for?
10 List two laws which are relevant to practices in a hair removal salon.

Activities

Conduct the following activities to practise your knowledge of health and safety for hair removal:

1 Create a layout of a hair removal room, clearly showing electric sockets, light switches, the layout of the furniture and where you intend the trolley(s) and equipment to be when in use.

2 Using a variety of resources find out what 'CE' stands for.

3 Visit a salon and see if there are any health and safety issues that you can see from reception.

4 Using headings only, create a draft health and safety document for a salon with all legislation and requirements covered.

Follow-up knowledge

To build on the knowledge of health and safety gained in this chapter, complete the following tasks to extend your hair removal skills and understanding:

1 Visit www.hse.gov.uk for information on health and safety.

2 Visit www.riddor.gov.uk for information on the regulations.

3 Visit www.directgov.uk for information on disability discrimination.

4 Visit www.cdc.gov/handhygiene for information on hand hygiene.

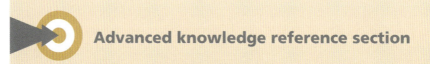

Advanced knowledge reference section

Are the gloves off in the salon?

Judy Jeffrey

Today, an increasing number of therapists are wearing gloves to perform treatments and some environmental health departments are encouraging this practice. We should, therefore, examine if it really is safer to wear gloves for treatments, or if we just think it is safer. In this article I will look at various issues relating to the use of gloves and then try to answer the question 'are the gloves off in the salon?'

Often, when wearing gloves, therapists feel safe and protected; tending to wear their gloves before and after treatments, touching other equipment, pens and consultation cards, etc. This carries the potential risk of 'cross-infection', which is the process of passing on an infection either directly from person to person or through contact with an inanimate object. When therapists are not wearing gloves, they tend to protect themselves and also their clients, by washing their hands immediately before and immediately after giving treatments so, in these instances, it can be safer without any gloves.

Wearing gloves is advised when a treatment involves, or could involve, the therapist coming into contact with blood, serum or body fluids that have a potential to carry diseases like hepatitis and HIV. Gloves are used to protect the therapist from contracting an infection from the client, the client contracting an infection from the therapist and to reduce the risk of passing on an infection to other clients or colleagues.

As with dental surgeries and medical centres, there are so many instances where the way gloves are worn poses a potential risk to clients and therapists. If gloves are not used and disposed of correctly they become a risk.

Despite these hazards, by imposing the following simple hygiene rules, these risks can be minimised resulting in an overall benefit to the client, therapist and the salon.

Choose suitable gloves (i.e. the 'right' type and fit)

- Fill in a consultation card and prepare equipment before putting on gloves.
- Wash and dry hands thoroughly.
- Fit gloves immediately before treatment.
- Remove gloves in a hygienic manner immediately after treatment.
- Dispose of gloves immediately in a clinical waste bin.

Wash and dry hands

Gloves are made in a variety of materials from latex to latex-free, without powder or with different types of powder – so there should be a type that will suit most needs. The quality must be effective against blood-borne pathogens, so thin polythene gloves are not appropriate, but very thick ones will be too clumsy. A good fit is essential. Gloves come in all shapes and sizes; if one is not suitable a different size or make should be tried. If they are too big, manual dexterity is hampered, bringing with it the increased risk of needle-stick injury and poor treatments. If they are too small, there is a risk that the gloves may split. A needle-stick injury whilst people are wearing gloves is reportedly not as dangerous as bare hands, as the blood is wiped off the needle onto the glove, prior to it entering the skin.

It is essential that the consultation card is completed and the working area is prepared prior to gloving, so that the therapist is not picking up dust, dirt or micro organisms on the gloves and transferring them to the client during a treatment.

Thorough washing of hands with liquid hand cleaner and drying on a paper towel or couch roll is a must immediately before putting on the gloves. This is to reduce the number of micro organisms on the hands to a minimum. Hand cream should not be applied to the hands as any perfumes may affect the rubber. Once the hand is in the glove it tends to become warm and moist and there is nothing micro organisms love more than damp, warm, dark environments to reproduce, so washing hands and drying thoroughly prior to using gloves reduces this activity.

Once the gloves are fitted over the hands, client skin preparation and treatment should commence immediately. The treatment should be completed without interruption. Even when wearing gloves it is advisable to avoid touching any areas where there is blood or serum as little as possible. If undertaking a different treatment on the same client, a new pair of gloves should be used.

Take care not to contaminate the work area with the glove after treatment. For instance, if an underarm wax is going to be performed, then it is better to have aftercare lotion previously prepared and ready to apply, so there is no risk of contaminating bottles or other items on the trolley with blood or serum from the gloves. Touching other equipment, pens, consultation cards, etc. whilst still wearing gloves poses a potential risk of cross-contamination to you, other colleagues and clients.

Immediately following the application of aftercare lotion, gloves should be taken off and disposed of in a manner that prohibits the contaminated outer surface of the glove coming in to contact with anything. The following is one way of doing this. With one hand pull the glove from the other hand down from the wrist, being careful not to touch bare skin with the glove, so that it is inside out. Hold the removed glove in the gloved hand and, with the bare hand, carefully remove the other glove, starting at the wrist to pull it off and encapsulate the held glove. This will result in the gloves being wrapped together, inside out, so any blood is inside the glove (if disposed of immediately) and is of little risk to you or other people. The hands should then be washed immediately to remove any micro organisms and to wash away any likely contamination on the skin. It also washes away any chemicals from the latex or powder that might cause an allergic reaction.

Used gloves are counted as 'clinical waste' because they are likely to be contaminated with blood or body fluids, so disposal should be into a yellow clinical waste bag in a foot operated bin. These bags should be removed from the salon by a licensed operator. A new pair of gloves should be used for each client and the cost built into the price of the treatment. Gloves should never be re-used.

It is known that, among people who wear latex gloves frequently, there is a risk of developing skin irritation or an allergy. This may take the form of an irritation, where the hand feels itchy and sore after wearing gloves, up to a full-blown allergy where there can be swelling of the eyes, difficulty in breathing and anaphylactic shock. This may be caused by the latex rubber, the chemicals remaining on the gloves after manufacture or to the powder inside. The risk of sensitisation can be reduced by washing hands prior to using gloves with a non-perfumed product, and washing thoroughly after using gloves. There are now a number of latex-free gloves, powdered or not, that are on the market to overcome this problem. If you are an employer, you may need to do a risk assessment to see if it is better to use latex-free gloves rather than have problems with staff becoming sensitive. Do not forget that it is not just you that this may affect – your client may have a latex allergy too. This should be checked when filling in the consultation card, and should be updated at every visit, as skin reactions can change over time. It is estimated that between 1 per cent and 6 per cent of the population may be sensitised to latex, but not all of them will develop symptoms.

Hygiene may not be an exciting subject but you can use good hygienic practices to attract clients and retain their loyalty. When a potential new client arrives, show her around the salon not only explaining treatments, but also showing how you are going to be hygienic and pointing out that these practices are for her protection.

If gloves are used in a hygienic way as described above, the answer to the question 'Are the gloves off in the salon?' is, 'NO – keep wearing them!' If gloves are not worn correctly or disposed of hygienically and they are a risk to both therapists and clients, then the response is to review the glove issue in the light of this article and start using them correctly. Can you afford to take the risk with your own safety or that of your clients?

Judy Jeffrey is Vice Chairman of BABTAC. Her background is in nursing and health education prior to setting up her own beauty therapy and image consultancy businesses.

Vitality, January 2005 21

Health and hygeine in the salon

By Janice Brown

Health and hygiene standards are of paramount importance in all health and beauty practices. The risk of cross-infection and contamination is high if good practice is not followed. Both the clients and the practitioners are at risk if poor hygiene standards exist.

What is good practice?

Comprehensive guidance can be obtained from your local environmental health department or the Hairdressing and Beauty Industry Authority (HABIA), who have produced a Health & Safety for Salons package which is recommended by environmental health officers. This will provide you with all of the information and guidance you need to ensure you stay within the law; information can be found on the web at www.habia.org

The general rule is that you should use disposable items wherever possible, dispose of waste carefully, and thoroughly clean and disinfect everything which has come into contact with the skin. Sterilise anything which has become contaminated by being inserted into the skin or by coming into contact with bodily fluids.

Practitioners should follow health and hygiene standards strictly, in particular:

● be clean, wear washable clothing

● wear a new pair of disposable latex or vinyl gloves for waxing and electrolysis for each client

● scrupulously clean hands before and after treatments and also if treatment is interrupted, particularly if the interruption involves touching other objects

● wear disposable face masks when suffering from a mild infection such as a common cold to avoid cross-infection.

Salon hygiene procedures in addition to personal hygiene

Every beauty therapist has a moral and legal obligation to ensure that their working environment and procedures are hygienic; all treatment couches should be covered with disposable paper sheets which must be changed for each client. All materials and equipment used on the premises must be cleaned, disinfected and/or sterilised to the appropriate standard.

There is significant misunderstanding regarding what is and is not required with regard to sterilisation and disinfection – up-to-date information can be found at www.habia.org

Sterilisation is the absolute destruction of all forms of microbial life, including spores. A sterile object is free from all living organisms. Examples of sterilisers are the autoclave, glass bead sterilisers and chemicals. Autoclaves sterilise by moist heat and are the most commonly used method of sterilisation. The process is quick and efficient. This method uses steam under pressure. It is economical to use compared to the regular purchase of chemical sterilising solutions. Glass bead sterilisers use dry heat; this method is only suitable for small objects such as tweezers. Tiny glass beads are heated in a chamber to approximately 250°C, and the glass beads conduct the heat to the items being sterilised.

Chemical methods

Specific chemicals can be utilised to reduce or destroy pathogenic micro organisms on items which are immersed in them. Gluteraldehyde, Cidex and Sporicidin are brands of gluteraldehyde which have, until recently, been extensively used in salons. Recent guidance, however, strongly discourages their use due to their potential as a skin irritant and as a carcinogen.

Disinfection is the destruction of the growing forms of infection and infectious microbes, but not spores. When the disinfection effect wears off the organism re-grows. Disinfectants should not be used on the skin; they are for inanimate objects only.

Examples of disinfectants are Barbicide or UV cabinet. Disinfection is adequate for uncontaminated items, for example facial or body sponges or mask brushes which have not been used on broken skin. Hypochlorite (bleach) solutions are recommended for disinfecting work surfaces and general equipment. An effective dilution is 1:100 dilution of household bleach in water. For clearing any body fluid spillage a dilution of 1:10 should be used. It is important to follow manufacturer's instructions when using sterilisation equipment. Antiseptics are similar to disinfectant and safe to use on living tissues. They kill bacteria and fungi completely, but not spores. Antiseptic is ideal for use on the skin; an example is Hibitaine or alcohols such as surgical spirit.

Re-usable equipment, for example tweezers, should be sterilised by:

- Cleaning thoroughly in water and detergent to remove organic materials such as skin, hair and grease.

- Rinsing thoroughly.

- Sterilising in an autoclave ensuring the pieces of equipment do not overlap each other, the autoclave should be CE marked.

- Once sterilised, items should be stored in sterile conditions (e.g. UV cabinet) ready for use.

- If the items are not used within 3 hours they should be re-sterilised.

- Hard surfaces, including equipment lamps and the trolley should be disinfected before and after each client.

glossary

abnormal systemic (causes of hair growth) hormonal stimulation of the follicle which is outside normal hormonal changes, i.e. endocrine disorders

acid mantle protective covering for the skin formed from sweat, sebum and cells of the stratum corneum

active electrode the electrode where the 'action' is taking place

adipose tissue fatty connective tissue found in the hypodermis

adrenalin stress hormone produced by the adrenal gland medulla

adrenocorticotrophic hormone (ACTH) hormone produced by the anterior lobe of the pituitary gland to stimulate the adrenal gland cortex

aldosterone steroid hormone produced in the adrenal gland cortex to help control the body's fluid balance

anagen fully growing follicle in the most mitotically active stage of growth

anaphoresis a technique used prior to epilation treatment to dilate the pores and increase local microcirculation which uses a direct current; the active electrode has a negative polarity while the inactive electrode has a positive polarity

anatomy structure

androgens steroid hormones that stimulate male characteristics

antidiuretic hormone (ADH) hormone produced in the posterior lobe of the pituitary gland to control absorption of water in the kidneys

aorta main artery leading from the heart

areola mammae a ring of pigmentation surrounding the nipple

arrector pili muscle small involuntary muscle in the skin responsible for 'goose bumps'

arteries blood vessels leading away from the heart

arterioles small arteries

aseptic hygienic way of working, the opposite of septic

atria upper chambers of the heart

axillae underarm area

bacteria microbes that can cause illness and disease

basement membrane point of attachment between two types of tissue

blend a combining together of alternating and direct current, i.e. thermolysis and galvanic, electrolysis techniques

blood pressure force associated with pumping action of the heart

bulge area of the follicle just below the sebaceous gland, which contains stem cells

calcitonin hormone produced by the thyroid gland to help control calcium levels in the body

capillaries single cell structures associated with blood and lymph vessels

carbon dioxide gas produced in the cells as a result of respiration

catagen second stage of follicle growth, following anagen and preceding telogen

cataphoresis a technique used after epilation treatment to reduce inflammation, tighten the pores and reduce reddening on the skin and to have a germicidal effect, which uses a direct current. The active electrode has a positive polarity while the inactive electrode has a negative polarity

cell microscopic part of an organism

chromophore an object which will absorb light energy

chromosome part of a cell containing genes

coherent all the photons of light are in phase

collagen a protein constituent of connective tissue, found in the dermal layer of the skin

collimated light waves are parallel

comedones commonly known as 'black-heads', a collection of sebum and keratinised cells which are oxidised at the surface, giving the black colour

compound follicles 'of two or more parts', a single follicle with two hairs and two dermal papillae

congenital a condition present at birth

connective tissue groups of cells providing a connective and protective function

cortex middle layer of hair

cortisol steroid hormone produced in the adrenal gland cortex

crusts result from dried bodily fluids and may consist of serum (yellow), blood (blackish) or pus (grey/green); usually however they consist of varying mixtures of these ingredients and are of a brown colour

cuticle outer layer of the hair and inner layer of the inner root sheath

depilation temporary removal of hair without destroying the lower part of the hair follicle

dermal cord connection between the dermal papilla and the hair bulb

dermal papilla a small nipple-shaped protuberance of the papillary layer, found at the base of the follicle, which provides nutrients via its blood supply to the follicle

dermis the second layer of the skin, often referred to as the 'true skin' as it performs many of the skin's main functions

desincrustation a method of deep cleansing the skin by galvanic current

desquamate the shedding of epithelial cells from the epidermis

diathermy a method of permanent hair removal using an alternating current

differentiation a process whereby cells specialise

disinfectant a chemical agent which destroys micro organisms but not usually bacterial spores. It does not kill all micro organisms but reduces them to a level at which they are not harmful

diuretic an agent which increases the flow of urine

down fine hair found all over the body, excluding palms of the hands and soles of the feet. May turn into terminal hair if stimulated

eccrine glands   sweat glands found on most parts of the body

electromagnetic spectrum   the range of electromagnetic radiations including visible and invisible light rays

embryo   early stages of a fertilised ovum

empathy   not to be confused with sympathy, it is the ability to identify with and comprehend another person's concerns and their situation

endocrine disorders   a disorder of the endocrine system, i.e. PCOS (polycystic ovarian syndrome)

endocrine glands   ductless glands secreting hormones directly into the blood

epidermis   the outer layer of the skin, consisting of 5 layers

epilation   permanent removal of unwanted hair

epithelial tissue   groups of cells providing a protective function

erythema   vasodilation; a superficial reddening of the skin

ethnic skin type   the classification of skin based on ethnic origin

excretion   the process of eliminating waste from the body

exfoliation   the removal of dead skin cells and debris from the surface of the skin

exocrine glands   a gland that secretes its substance into a duct

FDA (Food and Drug Administration)   the FDA is responsible for protecting public health and giving licence to certain equipment, drugs and cosmetics in the USA

fibroma   a benign tumour of connective tissue

Fitzpatrick skin classification system   system developed to assist in the prediction of the skin's pigmentary responsiveness and the person's lifetime risk of developing skin cancer

fluence   the energy density generated by the laser

foetus   developing baby in the womb

follicle   the opening into the skin which houses a hair

follicle stimulating hormone (FHS)   hormone produced in the anterior lobe of the pituitary gland to stimulate the ovaries and testes

folliculitis   a bacterial infection in the hair follicle

fungi   a microbe that causes illness and disease

galvanic current   direct current – the constant flow of electrons along a conductor in one direction with no change of polarity

gender dysphoria   sex is the physical form and function of the body, whilst gender is the identity of the body and so the dilemma of the gender dysphoriac (the person with gender dysphoria) is the difference between sex and gender

gene   the basic unit of genetic material

genetic   inherited

germinal matrix   living, reproducing part of the hair

gland   a structure lined with epithelial tissue capable of producing a substance

glucagon   a hormone produced in the islets of Langerhans in the pancreas to help maintain blood sugar levels

gonadotrophins   hormones produced in the anterior lobe of the pituitary gland which affect the ovaries and testes

growth hormone (GH)   hormone produced in the anterior lobe of the
  pituitary gland

hair bulb   base of the follicle
herpes simplex   commonly known as a 'cold sore', this is an eruption
  showing small vesicles found around moist openings
hirsuitism   male hair growth pattern found in females
histamine   present in body tissue and released in the skin in response to
  sensitivity
holistic   considering the whole person
homeostasis   physiological stability
hormones   chemical messengers
host practice   when the hair removal practitioner carries out her/his trade
  within another business practice
HRP   hair removal practitioner
hypersecretion   undersecretion
hyper pigmentation   increase of pigmentation in a given area
hypertrichosis   hormone stimulated hair growth considered abnormal for
  age, gender and race
hypodermis   fatty layer lying directly below the dermis
hypo pigmentation   decrease of pigmentation in a given area
hypothalamus   part of the brain that links the nervous and endocrine
  systems

in-growing hairs   a hair which turns back on itself in the follicle, often
  found in curly follicles and due to over keratinisation of the follicle
  opening; can cause infection
insulin   hormone produced in the islets of Langerhans in the pancreas and
  responsible for maintaining blood sugar levels
intense pulsed light (IPL)/flash lamp   a light source which emits the full
  spectrum of light; it is broadband or white light
interstitual fluid   fluid that bathes the cells
iontophoresis   introduction of ionised products into the deeper layers of
  the skin

joules   measurement of the energy density of light (fluence) as used in IPL

keratin   protein which forms the base of all horny tissues, e.g. hair, nails
keratinisation   hardening of cells with the formation of keratin
keratinocytes   cells that produce keratin

lanugo hair   fine hair present on the body prior to birth
laser   acronym for Light Amplification by Stimulated Emission of Radiation;
  an optical device that produces an intense monochromatic beam of
  coherent light
light systems   any system which emits light energy; e.g. laser or intense
  pulsed light
luteinising hormone (LH)   hormone produced in the anterior lobe of the
  pituitary gland
lye   common term for sodium hydroxide (NaOH)

mast cells   produce histamine when the skin is damaged or irritated

melanin   a dark pigment found in the hair, the eye and the skin. In the skin the pigment is stimulated by ultra violet light which causes darkening of the skin (tan)

melanocyte   a cell responsible for the formation of the pigment melanin

melanocyte stimulating hormone (MSH)   hormone produced in the anterior lobe of the pituitary gland

melasma   another term for pigmentation of the skin

menarche   the start of the menstrual cycle

menopause   the normal stopping of menstruation (periods). The ovaries stop producing oestrogen so there is a hormonal imbalance which often causes facial hair growth

milia   keratinised matter which is trapped under the skin, usually seen as a pearly white nodule

mineralocorticoids   hormones produced in the cortex of the adrenal glands

mitosis   simple cell division

mitotic/mitosis   cellular activity; a multiplication of cells by cellular division

monochromatic   all the photons of light are the same colour (wavelength)

nanometers (nm)   a unit of spatial measurement used to measure light

nasolabial fold   the fold of skin which lies between the nose and outer lips

National Occupational Standards   requirements devised by HABIA for all beauty therapy training

normal systemic   hormonal stimulation of the follicle which is within the normal hormonal changes of the body, i.e. puberty

oedema   an excessive amount of fluid in the body tissues, presenting as swelling

orbital ridge   the bony cavity containing the eyeball

organ   a structure formed from two or more tissue types

osmotic   the passage of fluid, from a lower concentration solution to one of a higher concentration, through a semi-permeable membrane

ovary   female endocrine gland producing hormones and female exocrine gland releasing ova

over-keratinised   thickening of the skin due to excess production of keratin

P&B   'papilla and bulge'; an insertion technique

papules   small superficial, raised, solid lesions of the skin; the skin is not broken

parameters   a range of variations from a process or policy which set limits or boundarys for a set of independent variables

parathormone (PTH)   hormone produced in the parathyroid glands

patch test   a small trial area which will help you to assess the likely reaction to treatment

peristaltis   involuntary movements (constriction and relaxation) of intestinal muscles which propel nutrients and waste through the intestine

photons   'energy bundles'; a quantity or amount of electromagnetic energy

physiology   function

pigmentation   colouration of tissues by pigment

pilo-sebaceous unit   the hair, the follicle, the sebaceous gland and erector pili muscle

polychromatic   many different wavelengths (colours)

protocols   a precise and detailed plan to define the codes of correct conduct for the use of a light system

pulse duration   the amount of time for which a pulse of light is emitted

pustule   pus-containing lesion of the skin with inflammation of surrounding skin

radiant   emitting heat or light

sanitiser   a product which cleanses the area to be treated and reduces the risk of infection

sebaceous gland   small gland opening onto a hair follicle responsible for secreting sebum

sebum   an oily substance secreted by the sebaceous gland

selective photothermolysis   the actual process used for laser hair removal

sex corticoids   hormones produced in the cortex of the adrenal glands

sexual hair   hair which is found in the pubis and axillae region of both male and female

spider naevi   a collection of telangiectasia presenting with a central 'body' and linear capillaries emanating from the centre

spot size   the size of the emitted beam used in IPL

STI   sexually transmitted infection, previously referred to as sexually transmitted disease

stem cells   stem cells are immature cells that have the ability to become any kind of tissue in the body

stratified   formed in layers

stratum corneum   the outer, keratinised layer of the epidermis

sudoriferous glands   sweat glands

superfluous   excess

sympathy   the ability to share another person's feelings, not to be confused with empathy

T-zone   forehead and nose area, sometimes referred to as 'central panel'

telangiectasia   persistent vasodilatation of superficial capillaries and venules, either singly or in a collection

telogen   the final stage of hair growth known as the resting stage, as the follicle is inactive until stimulated to reform

terminal hair   thick, coarse hair protecting underlying structures

thermal relaxation time (TRT)   the period of time a structure takes to lose a given percentage of generated heat

thermolysis   epilation carried out by oscillating, alternating current of high frequency

threading   hair removal method using strands of thread

thymosins   hormones produced by the thymus gland

thyroid stimulating hormone (TSH)   hormone produced by the anterior lobe of the pituitary gland

tissue   groups of specialist cells

tombstone hairs   remains of previously treated hair, which new anagen hair has pushed to the surface and made visible

transsexuals   old fashioned phrase for what is now called gender dysphoria, those who believe they have been born in the wrong body

urticaria   also known as 'nettle rash' or 'hives', an eruption of weals with great irritation, generally caused by a reaction to an allergen

vascular legions   structural change being caused by an injury or wound consisting of blood vessels

vaso-constriction   restricting blood flow through tightening of blood vessels

vaso-dilatation   enhancing blood flow through relaxing of blood vessels

vellus hair   fine downy hair covering most of the body

virus   a microbe responsible for illness and disease

vitiligo   a skin disorder, demonstrated by an absence of pigment which produces white patches on the face and body

watts   output power

wavelengths   the term used to describe the 'length' of a light wave

waxing   temporary removal of hair by mass plucking using product

zygote   a fertilised ovum

Index